★ CHAPPIE

★

America's First Black Four-Star General

★

The Life and Times of Daniel James, Jr.

★

by J. Alfred Phelps

Daniel "Chappie" James, Jr., began his military career as one of the original Tuskegee Airmen, a group of black aviators fighting discrimination in the segregated South. Years later, he became the first black four–star general in U.S. history.

Chappie and his fellow pilots at Tuskegee Institute in Alabama were among the first blacks anywhere to successfully resist discrimination, risking violent physical abuse and even death. As a result of their courage, the military became committed to equal opportunity years before society in general began to move in that direction.

Chappie was also a man of action, flying over a hundred combat missions in Korea and Vietnam — some of which are described with vivid clarity and unforgettable detail. Never daunted, he even confronted Muammar Khaddafy at the gates of Wheelus Air Force Base in Libya.

During and after Vietnam, as the Air Force's public affairs chief, Chappie was in a unique position to ease the agony and indirection America was suffering. He made a difference through voicing his passionate belief in ideals that were in danger of being lost in the angry turmoil. He understood the black soldiers who resented having to fight what they felt was a white man's war and had a keen understanding of the resentment all m felt about fighting a war that so bitterly di

Chappie drew inspiratior from the culture to which h These influences are traced in u reader is able to understand Chappie Jan

continued on back flap

CHAPPIE

Gen. Daniel "Chappie" James, Jr., as Commander, North American Air Defense Command. (Official U.S. Air Force photograph.)

CHAPPIE

America's First Black Four-Star General
The Life and Times of Daniel James, Jr.

J. Alfred Phelps

PRESIDIO

Copyright © 1991 by Joseph A. Phelps

Published by Presidio Press
31 Pamaron Way, Novato, CA 94949

Library of Congress Cataloging-in-Publication Data

Phelps, J. Alfred.
   Chappie : America's first black four-star general / by J. Alfred
Phelps.
    p. cm.
  Includes bibliographical references and index.
  ISBN 0-89141-396-0
    1. James, Daniel, 1920–1978.   2. Generals—United States-
Biography.   3. United States.   Air Force—Biography.   4. Afro-
American generals—Biography.   I. Title.
UG626.2.J36P48   1991
355′.0092—dc20
[B]   90–43537
                                        CIP

Printed in the United States of America

For my grandchildren
Alexander, David, Jr., Therese, Jacqueline, Linda and Hadascha

The sun shines right
  Where things are bright;
When the wind blows
  Strong and free.

. . . Go down there black boy . . . way down in Alabama.
  Sweat out your days and sit on your nights.
And show me . . . black boy . . .
  Show me you can fly.

Hold that nose down, Mister.
  Damnit, get that wing up!
Can't you see the horizon, Mister?
  Quit holding that rudder in turns.

From plane to plane,
  From light to heavy . . .
From Stearman to Beetee to Ayetee
  To Thunderbolt . . . from Tuskegee to Italy.

Pretty good, black boy, p-r-e-t-t-y g-o-o-d.
  But wait a minute. That's not all.
Can you FIGHT in planes?
  Will you come scudding home with the first burst of fire?

Better take it easy for a while black boy . . .
  Right now, better just
Fly over yonder and
  Shoot up some trains.

O tell me, lad, of that day long ago;
  Of the "black boy" from Tuskegee over Anzio
When shall we . . . meet again—
  In thunder, lightning or in rain?

—John H. Young, III
These Are Our Finest
Program, Seventh National
Convention, Tuskegee Airmen, Inc.
(Sacramento, CA: 1978)

Contents

Preface

A great amount of the material relating to General James's career during and after his Libyan assignment has been drawn from the Tuskegee University Archives, which house an impressive collection of the *James Papers* and audiotapes of speeches by General James. As importantly, United States Air Force research material contained in the Alfred F. Simpson Research Center at Maxwell Air Force Base, near Montgomery, Alabama, and the Office of Air Force History at Bolling Air Force Base, D.C., provided interfacing groups of data covering the same periods. Additionally, they contained a tremendous amount of official air force data pertaining to the Libyan period as well as the Korean and Vietnam conflicts, in which James was deeply involved.

Other sources covering the background and early years of the Tuskegee Airman "experiment" and its developmental stages when the air force was an integral part of the United States Army, were found in the National Archives in Washington, D.C. and the National Records Center in Suiteland, Maryland. Copies of the original trial transcripts recording the court martials of the three Tuskegee Airmen tried because of the officers' club fiasco were provided by the army's Judge Advocate General Archives in Virginia, allowing for what is believed to be the first in-depth recording of these trials for public airing.

Source material pertaining to James's early life included use of data included in the only other James biography to date, by James R. McGovern of West Florida University (*Black Eagle: General Daniel "Chappie" James, Jr.*, University of Alabama Press, 1985, 168 pages), and long, in-depth interviews with the general's widow, Dorothy Watkins James of Falls Church, Virginia; and his daughter and her husband, Danice and Frank Berry of Merced, California. This material was widely expanded upon through further interviews with other members of the James family, both in person and by telephone.

Members of the Tuskegee Airmen from coast to coast, and especially those who knew General James personally and many who served with him in later years, provided important insights and material. United States Air Force combat veterans of the Korean and Vietnam conflicts who served with General James contributed heavily to insights regarding General James. Their interviews and correspondence provided further understanding and knowledge, not only of the Tuskegee years, but of the experiences of which James was a part at Selfridge Field, Michigan, Godman Field in Kentucky, Freeman Field in Indiana and finally, Lockbourne Army Air Base in Columbus, Ohio—all of which represented critical turning points in the lives of all Tuskegee Airmen, including General James.

Other libraries provided materials for extensive background research: The Marin County Free Library, San Rafael, California; San Francisco State University Library, San Francisco, California; Brown-Daniel Library, Tennessee State University, Nashville; Hollis Burke-Frissell Library, Tuskegee University, Tuskegee, Alabama, which houses the *James Papers*.

Acknowledgments

The author wishes to thank all of the following who in one way or another contributed so much to the realization of this project: Mrs. Dorothy Watkins James, Danice Berry James, Dr. Frank Berry, Gloria Hunter, Cecil Hunter, Mabel Bates, Deonice Lucky, Vernel Steen, James R. McGovern, Roger Terry, James T. Wiley, Fitzroy Newsum, L. Gen. Benjamin O. Davis, Jr., Col. William Campbell, William B. Ellis, Maj. Al Downing, Maj. Thomas J. Money, "Chief" Alfred Anderson, Col. Dennis Sharon, Col. Dick Jonas, C.M.Sgt. Jessie O. Helms, T.Sgt. John Trammel, T.Sgt. Herbert C. Harper, C.M.Sgt. James H. Edmonson, Maj. Ted W. Johnson, Col. Ralph Hodges, Jerry Friedheim, M.Sgt. Roger A. Jernigan, William Heimdahl, Dr. James H. Kitchens III, the late Mr. Presley Bickerstaff, Lynn O. Gamma, Dr. Daniel Williams, Dr. Evelyn P. Fancher, William D. Madsen, Mrs. Lilli Rollins, Tuskegee, Alabama, Mayor Johnny Ford, Elaine Thomas, Archie Williams, the late Della Raney, Mrs. Edith Roberts, Harold Beaulieu, George Fordham, W. Leon, Edward Woodward, Robert Wilson, John "Mr. Death" Whitehead, Mrs. Walnita D. Allen, Mark Boes, Maj. Roy "J.C." Thompson, Col. Lloyd Thomas, Col. James Randle, Lt. Col. Theodore W. Jones, Dr. Maurice Brooks, Col. Jimmie N. Murphy, Pres. Gerald R. Ford, Sen. Barry Goldwater, Congressman Ronald Dellums, Mark D. Weinberg, Brig. Gen. Robin Olds, Dick Johnson of the *Kansas City Star*, "Brenda" at the *Pensacola News-Journal*, Richard Hopper of the *Indianapolis Star*, George Douglas of the *Colorado Springs Gazette-Telegraph*, Col. Howard K. White, Hank Basham, Emmit H. Brooks, Hannibal Guidice, Mrs. Ruth Ellison, Mrs. Gertrude Dendy-McGee, Mrs. Gina Fisher, Linda Allen, and Ted Berkman. There may be those overlooked, but this was not intentional and is due to space considerations. These are also heartily thanked for their contributions.

Introduction

America has seen black generals in its history, each bursting with those vital juices that seem to flow from general officers. But none have had quite the bright sheen of the late Gen. Daniel "Chappie" James, Jr., of the United States Air Force. Big, blunt, and burly, he strode the precincts of officer country with a special kind of resolution, culminating a solid career with the sparkling insignia of a four-star general.

It is a resounding success when any officer in the military achieves such a rank. It was a *spectacular* achievement for a black man alive in General James' era (1920–1978) to officially append eight stars to his tunic, mute reminders of almost the ultimate in generalship.

There will be those who scoff at the achievement and say that this man just happened along at the right places and times. There is a modicum of truth in that. But seers say that whatever a man creates in his life is his unique design, his alone, never done before and never to be done exactly the same again. Nick Thimmesch, in the 18 March 1978 issue of the *Los Angeles Times* called General James "a remarkable human being . . . a triumph of will . . . [who] . . . bulled his way through prejudice and closed doors . . . and at the end of his career, carried the responsibility of protecting us all from air or missile attack—Commander-in-Chief of the North American Defense Command . . . ."

No matter what the scoffers may suggest, it was a feat comparable to the first successful assault on Mount Everest or the first completed English Channel swim. A special kind of zeal seized Daniel "Chappie" James, Jr., at the beginning of a career spanning thirty-five years. He was to refer to it in a milestone speech before the Daughters of the American Revolution convention. "When I came into this man's Air Force", he said, "I vowed I would become a general officer, and I am, as you can see."

One wonders what would have happened to his resolve had he stopped to look longer at past experiences of blacks in America's military forces. He would have seen valor, bravery, sacrifice, and dedication. But he would have seen no universally admired black heroes like Hanno and his son Hamilcar of Carthage, or Hannibal the Great, the greatest Carthaginian general, openly admired by Napoleon for his military genius. He would have seen instead black men, slave and free, fighting and dying in the Revolutionary War; at the battles of Lexington and Concord; with Ethan Allen's Green Mountain Boys; at Fort Ticonderoga and Bunker Hill. Even as they fought and bled, he would have heard distinguished leaders of the Revolution, including General Washington himself, express their unwillingness to allow blacks to be soldiers because they were thought to be cowardly, servile, and below other men.

He would have heard colonial slaveowners push for exclusion of blacks from the military, as, filled with apprehensions and wild imaginings, they dreamed of armed revolt by slaves and sympathetic Indians with Spanish and French backing. When the War of Independence was over, he would have seen blacks excluded almost entirely from the American military establishment until the next war. And he would have heard those same colonialists animatedly reason over fat cigars and jiggers of whiskey that blacks could not be excluded from military services because *that* would "privilege" them. So make them drummers and fifers and trumpeter boys! Make them road and highway laborers! Give them guard duties!

In spite of whimsical notions of their soldierly abilities and trustworthiness, in spite of official policies barring them from the militia or regular armed forces after the Revolution, he would have seen black men serve in the naval war with France in the late 1700s and, in the War of 1812, heard Gen. Andrew Jackson refer to black officers and enlisted men as "adopted children." He would have seen them again excluded from the military from 1820–1863.

Come the Civil War, he would have seen his black military predecessors finally become a permanent part of the United States Armed Forces. He would have watched General T. J. Morgan organize and command four black regiments and the 1st Colored Brigade of the Army of the Cumberland. Their noncommissioned officers were pulled from the black ranks, while their field and line officers were assigned from the ranks of white men who "cared nothing for the niggers except for the Army rank they enabled them to attain."[1] He would have heard army officers speculate that southern, white officers made the best leaders of blacks because they "understood" black men, and he would have heard these same officers call the men under their command "niggers," and "coons," and "darkies." He would have watched his black military forebears chafe at their emasculated condition, unable to claim legitimate rights because someone white didn't extend them. He would have smiled at the end of the Civil War as, in spite of it all, of the ninety-three medals and commendations awarded to army enlisted men, blacks won twenty. Twenty-two black soldiers won the Congressional Medal of Honor. He would see some blacks remain to serve in the post-Civil War army, harassed within it and set upon outside it by a hostile citizenry. He would have heard the loud objections voiced by white citizens because black soldiers were stationed nearby. In 1877, he would have seen a black holder of the Medal of Honor shot in the back by a Texas sheriff. He would have seen other black soldiers lynched, denied accommodations, and murdered. He would perhaps have shaken his head in disgust to see how little had changed in racial relationships and attitudes by the time of the Spanish-American War. Black enlisted men promoted to officer rank were in regiments that were temporary and therefore could not retain the rank if they later elected to become regular army. He would have smiled again as, in spite of prejudice, black soldiers distinguished themselves in Cuba, while in the U.S., prominent citizenry and the general public cheered the exploits of black infantry and 10th Cavalry. Imagine a tear in Chappie's eye to see white Americans suddenly resent the praise heaped upon these black men and begin to regenerate racial hostilities.

If the historical view of black military experience had been bleak for Chappie up to this point, it would have become bleaker in World War I, especially for black officers. He could have heard the voice of experience in Allen Allensworth, a black chaplain who served twenty years in the United States Army (1886–1906): "There is no place on earth where the crucible is hotter for a negro officer than the Army. He is completely isolated from social companionship, except that of his immediate family. . . ."[2] The armed forces have almost always mirrored American society. What Chappie might have seen reflected the continuing Caucasian response. The general idea seemed to be to keep blacks out of the military until a conflict erupted and, as the struggle became difficult, welcome them with open arms. The blacks, on the other hand, seemed to feel a need to "prove their worth" and flocked to join. Having done so, they were then met by whites who were busy keeping them "in their place," crowning them with humiliation, indignity, and scorn.

A rationale concerning blacks (and especially black officers) developed in the military among whites. Generally it went something like this: *Problems in the use and assignment of black officers exist because the nature of segregation itself dictates limited use of black officers. The dictum of limited use is based upon continuing disbelief in their abilities by their white counterparts. Tradition says that blacks prefer to serve under white officers and actually perform better under white officers.*

Perhaps in recounting his vow to become a general officer on that glorious day he stood tall as the first black man to address the Daughters of the American Revolution, General James sought to undersocre the meaning of service by black Americans in the armed forces of the United States. It was a variation on a theme, a startling realization shared by a black corporal named Thomas Long, of the 1st South Carolina Regiment, during the Civil War:

If we hadn't become sojers, all might have gone back as it was before; our freedom might have slipped through de two houses of Congress and president Linkum's four years might have passed by and notin' been done for we. But now tings can never go back, because we have showed our energy and our courage and our naturally manhood. . . . Anoder ting is, suppose you had kep' your freedom without enlisting in dis army, your chilen might have grownup free and been *well cultivated* so as to be equal to any business; but it would have been always flung in dere faces—"Your fader never fought for he own freedom"—and what could dey answer. *Neber can say that to dis African race anymore* (bringing down his hand with the greatest emphasis on the table). Tanks to dis regiment, neber can say dat anymore; because we first showed dem we could fight by dere side. . . ."[3]

And if, wars apart, Gen. Daniel "Chappie" James, Jr., and Cpl. Thomas Long made sure, each in his way, that "dey" could never look any black American in the face and accuse his ancestors of lack of patriotism, it must be said that General James went even further. He fought a kind of still-alive segregation lingering from the past that might have overwhelmed lesser men. He paid for those battles with slow promotions and personal slights. Wars came and went, as did varying intensities of prejudice; he survived. Things got better as blacks came out for freedom with Martin Luther King, Jr. Chappie spoke of patriotism, of "another mile to run in that race for equality," of how there's "a better track to run on and the trophies at the end are a lot better than they used to be." His own people pooh-poohed him, calling him "Oreo cookie" and "token." He growled back at them, accusing them of "making a career out of being black" and avowed that "they didn't know what suffering is."

But Chappie was no demigod. He had his share of human frailties. A big man with big appetites, he had like many of his air force buddies a quick eye for a pretty girl. He himself admitted to a hair-trigger temper, which could explode into dangerous rashness, a shortcoming which became a lifelong challenge to be conquered and controlled. These shortcomings were far overshadowed by his love of country and achievement, trailblazing him to the top of a profession where no black man had ever gone before.

His is a story of courage, panache and charisma, providing a role model from which future generations of Americans, regardless of hue, may profit.

I never met General James, even though I served in the United States Air Force for twenty-one of the thirty-five years of his career. Somehow, I feel that I knew him, like all of the thousands of black airmen of his time felt they knew him. He was like a blazing sunset to us, a glowing dawn. He was a darkling rumor, a choice conversation piece:

"Hey man, didja hear 'bout ole Chappie?"

"Naw. What?"

"Gittin' 'nother star!"

"Yeah?"

"Yeah."

"Right on!"

We all walked and talked a little prouder because we knew Chappie was in the force and making good. Somebody always knew where he was and what he was doing. He came across as "straight ahead." Somehow we knew he was being rewarded because he loved his country and thought it the greatest country, a land that had hope—for everybody. And no matter what we all thought about the things happening to our people in America, America still gained points in our estimation because of Chappie. He was real. And he *never* said out loud what another black general before him is alleged to have said to lower ranking blacks in the military: "I'm your color but not your kind."

We loved him for that.

J. Alfred Phelps
Rohnert Park, California

Chapter One
The Family and the Dream[4]

Weatherwise, it was a most peculiar 11 February 1920 when Daniel "Chappie" James, Jr., was born. About a mile or so from the James house at 1606 Alcaniz Street in Pensacola, Florida, one G. S. Kennedy, weather observer at the U.S. Department of Agriculture's weather station recorded, in that delightful Spencerian penmanship of the era, that the barometer reading was 29.939 and it was raining—thirty-seven hundredths of an inch had fallen, to be exact. The relative humidity rode at ninety-eight degrees. The wind whooshed in gusts, driving the cirrus clouds before it at speeds of eight to twenty-four miles per hour. Nobody saw the sun nor felt the sunshine until around ten o'clock in the morning as it came out to play hopscotch across the city until three in the afternoon. By four o'clock, it was gone. A thunderstorm was to hit the next day.

In a way, the weather resembled a particular life that began that day down in the ghetto on Alcaniz Street. They called him Daniel, after his father and later, "Chappie" for short with "Junior" tagged on to the family name of James. Born the youngest of seventeen children to Lillie Anna and Daniel, Sr., there was absolutely no doubt that he was special and loved. His coming was a gift, since only seven of the seventeen were still alive when "Chappie" was born. Three of those had left the house.

As a boy, James generated sunshine. People still remember the performances of a small, engaging, precocious, brown boy on the little stage in the school run by his mother, Lillie Anna James. Clad in a white tuxedo with pink lapels, he performed while his cousin, Mabel, sang a song she had written to him:

> —*Two, three, four!*—
> "Handsome is as handsome does
> So the wise man say
> Feathers fine may make fine birds
> But folks are not that way
> It's what is in your heart,
> Deny it if you can;
> I'm not impressed
> With how you dress,
> 'Cause clothes don't make the man!''
> —*Five, six, seven, eight!*

That was the beginning of an extremely public life. Playing to audiences. Singing. Dancing. Public speaking. Becoming a personality who would make a difference in the American scenario.

Almost from the time he was able to understand words, James was to remember his mother's counsel, driven deep into his psyche through countless repetitions: "Don't stand there banging on the door of opportunity, then when someone opens it, you say, wait a minute, I got to get my bags. You be prepared with your bags of knowledge, your patriotism, your honor, and when somebody opens the door, you charge in. . . . ''

A pacesetter, Daniel, Jr.'s, mother came from New Orleans, the daughter of servants. Possessed of a high school education, she was early convinced that the keystone for her children's success lay in education. So convinced was she of this fact that this light-complexioned, attractive woman, of medium height and penetrating gaze, decided that the segregated "colored" school in Pensacola was not good enough for her children. She began her own, the Lillie A. James Private School, at 1606 Alcaniz Street. Beginning with her own brood, the school mushroomed until as many as seventy of her neighbor's children (who shared her dissatisfaction about the public schools) were in attendance. If the parents could pay, tuition was five cents a day. If they couldn't pay, the tuition was waived, and the children attended on credit.

Mrs. James taught more in her school than the three "R"'s. She was a homespun philosopher, her thoughts as cogent as those of any Aristotelian. Daniel, Jr., made them the cornerstones of his life. "For you, my son, there is an 11th Commandment, thou shalt not quit. . . . Prove to the world that you can compete on an equal basis . . . see that your children get a better education than you got. . . . ''

Daniel, Sr., a tall, dark-skinned and handsome Alabaman of medium-heavy build, a migrant laborer with little formal schooling, believed in hard work. It was the only way he knew. He was tough and uncompromising, and imbued Daniel, Jr., with those tenets, teaching him to ignore people who called him names because he belonged to a minority. "My father used to say," James was later to recall, "if a fight is inevitable, start it." "And," James was to add, "I believed in that."

By any measuring stick the James family was poor. The father pushed a coal dolly at the gas plant and worked as a lamplighter on the streets of the city. There were no sidewalks in front of their frame house, nor were there streetlights. The pavement ended where majority people lived; people like the Jameses lived in what everybody called the "sandbed." It was the local custom. The family was poor, but "Chappie" never knew it. His mother never let him know it. That was a Lillie Anna James custom.

Both parents were tough taskmasters. Daniel, Jr., was often required to bring his father's lunch to the gas plant. The trip was critical on the long Saturdays. To dawdle meant paying the piper, for a cool dinner on Saturdays meant unauthorized daydreaming had taken place on the way. Dawdling with the lunch could result in whacks in the nether regions of the anatomy, for his father never wanted to wait until late evenings for a hot meal. He was often accompanied on these "refueling" missions by his cousin Mabel, likewise charged with taking lunch to her uncle who worked at the gas plant alongside Daniel, Sr. Once there, the two of them often spent long minutes listening to Daniel's father talk of the importance of staying in school and doing well. He would look sternly at Daniel, Jr., and say, "I'm especially talking to you, Dan Baby." Daniel, Jr., was particularly impressed by his father's "stick-to-it attitude" in the way he worked long and hard at the gas plant and whatever else he was about.

It should be remarked that he was as naughty as other children, especially when soda pop trucks would get stuck in front of the house in the sandy loam called the "sandbed." "I remember," James was to recall years later in an interview with William Greider, *Washington Post* staff writer, "pop trucks would get stuck down there and the kids loved that! We'd run up and grab pop!" Almost as an afterthought, he recalled, "If my mother caught me, I'd get it. That's one thing, we didn't steal and we didn't lie."

Before the coming of Daniel, Jr., the family had been beset by tragedy of another sort, for, of the ten sibling deaths, perhaps the most tragic were those of the twins, dead of pneumonia in their infancy. Stricken in the middle of the night with chills and headache, scorching fever and chest pain, the twins were rushed to the offices of the family doctor.

They were among the first to arrive. The family doctor, in the tradition of the times, maintained two waiting rooms: one for the majority patients, light of hue; the other, for minority patients whose skins were the color of the coffee bean. The majority waiting room filled quickly and, as was the custom, its patients were seen first; while in the adjacent waiting room, on rickety and worn furniture, Lillie Anna and Daniel James, Sr., cuddled their twins, full of pneumonia, temperatures soaring. Late in the day, after the last patients from that other waiting room had been seen, Lillie Anna and the twins were called. It was the custom. Intervention came too late. Too much fever, inflammation of the lungs and edema. Days later, the twins were dead.

As "Chappie" became larger and able to walk around Pensacola on his own, the caste system into which he was born became painfully obvious. He was to recall those impressions before the Commonwealth Club in San Francisco: "There were parks in Pensacola, with green grass and park benches. The benches were labeled 'colored' and 'white.' To make sure I didn't sit on the wrong one, they were painted black and white. The water fountains—'colored'—'white'—the waiting rooms, 'colored' and 'white'; the latrines 'colored' and 'white'; the buses themselves white and 'colored' to the rear. . . ."

If Daniel "Chappie" James, Jr., was discouraged by what he saw in the larger world of Pensacola, Lillie Anna James had the answer: "Don't go somewhere else looking for your piece of the pie. Your piece is right here! You're an American, you're not an African and don't listen to any of this stuff about niggers going back to Africa. You answer: 'I didn't come from Africa. I came from North Alcaniz Street, Pensacola, Florida. . . .' "[5]

"Looking for [his] piece of the pie . . . right here!" is precisely what Daniel, Jr., did as his gaze wandered over the Pensacola he knew. It was immediately clear that the world contained other races of people. Pensacola was an American melting pot. The influences of the French, Spanish, and English, who conquered the town when their ships sailed down the Main, had resulted in integrated neighborhoods and a surreptitious social intercourse based on southern biases. As the numbers of whites increased, Daniel, Jr., would see fewer integrated neighborhoods, creation of a new, black "middle class" (of which his family became a part), while the Cajuns lost their "particular" identifiers to simply be called "colored."

Pensacola was exciting to Daniel, Jr., from another point of view. It was a restless place. From the right vantage points, one could see that the city had been fortressed. Forts called Pickens, McRae, and Barrancas protected it from the sea. Fort Redoubt stood watch to protect from land attack.

There were rumors of the times Pensacola was a link in the underground that helped Negroes escape to freedom during slavery. Of Pensacola's mean times, when citizens stormed the jail to drag out an accused rapist, hanging him from a lamp post while they took pot shots at his corpse. Pensacola was a place in which to be wary. Daniel, Jr., grew, watched, and wondered about that curious concept of separate-but-not-equal in operation everywhere he looked.

Something else about Pensacola caught his eye and then his heart. Pensacola had airplanes, lots of them. "Those airplanes," his widow recalls, "probably frightened him when he was so small, but he loved the sight of them." Somehow, the planes made the forts seem useless, the restlessness of Pensacola meaningless and the nearby squalor inconsequential. They made escape viable and not merely a dream. He spent hours gazing out towards the Pensacola Naval Air Station where navy pilots sliced through the air in silvered planes. They had been there since 1914, when the American navy decided to fly. In that year, nine officers and something less than twenty-five men appeared, with flying machines that seemed akin to matchsticks held together by magic glue. The townspeople were full of wonder; fascinated by the "glamorous, begoggled men" in their "aerial machines," sweeping across the skies. "Chappie" was even more fascinated, for now, years later, the aircraft were more sophisticated and faster. The Pensacola Naval Air Station sparkled with the names of the famous and, in the 1920s, had become the naval aviation center of the United States. Charles Lindberg came there to do maintenance on his barnstorming airplane; Admiral Byrd and Amelia Earhart came by often; and Wallis Warfield, who was to marry a deposed king of England was connected, since her ex-husband, Lt. Winfield Spencer, was stationed there.

Heady stuff for a little boy who thought he wanted to fly!

Typical of James, he not only thought he wanted to fly; he did something about it. As a teenager, he went to a nearby Pensacola airfield to strike a deal with the flyers so as to get himself airborne. In return for odd jobs and chores, he was taken flying by the pilots in their old fighter aircraft and seaplanes.

It was something he had to do.

Were those empty aphorisms from Lillie Anna James? Impossible dreams for a little minority boy born in Pensacola, Florida, in 1920 down in the middle of the ghetto? Hardly. Each word was like a blood transfusion. It was as if Lillie Anna James had somewhere run across Martin R. Delaney's 1892 book concerning the destiny of the colored people of the United States: "Our common country is the United States. Here we were born, here raised and educated; here are the scenes of childhood; the pleasant association of our school-going days; the . . . enjoyments of our domestic and fireside relations, and the sacred graves of our departed fathers and mothers, and from there, we will not be driven by any policy that be schemed against us . . ."[6]

Chapter Two
The Dream Begins[7]

I

Before Daniel James, Jr., could ever go out to the nearby airfield to barter chores for aircraft rides, there was the very serious matter of completing his education at the Lillie Anna James Private School run by his mother. All of the James children were to attend it as were the children of scores of black families in Pensacola who yearned for an education better than that offered children of color in the Pensacola public schools of the day.

The school began in the 1900s without a great deal of fanfare, but was to provide a sound educational base for myriad black lawyers, doctors, teachers, and a four-star general. It began around the fireplace of the family home, and when acquaintances heard that Lillie Anna James was educating her own, they asked that she take in their children. She couldn't refuse. So Daniel, Sr., built her a little, red schoolhouse in the backyard adjacent to the tadpole-filled fish pond. As students enrolled, more room was needed. Daniel, Sr., and Lillie Anna bought the house next door, knocked down some walls, and the only black, private school in Pensacola, Florida, began. The younger children studied in the red schoolhouse, the older ones in the larger room near the back of the James residence.

If Daniel's life was to be filled with challenge, then surely this was a time he was never to forget. It was rigorous stuff, attending the Lillie Anna James school. No tardiness or sluffing off. Everything was no-nonsense and practical, from the plain, frame house to the unpretentious desks. There were few books with pretty pictures or artfully contrived children's primers; few separate, slick books on mathematics, English, or spelling. Instead, there was one primary storehouse of knowledge, and that was herself, Mrs. Lillie Anna James.

Mrs. James had an intelligent face with piercing eyes. She was a very firm lady, who felt that black kids and black adults alike needed to get out, work, and earn what they deserved in life. Discipline in the classroom was paramount; she was ever watchful, believing in the efficacy of the "switch," and, at times, in a very threatening ruler, wielded with purpose. One can almost imagine her somewhere in the wings, nodding in assent, when the old adage "Spare the rod and spoil the child" was coined. Her philosophy was simple and straightforward: "What you want is out there, you can go for it. You can get it, you just have to work for it!" Mrs. James enforced a strict regimen. One came to her school to learn, not to play around. Those who didn't make it were unceremoniously booted out.

And so Daniel, Jr., his brothers and sisters, and scores of other children came each day to this novel, private school for black children to listen and learn from Mrs. Lillie Anna James, who knew and taught reading, writing, and arithmetic; as well as manners, patriotism, religion, English, spelling, literature, physical education, and, most importantly, good, down-to-earth common sense. She was a fountain of knowledge and rhetoric—things learned from a high school equivalency education in Catholic school.

The children came to the classroom with pencils, pads, innate intelligence, and lunch bags often containing only meager portions of food. They wore calico clothes and prints, short pants and long. When the Pensacola weather turned to frost, slanting rains, and whistling winds, they were wrapped in scarves, tattered caps, and raincoats, and they clustered around a lone, pot-bellied stove. They greeted Mrs. James with song:

> Good morning dear teacher
> Good morning to you!
> Good morning dear teacher!
> And how do you do . . .

Mrs. James responded:

> Good morning dear children!
> Good morning to you!
> I'm glad as your teacher
> I'm glad to see you!

It was a first lesson in reciprocity, teaching the young charges to be friendly towards authority figures. With fervor, they recited the pledge of allegiance and sang "My Country 'tis of Thee" and sometimes, "America, America!

God Shed His Grace on Thee.'' Patriotism was the ticket. This is *your* country. Love it! Do your lessons well. Get your education. You can survive and make it! Because your skin is darker doesn't make one bit of difference—and don't you ever forget it!

Daniel, Jr., heard even more at home. He was taught that he had come from parents who didn't know the meaning of giving up, who believed in country, God, the flag, and the power of excellence.

His mother used to say, ''Don't you dare sacrifice your abilities on the dubious altar of despair. Take whatever opportunities that are available to you, right here, and you develop them to the best of your ability. Get to the top of your chosen field, whatever it is. You can exert more influence from the top than you can from the bottom with a brick or torch. And don't get so busy along the way exercising your right to dissent that you forget your responsibility to contribute through your own excellence. People will reach out to help because excellence is a standard throughout the world and no one questions its color. Remember, you're an American, not an African. Loyalty, responsibility and future lay in America!''[8]

He thrived on his mother's words and teachings, from singing down the alphabet to rippling down the times tables in song, done with a kind of indomitable rhythm from ancestral memory, roman numerals leading the way:

> One-eye-One!
> Two-eye-Two!
> Three-eye-Three!
> Eye-vee-Four
> Vee-FIVE!

Gloria Hunter, Daniel, Jr.'s niece, remembers the witchery: ''There would be students who became engrossed in the rhythm . . . and they'd want to pat their feet!''

Ever-watchful, Mrs. James saw everything. Patting the feet in rhythm was the greatest of transgressions, Gloria remembers: ''. . . and if she caught anybody patting their feet, she'd call (them) up . . . and spank them, 'cause you weren't supposed to be *pleasurizing*—it was serious business!''

James was to learn addition, subtraction, and the multiplication tables next, done in the same, singsong rhythm. The ''ones,'' ''twos,'' ''threes,'' and ''fours'' were thrilling enough, but those *fives* provided the best rhythm of all! Gloria remembers the parody on jazz:

> Five times one is five!
> Five times two are ten!

Three times five are—FIFTEEN!
Four times five are twenty!
Five times five are—TWENTY-FIVE!

Daniel, Jr., exulted with the rest when they reached the monumental "twelves" and twelve times twelve. It was the ultimate release. "You'd be so tired, you'd just *scream* it! Twelve times twelve is A HUNDRED AND FORTY-FOUR!"

It was a challenge. And through it all, Mrs. James was uncompromising but fair. Recess was a time to relax and have fun, but without fighting or other unruly behavior. Afterwards, she'd read stories from the great works to them, including poetry from great bards like Henry Wadsworth Longfellow. Daniel, Jr., accepted the challenge eagerly, and seemed to want to excel. An especially enthusiastic student of civics, geography and history, he had no trouble remembering events and dates. He had the leading roles in the annual school plays. His ability to remember long recitations stood him in good stead. Competitive, he never wanted anyone *his size* to beat him doing anything.

He doted on his cousin Mabel, who had earlier been stricken with polio. They were only two months apart in age. Her family lived almost next door and they studied together after school, acting out what they had learned. Imagining themselves "the teacher," they used their dolls and dogs as students. Sometimes, one of them would be the "parent" bringing his dog "Honey Rags" and her dog "Grant" to school. The two hapless animals would become "pupils" along with their dolls "Luther" and "Jemina" and be sternly lectured on the correct ways to speak. Daniel and his cousin competed when the time came for the annual school plays, wondering who would learn their lines first.

"Play time" came only after household chores and completion of school assignments. On weekends, they played sandlot baseball, using oak trees and crocus sacks for bases. Mabel could only haltingly walk and Daniel ran the bases for her whenever she'd hit a good ball. Together, they learned the social graces when Mrs. James would have a party in the large classroom. Mrs. James would chaperone the dances, and the boys would be instructed to ask for a dance politely, and be shown how to hold the girls while dancing. "Dan Baby" and cousin Mabel would be the models. There would be games from game books and games made up on the spot to the delight of these new citizens.

Such was the greening of Daniel "Dan Baby" James, Jr., and scores of others like him, discovering singing, dancing, and participation in school plays before large audiences on special holidays. From these experiences, Daniel, Jr., was to learn an ease before audiences that would serve him well during his lifetime.

In the ghetto of Alcaniz Street, he learned about combating fear. Not infrequently, his mother put fifteen cents in his hand and sent him out into the

Alcaniz Street jungle to buy a loaf of bread for the family table. The store was only two blocks away, but they were long and terrifying blocks for a small boy who was often set upon by "big bastard" teenagers, stomachs empty, bent upon forcibly stealing the money. Only two options existed. Outrun the "big bastard," or "get to a rock fast enough to bloody his nose, turn him around, get to the store and back home with the loaf of bread." On occasion, "Chappie" exercised both options. It was a matter of learning to control fear and still function. Run like hell, stand, fight and survive, and turn the enemy away.

Dubbed "Dan Baby" by a doting mother, Daniel, Jr., was virtually raised by his mother and older sisters with little intervention by his father. Mrs. James was a scintillating cook, and Daniel, Jr., whiled away many hours in the kitchen. He loved his mother, and he loved good food, and he would cherish both all of his life.

Although his father's involvement was erratic because of the need to provide a livelihood, it was always filled with deep-seated wisdom born of hard-won lessons.

For example, Daniel looked forward to his father treating him to the movies on the weekend. Once, Daniel failed to come home on time for the great adventure into the world of celluloid imagery. A stickler for promptness, the elder James waited, pacing the floor, wondering where his young charge was. It was unusual for Daniel, Jr., to be late, because he knew he was expected. He had learned *that* through upbraidings received for failure to deliver his father's lunch to the gas plant while still hot. The lateness was inexcusable. His father continued to pace. The annoyance grew.

The door burst open, framing a breathless, bedraggled youngster.

"Where have you been? You *know* I've been waiting to carry you to the movies!"

"Well, there was this guy down the street—"

"What guy down the street?"

"He called me a nigger, Dad—and—and—I hadda punch him out! *I* won the fight!"

For a moment, they froze in the classic father-son confrontation. The father regarded his son, whose countenance sought parental approval. After all he *had* successfully defended himself!

"You wasted your time! *You wasted your time!* You don't have time to waste! You can't stop and take issue with every idiot who hurls an epithet your way! If you move forward at the rate I've got programmed for you, you'll soon be too far to hear him! Pass him by, and he'll still be standing on that corner wrapped in his bigotry and his ignorance and his hate when you drive back by him in your limousine of success! *Pass him by!*"

There was a pause. The silence was palpable.

"Now, get cleaned up, and let's go!"

As observed by James McGovern in his book, *Black Eagle* (University of Alabama Press), the perfection expected by Lillie Anna James and his father was probably responsible for the intense drive evident in whatever her youngest boy did. The immediate challenge was to please his mother, who seemed, according to McGovern, to withhold her love until "Dan Baby" achieved, or came very close to achieving, a goal.

The sobriquet of "Dan Baby," although full of affection as used by family and friends, somehow rankled Daniel, Jr., as he left his mother's school and entered Pensacola's Washington High School in 1933. All the James children had gone to Florida A & M and, among those, the one who perhaps stood highest in Daniel, Jr.'s, approbation was his older brother, Charles, who had become an outstanding athlete. Daniel, Jr., was proud of his brother, and was particularly fascinated by his nickname, "Chappie," for Charles was the family centerpiece. First of the family to graduate from college. Football star. Baseball star. Teacher. Athletic coach. Charles had been a shooting star and now, Daniel, Jr., would be a satellite of that star. No more "Dan Baby" for him! "Call me 'Chappie,'" he insisted, "like my big brother!" And they did. They called him "Little Chappie."

"Little Chappie" was well liked and active in a variety of high school activities. He sang in the school glee club and chorus, played football and basketball. He bragged a lot. It was important because *he* was the greatest, and it was necessary that everyone know that! The attitude seemed to fire his confidence until, one dreadful evening, he competed in a locally produced "Major Bowes's Amateur Hour." The idea was to gong the contestant off if the performance was not considered up to par by the judges. Suddenly, as the first strains of "Alone" wafted from a throat that was to eventually thrill large audiences with its melodic singing quality, the gong sounded in startling finality, with no second chance to make amends for this horrible moment of "incompetency." The embarrassment and hurt were to rankle for years.

That had been a humiliation, but it was a tragedy when his friend and constant companion, Honey Rags, the nondescript dog he loved so much, was killed by a passing motorist. "Dan was delivering papers on his paper route," his niece, Gloria Hunter of Pensacola remembers. "He had just run across Alcaniz Street and Honey Rags followed."

Nobody had ever seen Daniel, Jr., cry that much about anything.

"Dan was overwhelmed," Gloria remembers. "It was one of the few times I ever saw him lean on his Mother's shoulders and cry like that. She just put her arms around him, holding and comforting him in his grief."

As "Chappie" knelt alongside his mangled pet, he looked up to see an image that made his world even darker.

"And what made it so bad," Gloria continues, commenting on the way things were then, "was that the driver was white!"

Even darker clouds were to arrive, for in 1937, just prior to "Chappie's" graduation from high school, his father died of a heart attack. It was a quiet, reflective time for "Little Chappie" that lasted for days.

But if these were storm-clouded days for him, they also signaled the beginning of a new sunlight. Because of his interest and participation in basketball tournaments, his life began to take on other dimensions. A basketball tournament took him to Tuskegee Institute in Tuskegee, Alabama, where high school students lived on campus under certain conditions: The female high school students lived in dormitories with the nurses if they were boarding-students, and male students lived in the dormitory with the athletes.

"Little Chappie" was thrilled with Tuskegee Institute: the bright sophistication of academia, the wide, green lawns, the ivy-covered, colonnaded buildings of brick and mortar, black students behaving like no black students he had ever seen, sparkling, sophisticated girls strolling about the campus. In fact, it was while playing in a high school basketball tournament there, that he had actually seen the young student who would become the mother of his children and hold his hand to the end.

Daniel, Jr.'s, excitement about the campus was so great, he rushed back home to confront his mother.

"Mom!" he exclaimed, "*That's* where I want to go to college!"

"Well, son," Lillie Anna James replied in her sage way, knowing that it would be a struggle, "we'll see. We'll see!"

In June 1937, "Little Chappie" graduated from Pensacola's Washington High School. In January of that year, Franklin Delano Roosevelt began his second term as president of the United States. President Roosevelt would greatly affect the future of this young man and thousands like him across the country.

Out there, over the coastline and wide expanse of Pensacola Bay, navy pilots earned their wings, slashing through the Florida air, their planes twinkling in the reflected sunlight. "Little Chappie's" dream had begun. The die was cast:

"I didn't want to go into the navy, although that was my first love, because I wanted to fly—I didn't want to cook!"

Chapter Three
Into the Clouds

I

" "Booker T. Washington," Bernard T. Weisberger wrote, quoting a reporter in his 1972 book on the man who founded Tuskegee Normal and Industrial Institute, "was a man of the soil, who has come up fighting, dealing with the world, not as he would like to have it, but as it had overtaken him. Many great leaders have been like that."

The leading black school in the South no doubt reflected that scrappy quality of its founder, and this could have been at least partially responsible for Daniel, Jr.'s, selection of Tuskegee Institute as the college of his choice. Athletically inclined, he found the school a natural, for it was a power in black sports. The meager beginnings of the school had to be an inspiration to a young, black mind seeking greatness. Booker T. Washington had begun life in 1856 as a slave in Franklin County, Virginia, the son of a slave called Jane and an unknown white man. He started Tuskegee Institute with little more than determination and a prayer in two loaned buildings—an old church for assembly and a ramshackle shanty. He literally had to recruit students for his foundling school, and even so, there were only thirty students in the first class. Because of the patriotism instilled by his mother, Chappie would have appreciated the fact that Tuskegee Institute was begun on the Fourth of July 1881, a beacon for another kind of independence.

The Washingtonian philosophy might have also been fascinating to Daniel, Jr., because its concepts were as down-to-earth and straightforward as he was. For Booker T. Washington realized, based on things he knew about his own people, that the Emancipation Proclamation and freedom from slavery were not, in themselves, the ultimate panacea. He knew that there was practically no hope that these new freemen would achieve equality at once since, by definition, slavery had left his people inferior culturally, socially, and economically, although they were intrinsically equal as human beings.

Washington realized that in order to compete in American society, his people needed more than mere academic learning. "[There are] scores of young men," he said, "learned in Greek, but few carpenters or [experts in] mechanical drawing. [Learned in] Latin, but no engineers, bridge-builders and machinists . . . or [experts] in agriculture."

So Tuskegee Institute was steeped in the theory of "an integrated training of the head, heart, and hand" that would elevate the race beyond the menial by teaching it to have a role in harnessing nature, learning the intricacies of modern science, and making these God-given gifts work for the race. There were few, if any, black students at Tuskegee, or serious candidates for admission, who did not know of Booker T. Washington's counsel: "Cast down your buckets where you are. . . . Cast [them] down in agriculture, mechanics, in commerce, in domestic services, and in the professions . . . *we shall prosper in proportion as we learn to dignify and glorify common labor and put brains and skill into the common occupation of life . . .*"[9]

Those stirring words were nothing new to Daniel, Jr. He had heard them all before at his mother's knee and in her classroom. Washington's words were simply validation: "Don't you ever make a profession of being black and don't you ever turn your back on your God or your country or the flag. That's *your* flag—red, white and blue, not black, green and red. Don't get so busy practicing your right to dissent that you forget your responsibility to contribute. *And you will prosper in proportion as you contribute to this great nation of ours . . .*"

"Little Chappie" enrolled in Tuskegee Institute in September 1937 and entered a black middle-class, intellectual oasis. Buildings bore the names of famous benefactors: Rockefeller Hall, Carnegie Hall, Huntington Hall, Phelps Hall, and White Hall. The names of campus sites reflected the cream of American society. College was a place insulated against the horrors of poverty resulting from lack of opportunity, rampant illiteracy, and stultifying need. It was a place to formulate dreams and prepare to carry them out. It was also a place to remember God and one's place in the universe. In those days, Tuskegee Institute required its students to attend church each Sunday. Male members of "The Drill" (forerunner of the ROTC) would march to church, along with the other students. And Chappie would be there, in his navy-blue uniform, white shirt, and tie, the metal buttons shining and the "Sam Brown" belt securely buckled.

"They looked," remembers a fellow student, "like policemen in those uniforms!"

Tuskegee Institute sparkled in those days and had gained national reknown, with its colonnaded buildings, wide green lawns, and polished military "Drill." Even the president of the United States, Franklin Delano Roosevelt, had come to see this wonder, this black diamond in a desert of minority depression. It was a glorious day when Roosevelt came to see this wonder of wonders. Some who were there will never forget the expression on the president's face. "He never closed his mouth," they remember. "We were in uniforms; we had our drill. Our guys were polished, swords at their sides, and we were standing in front of White Hall with its columns. The long car drove up and he looked and looked and never closed his mouth. It was as if he was thinking: 'I can't believe it; I can't believe there's a place like this in the South!' "

Choosing physical education as his major, "Little Chappie" lived in the dormitory with the athletes and played center and, sometimes, tackle on the powerful Tuskegee football team. He played basketball as well, following in the footsteps of his older brother. Tall, handsome, well-liked, six-four and 225–230 pounds bone-dry, he became an outstanding personality and athlete. Everybody knew him; most liked him. In spite of his own prowess, he rode, in a way, on the shirttails of his brother, Charles, for when people from Florida A & M would come to Tuskegee, they would greet him as if he resided within his brother's aura.

"Oh, you're Chappie James's little brother!" Even the football coach recognized him as such. And "Little Chappie" would beam, because he, too, was proud of his brother. It was an honor, this being known by his brother's nickname.

If "Little Chappie's" mother taught him the rudiments of being human and the need to excel and maintain loyalty to God, country, and flag, then his football coach rounded out his education. "Cleve Abbott," he was to recall in later life, "my football coach, taught me to be a man and be proud. When the national anthem was being played, we didn't stand around kicking the sod, we stood at attention with our helmets over our hearts."

In spite of his athletic prowess and dazzling, on-campus popularity, it was not easy for "Little Chappie." Although the family provided him what assistance and help it could, he had to supplement that with hard work. During the summer months on campus, he taught swimming, kept the tennis courts clean, and helped clean the gymnasium. Tuskegee Institute paid no money for this work, but gave its students "credits" towards their tuition, thus allowing them to work their way through school.

II

Meanwhile, events were occurring at a national level which would seriously impact "Little Chappie's" career. President Roosevelt's visit to the Tuskegee campus involved more than mere wonder at the exemplary deportment of blacks there. Other winds were blowing.

In the War Department, battle lines were being drawn concerning policies on the use of blacks in the military. From its evaluation of black soldiers during World War I, the War Department was generally not satisfied with what it perceived as their mediocre performance. Its evolving policies were apparently based on an Army War College study done in 1925. That study exemplified the army's racial biases, born of American society at large. It became the fulcrum upon which War Department policy towards blacks was based, and caused a change in the General Mobilization Plan designed to attain military efficiency. In general, the study mirrored the views that blacks were mentally inferior to whites; that they were "physically unqualified for combat duty; were, by nature, subservient, mentally inferior; believed themselves to be inferior to the white man; were susceptible to the influence of crowd psychology; could not control themselves in the face of danger and did not have the initiative and resourcefulness of the white man."

Additionally, the War Department relied heavily on so-called intelligence testing, without considering differences in educational opportunity, or economic and environmental background. It concluded that, for the average black, "the cranial cavity of the Negro is smaller than the white; his brain weighing 25 ounces contrasted with 45 for the white," and that "the black was immoral," since "his ideas with relation to honor and sex relations are not on the same plane as those of our white population," and "petty thieving, lying, and promiscuity are much more common among Negroes than among whites."[10]

Against this dark background, the president, as commander in chief, was being pressured by a new kind of black activist, coming from schools like Tuskegee and from parentages exemplified by the likes of Lillie Anna James, reaching for the full promise of the American dream. Within that group, a stellar goal existed: acquisition of rights by black citizens equal to their input to the national effort—extending to and existing even as soldiers of the country.

In Europe, Hitler's voice was becoming ever more strident. German armies were on the move.

On the basis of the War Department's stance, the army air corps, ultimately to be "Little Chappie's" service, unconditionally rejected blacks as a matter of policy. "There are no organizations in the Army Air Corps made up of colored men," it said petulantly, "and none are contemplated. . . . [Therefore] there are no colored soldiers in the Army Air Corps . . ."[11] Nor was the air corps to be swayed by father-son tradition or successful United States Military Academy graduation by a black. It initially turned down Cadet Benjamin O. Davis, Jr., the son of America's first black general, who submitted an application for flying training. The acting chief of the air corps wrote, "there would be no unit to which to assign this officer . . ."

People were already dying in Europe while the Japanese threat grew. World War II loomed ever larger on America's horizons.

III

It was now the summer of 1939. She had seen him around the campus, this ever-popular "Little Chappie" James. Socializing. Playing football and basketball. She had been watching him pass by with other young men on their way to the dining hall. Just graduated from high school, she was enjoying a time of celebration and coming leisure. May Day and ribbons, flagpoles and Memorial Day. Many students had already fled the campus for home and summer break.

It was the time of the usual weekend dance in the school gymnasium, and Dorothy Watkins had gone there with her friends. The chairs used for the basketball games had been removed from the center of the gym floor and placed around the sides of the gym turned dance floor. It was a time of expectations for Dorothy Watkins, a Tuskegee native, daughter of a teacher associated with the Institute and who was to eventually be employed by the Veterans' Hospital. She was shy and unspoken for.

"Little Chappie" was there, all six feet, four inches of him; surrounded as usual by his friends; inundated with kidding and laughter, carrying himself in that special way of his—as if he were already really somebody of real consequence. He swept through doorways with a special electricity, a fact not lost on the distaff members of the student body.

Dorothy Watkins knew, with a sort of prescience, that a change involving love was soon to enter her life. Once, eavesdropping at home, as young people do, on a conversation between one of her aunts and her father, she heard what she probably already knew about herself.

"Jim," she overheard, "Dorothy's growing up. She's going to be courting before too long!"

"Oh," her father began, in that overly protective fashion fathers exude when speaking of pretty, dewy young daughters, "none of that courting business until she graduates from high school!"

And *that* was precisely the point on the occasion of this Memorial Day dance! She *had* just graduated from high school and knew she'd be all right if something wonderful happened.

It didn't take long. From his vantage point of great height, "Little Chappie" surveyed the gymnasium. His gaze fell on Dorothy Watkins. With his usual confidence, he strode over to her and, with his best "I'm the greatest" look, held out his hand.

"May I have this dance?" he asked, in that gentlemanly and now slightly antiquated way of asking a lady's permission for a dance.

"No, thank you," Dorothy replied. "First time I've met this man," she thought.

The music played and the dancers whirled. Before she knew it, "Little Chappie" was back. She turned him down again. Three times he returned, holding out his hand, asking permission. The third time, he had come with not a little concern and puzzlement, wondering why he'd been turned down in the first place!

"May I have this dance?" he again intoned.

Dorothy Watkins smiled and thought, "Oh, this is the same guy. Oh, he's nice and tall—maybe—maybe—"

And they danced the way people did in the Thirties. Close, but not too close. Eagerly, but not too eagerly. It was a nice dance. Chatting, they noted that there weren't many students around. "It's just a dance," Dorothy thought, "because my father's coming to pick me up!" She remembers that she let him walk her to her father's car that night.

"Little Chappie" was all agog after that night. "Who *is* she?" he asked his fellow students. He corraled her best friend and browbeat her in a nice way: "Have you talked to her? Tell her I'm a nice guy, ok?"

They began to see each other at the "entertainments" on Saturday evenings, which included concerts by the likes of Marian Anderson. Love bloomed as she began to let him walk her home—just before dark.

On one of those delicious, summer evenings, after a slow walk home, they sat together in the front porch swing. Close. Speaking the words that lovers speak. Swinging, gently swinging, in the summer air. Her father was off to a meeting. It was a nice, close, private kind of moment.

Suddenly, her father was home and, as he came up the steps, "Little Chappie" decided to seal it. As Mr. Watkins topped the stairs, "Little Chappie" stood up and faced him.

"Sir!" he began, "I'm Daniel James! I'm a student at Tuskegee; a physical education major and I'm going to be a senior. I'd like to call on your daughter!"

Mr. Watkins stopped, turned, looked "Little Chappie" up and down, then shook the hand of his daughter's would-be suitor with a twinkle in his eye. "Well, I guess that'd be all right," he said, "as long as you can conduct yourself as a gentleman should!" Not until then, not until Mr. Watkins gave it his blessing, did the courtship begin in earnest. Inseparables and born-to-be-togethers, now. Football games. The movies. She a majorette, he a star football player. Watching the drill team together. Slow dancing. Shadows on the ceiling. Slow dancing, like lovers do.

Although Cupid had clearly run "Little Chappie" through with every arrow from his quiver, this had not dampened his ebulliency or aggressiveness. Retired

Col. William Campbell, of Seaside, California, then on the Tuskegee Institute staff, knew "Little Chappie" well, having met him in the summer of 1937, and remembers that "Chappie was always up to something. He was mischievous, and was always involved in anything going on around the campus." It was this mischievousness, this yearning for untrammeled involvement, and his size (constituting a threat to average-sized people), which almost ended his college career.

Somebody made him mad, and, according to James McGovern in his book *Black Eagle,* "Big Lumbering Dan" did not take kindly to insult. Perhaps it was his father's counsel ("If there's going to be a fight, you start it.") that caused him to respond to insinuations about his attentions to a coed by challenging the loudmouth to a fight. Fighting was against campus policy, of course, but it must have been splendiferous. The taunt. The gauntlet thrown down. The group of special friends egging the gladiators on, locking their arms to form a circle around the warriors. It was a flashback to original man. A brawl, that "Little Chappie" won. Even "Little Chappie" thought that his number was up as far as Tuskegee Institute was concerned. And above all, he worried about what his mother would think and say. It was a legitimate worry.

"Tuskegee Institute," says the retired Colonel Campbell, "had a warning system. Before they would suspend you, there were three warnings for missing classes, insubordination to teachers, fighting, etc." Among other things, suspension "meant going home, so unless you lived in the area, it was a problem. If you had to go home, it was tougher, because in those days, parents sacrificed a lot to send you to college." "If I ever got kicked out of the place," Little Chappie moaned, "mother would die!"

Events were to save his hide, in spite of the punishment of being expelled.

IV

World events, Congress, an activated black population, the black press, and political expediency were to save "Little Chappie's" hide.

During September 1939, a scant four months after Daniel James, Jr., and Dorothy Watkins discovered their great love, four German armies struck across the face of Europe. Hitler's *Fall Weiss** left Polish villages in ruins, children screaming alongside the charred bodies of their mothers, while the Luftwaffe showered Warsaw with steel and fire.

* Code name (Plan White) for Hitler's invasion of Poland.

In Washington, the army thought it time to rethink the role of blacks within its ranks. Should it expand past the four black regiments already in existence? The Negro community and black press criticized the army for its vacillation. Feeling set upon, the army responded that "its primary concern was . . . to maintain a fighting machine . . . it was not interested in changing social customs," and "segregation is required; discrimination is prohibited," thus its separate-but-equal stance would be maintained. Efforts by blacks to enter aviation were stymied by the army air corps, which responded that it could not use blacks because it "required men of technical and mechanical experience [and] as a rule, the colored man has not been attracted to this field as has the white man."[12]

However, in that year, Congress shot two arrows into the rump of the hidebound army air corps. In April 1939, it passed Public Law 18, providing for the large-scale build-up of the air corps, stipulating that civilian schools would be contracted to conduct primary flying training and that at least one of these schools would be dedicated to the training of blacks. In June of that year, the Civilian Pilot Training Act called for the establishment of the Civilian Pilot Training Program (CPTP), to be run by the Civil Aeronautic Authority (CAA). The rationale called for the establishment of a flying cadre should the country become embroiled in the war. Programs were established at six black colleges: Howard, Hampton, North Carolina A & T, Delaware State, West Virginia State, and Tuskegee Institute.

With the formation of the Civilian Pilot Training Program at Tuskegee, the realization of Chappie's long-wished-for dream of one day becoming a pilot could become a reality. The dance that was to become his life could not have been choreographed more perfectly.

He entered the program in his senior year with gusto, leaving the consequences of threatened suspension behind him. "Chief" Charles A. Anderson, his flight instructor, was overjoyed at the innate abilities of his new charge. "I could tell," said the Chief, "the first time I took him up, he was going to be a good pilot, he had more guts than anyone I had ever seen!"

It was Chappie's dream. He wanted it.

Eleanor Roosevelt wanted it, too, for it was at this time that the president's wife came to Tuskegee to witness this phenomenon of black men flying. Chief Anderson took her up for a ride. "She looked down," they recall, "and saw all the land and the beauty. Nobody knows for sure, but maybe she might have gone back to Washington and said to the President, 'Mr. President, there's plenty of land—why don't you let the blacks fly?' "[13]

Chapter Four
"They Shall Mount Up Their Wings Like Eagles"

I

" "Little more than a cow pasture" at the time, Moton Field, situated a few miles north of Tuskegee, a little east of the little town of Notasulga, Alabama, was the site of the beginning of the Civilian Pilot Training Program at Tuskegee Institute.[14] Chappie's basic flight training was done in the old Piper Cub. Primary training, when it was time, was to begin in the old Stearman aircraft, the PT-17 (and PT-19s, until they fell apart).

Still in college, he retained his reputation as big man on campus. He was the consummate politician and football player, ranging the line as guard or tackle or center, playing where he was needed to fill the gap; for in small schools such as Tuskegee, one was a "linesman" first of all. It was basic, bone-rattling, rough football. The single wing. A "balls-to-the-wall, go-for-it" kind of football. He played guard on the basketball team the way he played football, uncompromisingly and rough. It was all the same to him, because that was the way he approached life.

Early in 1941, a Californian named Archie Williams came into Chappie's life as he signed on for advanced instructor classes in the Civilian Pilot Training Program. A new arrival at Tuskegee, Williams had already completed CPT at the University of California, Berkeley, an engineering degree in one pocket, a pilot's license in the other and an Olympic Gold Medal around his neck, having won the 400-meter competition in 1936. After a checkout ride, he had been certified as an instructor pilot. Chappie became one of his student trainees.

It was time now to leave the little Cubs behind. Acrobatics was the name of the game, calling for the faster biplanes. There might have been another reason for the switch.

"Chappie and I," Williams recalls, "used to go up in this little Cub. Chappie weighed about 210 pounds, and I wasn't too small. That little Cub was just— *squatting!*"

Williams began Chappie's introduction to acrobatics and advanced flying gently. "The main thing to realize is that everybody's scared when you get into one of those things, I don't care who you are," Williams reminisces. "Chappie was a big, old, rough, teddy-bear kind of guy. You'd think that *this* guy's too clumsy to do this, but no, he had a good touch," he remembers.

So the "confidence maneuvers" began. Teaching Chappie to be an instructor pilot. Take-off procedures. Circle into slow, gentle turns. Show Chappie that the plane wouldn't fall apart when the power was cut back. Demonstrate and teach him the mechanics of the steep turn and other maneuvers he could handle. All of it done gently, ever so gently, so as not to panic his students.

"Chappie had great flying ability," Williams says, echoing "Chief" Anderson's initial evaluation. "He was a natural. He caught on to anything real quick. In fact, he could improvise!"

Chappie's quick grasp of instruction was to stand him in good stead, for now his confidence was building. He was, as were most of the flying students at this stage of civilian pilot training, anxious to keep going. This was necessary, because other students were doing those slow rolls and snap rolls. One had to measure up. They even invented maneuvers that weren't in the book, "just for the hell of it." Converted snap rolls, for example, they christened "dillies" (as in, "Damn, wasn't *that* a dilly!")

By now, Chappie and his fellow students were excited about what they did in the air. It seemed natural, almost easy.

But it was more than that. It was, in effect, part of the greatest challenge Chappie and the rest of his fellow students had faced thus far in their young lives. The challenge was real, because *everyone* was watching: the black press, the civil rights activists, Congress, the jaundiced eyes of the military, and even the president of the United States, who was running for another term and sharply felt the need to ensure the black vote. Almost to a man, the people with the power had said that black men couldn't fly. Somebody had even made the sarcastic but succinct observation that "the jump from the plough to the plane was too much for the average nigger."

Chappie and his fellow trainees had to prove people like that wrong. So great was this challenge, it had become almost an obsession that drove some blacks in the program over the edge to the kind of brinksmanship that bespoke danger and death itself.

Such a driven man was Butch Dawson (Cadet Robert Dawson) who had become a friend of Chappie's. More than friends, they were, in Williams's terms, "real good buddies." So intent was Butch Dawson in his zeal to fly and excel, he had become an inspiration to the other students. Later, after other hurdles to cadet training were overcome, they were to be shocked and saddened.

"Butch," remembers Williams, "was on his last team ride in advance training before graduation. He and this other guy used to fly under this damned little bridge at the end of the ride, pull up and do a roll. Well, he hadn't done it for two or three months, and this was to be his last chance at it." It was 8 June 1942. Butch rode the front cockpit, Cadet William I. Lawson in the rear.

Coming around high above the Alabama landscape that last time, they looked down and saw the damnable, little bridge sitting there like a little toy. It looked completely harmless. A play bridge on a train set some kid had just gotten for Christmas. They began their long descent.

"Let's do it one more time!" Butch yelled.

"Well," Williams continued, "what happened was that he didn't know that they had put a damned power line right in front of the bridge. He hit the power line and that was it. All you can say is that he put out all the lights in southern Alabama—but he put his lights out, too!" Butch was dead. The AT-6 was sundered in half. Lawson was found in a disoriented state a mile from impact, his survival earning him the nickname "Ghost," which was to follow him in perpetuity.

The friendship between Chappie and Archie Williams grew, and, as Williams watched Chappie's flying progress, he knew it was just a matter of time before his student would be trying for further training. Chappie's immediate goal was to complete the instructor cycle and ultimately obtain an instructor's rating.

Williams and his wife befriended Chappie, still a struggling student. He was, even at that young age, the kind of person you had to like. Even if he did something you didn't like, people remember that you *had* to like him "because he was just that kind of guy"—until somebody pushed too long, too hard. Then the quick, tornado-like temper would rise. Though he picked his spots to lose his temper, his sheer size numbed most opponents and usually served as a catalyst for peace. He might have growled in counterpoint at such times, exercising that marvelous, rheumy voice of his, "If you don't start some 'SH'—
—there ain't gonna be no 'IT'!"

The two of them were denizens of the campus pool hall where Chappie excelled. It was no difficult feat for him to hold three pool balls in one huge hand. "You couldn't beat him at nickel nine ball," Williams remembers, "no way!" Fondly dubbing Williams "Pool-Hall Red," Chappie at times would stop by Williams's home to "sample the cooking." Hunger sometimes dogged the heels of working students with minimal help coming from home.

Elaine Thomas, Tuskegee native and lifelong friend of Dorothy Watkins James (they were look-alikes in their younger years, causing confusion and consternation "among the fellows," leading Chappie to jokingly remark to his children in later years, "See, if I'd made a *mistake, she* could have been your Mother!") remembers Chappie's bent toward well-meant mischief during his instructor pilot days. He awed them with his new-found flying skills. Gathering a group of students about him, he'd look them in the eyes in that easy, relaxed way of his and get their adventurous juices flowing.

"Now," he'd begin with a straight face, "if you're around tomorrow about two o'clock, I'm gonna buzz the campus and *land my airplane on top of the library!*" With that, he'd walk away, leaving them with eyes stretched wide with amazement and not a little fear.

"We *believed* Chappie," Elaine Thomas remembers, "because we knew he usually did what he said."

And at exactly two o'clock the next day, they'd hear an airplane engine coming closer. The students would look at each other nervously. By now, the sound of the airplane would be roaring and suddenly, *there he was,* coming in low, buzzing the library building as he promised.

"We were really afraid," Thomas remembers, "because we thought Chappie was *really* going to try landing that plane on top of the library!"

That's the way he was—jovial, fun-loving and a tease.

Although the CPT involvement was a giant step forward for Chappie, one more giant step remained—somehow to make the transition into the air corps itself.

II

In spite of the fact that the army air corps had its mandate to train black pilots under the auspices of Public Law 18 and the Civilian Pilot Training Program, it did not hasten to include them in flying programs. Although blacks like Daniel James, Jr., assumed that they would be allowed to enter the army air corps after completion of civilian pilot training, they were to be initially disappointed. Because the law did not state this clearly, they were excluded from entry for the next two years. Actually, the army air corps would not fully implement the law, its leaders calling its provisions "superfluous," confident that the War Department was itself opposed to the proviso of black inclusion in the program.

Civil rights and black activist groups began to exert pressure on Congress, which finally responded in 1940, amending the Selective Training and Service Act to include specifications outlawing "race or color" discrimination and providing for induction, selection, and training in the military for blacks. Thus the

War Department was required to accept blacks in "numerical proportion to whites."

Still the army air corps vacillated, falling back on the old theories. "No separate units had been set up to accommodate Negroes for training," it said, "and therefore, it would be impossible to accept people of that race." The chief of the air corps, Gen. Henry Arnold, supported the argument by saying that "Negro pilots cannot be used in our present Air Corps units since this would result in having Negro officers serving over white enlisted men, which," he continued, would create "an impossible social situation." And later, as if to simply close the matter, the army air corps concluded that "there are no Negro pilots in the armed services of *any* of the world powers."

However, civil rights pressures continued until, near the end of 1940, the army air corps was forced to plan for utilization of blacks and accept its numerical proportion of selective service blacks. Expediency had been the watchword. Chanute Field, in Illinois, an already established facility, was selected for black technical training, and Tuskegee was to be the site for black pilot training.

To its credit, once embarked on the project, the army air corps did insist that the facility at Tuskegee be "fully equivalent, with respect to the character of living conditions, facilities, equipment and training, to that provided white personnel under similar conditions."

Southeastern Air Corps Training Center at Maxwell Field, Alabama, commanded by Brigadier General W. R. Weaver, activated the army air corps plan. Guidelines were stringent, and in line with social norms. Blacks were to be supervised and trained by white officers and noncommissioned officers. The commanding officer at Tuskegee, by regulation, was to be white. The commander of the soon to be formed 99th Pursuit Squadron was "to be a white officer, for an indefinite length of time." Forty-seven black officers and 429 black enlisted men were to be trained in the first year. It was to be *an experiment,* fair-mindedly administered by General Weaver who "wanted a safe and satisfactory airfield," since "the negro population deserved a successful experiment in flying training; the success of negro youth in the air corps hinged upon the fate of the Tuskegee project." Additionally, the decision by the army air corps to select the pursuit squadron as the experimental vehicle further reflected the country's racial norms of the time. One pilot per single-seated fighter ensured limited black training. Bombers required larger crews.[15]

Later in his career, Chappie James, in an address, rather lightheartedly spoke about this early restriction: "A lot of people ask me today," he said, "they ask me, 'as big as you are, how did you get to be a fighter pilot?' Well, hell, baby, that's all there was, you know? If you were a black man, you *had* to be a fighter pilot and that's about it and—er—well, 'how do you get into 'em?' they ask. I say, *I don't get in 'em, I put 'em on!*" The jibe was received by his audience with uproarious laughter.

The air staff's back remained inflexible. "Blacks," it sniffed, "did not do well in World War I under their own officers due to the emotional characteristics of the race." But, in early 1941, the escarpment of air corps resistance began to crumble. It was the hour for blacks like Chappie James, who wanted to learn to fly, become air cadets and ultimately air corps officers. In January 1941, the War Department announced the formation of the 99th Pursuit Squadron, with the 100th Pursuit Squadron scheduled for the following year. It would be up to these units to prove that blacks had the ability to fly. And the only way to prove that, the training gurus intimated, was to provide "a test by fire—the only one of recordable worth." In March 1941, the first blacks were advised of acceptance into the air corps for training as flying cadets. And, in order to fulfill its quotas under the amended selective service legislation, the air corps activated "Aviation Squadrons" at its bases across the country, into which black men were assigned as members of trucking companies, base defense units, and medical or quartermaster detachments.

Tuskegee Army Airfield was established on 23 July 1941, and, on 1 November 1941, training began. The first class consisted of six men[16] who formed the crux of the now-famous Tuskegee Airmen. Five of these men were cadets and the other, a black officer, Benjamin O. Davis, Jr., was a West Point graduate and the son of a well-known black officer who himself was to become an army general. Benjamin O. Davis, Jr., graduated from West Point in 1936, having toughed out the four years in silence on the orders of an upperclassman who forbade his fellow cadets to speak to him because of his race. His very presence in this first class lent a special aura to it.

III

The man some called "Mr. Aviation for the Black race," "Chief" Charles Alfred Anderson, took the first air cadets through their paces, including then-Capt. Benjamin O. Davis, Jr. Anderson, from Bryn Mawr, Pennsylvania, had come to the institute in mid-1940, to teach flying under the Civilian Pilot Training Program and was selected to be the chief civilian flight instructor at Moton Field. The sobriquet, "Chief," stuck. Other black flying instructors (i.e., Wendell R. Lipscomb, Adolph Moret, Charles R. Foxx) involved in CPT training were to eventually become Chappie James's compatriots as his career unfolded.

November 1941 swept past. December came threateningly into view as Japan stirred menacingly in the Far East. On 7 December 1941, Japan attacked a slumbering American fleet at anchor, causing some 4,575 casualties.

Chappie James, his fellow pilot instructors, and the new cadets at Tuskegee

Institute listened incredulously the following afternoon as President Roosevelt's sonorous voice startled the world: "Yesterday, December 7, 1941—a date which will live in infamy . . ." And in Japan, its emperor intoned, "We, by the grace of heaven, Emperor of Japan, seated on the Throne for ages eternal . . . we hereby declare war on the United States of America and the British Empire . . ."

Noel F. Parrish, soon to become the long-term, revered commander of Tuskegee Army Air Field, looked at "Chief" Anderson in his steely way, but with an introspective smile.

"The Japs just attacked Pearl Harbor. Did you hear that, Chief?"

"Yes, sir, I did," the "Chief" answered.

"Y'know, Chief," Parrish continued thoughtfully, "they always said the Japs couldn't fly because their eyes weren't slanted right. Well, their eyes must be slanted right today!"

"Chief" Anderson was to remember those words the rest of his life.

Reeling, America assumed a war footing. At Tuskegee, Benjamin O. Davis, Jr., was promoted to major in one week and, never having an opportunity to put on his major's oak leaves (naming his dog "Major" instead), was promoted to lieutenant colonel within two weeks. While things that had mattered mightily the day before still mattered, they suddenly did not burn with the same peacetime incandescence. In Washington, selective service quotas were assigned to all military branches for greater numbers of blacks. The influx of new blacks into the army air corps severely impacted the Tuskegee complex, creating an applicant overflow for flying training against a quota system which admitted only ten to twelve blacks every five weeks.

During this period, Chappie James applied for admission to the air corps as an air cadet, but encountered constant delay because of the quotas. He continued working as a civilian pilot instructor. As work continued on the construction of Moton Field and the Tuskegee airfield complex (the War Department initially allocating one million dollars for its construction with a final cost of four million), he earned additional money as a construction worker.

He was deeply sentimental about Moton Field because he helped build it. He wielded a paint brush during the summer months. It was a windfall. The students worked for one or two dollars an hour, considered lots of money for the times. It was such a windfall, it enabled some students to buy their first car ever.

It was now November 1942, and the courtship that had begun between Chappie James and Dorothy Watkins at a Memorial Day dance in the spring of 1937 had blossomed into a full, serious romance.

It had early dawned on Chappie that, with the steady job of civilian pilot instructor, this might be the time to take a wife. In fact, to the best of his widow's recollection, it was this precise reasoning which led him to propose.

"We can get married, now," she recalls his remarking, "I've got a job now."

The date was set, and on Wednesday, 3 November 1942, Chappie James and Dorothy Watkins were married in a simple ceremony in the chaplain's home on the Tuskegee campus. The bride was lovely and sheathed in a gold, silk dress, pinned with a corsage of chrysanthemums. She wore Chappie's class ring on a golden chain around her neck. He couldn't afford to buy her a wedding ring. Dorothy's sister, Aubrey, was the only member of her family present. Dorothy had been afraid to tell her father. She feared his disapproval because she was so young. Her mother knew, but didn't come to the wedding, either, for fear her husband would find out. Later, a tense Chappie broke the news at a quiet dinner.

"It wasn't a big, formal wedding," Dorothy remembers, "because in those days people weren't doing that. Everybody was thinking about the war." Chappie's long-time friend, Archie Williams and his wife "stood up" for him. Archie was best man.

"We didn't have a honeymoon," Dorothy continues, "we didn't have time for those, it was wartime. Nobody was doing those things."

For the first few months after the marriage, Chappie continued his work as a civilian pilot instructor.

A breakthrough was coming.

IV

In January 1943, after Chappie had graduated from his last civilian pilot trainee class, the call came from the air corps to take the written examination as part of the application process. He and old friend Archie Williams went over to Maxwell Field in Montgomery to take it.

"We shocked those dudes!" Williams now exults. Chappie's brain was college-smart. Both were already expert pilot instructors. Archie was just out of engineering school.

"Y-You guys m-made the *h-h-highest* score!" sputtered the exasperated proctor, his face contorted in a kind of disbelief that Chappie and Archie read as saying, "God, these white guys didn't do *that* well!" To which Chappie and Archie mentally replied, "Well, hell, that's *their* problem!"

But no matter, the proctor sat them down to take the test again.

"We ate that thing up!" crowed Archie Williams in recollection, seated in his high school classroom in Marin County, California where, in 1987, he was teaching mathematics and computer science, his hair grown white, his body a little bit fragile with age, a look of extreme satisfaction wreathing his face.[17]

Chapter Five
"They Shall Run and Not Be Weary"

I

Chappie James and the men who were to become Class 43G must have felt a strange stirring of the soul when they first experienced serious military training. They heard the muffled staccato of marching feet, were dazzled by the swashbuckle and oomph-pa-pa. They watched the parades and unit flags flying, touched the sparkling, new insignia, attended the steely attitudes of the people with the rank, bent upon instilling a new discipline. They heard profanity and indulged in ribaldry and bawdy humor. Suddenly they were coming face-to-face with the real weapons of war, which, until now, they had known only through conversation. They had come in time to see and hear the glory of the all-new, first-ever, all-black 99th Pursuit Squadron, swinging smartly down the street, 120 steps a minute, uniforms crackling, arms swinging by their sides with every cadenced step. If that were not impressive enough, the very air was ripped asunder as they chanted their fight song, delivered with university-like fervor:

> *Fight! Fight! Fight—Fight—Fight!*
> The fighting Ninety-Ninth!
> We are the heroes of the night
> To hell with the Axis might!
> *Fight! Fight! Fight! Fight!*
> The fighting Ninety-Ninth!

Rat-tat! Rat-tat-tat!
Round in planes we go
When we fly, Ninety-Ninth
This is how we go

We are the heroes of the night
To hell with the Axis might
Fight! Fight! Fight! Fight!
The fighting Ninety-Ninth!

Enough to wake patriotism and pride in the hearts of any *real* American military man! And Chappie James was no exception.

But this road upon which he now embarked was not to be filled with sunlight only. It would abound with obstacles and challenges that had defeated many others.

The people in authority took a dim view of those who didn't make it and called them "washouts." It wasn't the place to be, for these men were to be the finest examples of what black American men could really do.

II

When Chappie entered air cadet training in the real world of January 1943, the color of his skin was a heavy load. Though he was born and reared in the South, and knew that the air cadet program for blacks was experimental, it was punishing to the psyche to hear that segregation was as much a problem as the tough training. To cope, one had to "think segregation" in order to survive.

In October 1941, for example, a little over a year before Chappie James was to enter the cadet program, the aviation mechanics and ground crews that were to support the 99th Pursuit Squadron arrived by troop train. They were quartered at nearby Maxwell Field, Alabama, because Tuskegee Army Airfield was still under construction. Their assignments involved cutting down trees and bulldozing water moccasins to death by the score. Living in tents, they built a new pistol-and-rifle range and set up bleachers in the base gym for entertainments they were not allowed to attend. They swept the streets, one survivor of the experience recalls, "from the main gate to the post exchange." "It was so bad," he recalls, "everybody thought we were prisoners." Local segregation stiffened with the influx of black troops. At many off-post establishments, it was no service at all or "back door service" if one was lucky.

Black soldiers were beaten and jailed for "attempts to cross the color line." Unless one lived in Montgomery, one did not go there on pass because "it was too dangerous." And true to its announcement, the first army air corps' commanding officer for Tuskegee Army Airfield was a caucasian major named James A. "Straight Arrow" Ellison, who, although competent in supervising the delay-ridden construction of the airfield, soon found, to his everlasting chagrin, that it was also dangerous to stand behind his men as commanding officers are usually expected to do.

He had posted a guard at a rented warehouse near the railhead to prevent vandalism of quartermaster lumber and supplies off-loaded for airfield construction. The overly energetic black soldier, posted without ammunition, took it upon himself to "direct traffic" on the nearby street. Irate citizens called the mayor to report that an armed soldier was stopping automobiles on the street. The sentinel was promptly arrested and jailed by the local sheriff for illegal possession of a firearm. Infuriated, Major Ellison retrieved his man from custody, informing the sheriff that he intended to post yet another guard that very night and, "this time," he roared, "he will have a rifle and this time he'll have live ammunition! Now, let's see you try to take his gun away from him!" Even an immediate conference with the mayor did not mend fences. The mayor bluntly demanded that black military police in Tuskegee not be armed with anything other than nightsticks because "the people did not trust Negroes with arms," and furthermore, "there was [no necessity for them to have side arms]." The major was quickly relieved from his duties and unceremoniously transferred when complaints were received from the local power structure.[18]

In January 1942, he was followed in command by Col. Frederick V. Kimble who, although a capable officer, soon earned a reputation for "catering to local racist policies" and being insensitive "to problems surrounding Negroes [he commanded]," maintaining strict segregation on Tuskegee Army Airfield, right down to signs designating "Colored" and "White" toilets—even though it was an installation established primarily for black pilot training.

Set into this matrix were three white men, who more than anybody else, were responsible for success or failure of new cadets. If a cadet heard a rangy, southern voice saying, "In the event of engine failure, don't you boys *never* try a 180 degree turn, 'cause this BT will sail like a rock!"—he knew that it was Capt. Gabe C. Hawkins, director of basic training. If a cadet wanted sympathy and understanding and an honest expression of hope for survival and success, there was always Capt. Robert M. Long, director of advanced training, whom some called "Mother Long" because of his apparently caring attitude. Then there was the devil himself, "old Major Donald G. McPherson," director of flight training, who looked, they say, "like the villain in the Buck Rogers comic strip of the times," because he never seemed to shave, presenting a "five o'clock shadow" anytime you saw him and who flew a plane as if he were "driving a truck." McPherson was not liked, and was perceived as being short of tact having apparently never learned the meaning of sensitivity.

And finally, on 26 December 1942, Lt. Col. Noel F. Parrish, former commander of primary training, became commander of Tuskegee Army Airfield. Although segregation was to continue under Parrish, his assignment to this position was to be a boon to every black man destined to serve at Tuskegee. Parrish, over time, established at the base command level an aura of understanding and patience, which included a studied awareness of the ultimate effect of southern practices on the psyches of black people. He became known for considerable tact and diplomacy, evidenced as he went out into the community to meet and talk with black leaders. Ultimately, he was to engender great respect for his fair-minded thinking.

This was the *mise en scene* when Chappie's Class 43G took the stage. The class consisted of Chappie, Archer, Ellis, Temple, Bailey, Mason, Wyatt, "Evil" Smith, Robert Nelson; Leahr, Bailey, and "Dopey" Hall; Wiggins, Curtis, and Steward; Melton, Westmoreland, Page, and Taylor; Holsclaw, McLaurin, Rogers, and Chubby Green; Claybourne Lockett and Daniels.

III

Five-thirty in the morning. Reveille. A fugue that soldier tune-crafters have long set to words: *"You gotta get up/you gotta get up/you gotta get up in the morning!"* That's how Chappie James and Class 43G began their cadet training day. Up and stirring before first cackle from Alabama chickens while the branches of pine trees raked the predawn sky. Reveille and the inevitable formation in the wide, company streets. Reveille and physical training, performed in front of the stark, spare barracks. Physical training, then marching to the mess hall, breakfast, and back to the barracks again.

Drill, and the cleaning of the barracks rooms. "Lowerclassmen, to the 'public' areas! Make those latrines shine! Sweep and mop down those hallways Mister, *if* you please!"

Depending on the individual schedule, cadets went either to the classroom or flight line. If it was the classroom, the morning was filled with meteorology and theory of flight, so they could understand what makes an airplane fly. There was Morse code and communications, radiotelephone and the history of the military, indoctrination into the officer ranks and what that meant.

After lunch, it was the Stearman with the open cockpit or the BT-13 (fondly called the "Vultee Vibrator") with its fixed gear, propellor, and a canopy that could close over its two seats housing instructor and student pilot. Students were required to fly these ships sixty to seventy hours. Beyond that lay the wonderful AT-6 (Advanced Trainer No. 6), a low-winged monoplane with retractable landing gear and controlled-pitch propellor.

The challenge was awesome, for out on the Tuskegee Air Field flight line reigned the volunteer terrors of the tarmac. Old, rough, ready McPherson, of the perpetual five o'clock shadow and the mean mouth. Captain Boyd, the nice guy from Indiana. A fellow named Dunn, from Union Springs, Alabama, of whom they said, "Hell, he's here 'cause he's close to home, what else?" The flying instructor from Texas, apparently nursing a perpetual grudge against guys like Chappie from the Civilian Pilot Training Program turned cadet. This guy had a personal vendetta against them, especially if they also had a college degree. *Their* days were particularly rough. He was nasty and mean. He'd curse, scream, and heap on the racial slurs, to include the ultimate ignominy. "He'd put you out of the airplane down on the end of the runway, screaming 'Get outta the goddamned airplane—I'm sick and tired of you and the way you fly!' *Then*, he'd swing the airplane around and dust you off with his tail as he taxied in and you've gotta walk all the way back in . . ." Cadets would look down the long runway to see a humped-over, solitary figure ambling in, and they'd know the son-of-a-bitch from Texas was doing his thing again.

Then would come the meticulous, razor-sharp debriefing, completing the debasement. It didn't happen to Chappie, but he watched it happen to another cadet. Silence, after all, was golden, if one wanted to have the coveted wings. "Suffer a few indignities if you have to, and get what you want!" his mother had said. Instead of telling the cadet what he'd done right, old "Texas" spewed venom: "Oh, you dumb nigger! I knew niggers couldn't fly! And here you are, you goddamned ape! It's just ridiculous! Get outta my sight! I don't wanna see you—ever again!"[19] And when somebody had a bad day, "Mother" Long's verbal syrup would be administered while old Gabe Hawkins repeated his soliloquy about how a BT-13 sailed like a rock if you ever tried a 180 degree turn just after take-off to come back where you were!

And if you were still in primary out on Moton Field, you could be backed into a corner by CPT instructor Wendell Lipscomb, growling in that special way of his: "So you think you've got it rough? Why, I used to walk twelve miles each day for flight instruction . . . so don't tell *me!*" That sounded laughable, but it was really true, he *had* walked that distance for private flying instruction, because he really wanted to fly, long before the Civilian Pilot Training Program.

It was *really* your unlucky day in the rear cockpit holding the stick if you'd drawn amiable Rodney Little (not his real name) as the instructor, who, having a "very juicy mouth," was known to spray the hapless student with spittle tinged with "halitosis" as he explained the mechanics of the aircraft. It may have been just after any of those episodes that Chappie came home, his heart dragging, ready to give up. Dorothy verbally upbraided him, sounding a bit like Miss Lillie.

"You told me from the first," she sizzled, "that you wanted to be an Air Corps pilot! You knew all along it wouldn't be easy. But I know you can do it! So go back there and face up to whatever it is that is making you unhappy! And don't come back to me until you bring me those *wings!*"

On payday, after evening chow, hard on the heels of the Alabama sunset and maybe a movie or a beer, the cadets would settle in for a bit of talk and friendly gambling. There would be the quiet shuffling of the cards. Rustling paper money and the jingle of change. Glaring eyes sealing in the bluff. Cussing and the finger-pops as the dice bounced through blue, nicotine-laden air across sound-dampering olive drab blankets.

"Harumphf! *Be* theah, baby!"

"Cra-a-a-p! Gimme those dice!"

"C'mon babee! Baby needs a new pair of shoes!"

"Harumphf!"

The dice slo-moed the blanket.[*]

Daniel "Chappie" James, Jr., probably shouldn't have been there. Dorothy was waiting out there on Franklin Road in the neat, little place. It was a challenge. He loved it. Often the outcomes of these games would be more than he had bargained for. More than once, he found himself broke, every cent gone. He'd stand up to his full height at such times.

"Hey, guys," he'd breathe, "nice game, but I've gotta take care of Momma! You guys've gotta help me!"

There would be silence and the plaintive voice again. Without a word, they'd all ante up. For Chappie. Because he had to take care of Momma.

That was more or less the routine that Chappie James and Class 43G followed. Something would happen sometimes that would distort the prism, portraying life in colors of happy, blue, hopeful, and even sad. Like the day Butch Dawson bought it back in 1942 trying to fly under that damned bridge. It could be *almost* funny and sad at the same time. Or the day old Gabe C. Hawkins forgot his own counsel about what a BT-13 would do if you tried a 180 degree turn to come back to the place from which you had just taken off.

The cadet training of Chappie James and Class 43G came to a temporary halt when Gabe did just that, and collided with a misplaced derrick. Having engine trouble on takeoff, he tried to come back to the place he'd just left, forgetting that the chances were he'd never make it. He didn't even have a

---

[*]This conversation is the author's invention, emanating from the observance of dice games during twenty-one years of active military service (USAF). However, the facts are correct according to Roger C. Terry.

thousand feet of altitude. The best that anybody could guess was that he'd figured it was better to come back than deal with all those pine trees and rocks out beyond the runway markers. Only trouble was that there was that infernal derrick some fool had left in his line of flight. He splattered himself all over the landscape.

"Splattered all over the landscape" is an understatement. According to William Ellis of Los Angeles, Hawkins was "pretty well messed up, [for] when they took him into the hospital, the chief surgeon gave him up for lost!" His injuries were grevious. The tremendous loss of blood made his survival tenuous. The two black doctors in attendance, Walter Scott Brown and Dr. Pinckney, head of orthopedics, literally put Gabe back together again, only to discover that all of their work would be in vain without an immediate blood transfusion. The nurses came, and they put the blood packets on the little, hanging stands there by Gabe's bed. The printed codes on the sides of the bloodpack showed from which "race" it was donated: "A" = American-Causasian donor; "AA" = Afro-American donor. Still in a semiconscious state, old Gabe looked up, just as the bloodpack was set to dangle above his arm, and he saw "AA" imprinted on the side. According to the chief nurse, he became really upset at the idea of "black" blood being given to him. He called in his wife, told her, and they say her blood pressure went off the charts as she demanded that her husband be transferred to another hospital. Frustrated, younger doctors were ready to abandon Hawkins, but older, more experienced doctors pressed on with their treatment, for the probability was high that he would not survive such a transfer.

Everybody watched to see what would happen. And before their very eyes, old Gabe began to get better, "black blood" and all. They say that after old Gabe recuperated, there was a noticeable change in him. All those dyed-in-the-wool, southern, segregationist fires seemed to die down. Gabe C. Hawkins mellowed out.

"Gee, Gabe," they used to say to him, "you sure have changed. Boy you're the nicest fellow! See what that 'black' blood did? Mellowed you out, is what it did!" And although it's getting ahead of the story a bit, Archie Williams says he saw old Gabe at the military terminal at Dayton, Ohio, years later, a colonel, and he was *still* mellowed out. Says he yelled, "Hey, Archie, how ya doin' man?" way across the wide terminal, and ran over to give him a great big bear hug!

Chappie James and Class 43G chuckled softly to themselves. So did the nurses and the doctors on duty in the hospital that night.[20]

Chapter Six
"They Shall Walk and Not Faint"

I

At twenty-three, Chappie was a new liquid, condensed from the vapor of his mother's and father's teachings. His black, middle-class face reflected his values. You could see it when they took the group picture of the primary CPT instructors back in December 1942. One of the most serious and determined faces in the group belonged to James. Robert Terry appeared dapper; Adolph Moret, thoughtful. Roscoe Draper cracked a smile while Linkwood Williams stared at the ground. C. R. Harris knelt on one knee next to "Chief" Anderson. Wendell Lipscomb, gloves in hand, a slight smile on his face, crouched alongside. Aviation-helmeted like the rest, Chappie stared straight into the camera, his face reflecting an immense inner resolve.

Big, strong, determined and smart, he cared about himself and others. Aggressive, he knew what he wanted. He had found himself, and the real Daniel "Chappie" James, Jr., was standing up.

Lillie Anna James's words formed the catalyst for the transformation. It was the "thou shalt not quit"; the "charge in that door of opportunity when it opens!" that did it. And Chappie had done it with a kind of ferocity uncommon in young men his age. To resolve never to quit and to mount a charge on doors of opportunity took daring for a young black in those days, because so many "doors of opportunity" were only mirages.

So he had dared, and applied for the Civilian Pilot Training Program, even as the army air corps and Congress itself had dilly-dallied on the issue. He did it, acquired a license, and now helped teach other black men to fly. He had dared, in the face of slow, almost nonexistent quotas, to apply for training as a flying cadet. He had done it, and here he was, riding a seemingly unquenchable resolve; nourishing a love affair with the United States of America—in spite of the apartheid-like face it presented to him.

But if that concerned him, there was not time to brood about it or to caterwaul about the separate-but-equal status the country seemed to impose as a way of life. Only one thing seemed important, and that was completing cadet training successfully with honor. It wasn't easy. It was tough.

"You were lower than the bottom of the ocean," recalls one ex-cadet, "you had no rights whatsoever for anything. It was 'Yes, sir! No, sir! No excuse, sir!' In short, underclassmen were nothing, while upperclassmen over on Tuskegee campus were top dog." The denizens of preflight were "simply warm bodies" heavily hazed and considered "not quite an entity."

And if this routine of tough cadet training was not treacherous enough, there was the problem of the old devil Link Trainer, which Chappie was now required to address. An odd contraption, the Link Trainer provided flight simulation for flying with instruments in adverse weather. Designed for "normal" people of "normal" size, it was named for the man who dreamed it into existence.

Concern and apprehension grew by leaps and bounds in John Wilson, the Link Trainer instructor, the day Chappie James presented his huge frame for the training.

"He kept hitting up against the sides of the trainer!" Wilson complained. On this first day, after watching Chappie cram his frame into the trainer, he tried to close the hood so Chappie couldn't see out. The hood kept banging him on the head. The outcry was immediate.

"What're you trying t'do, kill me?" Chappie roared.

"Well," replied Wilson, "we got a problem, then. I need to be sure that you're using instruments rather than looking out to see what's going on!" Wilson continued a bit testily.

Chappie looked at him with large and serious eyes.

"On my honor, Wilson," he basso-profundoed, "I will *not*—er—I will *not* look out!"

But Wilson knew that this was too easy. With the hood practically open, Chappie could make the training duck soup using his peripheral vision, Wilson thought. It appeared that he was right, because as Wilson recalls, "he flew it *so* perfectly!"

In spite of Chappie's solemn promises, Wilson's apprehension grew. "I *swear* Chappie is looking!" he lamented. "No one keeps that trainer that steady. I was trained in the thing and could never hold it that steady!"

Not one to be stymied, Wilson decided to act.

"Hey, soldier!" Wilson yelled, calling an enlisted man over. "I want you to go over to supply and get me an umbrella. You know, one of those big, GI umbrellas with the crook in the handle? Know what I mean?"

"Yes, sir!"

"Well, hop to it!"

Presently, the soldier returned with the umbrella.

"I popped that umbrella," Wilson recalls, "and covered up the space where the hood wouldn't close. I had to do that every time Chappie came in to do Link Training. Couldn't close that door with him *in* it!" It apparently made no difference to Chappie. He flew it just as well either way!

II

Everyone, including Chappie even though still in training, wondered when the 99th Pursuit Squadron would be sent into combat. As early as February 1943, the "spratmo"[21] around Tuskegee was that the 99th was to be sent to the North African theater. There had been other rumors. The 99th, for example, would be going to China to fly with Gen. Claire Channault's boys. The War Department had put that one to rest, deeming it politically unacceptable to risk the losses which would surely occur by pitting inexperienced pilots against an already accomplished enemy.

Since March 1942, when the first black cadet class (42C), the 99th, had been constantly involved in "combat refresher training," the air corps vacillated as to what to do with the unit. "Immediate movement" communications were received, automatically cancelling leaves and passes, only to blossom into nothing. They called themselves "Lonely Eagles"—whose future it was to fly alone, if ever at all. The delay was a blessing in disguise because of the additional training time it afforded to include upgrading of the skills of the ground crews.

But it was 1 April 1943 now, and the 99th Pursuit Squadron was really preparing to leave. Regret was evidenced in the hearts of Chappie's training flight, for here was a chance to *fly and fight*—and the air corps wasn't ready for them to go! Benjamin O. Davis, Jr., now a lieutenant colonel (in spite of the persistent rumors that he had almost washed out of flying training only to be saved by the War Department as its "handpicked" officer to lead the 99th) was its commander, replacing Capt. George "Spanky" Roberts, who became the operations officer. On this day, the sky was filled with the squadron's planes in perfect, low-altitude flybys and soaring chandelles. During the next two days the 99th Pursuit Squadron left the nearby Cheehaw Station amid farewells and tears as it entrained for Camp Shanks, New York, Casablanca harbor nine days later, and combat.

III

The training of Chappie's Class 43G continued. The boring repetitions of lessons would sometimes overload already short fuses, and it was time for a favorite pastime fondly remembered as "chasing them Alabama mules."

The name of the game was to get up high in a BT, spot a mule pulling a wagon, ease back on the throttle, then come down silent, cutting through the air like a Halloween hobgoblin; coming down low and slow and silent. "When you're right on top of that mule and that old boy driving the sucker," Archie Williams remembers, "give 'er the gas and climb out and UP! Then look down and watch that old mule go one way, the wagon another and that old boy driving the wagon still another. *Hot damn!* It was mean, but them old boys deserved it!"

Circumstances could, however, force cadets into embarrassing, and sometimes life-threatening situations. A forced landing, for example, into an open field was often cause for the jailing of an unfortunate cadet after he was arrested by the local sheriff for trespassing.

Colonel Parrish would get the call.

"Hey, Colonel, we got a nigger down here in one'a yo' sailin' buggies? He claims he's in the—er—air corps—but we know *that* ain't true! Found him out in this field. Got 'im locked up tight. Reckon he belongs to you. Well, he's your'n when you come to get him!"

And although Chappie is not remembered at Tuskegee as a heavy drinker, he undoubtedly knew and empathized about the problems the cadets were having in trying to get hold of a decent ration of booze. Everyone on station who drank was affected by the fact that Macon County, in which the base sat, was dry. But down in Union Springs, Alabama, lolling in the adjacent county of Bullock, the cadets could buy booze at the liquor store, or so they thought.

It turned out that the diabolical sheriff had a deal with the liquor store owner in Union Springs.

"If you went down to Bullock County to buy some liquor," Archie Williams and others remember, "the liquor store owner would write down your license number, exactly what you bought and advise the sheriff. As soon as you hit the city limits, that old sheriff would stop you."

"Okay, boy," the sheriff would growl, "pull over! Let's see, now. I know you got a six-pack of Greasy Dick beer in there, ain'tcha? You got a quart of Myers Rum in there, ain'tcha now, and you got *two* bottles of Jack Daniels!" he'd chortle, licking his lips. "Come on! Ain't no sense lying. I *know!* Awrite, let me have 'em!"

The cadets would dutifully hand over the booze, exactly as the sheriff had catalogued it. The sheriff wasn't finished.

"Okay," he'd rasp, "we gonna impound yo' car! Follow me, now!"

Once in the sheriff's office, the cadets were made to place their wallets on a table, then watch as the sheriff slowly counted out the amount of money in each.

"Wanta write this down," he cooed, "just how much money you got. You gonna get it back tomorrow morning after yo' case is heard, y'know."

The cadets knew from experience that the next morning in this kangaroo court, they'd say, "Well, boy, yo' fine happens t'be (the exact amount in the cadet's wallet). And, when y'all able, you can *buy* yo' car *back!*"

"Chief" Anderson's solution for the cadets was to fly down to Union Springs, buy and load up the booze, file a flight plan for Atlanta, then fly back to Tuskegee. A plan that filled the bill.

The enlisted men had it rougher. They had to run the same sheriff's gauntlet, using guile and speed. They were like pirates, driving a circuitous and wide route north of the base through surrounding towns in a big, long, Buick Roadmaster belonging to the assistant provost marshal. Slingshotting down a back road to the base leading to the rear gate, horn blaring, the sheriff in hot pursuit. The gate swung open as the Roadmaster zoomed through. The military police shut the gate as the sheriff burned rubber, his big, red light flaring devil rays across the landscape.

The training was tough. Relaxation was tougher, but it was fun sometimes. Shortly it would soon be over. Time for a final picture in flight togs. There was Bill Ellis, from Washington, D.C., and Ed Smith from Philly. "Dopey" Hall, from Albany, Georgia, and in the back row, center, almost as tall as the eye of the propellors of the aircraft parked behind them, stood Chappie James— from Pensacola, Florida. Even now, as graduation beckoned, the mechanics of the smile on the occasion of a photograph escaped him. Only the intensity remained, the lips firmly set. The eyes scanned the camera lens, while the aviator's helmet sat pushed back on his head, the goggles riding high. His compatriots might have remembered him, leading them as a choral group in the mess hall at Eglin Field in Florida during their last gunnery trials before graduation. He had them singing the Negro spiritual "Massa's in de Cold, Cold Ground," a song they weren't *too* pleased to sing, existing as they were on the cutting edges of a new kind of emancipation. But Chappie had led them in that song in spite of that as a white captain nodded patronizing approval across the wide room. They probably remembered, too, the two black student officers who took on this Chappie James afterwards.

"Chappie," they chorused in good-natured pique, "what the *hell* were you doing in there?"

"What?"

"What? You had those guys singing 'Massa's in de Cold, Cold Ground.' Hell, man, what kinda image is that?"

"Oh, yeah, man," Chappie responded, flinging aside their concerns. "But didja *see* the expression on that old white captain's face? Did you see how much he *liked* that?"

Little did they know that they had just witnessed the first demonstration of the astute political acumen possessed by Chappie James. *Get the people in charge on your side, and success was in the bag.* But then, they also suspected that this same man could sit down and figuratively scheme how to cut the throat of the captain who had smiled so patronizingly at the strains of "Massa's in de Cold, Cold Ground."

IV

On 2 June 1943, the 99th Pursuit Squadron flew its first combat mission, a strafing attack against the fortified island of Pantelleria. For seven days they flew without any enemy aircraft contact until, on 9 June, planes from the squadron were attacked by a flight of German fighters. Focke-Wulfs and Messerschmitts dove, from twelve thousand feet, straight through the American formation, firing as they made their passes. Crazy-quilt bullet patterns ripped through the wing of one American fighter. Responding, an American, Lt. Willie Ashley, returned the fire and at least one German plane was seen "gliding down towards the sea," smoking as it went. (Unfortunately, enemy ground fire precluded verification of what would probably have been the first kill by a black fighter pilot.)

Flying out of North Africa, the squadron later took part in the air battle against Sicily and flew strikes in support of the invasion of Italy. On 2 July 1943, Lt. Charles B. Hall, from Brazil, Indiana, became the first black American fighter pilot to down a German fighter. "Ghost" Lawson scored a probable on that day and, sadly, the 99th Pursuit Squadron sustained its first casualties. Hit by ground fire were Sherman White and James McCullis. Starting 19 July the squadron helped fly air support for General Montgomery's Eighth Army for eight days, helping make the summer of 1943 a different kind of scenario for the Germans—from that of offensive tactics to that of defensive thinking.

Nine days later, on 28 July 1943, Daniel "Chappie" James, Jr.'s, career as a commissioned officer in the army air corps began. It was a glorious day. Class 43G assembled in loose formation in front of cadet headquarters, dressed in their "pinks and greens"—the officer Class "A" dress uniform of the times. Chatter was subdued and amiable under the regulation, grommet-flattened, round-as-pancakes cadet hats.

The band and Class 43G moved down the street as one man, all those days of learning how to fly running through their minds. Learning what the aviator helmets, goggles, and parachutes were for. Learning about aircraft characteristics and what made airplanes fly. Boning up on meteorology, communications, instrument flying, acrobatics, and tactics. The tremendous pressure on them as black men involved in showing their countrymen that they had come far enough past a heritage of slavery that they could indeed fly airplanes in defense of their country. Remembering things from the underside of Tuskegee Army Air Base as they learned to fly, the things nobody talked about: the black officer of the day, pulled from his car, his driver attacked and how they had wanted to storm Montgomery, only to be talked out of it. Milton Henry, striking out against the travesty of having to ride in the back of the bus years before Rosa Parks did it, refusing to move, hearing the bus driver threaten as he fingered a pistol: "I ain't movin' this bus 'til you niggers move to the back!" while British cadets surrounded Milton, protecting him with their bodies while they gently pushed him off the bus. Remembering a black nurse, severely beaten on the bus for the same reasons by the driver and how, when they heard, they had broken into the MP station taking up weapons there and commandeering a truck, finally allowing themselves to be talked back into a sensible frame of mind. Wondering how the brigadier general, B. O. Davis, Sr., rationalized it on a visit to Tuskegee when he said: "You are in the South. There are certain laws and customs you must abide by. The Army is not to take part in any incident. Those who get involved do so at their own risk and must suffer the consequences . . ."[22] There was the instructor who tried to demonstrate a crash landing to a hapless cadet who actually crashed, striking trees on the way down, the engine sticking into the ground while he and his student pilot dangled upside down in an Alabama swamp.

The formation stopped in front of Chapel Number One, filed inside and into the front pews for graduation ceremonies. Friends had come to watch the presentation of certificates of course completion. They came to watch the presentation of orders promoting each cadet to the rank of second lieutenant, United States Army Air Corps. Came to see and hear the oath of office taken, words by which Chappie was to govern his military life, even to the emblazoning of parts of it on his tombstone decades later, so important were they.

It was magnificent. They had come, with Lillie Anna James, to hear and see the presentation of Aeronautical Orders. Come to see the lieutenant's bars appended. There were not many dry eyes in the faces of those close to Daniel James, Jr., as Lillie Anna "pinned" him, whispering in a voice filled with pride, "Do well, my son!" Those same eyes sparkled when the wings came. The wings, a license to soar, to go where not that many earthbound humans of the forties had ever gone—over and into puffy clouds, high across rivers and down high mountain passes. Gliding over great, wide lakes and even the very oceans themselves.

It was a proud moment. Tears gathered in the eyes of some family members come to see and hear and feel.

The instructors were there, too. Come to smile in approbation; to congratulate. "Mother" Long and Lieutenant Dunn. Old McPherson, perhaps, "a helluva pilot; rough, and a helluva man . . . a segregationist for sure . . . but Colonel Parrish kept [them] in line . . ."

Finally, it was over. Chappie and the rest of the class left the chapel warily, for tradition had it that the first man who took a salute from these new officers must be paid a dollar. Circuitous routes to the barracks were eagerly sought out. After running that gauntlet, the next chore down at the barracks, pursued with great ceremony, was doctoring "the hat." Turning the severe, stiff, regulation hat into a ninety-mission "crush" by removing the grommet, literally pounding it with relish until the desired "style" had been achieved.

The time for an extended leave was welcomed by Chappie. He and Dorothy proudly visited his beloved Pensacola. She stayed close as he sported his "pinks and greens," the wings, and the brand new bars of his lieutenancy.

Eugene Crenshaw, a former Washington High School classmate, had not been so lucky in the military. Home on leave, too, he wore the uniform of an army private. He was to later recall that when he saw Chappie coming down the street, a commissioned second lieutenant, he would dodge him to keep from having to salute, perhaps simply because he had not done as well. There was no malice involved, for he remembered Chappie with great affection from their school days. "[He] was an outstanding student," Crenshaw remembered, "always *driving* for something; he always had a *goal* he was trying to reach."

It was a difference that mattered. But there would be some things that would not budge for Chappie no matter how much drive he had.

V

Awaiting assignment, the proud graduates were allowed to try their wings in the powerful P-40 and P-39 aircraft. There were only a few in Tuskegee. Perhaps Chappie liked the cut of the P-39. At any rate, it was the ship he chose to fly. But there was a problem. It was just too small; he simply couldn't fit into it with a parachute on.

In typical Daniel "Chappie" James, Jr., style, he flew the ship anyway— *without* a parachute. He was so likeable, the line crews were in on his secret.

"There was a fuel booster pump on the left side behind the pilot," a line chief remembers, "and he couldn't turn that off, so we had to leave it running the whole time [he was airborne]. You were only supposed to turn it on during takeoffs and landings. He could fly by the stick and a little bit of leg movement."

Then, one day, the inevitable happened. After landing the P-39, he simply couldn't get out of the airplane. He was stuck. Twisting and turning, he tried to extricate himself. He couldn't.

"Chappie had to be cut out of the P-39. He'd flown his mission and couldn't get out," men who were there remember with some amusement, "so they started pulling doors off and [we think] it was Tony Jones [who was a sheet-metal man] who did most of the cutting of Chappie out with a big pair of metal shears!"

It was the beginning of a pattern for which he was to become famous. It was the way he was. A bit brash. Aggressive. A friend said it best: "A rule didn't mean a damned thing to Chappie. If it was there it was meant to be broken. He was a balls-to-the-wall kind of guy . . ."

It was late July 1943 and Chappie James had orders to join the newly formed 332d Fighter Group at Selfridge Field, Michigan, for combat training. Dorothy was pregnant with their first child. The "witches" who had hoped to cast a pox and pall on the idea of black men flying were gathering on the heath. The word was spreading everywhere that they had been right, that "the top air command was not altogether satisfied with the performance" of the 99th Pursuit Squadron. Col. William Momyer, 33d Fighter Group commander, to which the 99th had been attached, reported that "air discipline has not been completely satisfactory . . . [nor has] the ability to work and fight as a team been acquired. . . ."

The matter was to be brought before the Senate Advisory Committee in Washington. It now remained to be seen whether Secretary of War Stimson's assessment of this business of allowing black men to fly was valid in the first place:

"I had seen Woodrow Wilson yield to the same sorts of demands and appoint black officers that went to France [World War I]," he said, "and the poor fellows made perfect fools of themselves. . . . At least one of the Divisions behaved very badly. The others were turned into labor battalions. Leadership," he continued, "is not embedded in the Negro race yet and to try to make commissioned officers to lead the men into battle—colored men—is only to try to work disaster to both. . . . Colored troops do very well under white officers but every time we try to lift them a little beyond what they can do, disaster and confusion follow. . . . We are preparing to give the Negro a fair shot in every service, even to aviation where I doubt very much if they will not produce disaster there. . . . I hope for heavens sake they won't mix the white and the colored troops together in the same units for then we will certainly have trouble . . ."[23]

As Chappie James prepared to report to Selfridge Field, the struggle for black commissioned officers in the army air corps began to assume new dimensions.[24]

Chapter Seven
Trouble in Old River City

I

As Chappie prepared to transfer to Selfridge Field in the summer of 1943, World War II was in full cry. Americans were realizing their first major victory on Guadalcanal. The air war over Europe gained momentum. Rommel was being driven out of North Africa, and the Germans had reached the end of their tether in Russia.

Selfridge Field had been closed for construction during the last four months of 1942, with restricted military activity. As 1943 began, guilty consciences dogged the minds of thirty-five hundred men on station who "felt that they were marking time, while their brothers in uniform marched . . . to war." The base was like a still, silent sea; an idyll. Lolling with the thirty-five hundred, the only black unit on station, the 44th Aviation Squadron, opened its very own NCO club in February with a remarkable party, dancing with ladies imported from the great, smokestacked city of Detroit. "One would never guess," wrote the base historian of that period, "that this was the day that the War Department declared nothing stronger than 3.2 beer would be sold on Army posts . . ." Jake LaMotta donated five hundred dollars to the base recreation fund from his advance purse as he prepared to fight "Sugar" Ray Robinson. Black performers titillated the 44th Aviation Squadron with a plethora of traveling camp shows. It was the "calm before the storm" as, almost simultaneously with the 99th Pursuit Squadron's entry into overseas combat, Negro troops of the 332d Fighter Group and the 96th Service Group began to arrive near the end of March 1943; and "time," the base historian noted, began "marching on toward the day when Selfridge Field would be getting its share of notoriety throughout the nation . . .''

The historian was correct. It was not only the arrival of the 332d Fighter Group that presaged change. Nearby Detroit, where the Negro population had been steadily increasing over the last ten years, pulsated with a new, black presence. The war industry had been a catalyst for increased minority migration. This new population began to push for racial equality. Civil rights organizations agitated for further assignment of black flying personnel to bases in the North.

The calm and peaceful atmosphere of the base was shattered in April 1943, as the 332d Fighter and 96th Service Groups arrived, commanded by Lt. Col. Sam W. Westbrook, a white officer with a white staff of ''supervisory'' officers and a squadron of white enlisted men in support. One black 44th Aviation Squadron doing housekeeping chores was one thing, but an *entire* black fighter group? An *entire* black service group? It was unheard of in the annals of army air corps history. In May 1943, an ominous pall began to settle over Selfridge Field.

II

On Tuesday, 4 May 1943, Colonel William T. Colman, the Selfridge Field base commander, took the afternoon off. He went on a picnic with his family and several officer friends. Sam Westbrook, the commander of the 332d Fighter Group, was there. Colman held forth at the barbecue, turning sizzling steaks from side to side, as he drank like a fish. He saw the ''bone in the steak'' as he turned them, so intent was he on the job at hand. But then, the alcohol took over and, as he was later to admit, ''from that time on, the only thing [he] could remember seeing was Major John R. Lucas, and for the life of [him], so help [him] God, [he could not] remember one other thing.''

His mind a blank, he ''leaned over that fireplace to cook a big, juicy steak . . . [remembering] it as if it were yesterday . . . [he didn't] remember eating the steak and didn't remember returning to base headquarters.'' He quaffed mightily. Suddenly, it was midnight, and he had indeed found himself at his offices at the Selfridge Field headquarters. There, he had more to drink from a bottle of liquor in his desk, absentmindedly seeing his pistol in a desk drawer.

If it were not for what was about to happen, Colman might have been commended for refusing to drive while intoxicated. He did make that decision, directing the officer of the day to call for a staff car to take him and his family home. The clock inched past midnight.

A black private first class named Willie McRae was the staff car driver assigned to chauffeur the colonel home. Private McRae parked the staff car, entered the headquarters building, then went upstairs, where he encountered Capt. Will Orr Ross, the officer of the day.

"Where's the Colonel, sir?" McRae asked.

"He's in his office," Captain Ross replied, "I'll go and get him." By now Colman was staggering about. McRae went back downstairs and waited in the staff car.

Within minutes, Captain Ross came downstairs with Colonel Colman and the colonel's four-year-old son, Harmer. Together, they put the boy in the staff car, where he promptly fell asleep. Captain Ross and the colonel reentered the building, leaving Private McRae alone with the child who, within a few minutes began to stir and cry, saying that he had to go to the bathroom. McRae took the child to relieve himself. Then both of them returned to the car.

Colonel Colman reappeared. Staggering badly, he ambled over to the staff car and drunkenly began to play with his son.

"Say, driver," Colman slurred, "why don'tcha take t'kid and put him in my car? Right now!"

"Yes, sir!" McRae dutifully replied, getting out and carrying the boy over to the colonel's car. McRae paused, waiting for further orders from the colonel.

"Tha's okay," the colonel said, "go ahead and leave 'im there!" McRae walked back to the car, got in, and sat down.

Colman animatedly talked with the officer of the day for three or four minutes, only to turn towards McRae, his face red, teeter-tottering as he began to speak.

"H-Hey!" he roared to McRae, "H-Hey! Get the kid outta my car, why don'tcha?"

Sighing, McRae opened the car door, got out, and started to obey the order. It was a mistake, for as McRae began to move, Colonel Colman whirled, pistol in hand, sighting on McRae.

"G'dam you!" he whooped, weaving inebriatedly, "I made it perfectly clear that I didn't want a colored chauffeur!" pulling the trigger at almost point-blank range. McRae was hit in the stomach. He whirled about crazily, grasping at his abdomen, trying to run away, pitifully circling the flagpole. A Pvt. Carl E. Blankenship, on duty at the headquarters building, ran to McRae's aid, only to look up in horror as Colman appeared to be aiming the gun at him for a second shot. Blankenship stepped behind McRae. Colman fired again, this time discharging the weapon into the air, shouting maniacally, *"That* one was for the British! I wish I was there with them!"

Ambulance lights flashed red as the wounded McRae was whisked away to the hospital. Colonel Colman was arrested and temporarily confined at nearby Percy Jones General Hospital. Col. Sam Westbrook, the 332d Fighter Group commander, assumed command of Selfridge Field, clamping down a news blackout; for it was not every day that an army colonel with the responsibility of a base commander shot a private first class of any color. Nevertheless, the news leaked and newspapers began calling less than ten hours after Colman shot McRae. It would be thirty-five hours before an official announcement would be made of the occurrence. Newspapers, after all, only printed "gossip and rumor." Finally, on 6 May, as Colonel Westbrook was relieved by Col. William B. Wright, authority was received to release the story: Colonel Colman, Selfridge Field commander, had shot a Negro soldier. He had been replaced as commander.[25]

Two nights later, 7 May 1943, a civilian trespasser on Selfridge, badly intoxicated and on his way home from a party, was shot by a Negro guard, acting in the line of duty. The civilian was placed in the station hospital along with Private McRae, whose condition remained guarded. Gossip and speculation were rampant. The Selfridge environment grew more ominous.

An uneasy quiet settled over the base. Third Air Force established the Selfridge Field Air Base Command, the components of which were Selfridge Field and Oscoda Army Air Field at Mt. Clemens, Michigan. During this second quarter of 1943, most of the 332d Fighter Group was stationed at Oscoda for gunnery training in tandem with ground crews and service elements so as to simulate field conditions. Bomber groups from the rest of the army air corps which *used* to land at Selfridge were suddenly routed to other airfields. Most of the summer, the 332d maintained a skeleton crew at Selfridge.

An unholy alliance was consummated as Col. Robert R. Selway, Jr., assumed command of the 332d Fighter Group on 17 May 1943, with Lieutenant Colonel Westbrook remaining as executive officer until June. Although Colonel Selway was not to command the fighter group in combat, his coming on the scene to train it was a harbinger of trial and tribulation for black pilots. He was to epitomize the separate-but-not-so-equal credo espoused by the army air corps doctrine of the day. Educated at Kentucky Military Institute, he had graduated with honor in 1920, the year Chappie was born. He graduated West Point in 1924, when Chappie was four years old, and was commissioned a second lieutenant that summer, earning promotions through the ranks until, in 1941, he became a lieutenant colonel, ultimately attaining the rank of full colonel.

He was to represent all that could be defined as demonic in the minds of the black officers he was to command. Although he was thoroughly competent in many ways, his attitude towards blacks was known even before there was an air cadet program for blacks at Tuskegee. No less an individual than Noel R. Parrish, long-term commander at Tuskegee, when asked, as a brigadier general, about the attitudes of men like Selway toward Tuskegee, had replied, "I knew what Selway's attitude was—he was incensed about it, because he took the position that he could not have black crew chiefs on airplanes. It was all right to have black mechanics, but all the crew chiefs had to be white. So he was setting up various levels [as he went]—arbitrary levels of black employment. You mentioned somebody being hostile—that's what he was . . . ."

But regardless of Selway's mores and attitudes about blacks, the big job for him during the last half of 1943 was preparation of the 332d Fighter and 96th Service Groups for shipment overseas and combat.

On Sunday, 20 June 1943, somewhere amid Detroit's industrial haze, a black man and a white man had a fistfight on a teeming street. It was a fistfight that caused a human explosion of such magnitude it was to be later termed one of the most vicious riots America had ever seen. In short order, twenty-five blacks and nine caucasians died. Seven hundred people were injured. By four-thirty in the afternoon on Monday, the twenty-first, the army called upon Selfridge Field to send troops to Detroit to protect life and property. The entire field, except the black troops who were not regarded as a resource, was alerted, and a convoy made up of station complement personnel moved into the city with three M-4 tanks. A cordon of white infantry was thrown around the squadron areas where the black troops lived, effectively placing them under guard.

The next day, reinforcements were sent into Detroit from the 4th Base headquarters and air base units. In all, about two thousand men, commanded by the base executive officer, were on station in Grand Circus Park in the city and others at Fort Wayne.

Incensed by their exclusion as part of the riot force, the decision by the command structure to consider them a threat and not a viable military troop resource, some eighty Negro soldiers at Oscoda wrote a letter to President Roosevelt protesting their lack of participation and charging that "the Army was unjust to Negroes."

But the 332d Fighter Group was having more serious problems as they pursued their combat training at Oscoda. Flying old P-40Cs, some still painted with the shark's mouth of the famed "Flying Tigers," they found themselves constantly at risk. A former line chief, M. Sgt. James Jones remembers:

> In a few cases, we had to hold hoses on those old Allisons due to overheating while warming up. It was a shame to think that our boys were expected to fly those things. It was all my men could do to keep them airworthy. We lived in continual fear that someone wouldn't return due to a failure beyond our control. When they returned from a flight, it appeared quite frequently as though they'd flown through an oil storm . . .[26]

The black press began to castigate the army air corps for the assignment of aircraft due for retirement to the fighter group. These were, according to the Selfridge Field historian of the period, "gossip mongers [who] paid more attention to the accidents, because the outfit was the first Negro flying group, but there was never an *authentic* statement to show the Negro fliers differed essentially from white flyers," and cited the news release of a misled, black reporter from the *Pittsburgh Courier* who, on 30 October 1943, was to write: "The colored pilots at Selfridge Field and at the Oscoda were quite disturbed over

the stories . . . charging the Army with delivering inferior . . . obsolete planes
to the colored flyers. . . . The truth . . . was that the planes sent to both the
squadrons were identically the same planes sent to other squadrons using this
type . . ."[27]

It is an issue that black airmen may wish to discuss and conjecture about
in years to come, perhaps. The airplanes they flew were old and accident-
prone. During the very first week of his assignment to Oscoda flying the old
P-40Cs, Lt. Jerome T. Edwards was killed at Oscoda, his aircraft in flames.
On 9 May 1943, Lt. Wilmeth Sidat-Singh had been forced to bail out over
Lake Huron, crashing into Saginaw Bay, his P-40C engulfed in flames. After
forty days of searching, they found his body around three o'clock in the afternoon
on 27 June 1943.

The death of Lieutenant Sidat-Singh may not only have been of consequence
because he had been a fellow cadet and officer, but it would have also been
of special significance to Daniel "Chappie" James, Jr., since Sidat-Singh had
been, as was Chappie, an athlete of note. Sidat-Singh, an ex-Washington, D.C.
police officer, had graduated from Tuskegee in March 1943. America knew
him for his athletic prowess at Syracuse University in football and basketball.
As Chappie was arriving at Selfridge Field for his assignment to the 100th
Fighter Squadron, they buried Sidat-Singh at Arlington National Cemetery with
full military honors. It was a sad day for the Tuskegee Airmen and athletes
everywhere.

III

For Chappie and the other pilots transferring with him to Selfridge in early
July 1943, going to this army air field in Michigan was considered passage
into "God's country" after Tuskegee. Racism and oppression were not at issue,
or so they thought. But they were wrong. Selfridge seethed.

Instead, Daniel James, Jr.'s, assignment to combat flying training at Selfridge
Army Air Field was the beginning of a period of high drama, great risk, personal
fortitude, and sheer luck of the draw. Survival as a black, newly minted second
lieutenant in the United States Army Air Corps required a special level of
resolve. In James's mind, there were virgin territories to contemplate that no
black man had crossed in American history. The spotlight was on him and his
fellows, and they were at center stage. He must have felt the eyes of Americans
watching: some full of hate and disbelief, some cheering and applauding, and
some who didn't really give a damn.

There was something exciting about being at Selfridge Army Air Field just up the road from big, brassy Detroit. Compared to Pensacola and Tuskegee, it was more than hustle and bustle. It was a cacophony; a study in grey concrete, shining steel, and cascading glass. It was flying the "Luftberry" circle around the top of the Maccabees Building, or under the Blue Water Bridge between Port Huron and Sarnia, over in Canada; flying single-file under the Ambassador Bridge because it was there. It was wide lakes, motor cars, steaming ghettos, and for the unattached officers, fine, bronzed ladies from the environs of Detroit.

The Selfridge Field brass were busy now reassessing their position after the Detroit riots. Although they had thought themselves justified concerning their treatment of the black troops during the riots, the letter from the eighty at Oscoda to President Roosevelt had stung them. They lifted the restrictions on the field on 27 June 1943. Colonel Colman's shooting of Private McRae had complicated matters, not to mention the shooting of the white trespasser by the black sentry. At any rate, they had regarded their handling of the riot fiasco as satisfactory, and, with a flourish, sanctioned a kind of "victory parade" for the troops returning from Detroit on the fifth of July.

But what had really happened?

According to Professor Allen Grimshaw, then of Indiana University, that riot, like other major disturbances of the era, resulted from "threats to the security of whites . . . by the Negro's gains in economic, political and social status; Negro resentment of attempts to 'kick him back into his place.' "[28]

Since the military usually mirrored the larger society, the drama of the riot was keenly felt. In military circles, there was a great fear. Chappie and his fellow officers could not help but feel it, as did their white commanders. What influences would the Detroit riot have on the lot of them? Especially now, when the goal was the activation and training of an entire fighter group of black airmen and officers at Selfridge and, rumor had it, an all-black bomber group was on the drawing boards.

If the commanders at Selfridge and First Air Force at Mitchel Field in New York were moved by this new, wild electricity, they did nothing to control it. Their actions, which sought to contain it, only sowed seeds of discontent. When Chappie arrived, he was greeted by the same separate-but-equal—really racially unequal status quo he had left at Tuskegee. Comparison of the separate officer clubs, the paucity of promotional opportunity, and the exclusionist social arena were the proofs.

These factors, however, were not the focus of the Selfridge Field command. It sought instead, to find ways to divert the attention of the black pilots and enlisted men from the problems of racism, the diatribes of the black press on the subject, and "racial agitators" ensconced in the "Negro Mecca" of Detroit. The focus was centered on "keeping Negro troops at the business of training for combat."

On 24 July 1943, a major player destined to impact the lives of the black pilots arrived at Selfridge. Col. William L. Boyd became the new Selfridge Field base commander. Robust and well fed, sporting a neat moustache, Boyd hailed from Pittsburgh, Pennsylvania, born two days before Christmas in 1896, twenty-three years before Chappie was born. A "decorated hero of Hickam Field during Japan's attack on Pearl Harbor," Boyd was a veteran of World War I, a command pilot who had been an army air corps officer for twenty-five years. He was therefore steeped, regardless of his Pennsylvania roots, in army air corps doctrine governing the treatment of Negro troops, instruction which was soon to be made painfully obvious to the black pilots and enlisted men assigned to Selfridge.

James had arrived in time to be a recipient of Colonel Selway's master strategy intended to focus the black troops' attention on combat training. The colonel began by requiring that all military personnel take an hour of physical training six days a week. On 10 August 1943, he directed a simulated aerial attack on the city of Detroit, combining 332d Fighter Group aircraft with those of the Civil Air Patrol. He followed with another similar maneuver on 13 August, as the 332d flew thirty-seven P-40C Warhawks in formation, controlled by radio mounted on a field vehicle. All this wasn't good enough for Colonel Selway, the Selfridge historian notes: "Colonel . . . Selway . . . was dissatisfied with the progress of the training, and a new program was drafted as . . . the 332d . . . returned from Oscoda. The keynote . . . was 'Get to your Damn' Guns'—an idea intended to get the Negroes to concentrate on the business at hand rather than wasting time with racial matters . . ."

Selway stepped up the training schedule. There were fewer and fewer hours of leisure. He directed that signs be placed all over the 332d Fighter Group area reading: "GET TO YOUR DAMN' GUNS!" It was, he thought, a turning point in the training of the group and proof of his theory based upon an old provincialism: "An idle mind is the Devil's workshop."

Meanwhile, an aircraft retrofit was in progress, switching from the outmoded P-40 fighters to the new P-39 Airacobra fighters. New P-39 fighters or not, it was no different for Daniel James, Jr. Because of his size, the P-39 was "like a Volkswagen" to him, "with a little door on the side." It simply wasn't possible for him to get into the plane with a parachute on. The solution was the same: fly it without the parachute. He flew it that way for a month until, one day, the colonel spotted him.

"Get *out* of that thing, Chappie!" he roared, assigning him to fly a P-40. At last! A plane with enough room. To Chappie, it probably was like loosening the belt after a good meal.

In spite of that bright spot, the witches' brew continued to bubble. Housing for the wives and families of black officers was nonexistent on the base, its top brass electing to let officer housing sit vacant rather than allow them to live in it. Dorothy delivered Danice, their first born, in the Tuskegee campus hospital while Chappie was away on a cross-country flight. The child was two days old before Chappie knew. The familial tie grew stronger than ever. He wanted them near.

"Dottie?"

"Yes?"

"You check with your doctor and see if you can come up here," he suggested.

The doctor's response was positive: "Yes, and wrap up good, because Detroit is very, very cold!"

They were forced to find housing off base. Daniel, Jr., Dorothy, and Danice settled, along with the families of four officer friends, on Gratiot Avenue in nearby Detroit.

"Yes," Dorothy remembers, "we stayed in Detroit. There was Chappie, C. I. Williams, J. Y. Carter, Terry Hunter from Atlanta." They would drive to Selfridge in a carpool. "There was no place to stay on base."

Although the arrival of the families gave some relief, segregation continued to be a problem. Not only was there no housing on the base for black officers and their families, it was evident that the majority commanders meant to maintain the separate-but-equal doctrine. Black officers were a "problem" to be "handled."

As the summer of 1943 wound down in August, Lt. Col. Benjamin O. Davis, Jr., until then commander of the famed 99th Pursuit Squadron at Licata, Sicily, received orders to return to the United States and take command of the all-black 332d Fighter Group and its 301st, 302d, and 100th Fighter Squadrons. It was a bittersweet parting as Davis turned command over to Capt. George "Spanky" Roberts.

"Spanky," Davis said stoutly as he prepared to leave, "the destiny of the squadron is in your hands."

As Davis' C-54 took off, Roberts turned to his new charges, a touch of melancholy in his voice.

"The 99th," he said, "will never have as fine a commander as the skipper. I hate to see him go."

Although a competent officer, Roberts was to feel the ire born of suspicion and distrust in the breast of the top echelon of the army air corps as its chief of staff, Gen. "Hap" Arnold, visited the squadron only to stand Captain Roberts in a brace.

"George said," his widow Edith Roberts recalls, "that the general said the most awful, racist things to him under his breath so others nearby couldn't understand what he was saying. I have a picture of it and I could tell the way George's chin jutted out that George was *so* mad!"

"I never felt so bad in my life," Robert Rose quotes Roberts in his book, *Lonely Eagles*. "It was extremely difficult for me as he stood there discrediting and maligning the men who were doing their best under the circumstances. Whether right or wrong in his assessment of the unit, his manner was not what should be expected from the Chief of the Air Corps!"[29]

Chapter Eight
Escalation

I

The pall over Selfridge Field during the last several months grew thicker as Col. William T. Colman was brought to trial before a general court-martial on 6 September 1943.[30] The charges brought against Colman involved violations of five Articles of War, including twenty-nine specifications. He had committed an assault with intent to do bodily harm to the black private first class McRae by carelessly discharging a pistol, wounding him. He had misappropriated an engine generator near Oscoda Army Air Field, had been drunk and disorderly on five specific occasions, and had fraudulently and unlawfully procured transfers of eight enlisted men to Selfridge Field (one alleged to have been Benson Ford of the Ford Motor Company clan). He had testified to false statements in eight cases in order to procure transfers to enlistees at the base and had accepted the personal use of a vacation lodge at Foote Dam Lake from a company engaged in setting up prefabricated huts at Oscoda. Finally, it was charged that he had misappropriated the labor and services of three civilian employees.

Not only were Michiganders shocked at what seemed to be the almost callous way the court handled the case, but the black pilots and enlisted men of the 332d where Chappie was assigned were aghast as well when it became obvious that Colman's hands were to only be slapped. Found guilty only of an assault upon Private McRae; misappropriation of government property and drunkness in a manner that somehow absolved him of "conduct unbecoming an officer and a gentleman," he was broken to his permanent grade of captain and suspended

59

from eligibility for further temporary promotions for a period of three years.

"I wonder," asked Congressman Paul W. Shafer, Michigan member of the House Military Affairs Committee in Washington, "what this court-martial would have done if a drunken private shot his commanding officer?"[31] Over in the barracks of black airmen and officers like Chappie James, in the northwest corner of Selfridge in "Boom Town," and up at Oscoda, the question was undoubtedly rephrased: "What would have happened if a drunken *Negro* private shot his commanding officer?" It was an act that provided positive proof to them that the web of racism which they faced was rife with injustices and more than simple human error.

Private first class McRae eventually recovered from the gunshot wound and, after further investigation prompted by editorials in the *Detroit Free Press,* Colman was later retired from the service. The tension at Selfridge became tauter, and feelings in the 332d Fighter Group grew more bitter. It was only the beginning.

II

Three important things took place during the fall of 1943 which were to have long-term effects on Daniel "Chappie" James, Jr.'s, military career.

The first was the appearance of Lt. Col. Benjamin O. Davis, Jr., upon his return to the United States, before the McCloy Committee, a special advisory committee regarding black troop policy in the War Department. In official reports from line combat officers, endorsed by command-level, general officers, and a critical press, all evaluating the 99th Pursuit Squadron's combat performance, the future of the black flying program was at least suspect. On 13 October 1943, the committee reviewed army air corps evaluations and also listened with interest to the thoughts of black advisor Truman Gibson of the War Department and General B. O. Davis, Sr., inspector general's office (and father of Colonel Davis).

Three factors pertaining to the 99th Pursuit Squadron's performance record were pointed out. First, the squadron could not help but be inexperienced in combat because these black pilots had been barred from combat duty. Second, after arrival in the combat zone it was teamed with a veteran fighter unit whose performance it could not match because of that inexperience (hence, any comparative analysis was probably faulty). Finally, because segregation had to be maintained, the unit was denied the experience of seasoned flight leaders. Even though Gen. Ray Porter, army air corps operations representative on the committee, recommended that the black leaders of the squadron be immediately "re-

The Stain Remains

From the Detroit Free Press, 16 September 1943 Editorial page. By Permission.

placed by whites,'' the senior Davis recommended against it. It is not clear whether the committee motive was to respect the fact that General Davis's son had commanded the 99th Pursuit Squadron, but, based on his recommendation, the committee agreed to withhold judgment until Colonel Davis could state his case before them. Appearing before the committee on 16 October 1943, he gained some points by immediately praising his chief critic, Col. William Momyer, whose initial report had brought things to the present impasse. Davis admitted that the squadron was handicapped because no one in the unit had combat experience and that, he asserted, made for a certain lack of confidence. The quality of training was adequate, and, at first, mistakes were made. After these opening comments, Davis moved to the crux of the matter: ''After that, confidence picked up and became part of the squadron. . . . If there was a lack of aggressive spirit . . . later, we had it . . .''

He went on to profess surprise at Momyer's observation that his squadron had ''disintegrated'' when jumped by enemy aircraft, with one exception, for which he offered no excuse, as, during its first encounter with the enemy over Pantelleria, it failed to maintain a flight of sixes, breaking down into twos. Stand-downs, he asserted, were due to failures to receive replacement pilots in a timely fashion (''We were in combat two months before we received replacements . . .'') and, in no uncertain terms, indicated that he ''had no doubts'' about the squadron's ultimate success. The 99th Pursuit Squadron was thus allowed to remain and under the command of black officers in combat, even though the War Department and army air corps still believed that the 99th ''experiment'' was not a success, regardless of the Davis rhetoric.

The second incident of note impacting James's career was the decision, also in October 1943, by the chief of the air staff, Gen. ''Hap'' Arnold, to authorize formation of a black medium bombardment group. Its station was to be Selfridge Field. General Arnold's decision to allow formation of the 477th Bombardment Group was in response to political pressure, primarily, which held that black troops would be used in more than one kind of aviation. The 477th satisfied that demand.

The news of General Arnold's decision, regarding the formation of the bombardment group, presaged the third important event impacting James's career. Multi-engine training would open a new option for fighter pilots who were large in build. Chappie, at six feet four and two hundred pounds plus with flying gear, was certainly one of those. Wishing to ensure a future as combat pilots, Chappie and other large pilots, knowing that the P-40 and P-39 weren't built with them in mind, became involved in the program. Chappie, C. I. Williams, Peter Verwayne, Bill Ellis, George Knox, and others were pegged for B-25 transitional training at Mather Field in California.

While these events were taking place, the racial climate on Selfridge sank to lower levels. Of chief concern to Chappie James and other black officers on station was the steadfast refusal by those in charge to address the obvious solution to racial conflict over the officer's club utilization issue. Army Regulation 210-10 made it as clear as day. The right to full membership in "officer's clubs, messes and similar social organizations" was to be extended to *all* officers, permanent or temporary, on duty at a post. At Selfridge, the right to membership in the officer's club was expressly denied. James remembered the scenario:

> I took part in the sit-ins. We would start by going into the club at Selfridge and ordering a drink and the bartender would say, "I can't serve you here. We just can't serve you here, this is the Supervisory Officer's Club." We would reply, "Well then, we'll sit here until you serve us." They then would close the bar. We would leave and later one of our white friends would call us and say, "Hey, they just opened the bar, come on back." We would dash back up, and as soon as we walked in again they said the bar was closed.

Early attempts by black officers to attend the main officer's club could result in reprimand. The black officers were further embarrassed and humiliated by directives from the base commander to the Women's Army Corps (WAC) squadron on base to the effect that they should not wander the base unescorted between their barracks and work on the flightline because of the "threat" from black officers and enlisted men.

Chappie James and his fellow black officers could not see a movie in peace without first addressing the problem of racism. General Hunter, the First Air Force commander, who nurtured a special kind of fury which translated into an inbred mistrust of blacks, had thrown down the gauntlet. His Charlie Chaplin moustache quivering, General Hunter said that he "would not tolerate blacks and whites using the same facilities or even sitting beside one another in the theater." It was almost surreal, as James remembers:

> They had drawn a line down the middle of the theater . . . (where even the theaters in downtown Detroit were not segregated), and said, 'the blacks will sit on one side of this line, and the whites on the other.' And so when we, with the full cooperation of most of the whites (who were not in authority and did not agree with this sort of enforced segregation) decided to go on what we called "Operation Checkerboard" after the lights went out in the movie, they turned the movie off and made us go back to our segregated seat. This was a very stupid thing to do, but they did it two or three times a night . . .

The framework of this intense racial pressure became larger and more complex. Colonel Selway, commander of the base and, in James's words, a "master segregationist," reported the theater incidents to General F. O'D. Hunter. "It was," Chappie remembered, "just one of the things we had done to try to speed up the breakdown of this idiocracy."

The commute home was grim for James and the officers sharing the carpool each working day between Detroit and Selfridge underneath forced smiles. They'd get together weekends and talk about it, tensions rising, frustrations overwhelming, but always with a caveat: *They would discuss it among themselves and not with their wives.*

"The guys would come by," Dorothy James remembers, "and they'd say, 'let's go over here and talk.' " And that usually meant the gender separation expected when military families got together in those times. The men would be in the kitchen with the booze, talking "shop," while the women held forth in the living room talking babies, patterns, recipes, and private goals suppressed for the moment.

"Yes," Dorothy continues, "there were racial problems at Selfridge. But our husbands would try not to worry their wives. We knew they were going through problems. Always. That was a part of living for us," as their husbands persisted in trying to solve the problems they were experiencing.

III

On 7 October 1943, Lt. Col. Benjamin O. Davis, Jr., reported to Selfridge Field to take command of the 332d Fighter Group, relieving Colonel Selway. Selway became the officer in charge of all units in the First Fighter Command.

Davis's arrival, amid the usual military protocol involved in welcoming a new commander, was the catalyst for initiation of a twenty-four-hour, seven-day-a-week, intensive combat training regimen for the group. "Nothing," said Gen. Frank O'D. Hunter, visiting the base on 11 October 1943, "should be allowed to interfere with the preparation of the 332nd Fighter Group for combat."

Davis took him literally, establishing (with Colonel Selway, in charge of First Fighter Command training) an "Airacobra College" to ensure that his pilots were schooled in the operation of the P-39 Airacobra. Twelve civilian instructors from the Bell Aircraft Corporation, technical representatives, and combat-tested military veterans assisted Army Air Corps instructors. Films flickered, demonstrating reactions of the P-39 in combat, how its cannon worked and how ground crews could repair damaged aircraft at forward air bases. There were bigger-than-life mock-ups of the fighter's mechanical systems, showing pilots and mechanics exactly how the ship worked. Over in hangar seven, ground crewmen studied maintenance and repair while pilots listened to flight characteristics lectures. And, on one glorious day, a test pilot visited and presented a thrilling demonstration of expert handling of the P-39 Airacobra. It was an exciting time.

The *Columbus Georgia World* noted, on 13 October 1943, that

Selfridge Field's "Airacobra College," most elaborate ever arranged by the Bell Corporation for the AAF, was set up and operating when Colonel Selway was succeeded as group commander by Lt. Col. Benjamin O. Davis, Jr., son of the Brigadier General. . . . Instructors, who have been overseas, are showing 332nd Fighter Group men how they learned to repair planes with Spam cans, linoleum or a can-opener—the short-cuts and time-savers that these ground crews must depend upon . . .

It was serious business. Gone were the boring days of interminable flight into the Michigan haze à la Selway's game plan. Boredom had made these pilots seek "unauthorized" excitement. They played peek-a-boo with a train— flying down the tracks towards the oncoming engine, then pulling up at the last minute as the engineer cringed in terror.[32] They buzzed nearby chicken farms, shattering china as it fell down from hapless farmers' kitchen walls while terrified chickens went "on strike," refusing to lay any more eggs. They flew circles around the Maccabees Building in Detroit in the middle of the night "showing off their flying ability" to the black girls down below, except that there were no black girls living in *that* part of town *then*. Colonel Selway had been furious, verbally ripping them up one side and down the other. They were to "walk around the entire base with parachutes on [their] backs until he said stop!" But they hadn't given a damn. It was fun, doing acrobatics in front of that train and backing up eggs inside those chickens, or maybe turning over a sailboat or two out on Lake Huron, or landing "hot" on a highway, engine sputtering, watching motorists' eyes widen into frightened orbs. "Hell! It wasn't nothing but somethin' to do!"

But with Davis in command, for the most part, all that foolishness came to an end. The real world of combat was coming ever closer, except for those men like Chappie who had been tagged for transition training into B-25 bombers and those culled out for other reasons. Black enlisted men in this category were assigned to the greatly expanded 44th Aviation Squadron, and officers were assigned to the 553d Fighter Squadron, newly activated on 1 November 1943, commanded by Lt. Col. Charles Gayle, Selway's "hatchet man." It became the replacement squadron for black combat units overseas.

Around 1 December 1943, the full complement of the 332d Fighter Group came together at Selfridge Field. The hangars were used to update individual personnel records and double-check supplies and equipment. The final alert was given, the white officers and "supervisors" were withdrawn, and the all-black 332d Fighter Group was on its own, leaving Selfridge Field by train deep in the night of 22 December 1943.

The movement of the 332d Fighter Group to Fort Patrick Henry, Virginia, would have been relatively uneventful except for the unfortunate experiences of a group of eighteen black pilot replacements destined to join the group from Walterboro Gunnery Base in South Carolina. Getting off the bus at a ramshackle train station awaiting arrival of their train, these pilots were surrounded by a mob of whites from the nearby community after taking offense at being told "we don't serve niggers in here" when they attempted to purchase a cold beer in a local restaurant. Unslinging Thompson submachine guns and taking over the signal tower, recognized as the communications hub of the area, they saved themselves from a mob armed with pitchforks, blunderbusses, and high-powered, telescopic-sighted rifles. Making it to Camp Patrick Henry, they never caught up with the 332d. The FBI met them instead, ensuring their processing out of the United States in a record eight hours, to be locked up aboard ship until the transport was thirty miles out to sea.[32]

James, Bill Ellis and others were still waiting at Selfridge for orders sending them to Mather Air Field in California for B-25 transitional training.

IV

Lt. Gen. Frank O'D. Hunter groaned as he discovered that forty or fifty of the black officers had applied for membership in the white officer's club. To add insult to injury, on New Year's Day, 1944, three of these officers had the temerity to visit the club. They were met by the plump base commander, Col. William L. Boyd, in the company of another officer.

"You men must leave this club immediately," Colonel Boyd growled, his flight cap pushed high on his ample forehead. "You are not welcome here and you are forbidden to use this club or its facilities! And if anybody asks you who told you, you tell 'em I'm the big sonofabitch who said so!"

And to be sure that everyone knew that he was on the winning team, Lt. Col. Charles Gayle, commander of the 553d Fighter Squadron and Selway's "hatchet man," laid down the law as it applied to the club, in all its red-bricked, well-appointed splendor.

"I will," he raged, "court-martial for inciting a riot, the first man who steps into the officer's club!"

The cauldron of racism bubbled over. The army air corps investigated. It defended Boyd and Gayle, took the responsibility, and said that it "had established as a cardinal policy, explicit and definite directions that recreational and social activities on each base, whereon colored and white troops are stationed jointly, should be so provided and handled as to avoid charges of discrimination or prejudice towards members of either race . . . further, construction of a gym, service club and officer's club was in progress . . ."

The air corps called in yet another inspector to assess the situation. There was talk of closing the club. Something about "going to the root of the problem." Meanwhile, Chappie, William Ellis, and Daniels were thoroughly incensed at the callous and embarrassing manner in which Lieutenant Colonel Gayle had responded about the officer's club incident. Enough was enough.

"That god-damned sonofabitch!" they groused.

"We oughta kill this bastard," said one of the three.

"Hey, well, listen," said the third one of the three, "why not?"[*]

"Yes, the three of us oughta be able to drive one pilot into the ground," said the second of the three.

"Yeah!" they chorused.

"Look, we're gettin' short," the first one said, with the full knowledge that they had volunteered to train as twin-engine pilots and were due for transition training at Mather Field in California any day now. "We don't have much time, why don't we do in old Gayle?"

"Right! But not too much later!"[33]

It was in the middle of January 1944, when Colonel Selway, appointed commander, activated the new 477th Bombardment Group (Colored), again with his "qualified" staff of white troops to supervise its training. Hardly more than a skeleton organization at the time, it suffered for lack of administrative staff, bombardiers, and navigators, the two latter groups still in training. The army air corps personnel pipeline slowly began to man the unit. As more men arrived and their numbers grew, so did the unrest. There was still no officer's club for the black pilots; and, almost as an afterthought a miserable substitute was provided, but few officers patronized it. Again, black officers attempted to enter the white officer's club, to no avail.

V

It was a cold Thursday in March. Loudspeaker systems blared the message. Pilots in the air were recalled by radio. All officers were to assemble immediately in the base theater.

---

[*] Although the choice of words used here to describe the anger felt by the three pilots may offend, the sole surviving member of the group (William Ellis) vouches for its accuracy and allows that even more vehement language was used.

"Ten-Hut!" an officer roared. They stood in place like ramrods.

And there he was. Old two-star Gen. Frank O'D. Hunter, Chaplinesque moustache atwitter, a small rainbow of medals riding his chest, swagger stick in hand, striding widely down the center aisle of the theater, with Selway doing a tag-along.

"At ease, gentlemen!" he began. They sat, en masse. A few coughed. It seemed a good time to clear the throat since nobody could quite figure out just what the hell *this* was all about. Frank O'D. Hunter, lieutenant general, faced them.

"Gentlemen," he began, "this is *my* airfield! As long as I am commander of First Air Force, there will be no racial mixing at any post under my command. There *is* no racial problem on this base and there will *be* none!" And he concluded with even more bombast.

One black officer remembers that "he stood there, looking at us and we looked at each other. The officer's club hadn't been mentioned—but he had gone straight to the heart of the problem."

"Ten-Hut!" came the roared command, and he was gone, like a fingersnap!

"Outside agitators," Frank O'D. Hunter said later, "had made [my] Negroes surly!"

It was a thing emblazoned forever on Chappie James' mind:

. . . General F.O.D. [sic] Hunter came to Selfridge Field, and I'll never forget him, with his big, black moustache, standing up there, telling us that the world was not willing to accept us socially. He started out—I am paraphrasing a bit—saying that they were willing to let us fight beside them, and they were willing to let us fly, but the world was not willing— society was not willing—and that *he* was not willing to accept us socially. That what we were trying to do was ahead of the game, and not only were they not ready, but he wasn't going to stand for it, and if we didn't stay "in our place" he had other means that could be used to keep us in our place!

"We were," James continued in retrospect, "only spurred to go on further, and to keep the pressure on him, because we knew that he had been charged by Headquarters—the War Department—to press on with this project."

Almost at the very instant Frank O'D. Hunter was giving this speech, Congress had appropriated seventy-five thousand dollars to build the black officers a club of their own, right there on Selfridge Field.

James, Ellis, and Daniels continued their plan to rid the earth of at least *one* witch named Lt. Col. Charles Gayle.

"Okay, we'll get some P-40Ns, 'cause they're highly maneuverable and can handle a P-39—and we'll run him into the ground!" came the grim decision from one of the plotters.

"The thing about it," cautioned another, "is that once you commit, you can't quit, 'cause after he knows that you're really trying to do him in, he's smart enough to figure who it is!"

It was, after all, a matter of principle, and besides, "we were crazy enough to try!"

VI

It was early when one of the trio checked base operations to be sure that Colonel Gayle was up for a flight. He was. Warm sun tracked down the cold Michigan haze as the three would-be assassins locked down their brakes and spooled-up to takeoff power. The tower cleared them. They roared down the pavement into the cold air. Radio chatter was minimal, then silenced. This mission was clear: Get rid of Selway's hatchet man. The world's going to be a better place without him. Drive him into the ground, a P-40N riding each wing of the P-39 Airacobra; a P-40N almost sitting on his canopy. Can't quit once we start. *Get rid of him!*

The three P-40Ns pitched out into wide turns over the bottom half of Lake Huron and settled into orbit over Lake Sinclair, radios silent. Tuned to the base frequencies, they waited for Gayle to roll up for takeoff.

Minutes ticked. They could hear the wind whining and the raucous Allison V-1710s growling, punctuated by the periodic crackle of the radio out of Selfridge. More minutes raced by and then—

"Selfridge tower . . ." It was old Gayle's voice!

"Selfridge tower, this is Baker 4-2-1-0, out local, request taxi and takeoff instructions for one P-39 and your altimeter, over."

"Roger, Baker 4-2-1-0—You are clear to taxi to takeoff runway two seven and hold—Wind—west at eight—altimeter is 0-0-4. Contact tower when ready to roll—Over!"

"4-2-1-0 Wilco!"

Static. Chatter. More chatter. Chappie breathed harder. Ellis clinched his fist. Daniels smiled crookedly.

"Tower, this is Baker 4-2-1-0, am I clear?—Over!"

"Clear—4-2-1-0!"

"2-1-0—rolling!"

As they heard Gayle gather himself together and head for the wild, blue yonder, the three P-40Ns swept majestically up and around on a new heading which would allow them intercept. But at intercept point, Gayle's P-39 was nowhere in sight. Swearing silently, each climbed and circled, searching another small quadrant of the sky. It was as if Gayle had suddenly landed at some unmarked airstrip immediately after takeoff. He simply wasn't where he was supposed to be. Did he somehow slide right off the planet? The search continued without results. They had missed him in the wide reaches of the Michigan sky. It was just as well. He could have survived it, and then where would they have been? Frustrated, but perhaps a bit relieved, they took the P-40Ns back to Selfridge and themselves back home to their wives for love and more small talk in the warmth of one another's kitchens. They allowed as how it wasn't always the prejudice they talked about at such times out of earshot of the women. It was:

> Pilot chit-chat . . . technical problems . . . about troubles with the aircraft that you relate to other pilots. . . . Wives weren't part of [that]. Women can't understand the love affair between pilot and plane. It has no sense. It will kill you if you don't do what you should. . . . Can't make [my woman] part of something I don't understand myself. Women rebel. Airplane? Mind. Reflexes. All relative. At first, it's all a blur, then later, at 340–400 miles per hour, you can see every rock . . . every tree. . . . The women didn't understand . . .

Chapter Nine
Flash Point!

I

Not all black officers at Selfridge Field saw any virtue in challenging the existing racial bias. This was especially true of a percentage of those who could be called "senior" officers. But in spite of their counsel, the young "firebrands" continued to exert pressure from the bottom of the heap. Since the 99th Pursuit Squadron was doing well overseas, logic dictated that, in Chappie's words, "the War Department couldn't throw us out of the flying business at the time because we weren't sitting on the right side of the theater or staying out of the white officer's club."

Senior black officer cautiousness whispered "cool it!" The firebrands answered, "cool it, hell!" and pressed on with their harassments which served to embarrass the establishment and attract media attention. The establishment tried as hard as it could to stop them and *suppress* media attention. "We knew," James remembered, "that their policies could not be supported under constitutional law." James continues: "We had some pretty good advice, mainly from the NAACP. That's all there was to look forward to on how far we could go. We had some pretty good lawyers in our midst, young men who had come from law school. Many of them had not passed the bar, but were good 'guardhouse' lawyers, as they were called in those days. They knew the law extremely well and they were reading like mad to keep up with it . . ." Some had begun to wonder where the then Lt. Col. Benjamin O. Davis, Jr., was in all of this. His people were being victimized all over the Army Air Corps. He had become a successful fighter squadron commander and had brilliantly defended his officers before the select McCloy Committee, thus ensuring retention of black command of the 99th Pursuit Squadron. Then he had assumed command of the 332d Fighter Group, overseeing its training, then taking it into combat. Of what possible value now were his austere, stiff attitudes? Was he now to espouse, as his father had before him, the "company line" to his black compatriots and counsel: "There are certain laws you must obey"? Why his silence on the subject?

As a brigadier general, Daniel "Chappie" James, Jr., addressed this issue. "Sometimes," he said, "I feel that Colonel Davis was really with us but he couldn't come out publicly and say so, naturally." James's comments regarding Davis's approach to the problem provides this further retrospective:

> . . . I would like [to say] . . . that I have the greatest respect for the influence of . . . different approaches . . . for instance the approach of General Davis, who was very moderate. He was a product of a military environment, a product of West Point, and he had a job to do. At this time, most young firebrands had no patience with that approach, but he recognized the job to be done. There are many who will damn him today for the seemingly impersonal approach he took towards us, and a really hardline approach in many things in trying to "keep us in line." I don't take that stand now. I did feel that way at a time, but in the maturity of years . . . I know now General Davis had a job to do . . . and if he hadn't held a pretty tight rein on those of us who were trying to speed ahead in a different direction—to gain the same ends, of course—that unit would have been taken away from him . . .

Of course, James did not feel that way in 1943–44, as the struggle for black officer racial parity raged at Selfridge Field. Then, he felt that "our continued pressure was the only thing which caused the establishment to continue to move ahead with some deliberate speed in my lifetime. If we had attacked the problem strictly from the point of view of the moderates, we wouldn't have been there yet . . ."

According to "Chief" Alfred Anderson, (although he didn't see it personally) B. O. Davis, Jr., had found it necessary to quell Daniel James, Jr., in the boxing ring, to "keep him in line." The "Chief" remembers the "spratmo": "You know, B. O. and Chappie went a round in the gym! Put on the boxing gloves. Somebody said that after it was over, Chappie couldn't put his hat on, his head [was swollen up] so big! B. O. got in a *good* lick!"

The pressure from the "bottom" *had* worked. In spite of efforts by the command structure to protect Colonel Boyd, the pressure resulted in official censure. Lieutenant Colonel Gayle had been relieved and reassigned. His going sent minor shock waves up the command ladder, as Col. Max Schneider, of the army air corps's air inspector's office telephoned the First Air Force chief of staff, Colonel Caldwell, on 8 March 1944, to "discuss the embarrassment out there." In subdued tones, they spoke of 2d Lt. Milton Henry of the 553d Fighter RTU Squadron, "a professional Negro agitator . . . [who] made a bet some time ago, as a result of some complaints, he had said that he would get Colonel Gayle relieved."

"It's further complicated by the fact," Colonel Schneider went on, "that the First Fighter Command has relieved Colonel Gayle . . . and ordered him down to Richmond. It leaves the impression out there among the *other* side of the garrison and *that* side of the garrison too, that a 2d Lieutenant, working on his own . . . can get rid of his squadron commander whenever he wants to and this lad is making the most of that particular boast."

"I'm not fully qualified to explain that to you because something happened up there in which Colonel Gayle—"Colonel Caldwell began.

"I understand he's *Lieutenant Colonel* Gayle," Schneider interrupted with an elitist bent, "and Bill Boyd claims he's been doing a swell job."

Colonel Caldwell provided the answer to the riddle.

"General Barcus came over here," he intoned, "there was something up there [Selfridge Field] and General Hunter made the remark that Gayle had been very tactless in handling the situation . . . and it was recommended that they bring . . . Triffy down here [probably First Air Force headquarters] to take command. . . . That's just in line with the general's policy of trying to get along up there, that if a man shows any ineptitude or inability to handle that particular situation . . . he would rather get them out and without prejudice . . . put them in another job."

It was a conversation filled with chagrin, words with hidden meanings, a modicum of controlled anger, and perhaps a bit of helplessness. A new thing under the army air corps sun seemed to be emerging.

By now, Chappie James, George Knox, Charles Stanton, C. I. Williams, Peter Verwayne, Jim Mason, and Bill Ellis were off to Mather Field, California, for B-25 transitional training. They were to return in the spring after one hundred hours of flying time. The 477th Bombardment Group (Colored) continued to grow, its ranks filled in by graduates of multi-engine classes at Tuskegee.

But Colonel Selway and General Hunter would not be denied their revenge for the embarrassment of the official censure of Colonel Boyd, whom General Hunter had backed on the officer's club issue, ordering that the single officer's club on the base be used *only* by whites and "declaring that blacks would have to wait until one was built for them." Embarrassment, because even when Hunter had tried to save Boyd by asking that the reprimand be directed at him instead, the air staff would have none of it, even though sympathetic to his position.

Both admitted segregationists, Hunter and Selway seethed. Hunter, in particular, seemed beset by a strange, racially oriented sort of schizophrenia, constantly deluding himself. On the one hand, he fostered racism by his attitudes, declaring that "there will be no racial mixing in my command," then denied existence of the problem on the other, ordering his subordinates by telephone: "don't mention colored or white." He constantly referred to the pilots as *them*, and *those people*, the *other, colored officers*, and *those birds*—all entities against whom he was always prepared to "take disciplinary action" and whom he would "court-martial, if they stir up trouble," insisting at the same time that his real goal was "strict discipline" just like "the discipline administered to whites." His words fell on barren ground for all his bluster, even though he threatened, "I'll tell *them* exactly where I stand—we cannot handle *them* if we are going to be afraid of *them* and afraid of the papers downtown."

But it seemed that he and Selway *were* afraid. The pressure had built to unbearable limits. They blustered and threatened. They cursed and had been demeaning. Selway had sought resolution in a homespun provincialism: GET TO YOUR DAMN' GUNS!—only to create a searing boredom in his men such that they chased trains and aborted the laying of eggs by heretofore contented chickens. He and Selway had denied the families of these black officers government housing, even though that housing sat vacant. They had denied officer's club rights guaranteed them by military regulation. They had, under the auspices of the War Department, accepted these black men as commissioned officers and pilots with the authority to command, but had withheld command power from all but two or three of them because the granting of that power meant authority over white men, a situation they were not ready to accept. And they had denied all but one or two of these black pilots the rewards of promotion, using their peculiar circumstance to establish a "promotion mill" for their own kind, assigning black officers as "assistants" while the "supervisory" white charges did no work and got all the promotions.[34]

Their fear was justified. The firebrands pushed all the harder from the bottom of the heap—writing to the president, protesting to the media, challenging the constitutionality of Hunter and Selway's actions, further embarrassing them and ultimately, the War Department itself. With General Hunter's infamous speech in March 1944, the flash point had clearly been reached. Something had to be done. Hunter and Selway wasted no time.

Suddenly, all black officers who were not detailed to fly aircraft were restricted to the base. All gates to Selfridge Field were locked. Telephones, radios, and all other means of communication were blocked. The Saturday after Hunter's speech, the black officers were loaded on trains and given no destination.

"When we refused to stop protesting the segregated facilities at Selfridge," Chappie James remembered, "they loaded us on trains (except those few of us who were designated to fly the aircraft) and without telling us where we were going, they moved us all back down South, with the idea 'let's get them back down South where people know how to handle them, and they know how they'd better act down there.' "

Their train wended north to Point Huron, crossed to Sarnia, Ontario, and, with shades drawn, proceeded across Canada. Finally, it crossed into the United States at Buffalo, New York, and headed straight south. Told to detrain, the blacks still had no idea where they were. As they stepped down in dress uniforms from the train, their mouths fell open at what they saw. Facing them on the station platform, were armed white soldiers in battle dress, posted at twenty-foot intervals and poised for action.

"Where are we?" someone asked.

Silence.

"What's going on?" another shouted.

More silence.

Fifteen minutes later, the armed guard retired. They had been ordered into battle dress with live ammunition locked and loaded because as one white soldier later put it, "we had been told some *bad niggers* were coming in."

Daniel James, Jr., years later in an interview said:

We were sent to Godman Field, Kentucky, and to Walterboro, South Carolina. It was almost criminal the way they did it. They told us to send our families home and we thought that we might be going overseas, which was alright with us. But they put those guys on those trains and they rode them for days. They routed the train, I am told, all the way up through Canada. I don't know what the purpose of that was, but I know it took them twice or three times as long then as it would normally take a train, and the only way they could follow their progress was looking out through the shades every once in a while and catching a station sign as they went by, and they would say, "Well, we are moving South . . ."

II

"Racial friction," Gen. Frank O'D. Hunter was to write in December 1944, "will exist in a marked degree if colored and white pilots are trained together." The general marked time and hoped for the surfacing of some expedient that would blanket the real issues, so that they would not need addressing.

"Consistency in war aims," he continued, "[are] paramount in order to achieve white combat crew efficiency and handle the negro problem to the best of our ability, on as few bases as possible, [so as to avoid lowering] the combat training on all bases . . . to appease . . . agitators."[35]

But Daniel James, Jr., and his fellow officers were to see through the Hunter rhetoric. If their penetration of it was only subliminal at the time, James later drew a bead on it. "If you allow those in authority—who incidentally have always been white because of the nature of the system—their own choice of time, you find that too often their choice is *never*. They appreciate, I have found, the moderate and conservative approach because it gives them time to try to outlive it or employ some other cop out . . ."

The transfer of the 477th Bombardment Group (Colored) to Godman Field, Kentucky, in May 1944, was a "cop out" of the first magnitude. This avoided facing the issues that had caused the agitations at Selfridge Field. It provided an easy escape from the outrage of the Detroit community, the press, and civilian organizations pleading the cause of the black officers. The situation at Godman Field was an exercise in polemics which addressed the singular issue of racism. The base was not located in an urban area and thus was isolated from community pressures. It was in the South, where, as James later remarked, "people (allegedly) knew how to handle them." Most importantly, it was adjacent to sprawling army Fort Knox, where a large military police contingent sat alongside a tank battalion, making it easy to contain the blacks should their pseudo-rebellion explode into violence.

Years before, the airbase at Godman Field had been a polo field which had been converted to a grassy landing strip by the United States Army. Airplanes parked in the building where polo ponies once resided, until a large, brick hangar was built in 1938. When war came, the base was expanded. Now the army at adjacent Fort Knox maintained two airplanes for the Armored commanding general. Two pilots, formerly with the 115th Army Air Base Unit, were assigned. It was a sweetheart affair, with Godman Field regularly assisting Fort Knox by providing liaison aircraft for spotting artillery fire, aerial photography, camouflage, and chemical warfare activity.

Godman Field was too small and inadequate for the effective operation of the bombardment and service groups. Its runways were too short, and had deteriorated so that they could not properly handle bombers. Hangar and apron space were inadequate. The surrounding terrain was unsuitable for night flying and no air-to-ground gunnery range was locally available.

As far as Colonel Selway and his base officers and enlisted men were concerned, these were not unsolvable problems. During the remainder of 1944, according to the unit historian, increased facilities and training curriculums were installed. Selway counseled his supervisors that no training or equipage of the 477th Bombardment Group would be omitted or impeded and that the primary duty remained preparation for combat. His pet motto, "Get to your damn guns" still emblazoned itself on all their minds with new emphasis on its meaning: "Realize that winning the war depends on each man doing his job to the best of his ability." And each Saturday morning, all officers were briefed on problems and action needed. "No one," suggested the historian, "was kept in the dark."

III

Over fifteen hundred flights were flown out of Godman Field in 1944 as a result of Colonel Selway's regimen. As intense as the training had been at Selfridge with the fighter pilots, the repetitiveness of the bomber training had become a great metronome ticking, the B-25s the pendulums by which it swung.

That is why Chappie James and the 477th Bombardment Group pilots, winging high across the Kentucky skies on weekend training flights, tuned their radios to a Kentucky radio station and waited. Up there above the clouds they were in "box formation"—that infamous, hated flight of four B-25s, three up and one in "the slot" nobody wanted to fly. The slot was the hardest to fly because those pilots always had to look up to maintain position, to pivot and turn. They waited for two o'clock on a Saturday afternoon, listening for "The Nat 'King' Cole Show." Waited and listened for Cole's dulcet tones so that they could syncopate the B-25s in rhythm with the haunting melodies as they flew. Wagging their wings. Tilting the big ships from side to side, undulating with the music.

Maj. Ted W. Johnson (Retired) of Oxnard, California, smiles at the memory: "I remember that [when] the "Nat 'King' Cole Show" came on the air . . . we all used to listen. Sometimes there'd be two flights of us . . . listening. Can you imagine watching eight B-25s keeping time with Nat "King" Cole? I mean *"Str-raighten up and fly right . . . straighten up and sta-a-y right. . . . Cool down, poppa, dont'cha blow your top . . . !"* It was a sight to see! Sometimes it'd be: *"It's only a paper moon . . . shining over a cardboard sea . . . but it wouldn't be make-believe . . . if you believed in me-e-e!"*

On the ground, the enlisted men and officers found solace within their own ranks, partaking of the usual camaraderie of men thrown together in military life. The *Beacon,* the base newspaper, provided a conduit for togetherness, caring, and nostalgia. James, always carrying a soft spot in his heart for animals, probably read with great interest Rufus Wells's story in the *Beacon* about an errant squadron mascot named "Bolt-Stud" as he told how the dog "joined up." Seems he came upon the 619th quite by chance, following civilian workers around as they replaced a broken window in the hangar down on the line. The workmen left, but he stayed, "surrendering to the warmth of the shop and cordial reception extended him by the troops." One Norman Fletcher of New York City, decided to adopt the hungry canine, feeding him "GI chow" and laying on the monicker of "Bolt-Stud."

Bolt-Stud liked meeting all the mechanics and bomber crews. "He seemed," Wells reminisces, "to love the whine of props, the roar of powerful engines and watched with interest [the] blue flame discharged in the predawn darkness as the engines warmed up . . ." Everybody loved old Bolt-Stud. White furred, a sort of cross between a "police dog, rat terrier or just plain hound," he was a true mongrel.

But one night old Bolt-Stud decided to end the relationship. Maybe it was the GI chow. S—— on a shingle and all that.[36] Or maybe it was too much of the shattering roar of the B-25 engines, or the blue flames sparking. Maybe old Bolt-Stud wanted to fly, too. Go way up there, in the blue, with those pilots who seemed strange personages from outer space to a wee entity like Bolt-Stud. Perhaps they came from another planet, because to Bolt-Stud they were so big and powerful, with their fur-lined boots, flying goggles, and those parachutes growing out of their backs!

Bolt-Stud just—bolted, and Wells wrote, with great nostalgia: "We haven't seen or heard from him since—so the Sergeant has marked him AWOL." Wells tacked on a touching postscript: "P.S.—If you should read this, Bolt-Stud, don't bother to return. All is forgiven. You won't have to sign [an Article] 104 . . ."

IV

Unlike the situation of Selfridge Field, Chappie James and his black compatriots had relatively free access to Godman's facilities. The problem was that these were extremely limited. A central recreation hall was theater, gym, dance hall, and classroom. The nearby towns of Louisville and Elizabethtown, unlike bustling Detroit, had few recreational facilities for blacks. Demeaning treatment at the hands of the inhabitants was rampant. It was a climate in which the citizenry "ignored them at best, or tolerated, resented or discriminated openly or (unless they were watchful), [threatened] to destroy them."[37]

Against this backdrop of southern hostility, circumstances on the base began to go downhill, and morale quickly deteriorated. Although the officer's club on Godman was inadequate, one did exist. Other issues presaged the downturn.

Of primary concern to the black officers was the problem of nonexistent promotions. Black officers were simply not promoted above certain grades *in their own units*, while white officers who "supervised" them zoomed into the higher grades. Nor did it matter that there were black officers recently returned from combat. They were not promoted either. It was degrading and an insult. It was obvious to all but the most dense that the men in charge had fashioned and were operating a "promotion mill" for whites at the expense of the black officers who were going no place. Lt. Col. Spann Watson (Retired) remembers how it was: "You had a white power structure . . . that had all the positions and all the rank. . . . But you had black people doing all the work. The white people didn't even come to work . . . on most occasions. They just came in . . . got promoted and moved on. But the black people—'Chappie' Daniel James was one of them—they operated the assistant positions which called for 1st Lieutenant and no higher than Captain, and the job itself [called for a higher rating] . . ."

So great was the "cop out" that the vaunted "combat crew efficiency" General Hunter considered "paramount" for white pilots mysteriously fell by the wayside when applied to the black pilots. The transfer below the Mason-Dixon Line because they had tried to secure their rights as officers galled enough, and this failure to allow just promotions made morale plummet even faster. That was not all. Colonel Selway seemed impervious to their predicament, always pushing them further and further away from contact with the command structure, "as his ears turned to stone when altercations occurred between white and black officers."[38] Segregation slashed through the civilian community. Consciousness of it heightened when Selway created solid, segregated authority lines on the base by reorganizing the 115th AAF Base Unit into separate squadrons along lines of color, effectively driving a wedge between the races.

And across the railroad tracks separating Godman Field from mammoth Fort Knox were all the old bugaboos from Selfridge. There was the issue of the segregated army theater, which the army commander solved by installing "ushers" who escorted blacks to their seats.

But even this ruse was to be tested by black enlisted men from Godman as they challenged the neat "usher arrangement" by refusing to follow the usher's directions. A near-melee resulted at Fort Knox, and nearly riotous conditions exploded at Godman Field when the blacks returned. The NAACP sent a sharp protest to the army air corps, which responded with a disclaimer, saying that Fort Knox was an army base and therefore out of its jurisdiction. The army commander, in an interview with a black journalist, explained army policy: "Well, listen, I have known colored people all my life—grew up with them. And frankly, they haven't any desire to sit scattered around in the audience anymore than any other people have. . . . What is creating the problem is a lot of goddamn agitators. This thing crops up every now and then here. . . . We got along all right at Fort Knox until this Air Corps came in here . . ."[39] The lightning bolts were again to strike, as both service elements pointed fingers at the other.

Until this time, the officer's club issue was not as hot as it had been at Selfridge Field, but shortly it became so. Colonel Selway's base and supervisory officers were members of the Fort Knox officer's club and did not attend the Godman Field club since that was for the black officers stationed there. Until now, the Fort Knox club had been a nonissue for the blacks because they could not legally challenge Army Regulation 210–10. They were not stationed there. The regulation was specific: everyone *assigned to a base* could use the facilities. *But the white officers went there, why couldn't they?* They decided to challenge the violated rule. It was a matter of principle. Lt. Col. Spann Watson (Retired) describes the thrust of it: "That's what the trouble . . . was all about . . . position and promotion—it wasn't the damn club at all; we didn't give a damn about the club, this was just one way of getting rid of the people out of the organization. It had to be done . . . ."

It *had* to be done, and Daniel "Chappie" James, Jr., agreed. Remembering Selfridge, he recalled *that* "charade until the moving business started," and

> then, the same thing repeated itself down at Godman. You see, they really thought they had it made down at Godman, because we were on one side of the tracks—Fort Knox, Kentucky, was on the other side. Therefore, they felt that in housing all the so-called trainee officers at Godman Field, we would not go to Fort Knox at night. In the evening, the white or supervisory officers would go to Fort Knox . . . they could because that's where their BOQs [Bachelor Officer Quarters] were. Our BOQs were former enlisted men's quarters at Godman Field and a little hut of a club, not much bigger than [my] office. So the same started all over again. We said, "Well we *are* going to go to Fort Knox. If they can go over so can we."
>
> We went through the same thing again. The Army Commander at Fort Knox got upset and told Colonel Selway that they'd better keep the black air corps troops away from over there because *"his boys"* [the black army officers] knew better than to come in the club, and with our antics we were going to ruin the good manners of "his boys" . . .

"Hey, how you doin' with them niggers over theah at Godman?" became the singsong, and there would stand another white army officer with a bloody nose. The mine fields grew thicker. It seemed an impossible task.

"There is a Brer Rabbit story," Arthur Larson says in his book, *When Nations Disagree: A Handbook on Peace Through Law,* "which aptly sums up this theme of doing the apparently impossible. The old man was telling the little boy about the time Brer Rabbit climbed a tree. The little boy objected, 'But Uncle Remus, you know rabbits can't climb trees.' 'Yeah, I know that,' said Uncle Remus, 'but Brer Fox was right behind. Brer Rabbit was just *obliged* to climb that tree!' So we, too," Larson continues, "in the presence of appalling danger may do the apparently impossible."

It was the circumstance in which Daniel "Chappie" James, Jr., and the host of black officers serving with him now found themselves. And the foxes were named Selway and Hunter.

Chapter Ten
Zenith

I

As early as the last days at Selfridge Field, anger among the black pilots heightened. It rose to fever pitch when their flight surgeon, Capt. Walter Scott Brown, somehow discovered that the move to Godman Field, Kentucky, was being planned before it had been announced. Dr. Brown briefed the rest. The news was considered a slap in the face. It was the catalyst for a concentrated effort by the black officers, including Chappie James, to fight back.

Walter Scott Brown is important because he wielded considerable power, having a direct connection to the White House and Eleanor Roosevelt. His "inside track" with Mrs. Roosevelt derived from medical help he accorded the first family while in Seattle, Washington. At the recommendation of the Roosevelt's doctor, he performed a very delicate operation involving an intestinal stricture on their daughter, Sissy. The fact that Brown was black hadn't mattered to Mrs. Roosevelt. Her only concern was that her daughter get well. The child recovered, and a thankful Mrs. Roosevelt told Brown that if he ever needed to get in touch with her, he could do so through her secretary. It was a providential offer. Walter Scott Brown would need the connection, both as a human being and as one of the black officers caught in segregation's web. For some time, first at Selfridge and now at Godman, Brown had been reporting conditions under which he was forced to serve in personal correspondence to persons such as Truman Gibson, a special aide in the War Department. Once, at Godman, he wrote that nothing had been done to solve any problem, that morale had plummeted, and that the results of the collective frustrations experienced by the pilots were so grievous that their minds were filled with "confusion" and that "they can't possibly do their best." Further, he feared the existence of undetected flying fatigue, since no air corps psychiatric staff was available to diagnose it.

Brown was very light complexioned; one-thirty-second part black blood coursed through his veins. Handsome, he looked Italian. Connected, he was outspoken. Squadron commanders tried more than once to "talk him out of being black," attempting to transfer him to the army's all-white Rainbow Division. "Why don't you forget that you're colored?" they asked. But the swarthy, Italian look-alike refused, using the White House connection to thwart the transfer attempts. Frustrated, the commanders finally relented: "Just put him out there where the blacks are; maybe he'll be satisfied!" General F. O'D. Hunter, First Air Force commander, mentioned Brown in a telephone conversation on 25 March 1944, with the now-deposed Colonel Boyd prior to the unit's transfer to Godman Field.

"You remember," the general roared, "when I was out there . . . I talked about . . . strict discipline! Now that goes for both blacks and whites . . . they have got to handle this stuff with discipline. . . . This Captain Brown you've got, why didn't Selway give him orders that he won't build up any of this controversial stuff and if he does—then court-martial him!"

"It's pretty hard to get that stuff on them," Boyd allowed.

After assuring Boyd that "he would back [him] to the limit on any disciplinary action you take towards these people" he referred to Brown by again threatening court-martial "if they stir up trouble."

"That bird [Brown] is pretty smooth," Boyd replied.

Brown was indeed smooth. As angry as the rest about the incipient transfer to Godman Field, he, William Ellis, Sam Lum, and other officers began to lay plans for the first important swipe at Selway and Hunter. They knew as much as Selway did, since their own people worked in the base communications center and passed them copies of incoming messages.

It was to be a letter of petition to the president about the treatment they were accorded. Signed by as many officer supporters as they could muster, the letter told how, as colored officers in the United States Army Air Corps, they would gladly give their lives for their country if it came to that, and as officers and gentlemen, they should be granted all corollary rights on an equal basis.

It was a bold stroke, but dangerous. Turncoats were about, black officers whose only goal was to survive by whatever means, even to betrayal by surreptitious passing of their plans to Colonel Selway. Because of this, the signatures were obtained in the most secret way. The plotters waited until nightfall. Creeping through the barracks when everyone was asleep, flashlights in hand, they quietly shook possible supporters awake to explain, read their letter, and hopefully, sign it. Chappie James was so awakened. With sleepy eyes, he read and signed the document. A lieutenant named Kennedy was the last of twenty-six officers to sign.

Two of them drove to the Louisville train station to await the arrival of the Washington, D.C., "Special" as it chugged in. There, they slipped the envelope addressed to Mrs. Roosevelt, in care of her secretary at the White House, into the slot in the side of the train's mail car. Their action might have been discovered had they mailed the letter on the base. The odds were high that it would have landed on Selway's desk the next day.

About three days later, an official teletype from the War Department arrived reiterating their complaints and positions. The final line read: "No reprisal action will be taken against any of the officers whose names are affixed hereto." Two capital letters near the end sealed it. "DP," they read, meaning "by direction of the president."

Consternation erupted throughout the First Air Force command heirarchy. Before the command could recuperate or respond to this swift kick in the shins, the acting chief of the air staff, Lt. Gen. Barney Giles, was personally on station to meet with the officers, Chappie James included. "What could he do to assuage their displeasures?" the general asked. The audience lasted for a half-hour, but because Colonel Selway was there, the main issues did not surface. Giles tried the usual separate-but-equal "fixes." A swimming pool? A putting green? One officer, he observed, wore boots. A riding facility?

Not much came of it all in the way of immediate relief. The army air corps did build a swimming pool, which was seldom used.

The odd thing was that, in spite of this outburst, the highest levels of the army air corps continued to think that the black officers were happy. To General Giles's credit, he honestly reported the low morale he had observed, citing the reasons for it as racial in nature. Giles pulled no punches. He noted that the discontent among the black officers was multifaceted. That the meaningful positions were held by white officers, with little or no chance for promotion among the blacks. That the blacks' assignment to a station below the Mason-Dixon line was a burr in their saddles. That Colonel Selway's uncaring attitude when differences arose between the races was intolerable, constituting an extension of an already wide gulf between the men under his command. The problem, General Giles thought, was "Colonel Selway's attitude." It seemed to many, including the black press, that Selway's manner had drastically changed from an initially progressive one to one of extreme caution. Perhaps, it was thought, he remembered what had happened to Colonel Boyd and Lieutenant Colonel Gayle at Selfridge. Both had been relieved of their commands. Somehow that may have haunted him. It would have been an important factor if he dreamed of promotion to brigadier general.

The tension became palpable as the Godman command became more stringently segregationist. Forays into the Fort Knox post exchange by the black enlisted men were only part of the explosive furor. As Chappie James noted, the black officers, incensed that their white counterparts could use the officer's club on Fort Knox, and they could not, began to challenge the army rule by attempting entry. And still, the army air corps demurred as the tension simmered.

Throughout this era, Daniel "Chappie" James, Jr., was a refuge in the storm for many. He was someone to talk with. While William Ellis and others had some legal training and advice, Chappie was endowed with a wealth of common sense. Big and outgoing, he was recognized as a natural leader, but there was a quality about him that made some black officers wary. They thought him something of an opportunist. Chappie picked his points of entry into controversy. He'd only get involved in things when he *knew* the circumstances were right. But in spite of his occasional reticence when others were creating maelstroms, he was always looking ahead. He had often said that he regarded the air force as a career and more than that, he planned to be a general officer. Many dismissed this as pure bravado. But most of the black officers liked him and became his "running buddies" on GI forays into the civilian worlds of Detroit and now, Louisville, Kentucky.

"Chappie was," they remember, "quite a character in many respects." He proved that as they looked for and found fun among the civilians. In spite of the fact that the enlisted men fought isolated, pitched battles in the Fort Knox post exchange about being made to wait for service, the officers made good their threats to enter the white Fort Knox officer's club, and more enlisted men beat Fort Knox taxi drivers who refused to take them back to Godman Field.

Down in Tuskegee, still waiting, the long-suffering Dorothy gave birth to a son, Daniel III. Chappie was pleased and proud as he went on a shopping spree for baby clothes and the diamond engagement ring he couldn't afford a few years before. He flew into Tuskegee, a duffle bag stuffed with baby clothes and a new ring for his lady's finger. They called their new son "Spike."

II

Louisville, Kentucky, they say, was a place in those days, where one "learned to drink whiskey continuously, a little at a time." Chappie was one to enjoy a social drink or two by now. In Kentucky at the time, however, imbibing could be risky business. "Whiskey in Kentucky," one black officer remembers, "was some of the worst in the world. They had some whiskey *guaranteed* not to be more than thirty days old! Even the whiskey drinkers wouldn't drink it. Stuff called 'Five Stripes,' and 'Nelson Springs'—brand new and just out of the boiler!''

Chappie was definitely not a teetotaler, but at the same time, he was not one who allowed alcohol to control him. Most of the time, he seemed in control of himself. It did not pay to be out of control in southern segregated society if you were black. There were other reasons to maintain that ability. The black people in Louisville were nice, for the most part. There were parties and a plethora of beautiful girls. It was a city of "fast horses and pretty women," some black officers remember. But wariness *was* necessary. Segregation was a monstrous aberration. Adversity could strike at any time or place. Some officers carried concealed .38-caliber pistols and others, the harder to conceal .45 automatic. Just in case.

Although the plight of the black officers was critical, it seemed minor in the framework of world events. It was D-Day, 6 June 1944, and the largest amphibious assault the world had ever seen was taking place on the beaches of Normandy. Millions of men were committed. Against this panoply of earth-shattering events, the drive for equality by a few black officers stuck below the Mason-Dixon line may have seemed trite to those with the power to intervene. The only exception seemed to be the black press, which kept in close contact with the Godman officers. It put their story on its pages, the headlines calling attention to the outrages that were occurring. On 1 July 1944, Chappie received the obligatory promotion to first lieutenant, a promotion all second lieutenants receive if they've kept their "noses clean."

During the last half of 1944, the 477th Bombardment Group repeatedly flew proficiency missions. Combat crew missions were practically nonexistent: nine months after activation, only twenty-three of an authorized 128 navigator-bombardiers had been assigned. By October, only half of the 176 pilots authorized the unit had arrived. And by mid-October, even though new pilots and bombardiers arrived, a significant number of the latter had not received navigator training, which further slowed down scheduled operations. In spite of these problems, however, the group racked up an impressive flying safety record, flying over fourteen thousand flying hours before the first accident, a squall contributing to the disaster. Winter arrived, reducing available flying hours.

If anything kept the lid from blowing off at Godman, it was the very real attempts by the base personnel services section to provide entertainment on the base. As the group historian noted during this period: "All 'C' Squadron and Group enlisted men [were] invited to attend a *free* dance [every] Monday night in the local gymnasium—good music, plenty of girls, plenty of dancing space . . ."

For officers like Chappie, the presence of wives and families, however temporary, became an additional morale factor. But it was tough going for the wives of the black officers. The shortage of adequate housing for them was "very,

very acute.'' Only two guest houses existed. These were split between officer and enlisted wives. Completely inadequate to handle visitors, each held only seventeen guests at a time. This meant, since 430 black officers were assigned to the base at large, and the base itself could only adequately house 240 of them, that the entire housing situation was one more "downer," as wives came in for weekend visits. It rankled when it was obvious that their white counterparts lived in "fat city" by comparison. They found housing in a housing project outside the gate to the base, the Fort Knox guest house, and in neighboring towns of Elizabethtown and West Point. The black population in these towns was almost zero, and since they could not use white facilities, there was no immediate solution.

As involved as Chappie was in being the best pilot that he could, in battling racism, and in the repetitive proficiency flying, he still found time for his family when they came to visit. What was to become a family ritual for the small fry of the James clan began.

He loved his children and shamelessly cuddled them. It was a time to play and tease. Time to pick up his little daughter, Danice, by her tiny waist and playfully toss her high into the air as she squealed in delight, then catch her in his huge arms. "He was so tall," Danice remembers, "he was our friendly giant. He was like Jack and the Beanstalk to us, and when he threw us up into the air, it seemed like *miles* down to his waiting arms! Dannie was so little then. When he threw him up, it seemed as if the thrill of it would take his breath away!''

Chappie was a father who told his children magnificent, tender stories from his past. Wonderful stories from his college days, about football cohorts whom he loved and never forgot. Chappie produced jelly beans as if by magic, and created memories his children would remember forever. First snowfall and "Daddy" pulling them on a sled. Winterscapes, warm kitchens, hot cocoa, and marshmallows. Meal time was the best of all, for it was a happy time. Good food was always important to Chappie. His children, Danice and the newborn, Daniel III, had a wonderful time with their charismatic father. They sat at their own little table in a corner of the dining area during dinner and were surprised by Dorothy with delicacies like pink cake. Home life for Chappie was magic. It was the place in which he was the tenderest, most lovable man in his family's world. He protected them from that "other" world of bitterness and anger. As his wife, Dorothy, constantly reiterates, "he never told us about those other things; none of them did—they didn't want to have the wives teary-eyed . . .''

But that "other" world was there to be dealt with, and this soft, tender man, who cuddled his children and his wife, was also a warrior bent on doing his part in achieving an equality too long denied his race. He was a warrior-to-be of the sternest stuff when his country needed him to defend her ramparts.

There were other joys waiting for Chappie out there in that "other" world, and things that were to try his very soul.

III

There is a theory in psychology that when human need exceeds the means of satisfying it the likelihood of rebellion increases. In this model, satisfaction of need becomes paramount. So it was at Godman Field, Kentucky, except that there were two needs to be satisfied.

One belonged to Colonel Selway and General F. O'D. Hunter. Their need to quell this upstart insistence by the black officers on racial parity, promotional opportunities and the rest, far exceeded any satisfactions provided by their dusky brothers. The other belonged to the latter, and their need burned with the incandescence of the sun! Satisfaction of *their* needs was never an issue with Selway and Hunter. Bending the recalcitrants to their will and training them for combat was. They had the power and authority. Their charges had an overwhelming need and willpower that translated into "a question of . . . fighting for our people to be given a just according of their induction into the war effort . . . that's all we were fighting for. . . . We were trying to do something for America; not just for our people. If we [were] going to fight; if we're going to do it—we're going to *do* it! That's all we were trying to say!"

Selway sought other avenues to mitigate the segregation and discrimination. Between the mandatory proficiency flights, he stepped up "morale activities," providing "an outstanding program of entertainment, special events and athletics." Horace Henderson, the pianist, squadron parties and dances, were all seen as "fine for morale" and for development of "pride in outfit."

On 1 December 1944, the *Beacon* reported that Godman Field enjoyed the dancing performances of "Janie McNair's Dancing Dolls" in the gym. "It was a sight to behold," as they "displayed veteran stage techniques!" And in its 11 December 1944 issue, the *Beacon* caused an uproar as its front page lead read: LENA HORNE TO VISIT HERE! MOVIE STAR TO ARRIVE SATURDAY FOR A 3-DAY STAY WITH BOMBER BOYS!

Godman Field was agog! It would not be amiss to suggest that even Colonel Selway was moved as he peered into that lovely face pictured on the front of his base newspaper. Dorothy James remembers Lena: "She was lovely . . . just absolutely lovely! She stayed in our guest house and I met her there, along with the other wives. Just lovely!"

Lena Horne's impact was felt in other arenas as well. Wearing a fur coat, she visited with black GI patients at nearby Nichols General Hospital. Even those on crutches hobbled in to see her. And there were the white GIs, watching from a distance. Their faces seemed to project that they regarded her as a black man's movie star, never in touch with the idea that she really belonged to America. Lena's visit ended on stage as she caressed a trumpet, surrounded by members of the Godman Field band.

Christmas came and went. In the 1 January 1945 *Godman Field Beacon*, Colonel Selway sent his command New Year's greetings, a continuation of his "Get to your damned guns!" diatribe:

> With the birth of a New Year, 1945, I extend to you my sincere greetings and best wishes. . . . I am . . . proud of the way in which you have contributed to the war effort . . . continuance of these efforts . . . will hasten the peace. . . . The 477th Bombardment Group (M) . . . has developed into an outstanding organization. . . . Such accomplishment can be attained only by absolute cooperation, tireless effort, and . . . the will to see things done . . . now is not the time for coasting; instead, bend that throttle of energy!

Capt. Franklin A. McLendon, his personnel services officer, made a gargantuan effort to bolster morale. But nothing had changed. Segregation was still as frisky as ever; the army still segregated the seating in its theater, and black officers were not allowed into the Fort Knox officer's club, though their white training officers were. Louisville citizenry were still as ornery as ever towards black officers and enlisted men visiting their fair city.

IV

Things were no better at Walterboro base in South Carolina, where the 553d Replacement Training Unit (RTU) was sent after Selfridge Field. Excerpts from a telephone conversation on 12 June 1944, between Generals F. O'D. Hunter, First Air Force commander, and Barney Giles, acting chief of the air staff, are enlightening.

"Barney," Hunter began, "I called you about Walterboro . . . my idea is to run things in these localities [South Carolina] about the same way they run them there, their laws . . . which is Army custom. . . . The command has been weak. *But I do not want to stop dividing that theater!* If I do, there's going to be trouble. It's a hot problem down there and I just wanted you to know. I will do anything I'm ordered to do."

"Well, you're not going to be ordered to do it as far as I know. . . . There's been no pressure . . . to make any change in the way you run that post, has there?"

"No, but I didn't want something to develop and explode in your face—"

"There will probably be some . . . they told me that they had . . . permanent party on one side and the RTU on the other—"

"What it actually is, *is white on one side and colored on the other*. That's the way they run things down in South Carolina . . . in my opinion . . . it's bad stuff to stop that and I won't do it unless I'm ordered to."

Hunter's concern then turned to the quality of the commander at Walterboro. The 553d Fighter RTU Squadron was his biggest problem. Discipline was poor. He'd sent a Colonel Massey in to check things out. He thought he'd have to relieve the current commander because, in his view, he was not forceful enough, "enforcing strict discipline of the whites and letting the colored do anything they want to." He was going to have, he said, "strict discipline for both," and "it has nothing to do with color, creed or race."

General Giles agreed, but speculated that perhaps the better part of valor might be a recommendation that the theater be open and "let those boys go in there." Giles allowed that the idea would be all right with him, "and maybe," he thought, "they will refuse to go to the theater."

"They did, the other day," Hunter grunted, "they tried to go in the wrong side and they told them that their side was the other side and they all got up and walked out."

Hunter recognized the tenor of the South Carolina friction. In his favor, he explained that he'd advised his representative, Colonel Massey, to "talk to the Mayor and . . . Chamber of Commerce . . . and try for a better feeling." He'd purposely stayed away because "if they start walking off when they're talking to me, they'll walk in the Guardhouse darned fast!"

The conversation ended with the two warlords sounding a bit like two members of a street gang screwing up their courage to take on the gang across town.

"Now, Monk," Giles began, "when I was there they asked me when they were going to move. I said, 'not during the war that I know of. You're going to stay here and train like the white people have taken it before you, and if I can do anything about it, you'll not move at all. You'll stay here and go on and do your training and the Army Air Corps will give you the best training we can give you with the equipment available, and we'll train you just as well as we train these white boys in preparing you to go to the war!' "

"That's what *I* told them!" Hunter yipped.

"That's what we're obligated to do for you and that's what we're going to do for you!"

"That's what *I* told them at Selfridge!"

"And that we're going to give them adequate [facilities] and the best chance for athletics, recreation, just the same as we had for white troops, and just as good meals as the white troops have!"

"Now, there's one other thing," Hunter chimed in, his voice probably rising with a new kind of conviction, since this was the acting chief of the air staff to whom he spoke, "I told them, I'm going to start slamming people in the guardhouse and preferring charges against them when they say—these colored troops say, if they're going to be treated like that, they won't fight for their country, they're fighting for their race to try to improve it. If they say that to me, they go to the guardhouse with charges preferred against them!"

"That's right, that's exactly right," Giles replied, mentally hitching up his pants.

"I'm not going to let them get by with anything the whites can't get by with!" Hunter stormed.

"That's exactly right!"

"All right, Barney!"[40]

General Hunter was to have his chance for positive action with these pilots sooner than expected. In less than ten months, the lid was to blow. Godman Field and Walterboro became snake pits for the black pilots. When the confrontation came, Walterboro would be the place Daniel "Chappie" James, Jr., had gone on a cross-country flight. This in itself was an accomplishment, for there were not many bases in the country to which these pilots could fly in those electric days. There were no quarters or other facilities for them. And at one base, WACs whose job it was to drive out to meet incoming pilots, simply turned their jeeps around, leaving the black bomber pilots stranded to await a ride into base operations in an old pickup truck someone would finally send.

The air staff finally agreed that Godman Field was too small for the entire 477th Bombardment Group complement and directed it to be moved to Freeman Field near Seymour, Indiana, temporarily leaving behind the 115th CCTS Squadron. It was to be a move that the air corps, Colonel Selway, and General Hunter, in particular, would soon regret. They were going to be hurt again, and they never saw it coming.

Chapter Eleven
Confrontation

I

Freeman Field, located in the southern part of Indiana, sat two miles southwest of the town of Seymour and a half-mile south of U.S. Highway 50. Straddling the merging tracks of the Pennsylvania and B & O Railroads, it had a population of eight to nine thousand, including "forty or fifty Negro porters and janitors" and their families. Seymour was a slumbering town in which "a misdemeanor [was] as eventful as a wedding." Like Indiana generally, Seymour was part of America's heartland, a region of mingled agriculture and industry. Its people originally came from East Coast colonies and Europe. A hundred and seventy years ago, it was fiercely defended Indian wilderness, finally wrested away by the encroaching new Americans. The land was unchanging, and like it the people were conservative and staid. It was a place "surrounded by leagues of farmland," producing "huge crops of corn, wheat, soy beans, poultry and cattle," amidst "green seas of corn and wheat" and "deep shades of bottom timber." On warm nights, insect sounds filled the air.

With a very small black population, Seymour was not ready for the influx of black men soon to arrive. It treated its Negroes as white people generally treated Negroes in those days.

On 1 March 1945, General Hunter's First Air Force assumed responsibility for Freeman Field, and on 15 March 2,500 men from the 477th Bombardment and Service Groups arrived with 300 supervisors to begin combat training, as Colonel Selway assumed command.

Clashes between the citizenry of Seymour, Indiana, and the black airmen were immediate. On Wednesday, 7 March 1945, a black officer and four enlisted men dropped by and sat down in the Modern Cafe, operated by a Mr. Brinkman and his helper, Mr. Davenport. Mr. Brinkman ambled over.

"Sorry, fellas, but around here, we're in the habit of selling folks like *you* food to take out—not *servin'* it to you!"

"What?"

"You heard me!" Brinkman spat as Mr. Davenport grunted his agreement.

"Well, hell," they heard, "you don't know where we're from, man! We're from the North, and you and this fella you got working here—this Davenport—don't understand that we've got rights, like every other American! You dig?"

"Yeah," a black enlisted man chimed in, "this Mr. Davenport you got heah is a son-of-a-bitch, that's what he is! And you, Brinkman, I hope you got a son in the Army and I hope he gets killed—that's what I hope!"

Had the black airmen known that Mr. Brinkman and Mr. Davenport were armed, they might not have been so vocal. Brinkman and Davenport fingered concealed weapons as they looked at each other, determined to maintain, as Mr. Brinkman later said, "their collectedness" so as to "prevent disastrous results."

And disastrous results it might have been had the provost marshal from the base (Major Baumgardner, rumored to have had problems with blacks, having been dismissed from an Ohio police force as a result) not been present. Baumgardner ordered the blacks from the cafe and the day was saved.[41]

Not far away from the Modern Cafe, a black officer took the family wash to a Seymour laundry. They turned him away "because the articles were such that they would have to be washed by hand and can't be put in the machine or the ironer." Signs reading "Colored Will Not Be Served," sprouted in merchant's windows.

Mini-clashes occurred all around the town, as the citizens reacted to the sudden influx of more black people than most of its citizens had ever seen in one place. The Chamber of Commerce called a meeting and, according to the record, the town "became very quiet." Soldiers were suddenly allowed to purchase items and leave. Citizens later observed that "they were not rude; in fact they were more orderly than the white soldiers who had formerly been there." Come Friday and Saturday nights, they crowded the bus station, "very orderly and quiet," on their way to their old stamping grounds in Louisville or now to Indianapolis and Cincinnati or back to Freeman Field. The signs in the windows slowly began to disappear.

Almost at once, Colonel Selway set the stage for crisis, attempting to promote the attitude among blacks that as long as they accepted "the system," everything would be fine, even though the system was intolerable. Issuing orders that divided the officer's clubs along previously determined lines of "supervisor" and "trainee," Selway fell into the biggest trap of his career. The "Negro club'' was designated officers' club number one, and all black officers, regardless of status or experience, were designated ''trainees'' and expected to use the converted noncommissioned officers' club they dubbed ''Uncle Tom's Cabin.'' The ''white'' club (officers' club number two) was off-limits to them. It was for ''instructor or supervisory'' personnel only.

The black officers immediately objected. Selway's logic was flawed, since the flight surgeon and chaplain, both professionals, could hardly be called ''trainees.'' Over it all, the loud voice of General Hunter was heard: ''Any insubordination means guardhouse!''

Hunter's threat did not matter. Selway's ''head in the sand'' attitude did not matter, nor did the words attributed to the secretary of war that Selway quoted: ''The secretary of war says there is no racial problem and there is no racial problem!''

On the evening that Mr. Brinkman and Mr. Davenport were busy ''preserving their collectedness,'' Maj. Andrew M. White was assigned the duty of club officer for the white officers' club. Several days before he received the assignment and the issuance of Selway's order, he had seen two black officers from the bombardment group in the white club with three women. They had bought beer, wandered around a bit, and drove away. White, then, was not too shocked to see black officers approach his club. By now, however, Selway's order was in place and no beer was to be served to these ''visitors.''

''We'd like to be served.''

''I'm sorry,'' White retorted, ''this club is not the Officers Training Unit Club.''

The black officers left.

At five-thirty the next evening, another group of officers came in and asked for service.

''Look,'' Major White responded with a bit more verve, ''there are two clubs on the base. One, on Colonel Selway's orders, is for the Officers Training Group (OTU). The other is for permanent party. So you see,'' White patiently explained, ''it's *impossible* to serve you!''

On Friday the ninth, Major White stopped by his club and found nearly twenty black officers inside. Some sat at tables, others played the slot machines. White repeated his speech, this time reading Selway's order aloud. For all his good intentions, White committed a faux pas.

''So you see,'' he said stridently, ''we can't serve you *boys* in here!'' The resentment at being called ''boys'' was immediate.

''Well, we're not leaving unless the colonel himself comes over here and orders us out!'' Fortunately or unfortunately, Selway couldn't. He was sick and in bed with the flu. Finally, they began to drift away, until all were gone, much to Major White's relief. More came later in the evening, and the routine was repeated. After this incident, all 477th Bombardment Group officers were called together and advised that they were to use officers' club number one, which was assigned to them.[42]

II

If it had not been for the crisis over the segregation and officers' club issue, Colonel Selway and "the powers that be" might have gotten good marks for the movement of the bombardment group to Freeman Field. There was no question it was desirable to combine the training of the 477th Bombardment Group (Medium), the 387th Air Service Group, and the Replacement Crew Training Program. The advantages were clear. It would provide centralized administration for the three related programs and a field with the capacity to handle a large influx of personnel. With reorganization of base functions, integrating them with those already in place at Freeman Field, it would provide much-needed homogeneity as Godman became the sub-base. The ultimate goal, "direction of all activities toward the final preparation of the bombardment group and related units for combat," might have been reached.

Instead, although some flying activity was in progress, Selway's energies were being funneled into the segregation issue. For the moment, things seemed quiet. The 477th Bombardment Group officers held elections for "their" club, electing Capt. Elmo Kennedy, president, and a white squadron commander to the board.

This action stymied Selway's plan. On 10 March he worried about the legality of the black officers' actions in a conversation with General Hunter. His immediate solution was to close the white officers' club, but Hunter disagreed, cautioning him to say nothing in his written orders "about color, race or creed." To Selway's concern about the white officer elected to the black officers' board in their club ("he's going around tearing his hair!") he allowed that the officer didn't have to go to their club if that was his problem. Hunter was extremely worried that Selway was losing his nerve as Boyd had done at Selfridge and advised that he was sending his inspector out as an added impetus to ensure compliance with his orders preserving segregation. And if there was any insubordination on the part of the black officers, he wanted them immediately placed in close arrest. Further, Hunter indicated that, if necessary, he'd "order troops in there" ("I'd be delighted for them to commit enough actions so I can court-martial them!")

James and his black officer colleagues would have, at this point in time, been amazed at Selway's real understanding of their plight as he expressed it to General Hunter, even though he never expressed it to them: "What they're

demanding is social equality . . . it's been boiling for quite a while! . . .
They say they don't want to fly with officers who won't associate with them
equally and socially and I have failed in my job because I have failed to do
it—they claimed I should have ordered my white officers to associate with
them!"[43]

Clearly caught between the old Air War College study and the civilian status
quo, Selway's panic was real, because in discussing racial problems with blacks,
he had broken War Department policy. Hunter had begun to wonder a bit
about Selway. It was valid. Even Selway had begun to wonder about himself.

III

Colonel Selway not only would have wondered about himself, he would
have felt stark terror had he known for sure what the mechanics back at Godman
had planned for him prior to his move to Freeman Field.

Frustrated but held in check by the black officers, the black enlisted men
sought satisfaction from their plight as they hit upon a plan to solve "the
Selway problem" once and for all. They'd kill him. They'd kill him so that
nobody would ever know for sure how it happened.

The mechanics dreamed it one evening down in line maintenance. The plan
was diabolically simple. Take tissue paper, thread it into the fuel line of Selway's
plane, strand by strand. Stuff the fuel lines. Eventually they would clog, cause
engine failure and—poof! Selway's ship was up for maintenance that night,
and they did it. It was easy.

Next day, they stood in the shadows of the great hangar, watching as Selway
and his crew fired up for takeoff. Nudging each other as the plane taxied to
the outer markers, they waited for the scenario to unfold. Selway would com-
mence the takeoff roll. He would gather speed down the wide runway to that
critical place in time, too far to stop, but not enough speed to really fly. He
would just be lifting off the runway, and then—engine failure! Torque takes
over. Centrifugal force jerks them round toward the right engine—and—oblivion!

Selway roared up the engines. The B-25 began to roll. Faster and faster it
went. Odd smiles creased the faces of the mechanics, and there seemed a
kind of sadness there. A strange admixture of tears that did not flow, a bright
happiness, mixed with a maniacal but still-silent laughter. The B-25 leapt down
the concrete. Another ten or fifteen seconds, he would be almost airborne,
and Selway would be history!

The engines coughed, then sputtered and stopped. Power was lost. Enough
runway was left for a safe stop.

They had missed him by seconds! Mere seconds, and they could have been rid of Selway. Just a *little* altitude was all they had needed, but they had missed him.[44]

Inspection uncovered the problem. Nothing was done about it because nobody knew anything. Selway did depart from an old practice, though. He made a grizzled, old, black veteran called ''Pops'' his crew chief. Still, it was progress— of a sort—that Selway had unwittingly almost bought with his life. He had sworn he'd *never* have a black crew chief.

IV

Training went on at Freeman Field in spite of the shattered morale. It was a bright, sunny day when Daniel ''Chappie'' James, Jr., took his B-25 crew out for a routine training flight. Nothing kept him from doing all those things required of him, in spite of the bad situation. He was always calm and in control. This day he would demonstrate those attributes.

As the B-25 accelerated down the runway for takeoff, Harold Smith, his copilot, concentrated on the assignment of retracting the landing gear at the proper moment—just as the main gear leaves the ground with enough airspeed generated—so that the plane, just above the deck, would allow Chappie to power it, swoop up, and chandelle to the right or left. Smith's cue for action was Chappie's stern request that he watch for his ''thumbs up'' signal. When Smith saw that thumb up, the drill was to retract the gear. Pundits recount that Smith ''let a bump in the runway fake him out'' on his assignment, but according to Smith, Chappie ''reached over for the throttle with his thumbs straight up! And I looked at him, and he kept those thumbs straight up in the air. I thought that he knew what he was doing, so I pulled the gear!'' Unfortunately, the ship was not quite airborne. It settled on the air as Chappie jammed the throttles all the way to the firewall and the propellors, turning eighteen inches below the fuselage, struck the runway, making a horrendous clatter, bending the tips back four to six inches.

A lesser pilot might have crashed, but Chappie completed the takeoff, flew the mission, and landed the ship later without crashing. It had been a marvelous but revolting thing.

''What did you put your thumb up for?'' Smith grated.

''Well,'' Chappie replied, ''I was reaching for the throttles and I didn't know my thumb was up!''

The incident became a celebrated and sometimes embellished story old bomber pilots of the era loved to tell over forty years later. About Chappie's cool attitude. How he swung down from the airplane once he'd parked it without saying a word. How he "looked up at the airplane" and the bent propellors and silently but vigorously dealt with the copilot. That he didn't say much is true, Smith remembers. They reported the incident to the operations officer. Maintenance checked the engines and found them out of synchronization. Once repaired, Chappie and Smith took the ship up for a test flight. Later, while Smith was away, Chappie told about the incident at the weekly "blooper" session designed to prevent the repeating of mistakes that could be serious if allowed to stand uncorrected. The butt of good-natured joshing, Smith took it all in stride.

James was maturing. No need for lots of words when action made the point. It would be fair to say that the copilot involved never, ever pulled another main landing gear up too soon.

Shortly, Chappie, William Ellis, and others went to Walterboro Gunnery Base in South Carolina on ground assignments. It would not be long before they were pulled into the eye of the brewing storm.

V

Meanwhile, over in Kentucky at Godman Field, Squadron E, 118th Base Unit (CCTS), the 477th Bombardment Squadron's administrative unit, was preparing for movement to Freeman Field, Indiana. The planning, however, went far beyond the mere movement of men and material.

The black officers at Godman were preparing the main assault on segregation as it related to the officers' clubs. It was a different approach, designed to draw attention to the army air corps' segregation policy toward black units, reveal the service's failure to implement War Department direction on racial matters, and attract media attention if at all possible.

They knew what they were about. A plan began to evolve. But before the officers could solidify their overall plan, a larger problem had to be tackled, and that was keeping the enlisted men in line. They were "volatile and hostile toward the system and ready to strike back at the white supervisors on the spur of the moment."[45] Meetings were called in the hangars and the philosophy explained.

"An officer," they were told, "could never be railroaded nor court-martialed as easily as an enlisted man. Success in challenging the system lay in *not* creating distasteful situations." These sessions went on until the very eve of the move to Freeman Field when Chappie James was to arrive from Walterboro. He remembers the importance of these meetings. "We made sure that we briefed our people: 'Let them call you anything they want; when those cracker MPs come up, don't turn around and punch one in the nose. I know that you will be tempted to do it but there is no win there!' We really had to ride herd on the enlisted men, because they really wanted to get physical. We said, 'Don't do it, baby, just cool it. If they want to take us to jail now let it be.' . . .''

The cooler heads among the black officers luckily prevailed, although inside, they struggled with very real concerns, not the least of which was arrest. The hope was that they could challenge the system without going to that extent, and worse, escalation to court-martial. It was a perplexity, revolving around their very image; a fear that their actions, if handled awkwardly, would make them look like deserters at least and traitors at the worst, because a war was in progress. To counter these concerns, part of their plan was to somehow present their case to the black press and favorable white editors while sending telegrams to activist organizations, such as the NAACP.

They would challenge the club issue, but they'd do it by the book and peacefully, without violence. They would not go as a mob, never alone and only in orderly groups. They would start no fights, stating that they were there to use the club; that they intended to use it and if they were to be arrested, then so be it, because Army Regulation 210–10, paragraph nineteen, was their basis of operation—and *that* said that they were entitled. They would go to the club in twos, with the rest of a group forty to one-hundred yards behind, and they would do it until the ''authority'' saw the light.

Hostility on both sides was growing. You could see, feel, and hear it in the white officers' club as they gathered in the evenings for a cold beer. Lounging, sprawling, and standing around the tables, their words came from deep inside.

''I'll tell ya, I'll do *anything* possible to get transferred out of here. I don't care if I have to take a break in rank—it'd be worth it!''

''Yeah, I'll turn in my letter asking to be relieved of duty before I'll go overseas with the colored outfit!''

And then what some later thought was the crux of the whole problem tumbled out.

''If one of them makes a crack at my wife, laughs or whistles at her, like I saw them do to some white girls downtown, so help me, I'll kill him.''

''Well, I killed two of 'em in my hometown, and I'll tell ya, it wouldn't bother me to do it again,'' spouted a lieutenant.

''Yeah, [it's not the club] they're looking for. What they want to do is stand at the bar with you, have a drink with you and be able to talk to your wife. They're insisting on equality. It doesn't matter how many clubs of their own they have or how much better they are than ours, they will never accept that!''

''I have heard,'' said an officer, his eyes a bit wide, ''that a lot of the officers carry guns on their off-duty hours as well as on duty.''

The last officer was partially correct. And the feeling was no better over in the black officers' club. Similar remarks polluted the air there. The only difference was that the remarks being made in the white officers' club also stated the positions of the white command authority.

But informers were everywhere it seemed, at Freeman Field and Godman as well. Selway called them his "spies." He knew that it was no longer "just a clique of Negro officers looking for trouble" that he could weed out as one does bad apples, but something more pervasive. And if he didn't know for sure, during the month of April 1945, the *Pittsburgh Courier* made it clear: "Both officers and men point unwavering fingers of blame at Colonel Selway. . . . In the words of a soft-spoken Lieutenant, 'We aren't mad, but just disgusted with the rewards of our efforts.' . . . [It is] a rut which they keep from sinking deeper into by maintaining silence. Silence in mess, silence in barracks. . . . 'We don't want to be babied. All we want is to be treated as an Army tactical unit.' "[46]

Mischief was clearly afoot and Selway gathered his defenses.

Chapter Twelve
Imbroglio

I

The struggle between the two groups did not cause a lot of noise. Training moved ahead. Operations were normal in spite of overwhelming ideological differences. Colonel Selway and his advisers knew that his original officers' club order left much to be desired and that the immediate objective was to somehow make the original order "unquestionably legal, then enforce it."

First Air Force investigators flew out to Freeman Field for firsthand review of the situation. Colonel Wold, inspector, concluded that the black officers were scrupulously correct and apparently "well-coached. There has been," he continued, "no evidence of insubordination or the employment of force in their demeanor." The First Air Force operations and training officer concluded that "the main problems affecting training were the racial and political issue[s]." The provost marshal's man delivered analyses purporting to explain *why* the black officers were acting that way. "The Bomb and Service Groups," he theorized, "have had a long training period and it is the concensus of [white officer] opinion they won't improve, but gradually grow stale since a certain amount of dissatisfaction now prevails among the colored troops." It was a dissatisfaction, he went on to explain, existing because the black officers felt they had been trained enough and their training should be put to use. Two things made it worse, he thought. These were nonacceptance by the people in the nearby town of Seymour, which they could do little to control, and the high percentage of absence without leave (AWOL), which caused a disciplinary problem greater than at any other predominantly colored base. "There was," he went on, "the matter of discipline . . . not being enforced," requiring white officers in charge to have to bend over backwards before attempting any kind of action. He could see that local racism was a factor and thought a change of command a distinct option: "The colored situation within the Town of Seymour," he wrote, "is in negative status, but conditions existing at the Freeman Base warrant further surveillance along the lines of corrective action . . . in regard to the discipline of the troops, and *placing efficient officer personnel into positions where enforcement of the disciplinary problems will be insured . . ."*[47]

In spite of these examinations, the black officers maintained faultless behavior. The inspector, Colonel Wold, thought there was a kind of irony in that, since under ordinary circumstances faultless behavior on the part of the officers would have been commendatory. But because the sabers were out over the racial problems, their behavior patterns were suspect at the very least. There might previously have been a chance to instill a "combat spirit in this group," he thought the white supervisors had felt, but *now* they were "convinced that the Group has no desire to fight and consequently, they have lost any desire to be associated with the organization. Dissension had been sown," he concluded, "but the situation is not now explosive." The inspector general's man even went on record to suggest *the possibility of black command,* but backed away from the idea because "acceding to a portion of their campaign might give rise to further unacceptable demands."

Colonels Selway and Wold and the local staff hammered out a new club order, working against a backdrop of careful watchfulness, the nearness and readiness of white military police units, useful as an aid to "new and vigorous command."

The new order was of crafty device. Designed to be all-inclusive, it was replete with expedience and strategem, literally girded about with iron-bound words designed to control this new avarice on the part of black officers. Entitled *Assignment of Buildings and Areas at Freeman Field, Seymour, Indiana, Effective 1 April 1945,* it first justified its existence. It was based, it read, on army air corps standards relating to the control of personnel in training units. Not only was this the master design, it was also meant to be instrumental in the "development of the individual and . . . unit combat spirit of personnel undergoing overseas and combat crew training," and further, "was intended to *conserve fuel and power.* Compact organization of units and personnel," it noted, was the ultimate goal.[48]

The order assigned separate facilities to separate units; permanent party to one officers' club; the 477th Bombardment Group and the expected CCTS Unit from Godman Field to the other. It separated facilities by "supervisor" and "trainee." Assignment of the OTC and CC trainee officers to the recreational building rescued the commander the black officers had elected to their board. "OTU" put him in; "trainee" got him out. All white officers were "supervisors" and thus, key officers. What appeared to be a "minor" problem existed. There were "key" black officers such as Major Ramsey, group surgeon. The solution was simple—transfer—for a surgeon could hardly be called a "trainee."

An even more direct specification of intent in this area was considered by Colonel Selway. Deciding that additional revision of the order was needed to define who the affected officers were by name, he discussed the matter with General Hunter, who quickly settled the matter. "I do not consider them *under* training, they are *giving* training!" said the general. So the order survived as it was, and paragraph 1-b of the now-famous 1 April 1945 order went on to direct that: "Personnel, commissioned and enlisted, will use the housing, quarters, messing, recreational facilities, and areas as designated by paragraph 2, below; and at the time and within the restrictions as may be required by the Base Commander . . ."

The listing of all the facilities went on for five-and-one-quarter pages by building numbers, name of the facility, who used it, and in a last column, cited the officer responsible for each facility. The Freeman Field list was more than specific:

Building Number	Using Activities	Responsible Officer
T-2	Flag Pole	Post Engineer
T-810	Tennis Courts	Post PT Engineer
T-885	OTU and CC Trainee Officers' Club	OTU and CCTS Club Officer
T-915 thru T-951	Base and Supervisor Club and BOQs	Officer Club Mess Officer

Published on 1 April 1945, the order seemed to stick. There were no visitations from the bombardment group at the white officers' club. They flew their airplanes industriously. Colonel Selway and his staff officers may have chuckled a bit over in building T-951. They'd "slapped it to them!" it seemed. But it wasn't over. They had committed a tactical error, failing to see what the black officers were doing behind their backs. Squadron E, 118th AAF Base Unit (CCTS-M), would be arriving from Godman Field on the fifth of April, hardly a week away.

II

Colonel Selway's rosy world turned into swamplands around Tuesday of the following week. His spies made him aware that trouble concerning officers' club number two might erupt on the evening the combat training squadron was to arrive. Wily strategist, he immediately ordered his base provost marshal to station men at the front door of the club, and lock all other doors to "prevent entry by the Negroes," and "exclude any trainee personnel under penalty of arrest."

Around three o'clock on the afternoon of the fifth, Freeman Field activity intensified. A reporter from the black *Indianapolis Recorder,* a Mr. Lowell M. Trice, appeared at the base to "do some illustrated publicity stories" on the bombardment group. Poking about the base a bit before calling the public relations officer, Trice caused his own downfall. The public relations officer possessed an army air corps intelligence message terming him extremely uncooperative, defiant, and obnoxious. He was immediately expelled from the base. On the heels of this activity, Squadron E, 118th AAF Base Unit (combat training unit), with black officers and enlisted men, with B, C, and D Squadrons, along with the 619th, 617th, and 616th Bombardment Squadrons, arrived on station around four-thirty in the afternoon, some having flown in, others arriving by train.

Although not briefed on Colonel Selway's 10 March and subsequent 1 April letter order, they were well aware of the tactics that had been taken relative to the club, what their main plan was, and what their roles were to be in the next few days. In fact, their plans were to be put into effect almost at once.

The newly arrived black 118th AAF Base Unit officers hastily dropped their baggage in their quarters and washed up. Shortly, they would begin infiltration of the white officers' club in earnest!

III

James, along with William Ellis and other officers, remained at Walterboro Gunnery Base in South Carolina. While he was there, word of what was happening at Godman Field and about to happen at Freeman Field once the 118th arrived had been filtering down for about six weeks through couriers who flew in and out of Walterboro. Not only had they heard that planning was going on at Godman to press the officers' club issue, but they knew that Freeman Field had been segregated by Colonel Selway, that blacks couldn't go into one of the clubs. The news signaled the return of the unwelcomed spectre of Selfridge Field.

Racism at Walterboro Gunnery Base was as oppressive as at any other base in the South. Hard-working airmen needed a rest, a chance for social intermixing, a drink or two, to make the body and spirit burn brightly for a delicious moment. So it was that the military police encountered the young Lieutenant James at a table in the bistro at closing time. They told him it was time to go. James refused to move, his lips forming words indicating that he had no intention of going anywhere. A standoff. As was usual, everybody knew and liked him, even the military police. And besides, he was so *big!* Instead of the roust, they called his fellow officers at the base, one of whom was Lt. William B. Ellis.

"Hey, Lieutenant," said the military police, "we've got Lieutenant James down here. We're trying to get him out of this club, but he won't go!"

"Yes?"

"Yeah, Lieutenant! We know him. We don't wanna roust or hurt him. Could you—"

"Right!" Ellis replied, "We'll be right there!"

That is how Chappie ended up at the base hospital in the company of officer friends, who talked him out of the bistro and finally succeeded in convincing the doctor on duty to authorize the administering of a B-1 shot to hasten the departure of the bright fires searing Chappie's mind and body. It was an exercise in diplomacy, since the doctor hinted at documenting James' problem as excessive use of alcohol.

A nurse approached, syringe in hand.

"Drop your pants, Lieutenant," she said in her best professional manner.

"Nope! Nope! Nope! *Nope!* Nobody's shooting me with that thing—and certainly not *there!*"

"Lieutenant!" cried the nurse exasperatedly.

It was obvious that Chappie had no intention of cooperating. What to do?

"Say, nurse," one of the officer friends whispered, "tell 'im yer gonna give him a short arms!"[*]

The nurse smiled knowingly, whispering the news to Chappie. A great smile suddenly wreathed his face. They heard the belt unbuckle and the fabric slide. The deed was done as Chappie flinched.

It was his way. What is practical and resourceful. What gets the job done. When they recount the story today, officer friends still chuckle and smile with

---

[*] G.I. slang for a standard medical inspection conducted by the military to detect urethritis in the male soldier.

a certain admiration for this lovable man who, in spite of it all, had a sense of humor and could go with the bamboozle.

The weather had been foul when Bill Ellis landed at Godman Field on the eve of the move of the 118th to Freeman Field. A big strategy meeting was in progress in the hangar across the runway. He went over to listen. The instructions were the same. Enlisted men stay put. Stay out of this effort. Let the officers handle it! The Articles of War were explained. The message to the officers was loud and clear: *"Go into that club! No matter what! Go into that club!"*

The scenario was about to unfold.

IV

Maj. Gerald F. Baumgardner, base provost marshal, carried out Colonel Selway's order around seven o'clock in the evening, directing one of his assistant provost marshals, a 1st Lt. Joseph D. Rogers, of D Squadron, to go to the officers' club and mess number two to forestall any problems with black officer infiltration. He was to "enforce orders." Clicking on his web belt from which hung a loaded .45, Lieutenant Rogers snapped a military police brassard securely on his left arm, arriving at the club and mess number two about eight-thirty. Colonel Selway went to bed.

Rogers stationed himself at the front door of the club, first ensuring that all other doors leading into the club were locked. All seemed serene until a little after eight-thirty, when he looked out to see four black lieutenants and one black flight officer appear at the club door.

"I recognized them," Rogers attested, "as members of the CCTS." He went outside to meet them. They asked him why they could not enter the club, and Rogers told them it was restricted from their use.[49]

"That's not good enough, Lieutenant," came the retort, "we want to see the Club Officer!"

Lieutenant Rogers entered the club. Finding Major A. M. White, the club officer, he sighed, "Major, those four colored officers out there want to talk to you!" White went out.

"Howdy, fellas! What can I do for you?"

"Why can't we come into this club?"

"Well, on the strength of the Freeman Field letter order, if you enter this club, I would be forced to put you under arrest in quarters for not using the facilities assigned to you as outlined in the letter order!"

"Are you refusing us admittance because we are colored?"

"Color isn't involved here," the major smiled, "it's simply that if you were to enter this club it would be a violation of the Commanding Officer's letter!''

''Well—Okay, Major! We're gonna wait out here for transportation!''

Major White went inside. A few minutes later, the black officers were gone, much to Major White's and Lieutenant Rogers' relief. If Major White thought at this point that this threat to integrate his club was an empty one, he was wrong. He simply sat for the moment in the calm eye of a swirling hurricane.

The clock inched past nine-thirty. A single, electric light bulb hung, burning forlornly from the roof overlooking the porch and vestibule at the club's entrance.

About a quarter to ten, nineteen black officers appeared at the club door. Lieutenant Rogers met them, stepping, as he did so, out the front door. A double door, it was made of two normal-sized doors, divided in the middle, each built to swing towards the wall from which it was hung. There were matching screen doors, about five feet across in all. The left door was closed. Rogers stood in front of the partially open right door, his right hand against the closed door at shoulder height; his left hand against the open door at hip level, thus effectively blocking the door—or so he thought.

''Lieutenant, you can't come in here, this club isn't for you fellas!''

''Why isn't it?''

''Lieutenant, step outside and I will explain it to you! This,'' Rogers began, ''is a private club and you men are not allowed in here!''

A lieutenant named Clinton said, ''I'm base personnel, why can't I use the club?''

''I can't answer that question. I have my orders from the Commanding Officer that this *is* a private club and only members and their guests are allowed to use the facilities here at the club!''

''Well,'' another black officer said, ''I am a visiting officer and what are you going to do about visiting officers?''

''You are not a guest of a member of the club,'' Rogers shot back, ''and according to my orders cannot be admitted!''[50]

Ominous rumbles of discontent came from the crowd. Rogers blinked, and blinked again.

''I would like,'' a Lieutenant Thompson said politely, ''to utilize my privileges as an officer of the United States Army and enter the club for a drink!''

''If you men come inside the club, I'll—I'll—have to arrest you!'' Rogers cried.

''Get out of my way, let me in so I can get arrested!'' growled Lieutenant Thompson.

A great tide of black officers, led by Lts. Marsden A. Thompson and Shirley R. Clinton, pushed past Lieutenant Rogers and into the hallowed space. In the rush of bodies, it looked, according to Capt. Franklin A. McLendon, a club patron at the time, as if they had ''pushed Lieutenant Rogers backwards into the building." As Lieutenant Thompson entered the club, Rogers grabbed his coat sleeve and pushed back.

"Take your hands off me!" Lieutenant Thompson spat.

"You're all under arrest!" sputtered Rogers, "Stop, while I take your names!"[51]

They ignored him, scattering through the club. They lounged against the bar and perched on the furniture. "Lieutenant Rogers," Captain McLendon later recounted, "did not offer any great degree of resistance."

Second Lt. Coleman A. Young, arriving after the influx into the club, simply followed suit, went into the bar, and asked for a beer. He was refused service.

"I have instructions," the bartender smugly said, "not to serve non-members!"

"How do you know I'm not a member?" countered Young.

"Well," the bartender replied, frankly laying it on the line, "no colored men belong to *this* club!"

Across the room, Lt. Marsden Thompson, after trying to use a public phone (it was busy), walked over to the pinball machine. A white lieutenant appeared with Major White in tow. As he entered the big room, the pinball machine dinged and a record played on the music box. He beckoned them to gather around.

"If you men refuse to leave," the major started, "I will have to place you under arrest in quarters!"

"Major, Sir, we are not refusing to leave, but we would like to know *why* we must leave!" Lieutenant Clinton replied.

"I have orders, and I'm ordering all of you to leave the club!" the major flatly replied, pulling out pencil and paper so as to record their names.

"Then you're giving that order, Major?"

"I am."

"What is *your* name, Major?"

"Major Andrew White, Army Air Corps."

The officer asking the question wrote it down.

"And what is *your* station, Lieutenant?"

"I just left Godman."

"Then you're not a base officer!"

"But what if I was?"

"I don't have to answer that question!"

Lt. Marsden Thompson leaned against the pinball machine, bracing himself with one arm. "I refuse to go!" he asserted. A Lieutenant Payton repeated the challenge.

This was serious business! Although he might not have been exactly correct, Major White emphasized the fact that *disobedience of a direct order in time of war before witnesses was punishable by death.*

"Very well, you are all under arrest in quarters!"

The black officers fell silent. Major White listed their names. As he did so, Capt. Anthony N. Chiappe, the squadron commander of the 118th, whispered that he'd like to speak to his men after the names were taken. The request was granted. Chiappe took them all aside. It amounted to a verbal reprimand.

"Understand," he lectured, "that I *am* your immediate Commanding Officer. I want you to understand that in the army one obeys a superior officer without question! You are not to question the order of any officer in charge who is acting under the orders of Colonel Selway, the base commander. You are all to report to me in the morning. I'll hear your side of the story and take it up with the proper authority! Am I understood? You are all ordered to leave this club immediately. Do what the major ordered and return to your quarters!"[52]

"Captain," came a plaintive voice, "is this a white officers' club?"

"No, this club is for supervisory base personnel and you are to use the club in Building T-885!"

"Remember," reiterated Major White as the black officers turned to go, "you are all in arrest in quarters!" The nineteen faded into the night.

About ten o'clock the same evening, another group of fourteen black officers approached Lieutenant Rogers at the front door of the club.

"Just a minute," he started, "this is the base officers' Club. CCTS and OTU students are not allowed in here!"

They insisted upon entering.

"If you persist in entering, I will be forced to place you in arrest!"

Muffled voices.

"I am an officer of the guard and I have my orders from my commanding officer!" Rogers cried, again blocking the door. Through sheer numbers, they again forced him to move. Entering the club, they walked around, savored the place, and enjoyed the forbidden ground.

Suddenly, Major White was there, telling them that they were not allowed; that he was ordering them out.

"You are ordering us outside, is that right, Major?" rasped a black officer. "What's *your* name, Major?"

"Major Andrew White," he obliged. "Now, I want all of your names, and I'm placing you in arrest in quarters!"

"By what authority are you placing us in arrest in quarters?" came the automatic challenge.

"You have violated a headquarters letter order by coming into the club. I am custodian of this club and in that capacity I am placing you in arrest in quarters. Leave this club and retire to your quarters immediately!"

Steely glances were exchanged as the black officers' names were taken, but they too disappeared into the night.

It had been a harrowing night for Major White, Lieutenant Rogers, and the "reinforcement" assistant provost marshals he'd called for—Lieutenants Rice and Harrison (neither of whom wore military police brassards). But it was still not over. Between ten-twenty and ten-thirty, two black commissioned officers and one black flight officer entered the club lounge. The scenario was essentially the same. Rogers reiterated that the club "was restricted from their use." ("Just a second, Lieutenant, are you OTU personnel?" "No, we ain't." "Well, this *is* a private club!")

This time, the leader was one Roger C. Terry, of Los Angeles, who informed Rogers that he *was* going to enter, and according to the record, pushed Rogers aside, opened the door, and, "pushing Rogers further out of the way with the door," entered the club. Lieutenant Kennedy and flight officer Goodman followed his lead.

They were immediately met by Major White, who took their names, ordered them in arrest in quarters, directed them to leave the club and retire to their quarters.

"Why are we under arrest?" inquired Lieutenant Kennedy.

"I don't have to answer that question," replied Major White, by now an extremely harried man.

Not long after, Capt. Clarence C. Jamison, Capt. John W. Rogers, and 1st Lt. Milton T. Hall came to the door of the club, but did not, for some reason, enter. They were not arrested.

In all, thirty-seven black commissioned and flight officers had challenged Colonel Selway's edict concerning the separate clubs for "base supervisory" officers versus "a trainee club," ostensibly for black officers alone, during their first evening on station. They had challenged Selway's assistant provost marshals Rogers, Rice, and Harrison at the door. They had verbally indicated refusal to comply with a direct order in the presence of witnesses while a war was being fought. Not a shot had been fired. No blows had been struck. And it still wasn't over. The struggle had really just begun, in an intricate, perplexing, and potentially dangerous state of affairs. For riding above the confusion was that question many may have thought about but did not voice. What would happen when the next group of black officers appeared? Would the frustrated Lieutenant Rogers and his other assistant provost marshals finally draw their loaded .45 pistols? And if they did, would they fire, and how would the black officers and enlisted men react?

Chapter Thirteen
Counterpoint

I

It isn't known how Colonel Selway felt when he awakened on the morning of 6 April 1945. He would doubtless have been wide awake after the episodes of the previous evening were recited to him by his officers. Panic reigned. The telephone lines between Freeman Field, First Air Force headquarters and Washington, D.C., were buzzing.

Colonel Selway summarized what had happened in a long opening recitation to General Glenn, First Air Force chief of staff.

"And they said," he went on, "they were going to enter anyway and the provost marshal gave them a direct order in the name of the commanding officer not to violate that order, and they pushed him aside and came in anyway!"

General Glenn wanted to know how many officers were involved. Selway estimated the number as thirty-three, and added that his evidence came from the "colored officer who was with them down at Godman before they combined the CCTS program."

"What was his name?" asked the general.

"Silvera," came the reply. Selway seemed a little proud to expose this alleged pipeline to the black officers' inner sanctum. "He's the one," he continued, "who is trying to give proof of loyalty because I fooled him a couple of times and he's a little scared. He told . . . another colored officer . . . that this had been organized in advance, essentially organized at Godman Field, and that they came up here prepared to do this in an organized manner!"

There was another black officer who told Captain Chiappe that "*he* went down with the thirty-three because the rest had threatened him and he was scared to go overseas with them if he didn't go along with the rest of the Negroes.'' He didn't have that officer's name.

Colonel Selway had already been in touch with General Hunter to clear which Articles of War he could use to court-martial the officers. The plan was to have the squadron commander read the order about the clubs to the newly arrived officers, to reinforce the idea that it was done at General Hunter's direction and coordinated with army air corps, and that it was *policy* on *numerous* other air force training stations in the continental United States for base and supervisory officers to have certain facilities; and those undergoing training, different facilities. He had been cleared by General Hunter, he went on, to ''charge them under the 64th Article of War for willful disobedience of an order, and the other charge under the 66th [Article of War] because we may be able to prove they were organizing such a stand.'' They were all, he pointed out, in arrest in quarters and charges were being preferred as quickly as possible. A complete report was to be flown to First Air Force headquarters.

Colonel Selway was quickly expanding the scope of possible charges to specify not only disobedience to direct orders, but possibly mutiny, sedition, and even conspiracy.

General Glenn approved these actions and points of view, intimating that bringing additional military police might or might not be a bad move, although Selway thought that might ''rile it up, because, after all, this was an organization of Negro officers.''

It was a ploy backed by the ''Society for the Advancement of the Race,'' thought Selway. It followed, because how else could a reporter from a Negro paper slip into the base at the precise time all this was about to happen? Wasn't it peculiar that he ''went all among them?'' Obviously, Trice was an agitator. He was to be there and ''write it all up.'' But he'd handled it. Trice was ''practically physically'' taken off the base. It was the newspapers that were fomenting trouble. Selway knew it, because ''all the articles pick on me and General Hunter as the symbols of segregation.''

If he could have ''eight or ten good, white MPs to head up the guard section,'' he would feel better, since he only had six or seven, and the rest were colored. General Glenn promised help on the issue and ''if anything comes up at all, General Hunter wants to have a general officer down there to help you . . . and . . . keep us informed!''

Meanwhile, General Hunter was talking to Brig. Gen. Ray L. Owens, deputy chief of the air corps air staff.

''I like to keep Washington advised when I have any trouble with these colored pilots,'' he began. He talked about the black newspaper reporter who had infiltrated the base under ''false pretenses.'' They ''caught him and kicked him off.'' It was all planned, ''a bunch of these colored officers forced their way into the *white* officers' club and the provost marshal was there and they pushed by him.''

Hunter was rabid.

"They have . . . them under arrest and [are] going to prefer charges against them. They're under arrest in their quarters now and if they won't stay there, if the guardhouse isn't big enough, we'll put them in that part of the hospital where they confine people with guards over them!''

"And if they get out of hand . . . I'll get a general officer out there right away!'' General Owens agreed.

Captain Chiappe read the order of 19 April to the black officers at ten o'clock in the morning, counseling them on the base regulations. They thought it was handled.

But the day was young. At three-fifteen in the afternoon, eyebrows arched as seventeen black officers paraded down to the club and ambled in: Lieutenants O'Neil, Johnson, Harris, Green, Lewis, Altemus, Sanders, Prioleau, and Watkins. Flight officers Williams, Jackson, Lawrence, Murphy, Marzette, Steele, Lum, and Miller.

The clock read twenty minutes past the hour when Lieutenant E. V. Hipps walked in. At twenty minutes to four, Lts. William B. Ellis, Spann Watson, L. F. Gillead, P. T. Anderson, and flight officer R. Dickinson marched in.

"You cannot use this club. It's illegal for you to enter this club! You have your own club and you are supposed to use it!''

"No, we *are* going to use this club!''

"I have no choice but to place you under arrest!''

"Fine, then place us under arrest!''

"Okay, consider yourself under arrest, return to your barracks. You are under house arrest! You are to go nowhere except to the mess hall and training, then back to your barracks!''

At fifteen minutes before the hour, Lieutenant A. B. Polite, Jr., and Lt. James W. Mason came into the club. And that wasn't all. Around ten o'clock that night, the old "bad penny," Mr. Trice, from "that Indianapolis newspaper" showed up again aboard a bus at the main gate. Lieutenant Rogers, the assistant provost marshal (of 5 April fame), stopped him.

"Sorry, Mr. Trice, but you can't come on the base.''

"What?''

"I said you can't come on this base, Mr. Trice. My orders!''

"Listen, Lieutenant, do you know who I am?''

"Yes, Mr. Trice, I know who you are.''

"Why, I'm representing a newspaper, as you well know, and that's not all! I'm representing a wire service *and* the NAACP!''

"No, Mr. Trice!''

"Well, I wanna see the Indianapolis Girls USO Show and program!''

Mr. Trice became very indignant.

"I wanna see what Colonel Robert R. Selway, Jr., is doing to the boys stationed at Freeman Field!"

"Nope, Mr. Trice, so please turn it around and catch the next bus back to town." Apparently Mr. Trice was again not admitted.

If the colonel didn't panic on the fifth, definite signs of panic were showing now. He was on the phone to General Glenn, First Air Force chief of staff, at once.

"We have some more trouble! Thirty-six last night . . . we read the order to them . . . [and after that] . . . twenty-one of them paraded down and went into the club. . . . We're rounding up those veins* and I will write arrest orders and . . . start charges . . . we're going to be a little jammed in . . . the legal department . . ."

"Fifty-seven of them?" the general incredulously asked.

"There were thirty-six and twenty-one more this afternoon!"

"That's a total of fifty-seven!"

"I haven't added it . . . I'm gathering . . . names." Selway was concerned that one of the thirty-six officers originally arrested couldn't be found. He was having thirty-six bunks set up in the detention ward of the base hospital but the twenty-one new arrests caused new space problems and the guardhouse was already full.

"I'm going to close the club, and just open up the back for mess. . . . We're going to need some legal help to help type. . . . I thought . . . we could get . . . legal help from First Air Force."

General Glenn agreed and promised to send legal clerks to Freeman Field to help prepare court-martial charges; even if they had to be pulled from nearby stations.

"It just seems," Colonel Selway moaned, "as though there is a clan . . . looks like they are trying to make a test of their social equality!"

"Yes," replied the General, "the whole works will probably try it."

Little did General Glenn know how right he was. Even as he spoke, the arrested officers were engrossed in a strategy session on how to achieve that very goal. And Chappie James, even though a bit late, went down to enter the club with Bill Ellis, but it had already been closed. Contacts were to be made with Edmund C. Hill and Walter Winchell. Letters were written to relatives and other agencies that might listen. Communications were to be sent to all the black newspapers and other newspapers as well. The NAACP and Urban League were to be contacted. Roger Terry called his mother, who had White House connections.

---

* An epithet of the times referring to blacks. Assumed to be a play on one of the literal definitions of the word, i.e., "a strain [or] streak of different color in wood or marble."

They called their wives and enlisted their help. Wives circled the arrest barracks in Watson's convertible so that the officers' news releases and letters could be thrown into the back seat. The women drove to the nearest mailbox and dropped them in. Their wives began what Lt. Col. Spann Watson (Retired) remembers as "a leg patrol," walking around the officers' club to see when it was open, for, after the last arrests, their goal was clear. "We have to get *everybody* arrested or we are ruined. . . . That was the idea. We approached some people . . . and we got some . . . in this effort to organize everybody and get everybody arrested . . ."

Headlines in black newspapers and several white papers carried the story in bold print. Sixty-nine black officers were in arrest in quarters. Selway was also concerned about the possibility of violence (although none had taken place as yet), and the prevailing attitude of his white officers.

General Glenn's response to the mass protest was to add every new arrival in the club to the arrest list. Colonel Selway took that as the solution to both problems. He'd give the blacks no quarter. Everyone entering the club would be stopped and, because "the white people here are watching," he'd "make the arrest." Glenn thought there would hardly be any violence, that it was a "test case" brought about by "agitators who have talked them into it." To Colonel Selway, it was all paradoxical. "[They] seemed to be going about their jobs, saluting and everything. . . . It is therefore definitely cooked up off this station; cooked up before they came here, down at Godman. They just had the thing arranged I think, and they wanted it to come off when that reporter was here but I got wise and got him off the post . . . it will break out in all the papers anyway . . ." And what if they all broke their arrest? Selway wondered.

"Just add additional charges," said General Glenn.

"[But it's] a question of securing the bodies!"

"If they take off, they're AWOL until you catch them!"

Colonel Selway closed the club on 7 April, and the Freeman Field director of intelligence fired off a memorandum reporting the tawdry affair of 6 April to the First Air Force's inspector general and counterintelligence. It ended with this paragraph: "No violence at any of these incidents, and the Negro officers left after invited to leave. All above officers have been placed in arrest in quarters. Any further action that may be taken has not yet been announced . . ."[53]

II

Freeman Field turned into a legal clerk assembly line. Legal officers and clerks descended on the place. The production line went to work. Legal experts from First Air Force headquarters at Mitchel Field, New York, flew in to review the charges already levied against the black officers and consider if evidence existed to justify more charges. Colonel Wold, the inspector general's man, was back again, analyzing the situation. The chief document reviewed by Colonel Wold was Colonel Selway's 1 April letter order. His conclusions may have sent chills up the latter's spine, since they tended to make him look, at the very least, inept.

"The subject letter," Colonel Wold wrote, "is obscure, inexact and ambiguous as to its meaning or purpose. Whereas those who composed the letter were aware of its intent and the implied provision, the uninitiated or casual person . . . would certainly have difficulty comprehending its contents, and would certainly not read into it any definite prohibitions."

Inexact? Ambiguous? No doubt Colonel Selway had secretly been proud of the fact that these adjectives describing his handiwork *did* accurately describe his intentions. "Definite prohibitions" were to be avoided at all costs, because that tendency towards prohibition was the snare that caught Colonel Boyd at Selfridge and resulted in reprimand and transfer under a cloud. *Positive* assignments were made and the "prohibitions"—although present, were left to the assistant provost marshal and club custodian.

In spite of Wold's clear assessment of Selway's order, he somehow managed to stay on the right side of General Hunter as he also wrote: "The intent [of the April 1, 1945, order] was quite obviously to separate colored from white officers in regard to certain base facilities. Though . . . racial separation was not specified, there can be no doubt as to the intent of the order . . . ." The black officers, Wold went on, must be held accountable for their ultimate intent, as they "did in fact band together to perpetuate an incident by forcing their entrance." Technically, there was the infraction of the intent of the letter order, but *even though* the letter order intended segregation in its most limited meaning, it intended segregation in accord with War Department policy. The order *as it stood* had emphasized the "spirit" of the War Department's slap at segregation and had thus complied with "the spirit and intent" of War Department directive (i.e., there will be no discrimination because of race or color) by only specifically prohibiting segregation "in the most important facilities," and, because that was so, the intent of the letter did carry out air corps directives at Freeman Field. Colonel Wold *made it sound as if* Hunter and Selway were, in some strange way, right. He finally argued that: "The directives effecting desired racial separation in some off-duty activities have been in accordance with War Department policy, which provides that facilities may be designated for the *use of particular military units* but *not for the use of a certain race or color group* . . . ." There should be instead, he recommended, "a clear, concise order . . . issued as a base regulation to effect the desired degree of separation necessary . . . ."[54]

The latter recommendation was, of course, the precise route selected by General Hunter, who, along with Colonel Selway and Colonel Wold, embarked on joint authorship of a new Base Regulation 85-2, to be entitled *Assignment of Housing, Messing and Recreational Facilities for Officers, Flight Officers and Warrant Officers*. At the same time, Colonel Wold and Major Osborne of the First Air Force legal department, privately advised Colonel Selway that his case against his "deliberately disobedient" black officers now incarcerated in the hospital detention ward was as thin as tissue paper.

"Colonel Wold and Major Osborne are out here and advise me that I've got *technical* cases against these people but not iron-bound cases, and they think that there are only three of them that I can convict," Selway moaned by telephone to General Hunter on 9 April. "Those are the ones that pushed the provost marshal. So it looks like I'm going to have to release the rest!"

"All right," General Hunter replied with some disgust. "I can't understand why you didn't . . . get out an order . . . other than this assignment of buildings, because those people [didn't] see that!"

"They all knew about it . . . the provost marshal [was] actually in front of the club [and] told them that they were included in there as trainees and CCTS—they'll deny the fact that they heard the provost marshal. They've got a man who's a lawyer behind them general, and anything we write, they're going to go out and test—"

But General Hunter was more concerned about the new base regulation, a draft of which had reached him.

"I want [this] written so that they are disobeying orders if they don't do it! . . . I've got it here and there are some things I don't like about it!"

"It ought to be written to actually forbid them to enter the building," Selway volunteered, "because they'll claim that they're not using our facilities; that they're going in there looking for their instructor, or—"

"They can be instructed that they will not use the building," General Hunter interrupted, "that the assignment of these recreational facilities is [specified]. . . . You are fully covered. . . . You can get out a post order that certain buildings will be used by permanent party and that they will refrain from entering those buildings and the order will be for both of them—*don't mention colored or white!*"

Colonel Selway agreed to the new wording.

"What I'll do then is go ahead and charge these three, release the rest and put them back in training, and then sit tight until I get something from you."

"Yes. You can tell them right now that the commanding general of the First Air Force says that trainees will use one club and the permanent party, which includes the instructor personnel in that group, will use another club!"

Selway then decided, with the general's blessing, to reopen the club, but not before one more review of the new draft base regulation. Once done, General

Hunter directed its issue and, further "make everyone initial it that he's received and read it and understands it. *And every new officer that comes in, white or colored, I'd give them the same thing!*"

Officers were being selected to sit on the court-martial board of the unfortunate three officers, Marsden A. Thompson, Shirley R. Clinton, and Roger C. Terry. Lieutenants Thompson and Clinton were charged under Articles of War 64 and 66. Lieutenant Terry remembers that he was to be charged under Article 64, punishable by death in time of war. The remainder of the 101 officers were released.

III

The new Base Regulation 85-2, dated 9 April 1945, began with an enumeration of unspecified authorities: "Army Air Forces standards govern the control and curfew of personnel undergoing training, as differentiated from standards governing permanent party base supervisory and instructor personnel, authorize separate housing, messing and recreational facilities assignment to those classes of personnel . . ." It cited the commanding general of First Air Force and army air force standards as the real authorities. It specified the quarters, messing, and recreational facilities the black officers would use (i.e., officer's training unit, combat-crew and ground-crew air replacement training), and assigned a different set of buildings for white officers. It limited the black officers to "their" buildings, and forbade them entry to any others (even to the "other" tennis courts) except on official business with prior approval of the base commander or his deputy. Page two contained a "fill-in" first endorsement in which each recipient was to "certify that I have read and fully understand the above order" and sign by name, rank, and organization.

Again, Hunter and Selway thought they had handled it. Instead, the drama escalated.

It was one of those magic moments in history when, through much confusion and pain, the scales which had blinded Americans for decades fell away. Perhaps these black pilots knew something the rest of America had only dimly perceived at this point in its history, something that R. Buckminster Fuller described in "Technology and the Human Environment," "Humans have high destiny, possibly the most important in the Universe. And if the human team aboard space vehicle Earth does not make good at this particular occupation of this particular planet there are probably billions times billions of other planets with human crews aboard who will reboard Earth at some time to operate it properly . . ."[55] In flight of fancy, then, perhaps this group of oppressed, black officers was such a "crew," destined to do their bit to help "operate [planet Earth] properly."

It certainly seemed validated. They reacted to General Hunter's order with intense fervor regarding the order to "initial the new order" contained in the Base Regulation 85-2 and certify that they "had read it and understand it."

Throughout these activities, James was off-station at Walterboro and on cross-country flights, thus escaping initial compliance with the new order.

On 10 April 1945, all black commissioned, flight, and warrant officers were called together by their squadron commanders and advised of the contents of Base Regulation 85-2. Lt. Col. John H. Patterson, deputy commander, after discussing its contents, gave each officer a copy of the regulation directing that each sign the preprinted first endorsement on the reverse. All read it, but most "expressed their unwillingness to sign the indorsement." Fourteen officers were then interviewed by the squadron commander and advised they could "merely certify that they had read the regulation, deleting any other words appearing on the final indorsement, or they could prepare their own indorsement stating that they had read Base Regulation 85-2 and include their reasons for not being able to understand it." Eleven of fourteen officers refused to sign.

Colonel Selway required the appearance of each officer refusing to sign at the Legal Boards and Claims office at base headquarters for another interview on 11 April 1945, before a board of officers. Composed of two lieutenant colonels, a captain, a first lieutenant and a flight officer, the board interviewed each officer individually.

"Lieutenant," droned the voice of one of the lieutenant colonels, "will you please state whether or not you have read Base Regulation 85-2, Subject: *Assignment of Housing, Messing and Recreational Facilities for Commissioned, Flight and Warrant Officers,* dated 9 April 1945?"

"Yes, sir!"

"Will you please state whether you are willing to voluntarily certify, over your signature, that you have read Base Regulation 85-2, either by signing the first indorsement written on the reverse with the words 'and fully understand' deleted from the indorsement, or by signing a separate indorsement prepared personally by you to the effect that you have read Base Regulation No. 85-2?"

"No, sir, I am not willing to certify in any manner that I have read Base Regulation No. 85-2!"

Embarrassed silence blanketed the board.

"Lieutenant," the first lieutenant board member began, "I'm going to read and fully explain the provisions of the 64th Article of War to you." He did it. All of it. Penalties involved in disobeying a direct order in time of war before witnesses was hit especially hard. The lieutenant-interviewee listened stoically, at ramrod attention, eyes staring into the farthest gloom of the room. Only his eyes blinked, jawbone muscles twitching over set teeth.

"Do you understand what has just been read to you?"

"Yes, sir!"

"Do you understand the gravity of the offense you will commit in the event your commanding officer is *compelled* to give you a direct order to certify over your signature that you have read Base Regulation No. 85-2, and you fail or refuse to obey that order?"

"Yes, sir, I do."

The lieutenant sitting on the board took a deep breath as he turned to the captain who was the interviewee's squadron commander. "I suggest, sir, that you give this officer a direct order to certify over his signature that he has read Base Regulation No. 85-2."

"Lieutenant [Name], I, as your commanding officer, order you to certify over your signature that you have read Base Regulation No. 85-2."

"No, sir, I cannot." The officer's Adam's apple bobbled a bit.

"Lieutenant, by failing to so certify over your signature, you have refused to obey an order given you by your commanding officer. You are now placed in arrest in quarters."

"Yes, sir!"

"Do you understand?"

"Yes, sir!"

"Dismissed!"

And so it went, all of an April afternoon. One hundred and one officers from the 619th Bombardment Squadron, 477th Bombardment Group and E Squadron (Trainee), 118th AAF Base Unit, refused to sign. They were placed in arrest in quarters. Charges were prepared against them, even those who provided special endorsements of their own, outlining why they refused to sign. Among many officers, Capt. Edward Woodward and Lt. James V. Kennedy, submitted this universally accepted indorsement written by Coleman Young and others, the core of which read:

Undersigned felt and feels, that to have signed an indorsement signifying that he understood the regulation in question as required by paragraph 6 thereof, would have constituted a false official statement, inasmuch as undersigned did not, and does not, understand the cited regulation. Such an act would not only have, in itself, rendered the undersigned liable to trial by a general court-martial; it would have done violence to the conscience of the undersigned; it would have constituted moral conduct less than that requested of an officer and a gentleman in the Army of the United States. To have signed a statement to the effect that the undersigned had read, but did not understand, the document would have been a half-truth, and certainly would not have effected compliance with the written order contained in paragraph 6 of the cited regulation. Such an act would have constituted moral "weasling" and would have been no less con-

temptible or dishonest, than to have signed the statement in full. To
have affixed a signature to the document without further comment, would
have been equally dishonest. . . . Hence, any course of action available
to the undersigned other than one of manifest moral dishonesty, would
have rendered him liable to trial by general courts-martial. Knowing this
full well, undersigned in consonance with his conscience, could only
decline to sign the document, and thereafter, knowing himself in connection
with any offense that might conceivably have been alleged against him.
. . . For the record, undersigned wishes to indicate . . . his unshakable
belief that racial bias is fascistic, un-American, and directly contrary to
the ideas for which he is willing to fight and die. There is no officer in
the Army who is willing to fight harder, or more honorably for his country
than the undersigned . . .[56]

Lt. Col. Spann Watson USAF (Retired) wrote: "I know what the regulation
is and I have no intention of not using the officers' club of my choice." "Special
endorsement" or not, all were arrested who failed to obey the direct order to
sign. (Those who signed their *own* endorsements were released, however.*)

The need to "get everybody arrested" still rode high on the agendas of the
arrested officers. *Everyone* then refused to sign any endorsements at all, since
it was evident that any signature meant release, but defeat of their purpose.
There were pilots still at Walterboro Gunnery Base on ground assignments,
including Daniel "Chappie" James, Jr. Spann Watson called Walterboro to
explain to these officers that at Freeman Field, they were under arrest for entering
the club, not signing the endorsement and, when they returned, they too, would
be required to sign it.

"Don't sign it," Watson pled, "because we haven't signed it. They're going
to use [it] to give us the royal screwing, so don't sign it!"

Unfortunately, one officer he contacted (then a captain, hoping to be promoted)
hit the ceiling, asking who the hell Watson thought he was, telling him what
to sign and what not to sign! He then thought of Chappie James, "a more
enlightened type of individual who had worked at higher levels." He called
James, explained the plan, and made the plea.

"Thank you," James replied, "I've got you covered!" James returned to
the fray within a few days: ". . . I wasn't there when the original arrests
were made as I was on a cross-country. I got the word when I returned that I

---

* Lt. William Ellis's "endorsement" read: "I have read and fully understand the contents
of Base Regulation 85-2 and perceive it to be nothing more than a clever attempt to
camouflage segregation and discrimination on this station and under no circumstances
will I affix my signature thereto." But he *had* signed, and that satisfied the "order."
Eight black officers (reducing the original number in arrest to sixty-one) were thus
released before a change in their tactics.

was also under arrest . . ." Upon his return, James refused to sign the endorsement and was also arrested. In spite of his arrest, James's name does not appear on the official list of the 101. One of the only pilots on station checked out to fly the C-47, he was quickly released to fly daily courier flights between Freeman Field (and later, Godman) to East Coast bases. He did not forsake his comrades, but used his freedom to pick up press releases slipped through the barbed wire from the officers still in arrest. These he flew to newspaper editors friendly to the cause, spreading the word about his 101 comrades, including pictures taken by military photographer Harold J. Beaulieu, Sr., under secret cover. His gregariousness helped James establish contacts in eastern cities, allowing him access to white and black presses. Their ultimate response was good.

In later years, James remembered a key participant who aided him in "getting out the word," William T. Coleman, Jr., (who would one day become the country's secretary of transportation), as one of the premier "barracks lawyers" who struck not a little fear in Colonel Selway's heart. Dubbed "Bumps" Coleman, he was remembered as a "curbstone strategist." "Coleman was smooth. He said, 'if you guys don't go too far, you listen to me, you won't get locked up!' So we listened to him and we got locked up. Next day, he comes in and says, 'You guys went too far. But don't worry, I'm going to get you out.'" And often, it was Coleman at the fence, dispatches in hand: ". . . Coleman would get the stuff out to me, and I'd drop it off in the big cities. Boy, they'd have killed me if they'd known I was doing that—using military aircraft . . ."[57]

IV

As 10 April 1945 faded, uncertainty gripped the highest echelons of First Air Force headquarters. If anyone's hands were to be caught in the cookie jar, General Hunter made certain that those hands weren't his.

"It looks like Selway handled things very poorly," he said over the telephone to General Kuter of the air corps air staff, "he had no orders out . . . he had a building order, which these people had never seen, so we released them all . . . no question that it was planned . . . we had nothing on them!"

As General Kuter wondered aloud that there was *really* nothing to try the mass of black officers for, General Hunter completely washed his hands of Selway.

". . . Selway was not picked by me!" he cried, explaining that Selway would never have had the command had it not been for a "buddy" and "classmate" who "fixed it up for him" while at Selfridge. "And I didn't ever think," he went on, "very much of him, but he had a lot of experience and so Washington picked him and wanted him to do it!"

By ten minutes after five on the afternoon of 11 April 1945, General Hunter was on the line to General Owens at air corps headquarters, reporting that there was "more excitement," that "they're all organized and banded together," that "they have refused to read" the latest regulation, and that Selway was placing these new recalcitrants under arrest in quarters.

The numbers were growing and Hunter wanted air corps backing because this failure to obey an order to sign the indorsement was really only the beginning. He dredged around for more charges to add. Mutiny. Conspiracy. Anything else he could find.

Later on the eleventh, Roger Terry's mother's exhortations had begun to bear fruit. Gen. Max Schneider, air corps deputy air inspector, called General Glenn, air staff.

"Had a call from the office of the special assistant to the secretary of war, Mr. McCloy's office, with reference to a Lieutenant Roger Perry or Perry Roger—Roger Perry, I guess he is, who is, I believe, out at Freeman Field and they're asking for his status!"

General Glenn checked and called back.

"That man's name is Terry, Roger C.; Roger C. Terry, and he is one of the three officers who are under arrest and charges are being prepared for forcing their way into the club in violation of orders."

Schneider made sure that Terry was only in arrest in quarters and not locked up in some dank cell. Mr. Truman Gibson, special assistant to the secretary of war and a black, was on his way up to his office to see him.

James's delivered messages to the news media were also bearing fruit, and relatives like Edith Terry, Roger Terry's mother, were contacting people with clout.

The army air corps seemed oblivious to the plight of the black officer's struggle for equality. That may have been the reason for the reaction at Langley Field, Virginia, when Chappie landed a B-25 there. A ground crewman guided his aircraft in for a landing. Later, Chappie and his copilot remembered the look of shocked surprise on the man's face when it dawned on him that the only faces he saw through the cockpit windows were black.

"He was looking so hard," Archie Williams, best man at Chappie's wedding remembers, "trying to see what he was certain would be a white pilot, the propellers almost cut his head off!"

After Chappie went into flight operations, the ground crewman boarded the aircraft, looking into "every nook and corner of the airplane—looking for the white pilot. They couldn't believe it," Williams continues, "they just couldn't believe it!"

And perhaps that explained the reaction to the stand by these black officers. Hunter, Selway, and others simply couldn't believe it. But it *was* real, *and* it was happening before their very eyes.

Chapter Fourteen
Towards Resolution

I

This man is dead,'' he said softly. He looked at his watch. The time was 3:35 P.M. Lieutenant Commander Fox got off the bed. Bruenn used his thumbs to press the tired eyes closed. . . . Dr. Paullin stood aside as Fox bent over one side of the bed and Bruenn the other. Tenderly, they composed the body, closed and buttoned the pajama top, and composed the hands across the stomach. They straightened the legs, and rolled the counterpane up and up, until it covered the face and the wispy gray hair . . .

—Jim Bishop, in *FDR's Last Year: April 1944–April 1945*. (New York: Morrow & Co., 1974.)

It was 12 April 1945, and the world seemed to stop as life ebbed from the body of the only president America had known since 1933. Franklin Delano Roosevelt, thirty-second president of the United States, was dead. Friend of the hapless and poor, he had commanded the majority support of American black citizens. While the world sorrowed at the news of the death, the little band of black officers out in Indiana at Freeman Field quaked, for the president's wife, Eleanor Roosevelt, was more than a friend. She had been an influence in the formation of the black fliers program and had, through her husband, interceded in their behalf. The Roosevelts were a trump card, a distant refuge for ultimate right, provided the message could get through. The news of the president's death made many a heart sink in the ranks of the 101. Lt. Col. Spann Watson, USAF (Retired) remembers: "We always considered FDR, Roosevelt, a friend of the depressed, of the deprived . . . while we were under arrest in Freeman, [he] died, and we said, 'We've had it now!' "

Watson was right. News of the president's death hardly slowed General Hunter. Early that day, he had reported the latest statistics on the black officers refusing to sign the endorsement to General Kuter. "They were given a direct order . . . with witnesses and everything . . . and they refused to do it. We've got them in arrest . . . we've got some more to go . . ." He continued to place the blame for the entire scenario on Lowell M. Trice, the black reporter from the *Indianapolis Recorder*. *He* was the one, "down in town . . . advising these people . . . encouraging these people to disobey orders . . . stirring up revolt in the Army . . . get the FBI on him and see just what he *is* doing!"

General Kuter pledged support and approved Hunter's approach, requesting clarification of reasons the officers were in arrest.

"For refusing to take a direct order to indorse that they have read it!" shot back General Hunter.

General Kuter put the brakes on Hunter.

"Our concern," he counseled, "is that there should be no trials until we are assured that the order itself will stand."

Obstructed a bit, General Hunter sought confirmation of his actions. "All right, but they're in arrest in quarters?"

"That's correct," said Kuter, "and they should stay that way. Mr. Lovett, particularly, realizes the fact that the final case will probably not be settled on the *military* aspect of signing or refusing to sign the statement that they have read this piece of paper, that the case probably will be settled on the *contents* of the piece of paper."

"Well, I know," Hunter replied, his hackles rising a bit, "but there are two *different* aspects! I cannot run anything in the Army if I have white or colored that refuse to obey an order, and I can't do anything when they do. So there are two aspects to this. One is the refusal to take a direct order and comply with it and the other one is [that] I'm trying to see—there is undoubtedly collusion and conspiracy and I'm trying to see if we can't work up a case on that . . ."

General Kuter began to caution Hunter again, only to be interrupted with the confirmation that charges *were* being preferred, but that court-martial would be held in abeyance until he heard further from Washington.

About three o'clock that afternoon, Colonel Selway telephoned General Hunter with "a report and recommendations."

Six hundred and fifty officers had signed the housing order. Over two hundred white and more than four hundred black. There were about 105 black officers in arrest in quarters. The charge: willful disobedience of a direct order.

But Selway was worried. He had heard that the black officers were asking when the white club would open. The ones who refused to sign were saying that a signature would keep them from entering the club. In his heart of hearts, the colonel knew exactly what he had done. "It's quite evident," he said to General Hunter, "that they are displeased with the fact that the racial question has not entered into any of the investigations or charges or orders, and they are displeased with the fact that each question has been handled as an individual case and not as a mass." And underneath that, the real terror beating in his breast surfaced. "I am certain," he went on, "that as sure as we were born, that upon opening of Officers Club #2, the Negro officers will move *en masse* to continue their test and crusade to force investigation of segregation based on any reason at all." And if *that* happened, his legal staff was too small; his white security force not large enough to handle it, especially if it led to violence. General Hunter doubted it, but Colonel Selway persisted. To Hunter, it was a fairy tale, an idle fantasy born of a skewed imagination because, "if they do," he asserted, "they're sticking their necks out a mile!" Colonel Selway agreed, but had a solution: "I therefore recommend . . . that the officers to be charged . . . under the 64th [Article of War] for willful disobedience . . . those under arrest . . . be moved to Godman Field . . ."

General Hunter bought it. McDowell would command Godman. There were twenty white military policemen and the provost marshal to check and secure them. Besides, Fort Knox was right next door and, if necessary, an entire MP battalion could be mustered—one wouldn't have to be moved in! If he didn't have enough white MPs, well, then, he'd use "mechanics and things!"

Hunter cleared the move with General Owens, deputy chief of the air staff, to "move them over to Godman, pending . . . your turning me loose to court-martial them . . . send them over to Godman to get the rotten apples out of that barrel so they won't stir up any anymore." They'd fly them back to Godman.

II

On 13 April 1945, 101 black officers, having dreamed a daring dream, had become criminals of a special sort.

"The 101," Spann Watson recalled,

who were still under arrest . . . were lined up as prisoners dressed in full dress uniforms with their baggage put in wagons and fleet of C-47s came tooling in and lined up, and all these people were loaded in trucks and driven to the flight line and loaded aboard the airplanes. . . . We still didn't know where they were going, we didn't have any idea. . . .

We stood there (and being a released individual, I was very much a part of it until the very last, and in conversation with these people) . . . and we had no idea where they were going. The C-47s came in and flew them away . . .

The small armada of C-47s sped down the runway, taking off in tandem, circling and settling into the heading for Godman Field in Kentucky. The black officers sat helplessly, eyeballing each other, hearts full of wonder and perhaps not a little concern about their immediate future. The engines hummed and growled as the C-47s moved through the air. On 14 April 1945, the six C-47s circled Godman Field and began to land. Ignominy was heaped upon ignominy. As the black officers deplaned, they were met by military policemen in battle array, backed by armed half-tracks. Whisked across the base to the bachelor officers' quarters hard by the base recreational hall, they were surrounded by heavily armed military police.

It seemed surreal, and to some, almost laughable. Paranoia was rife, reflecting Colonel Selway's agitation. From their place of confinement, the black officers could see the little base gas station, where unguarded German prisoners of war with huge "PW" letters stenciled across the backs of their striped fatigues, worked as service station attendants. "And here we were," Capt. Edward Woodward recalls, "officers of the United States Army, guarded and watched by armed soldiers as if we were the 'enemy'—while across the way, men who were supposedly 'the enemy'—were allowed to move freely about the base . . ."

Other black officers with marital responsibilities returned to Godman Field by train. The "security force" met them, too, escorting them to "the same old barracks that we had . . . before, only now, they had a barbed wire fence around it!" The train ride said something very important about the American paradox. Given what seemed to be prevailing attitudes towards blacks, it would appear to be absurd to even imagine that a significant number of whites would be sympathetic to the cause of these black officers. But it was true.

Span Watson recalled in interview: "I remember, coming through Louisville in this time of hostility—when German war prisoners were all around Fort Knox . . . all over Louisville . . . able to use the drive-ins and the hotels . . . but a black man, a black officer, couldn't even go in the damn place[s] . . ."

In the midst of the hostility, Watson was able to see something else as he gazed out the train window. He saw sympathy and support out there from eyes embedded in white faces; faces they had come to know only as "the enemy": "Still there were always a group of white people who were friendly towards what you were doing. . . . You could see the friendship, the sneaking friendship . . . while the train was snaking its way through Louisville . . .

you could see these people who'd give you a little, sneaky wave. . . . I never forgot that . . . [it] was quite a display . . .''

Later that afternoon, the president's funeral train inched along, close by the Rappahannock River in Virginia. When night fell, it stopped for water ''between the cliffs of farmland,'' wrote Jim Bishop in *FDR's Last Year: April 1944–April 1945*, where: ''The night was spangled with stars. The engines stood panting. Unseen, the face of a black man appeared on top of one of the cliffs. Soon he was back with other sleepy faces. They had not been able to vote for Roosevelt, but they felt he was their father, too. A deep voice began to sing the sad, sweet notes of 'Hand Me Down My Walkin' Cane.' Other voices . . . picked up the words . . .''

Finally, the train crossed the wide Potomac and entered Washington. The nation mourned. Businesses closed. Radio commentators could hardly bear to repeat the sad news. The casket was eased from the train. The mighty paused. Three hundred thousand and more mourned at the capitol. Flags flew fitfully in April winds. Guns saluted. Newspeople remarked about ''someone black''— peering round a soldier's shoulder, tears streaking his cheeks, mouthing ''good-byes.''

III

Colonel Selway shut down the white officers' club as the 101 black officers were flown from Freeman Field. If he thought it was time to relax, he was mistaken. ''One of the colored officers [who told] him things from time to time'' Selway remembered, advised that all of the remaining officers were forming over in the colored area, and they were going to come over and break into the white officers' club.

Fright probably gripped Selway's heart. This was, after all, the probable fulfillment of his earlier prediction to General Hunter. This *could* be an en masse action, overtaxing his ability to contain it. And what of the white women and children who would have been in the club had he left it open? At least he had closed it. And what of the attitudes of the white officers, still outnumbered, but still so explosive that they would be likely to start something?

He looked out to see black officers parading by the closed, darkened club in automobiles. ''There were carloads of them,'' said General Hunter as he reported the incident the next day to General Owens, deputy chief of the air staff, ''about fifteen to a car—driving by and the lights and all were out and they went back to their area.''

Selway, with Colonel Harris, the inspector, and Colonel Patterson, his deputy in tow, drove over to the colored officers' area and found them formed up in their blouses, standing there very sullenly.

The black officers saluted but said nothing.

"Is it your intent," Colonel Selway boomed, "to violate any regulations?" Silence.

"Is it your intent to test any regulations today?" he challenged.

Again, no reply. Selway entered the barracks where the 101 black officers were confined.

Nobody called attention as he entered, walking down the barracks floor boards. Officers standing, sat down. Some tossed knives into the still air, watching them pirouette, then fall point-first into the wooden floor: *"Ka-chunk!"* Others flipped pennies into the air, as if Selway and company weren't there. And outside, still others tossed rocks into the air, studiously catching them in outstretched palms. As Colonel Selway walked further down the floorboards, the black officers turned away from him, one by one, until all the colonel could see were backs and backs and backs. Not a voice was heard nor a cough nor a sigh. Thick silence prevailed, punctuated by an occasional *"ka-chunk!"* as a knife-point punctured the floorboards, or a rock thwacked another outstretched palm in the April air.

Down by the big latrine, he stopped, turned around, looked, and "nobody said a damn word." He must have felt awfully alone. They saluted as he left. There was nothing left to do but go back to headquarters and report the situation to his commander, General Hunter, at First Air Force headquarters.

"Why didn't you order them back to their quarters?" the general wanted to know.

"They broke up and we were talking to them in a group. They hadn't done anything wrong."

"Were they insolent? Insubordinate?"

"No, sir, they were very polite."

"Well, did they act surly?"

"That's what I mean. They salute and say the right words, but it's like somebody with a sneer on their face, you know?"

Perhaps the black officers felt justified in their behavior because of this sudden violation of their space by their commanding officer. It got no better during duty hours. They had to talk to their white authority figures, but their facial expressions spoke volumes.

General Hunter had not wanted the club closed in the first place. He had said that he would have gotten the women and children out of the club, let the black officers come in, and *then* he would have had them!

But Selway's focus was on the denial of the goals the black officers sought.

"What they want," he began, "is to cancel the program—they want all airplanes grounded!"

"You don't know that," retorted General Hunter, "that's just a report to you."

"And they wanted a mass incident, too," Selway pressed, quoting his informant verbatim.

"I think it would have been fine if they had a mass incident, if they want to have it. It would have clarified the air!"

For all his actions, Selway had a conscience of sorts.

"Well, the president not being buried—" he began.

"Now listen," exploded the general, "you stop worrying about the president. You've got a job to do there and a post to command. It has *nothing* to do with the president. We've got to carry on, just the same, whether the president— we have a new president!" he continued as an afterthought.

IV

That afternoon, General Owens called General Hunter, to advise that Washington was backing down, ordering him to get ready to move the 477th Bombardment Group back to Godman Field in Kentucky. Hunter thought there'd be problems, but the orders were firm. He telephoned the decision to Colonel Selway, ordering him to keep it quiet. But Selway was still riding high. It seemed that some black officers had advised Colonel Harris, the inspector, in a "blatant" manner, that the solution to their problem was "education and assimilation" and "there will be no assimilation except over my dead body!" The prophecy was wrong. Selway would live to see the assimilation he dreaded.

It was quiet for a while. The 101 officers remained in arrest for what was thought to be a capital offense. General Hunter tried to pry written confirmation out of the War Department that his order had been legal. The War Department continued to vacillate. Army air force, the inspector general, the ground forces, and service forces were all on the general's side, and still the War Department vacillated.

On 20 April 1945, the War Department overrode General Hunter's command authority. General Giles, telephoning General Owens, recommended, and General Marshall had approved, that the 101 black officers be released, and the charges against them be dropped. General Hunter was livid.

"Are those orders to me?" he howled. "They'd better get the judge advocate general. They can't issue orders like that, they haven't got the authority!"

"—And an administrative reprimand be given to each of these officers instead of a trial," Owens continued, sympathizing at the same time with Hunter. "I know they can't [issue an order like that]!"

"They can't *do* that," raged Hunter. "Now if they want to do it, I'm not a guardhouse lawyer, I'll do anything they say. But I will write a letter telling them I can't command under those circumstances! I have court-martial jurisdiction, and they cannot *tell* me whom I can try and whom I can't! They're backing water!"

"That's right," agreed General Owens. But the order stuck.

On 21 April 1945, a letter ordered the officers released and reprimanded, and the group moved to Godman Field. The three officers who had shoved the provost marshal were held for court-martial.[*]

V

The pace quickened. Messages came by wire from the judge advocate general indicating congressional involvement. Chappie James's courier trips bore fruit. The old newspaper in New York, *P.M.,* carried a piece about the plight of the 101 officers. The NAACP, the Urban League, and labor relations organizations fired off letters to members of Congress and the Senate. Of these, by far the most poignant came from parents and relatives of the black officers.

During April 1945, Mrs. W. White of New Orleans protested the arrest of the officers and her son to Senator Allen Ellender (D-La.). Mrs. White wrote:

I wish to protest through you the arrest of the 61 pilots at Freeman Field, Seymour, Indiana.

These young men, one of whom is my son, Flight Officer Haydel White, were arrested for visiting the officers' club located on the same post.

I am sure that you understand the role of a Mother who had another son in the United States Marines fighting on Iwo Jima for democracy while the other son is denied the right to exercise the privileges of that democracy.

I trust that you will use your influence to aid in the prevention of such miscarriages of democracy in the future . . .

On 24 April 1945, Senator Ellender referred her letter to the army's judge advocate general.

---

[*] For the record, 101 men were placed under house arrest. Sixty-two refused to sign the endorsement (minus those signing endorsements of their own invention). In all, 163 officers and enlisted men were arrested in this period, the enlisted men involved in related incidents around the base and in town.

Inez Clinton, sister of Lt. Shirley R. Clinton, being held for court-martial, wrote what was probably the most emotional letter of all to Congressman Charles A. Wolverton, on 21 April 1945:

Now above all, every individual of this nation must stick together for it is unity and only unity that can preserve that . . . which we are fighting for.

But this great urge for unity has been overshadowed upon my receiving a letter from my brother, Lieutenant Shirley R. Clinton, Intelligence Officer of the Army Air Forces (Sq. E., 118th B.U., Freeman Field, Seymour, Indiana) who together with sixty other officers and pilots, has been arrested for entering a white officers' club at Freeman Field, Seymour, Indiana. Such actions in my estimation could never mean a step forward in unity for democracy.

I humbly request . . . you to intercede and have this matter investigated for my brother's release. He has worked hard for nearly four years to earn the rating presented him. His father who is in great distress, is a veteran of World War I, and proud wearer of the *Croix De Guerre.*

Please, Sir, may I ask you to give this your undivided attention as soon as possible . . .

On 26 April 1945, Congressman Wolverton referred the matter to the army judge advocate general.

On the same day, Mrs. Edith Terry, mother of Roger C. Terry, sent a telegram to Congressman Vito Marcantonio inquiring about her son, while one Edwin Johnson, legislative director, Lodge 748, International Workers Order in Chicago, Illinois, directed a stinging letter to Senator Scott W. Lucas. He wrote:

The recent arrest and removal by the Army of Negro Officer Trainees at Freeman Field, for refusing to sign away their rights as citizens, is in direct violation of an order forbidding discrimination against Negroes in any army camp. It . . . serves to demoralize these Negro servicemen instead of building up their morale, making them feel that they have something to fight for. It is regrettable that such a thing could happen in the United States at this time. The ones who should have been arrested are those who tried to make them sign this undemocratic, discriminatory guarantee—it goes against everything democratic and liberal; it goes against all principles of justice and fair play. It smacks of the way our enemies treat their minorities. We want to protest most vigorously against such undemocratic and discriminatory practices in the armed forces of the United States . . .

Johnson even proposed, from his particular point of view, the proper solution to the problem, as he enjoined the senator to: "See that they be reinstated at their former posts, at Freeman Field and that the white officers be punished for their unlawful acts . . ."[58]

VI

Colonel Selway wasted no time in composing a letter of reprimand. The missive was delivered to the officers, including Daniel "Chappie" James, Jr., on 24 April 1945. It read:

On or about 11 April 1945, at Freeman Field, Seymour, Indiana, you displayed a stubborn and uncooperative attitude towards reasonable efforts of constituted authority to disseminate among officers and flight officers of the Command, information concerning necessary and proper measures adopted in the administration of the Officer's Clubs of that station. This action on your part indicates that you lack appreciation of the high standard of team-work expected of you as an Officer of the Army of the United States, and a failure to understand that you should so conduct yourself at all times so as to be a credit and a source of pride to the military service. In these respects, you have failed definitely in your obligations to your command and your country. It is hoped and expected that you will consider this reprimand . . . a stern reminder of the absolute require-ments of prompt and willing compliance with the policies of superior authority, and that there will be no repetition of such regrettable actions on your part . . . This reprimand will be made a part of your official record. . . . You will acknowledge receipt by endorsement hereon . . .[59]

Each squadron commander indorsed the reprimand to each of the 101, who acknowledged receipt. The deed was done and the matter closed.

On 26 April 1945, as congressmen, senators, and other outraged citizens forwarded more letters of protest to the army's judge advocate general, the 477th Bombardment Group, the 387th Service Group, and the colored sections of the 118th AAF Base Unit were returned to Godman Field, Kentucky.

The army air corps felt itself to be under pressure, since the War Department had forced the issue of racial prejudice. It did not wish to rankle those in high places and refused to provide General Hunter written indorsement of his actions, although it was willing to give verbal approval through certain of its high-ranking officers. The attitudes of these officers reflected the civilian status quo where racial matters were concerned. It was necessary, some felt, to protect the whites assigned to the black bomber group, themselves a minority. Deliberate delay in solving the problem was seriously considered, even to the extent of doing a staff study that would recommend additional training for the group. "And then," Gen. William W. Welsh of air staff training said in a telephone conversation to a First Air Force colonel: "if we can stave it in some way for a period of time . . . maybe we can eliminate the program gradually and accomplish our end . . . if this thing gets out of hand you may have some of the 'jigaboos' up there dropping in on you at Mitchel Field . . ."

The War Department finally explained its decision to release the majority of the black officers: "There is reasonable doubt," it said, "that these officers fully understood the implications of their actions nor is it certain, because of their recent arrival at Freeman Field, that they had been adequately apprised of existing regulations. For these reasons, it was determined that they should be released from arrest and suitable orders were accordingly issued for their restoration to duty following the administration of appropriate reprimand . . ."

That explanation, given to Senator Edwin Johnson, begged the question, since people who had followed the issue knew that the officers were cognizant of the probable results of their actions and had weighed the consequences.

The "big gun," however, that slowed resolution was the McCloy Committee, formed several years before to establish black troop policy. It had followed the Freeman Field events and, in the end, assumed almost complete control of the outcome.

On 19 May 1945, the McCloy Committee on Special Troop Policies met and considered the inspector general's recommendations. It concluded that (1) the actions taken by Colonel Selway were within his administrative police powers, (2) the arrest of the three Negro officers and subsequently the arrest and release of 101 other Negro officers was proper, and (3) it *"did not concur in the findings upholding the basis upon which a separation of the Officers' Club facilities was made by the post commander,"* and believed that "such basis was not in accord with existing Army Regulations and War Department policies prohibiting separation in the use of recreational activities on racial grounds."

The memorandum from the McCloy Committee to the secretary of war went on to make two recommendations. First, it wanted the report of investigation returned to the inspector general "with the request that the noncomformance with Army Regulations and War Department directives be brought to the attention of the Commanding General, Army Air Forces, for appropriate action." Secondly, it recommended that the army air force's commanding general be advised that the trial of the three black officers then in arrest in connection with the Freeman Field incident be expedited.

The McCloy Committee was not the only agency pushing with alacrity for swift justice and through other authority figures, perhaps a bit of leniency. As in the judge advocate general's office, where, in the middle of May 1945, an unidentified officer whose initials were "W. A. R.," penned in the margins of a draft confidential memorandum: "I again repeat what I said on May 14—that punishment under Article of War 104 is the solution of this case." The draft memorandum went on to say that the officers should be transferred "to some other station."

This entire scenario finally landed on the desk of one Colonel H. G. Culton, deputy chief of air staff, who, on 15 June 1945, returned General Hunter's court-martial cases on the three lieutenants, quoting the War Department directive as of that date: "The Secretary of War directs that the trial of the three Negro officers now in arrest in connection with the Freeman Field incident be expedited . . ." The delay in returning the files, said Colonel Culton, was because of the consideration given the cases by the McCloy Committee. He attached copies of the committee's recommendations as well as those of the judge advocate and the air judge advocate. The most important statement in his endorsement, soon to be totally ignored by General Hunter was that: "As to any apparent conflict between the recommendation of the judge advocate general and the directive of the secretary of war, the latter will prevail . . ."

On 26 June 1945 the secretary of war *amended* his earlier pronouncement regarding the trials which Colonel Culton duly transmitted to General Hunter: "The *Secretary of War* directs that *appropriate* disciplinary action be taken in the case of the three Negro officers now in arrest in connection with the Freeman Field incident and that the above action be expedited. *This does not preclude action under the 104th Article of War . . .*"

The "pound of flesh" obviously was to be gotten, as Culton added ominously: "The effect of this amendment merely is to leave to your discretion the type of disciplinary action to be taken." Hunter now had free rein. The courts-martial were still on, for, as Colonel Culton breezily noted in his prior endorsement returning the cases to General Hunter: "This Headquarters notes with approval that on the list of officers recommended by [Colonel Selway], for the general court-martial, *The Trial Judge Advocate, Defense Counsel, and five of the nine members are colored*. It is suggested that this proportion be followed in the composition of the court-martial when it is convened . . ."

Although Colonel Selway actually did it as the charging official, General Hunter took credit for the decision. The *original* court's senior officer was a white lieutenant colonel, Wilbur E. Bashore, plus four other white officers and lieutenants as trial judge advocate and defense counsel with six black officers. The injection of black officers on the court-martial board probably would help stifle charges of racism, the air corps thought.

The army air corps then called upon its only black colonel (who was to eventually end his career a lieutenant general), Benjamin O. Davis, Jr., former commander of the famed, all-black 99th Pursuit Squadron and recent commander of the 332d Fighter Squadron then returning from the European theater. Directed to report to Godman Field as commander of the 477th Bombardment Group, he was detailed to serve as president of a newly convened general court-martial board upon arrival, signaling the end for Colonel Selway: "A gentleman came from the Pentagon with orders relieving Selway. I forget this gentleman's name, I should remember it, he was from James C. Evans's office, he was an Army type, and I remember him by having an amputated arm (I believe the left arm), and *he threw the orders on Selway's desk*—relieving him . . .''

Colonel Selway remained at Freeman Field in a "nominal command status," as Colonel Davis assumed command of what had become a composite group, now including the returning 99th Fighter Squadron with two bombardment squadrons now deactivated.

Although the entire black contingent of officers and airmen at Godman breathed a sigh of relief at these new developments, it is doubtful that the three black officers awaiting court-martial felt quite that way. This thirty-four-year-old black colonel, Benjamin O. Davis, Jr., was no easy man to contend with.

The first Negro in fifty years to break through the wall of *de facto* segregation to enter West Point, he withstood the same unrelenting pressure his black predecessors had experienced while attending the academy during the days of Reconstruction. Davis survived, graduating thirty-fourth in his class in 1936. He was of the West Point "Band of Brothers," very intelligent, dignified, and uncompromisingly upright. He had the trust and respect of the highest military hierarchy, having led the Tuskegee Airmen in successful combat as commander of the 99th Pursuit Squadron and, later, the 332d Fighter. That his command was segregated (although privately he was against the pattern of it) did not matter; he desired that it would be one of the best. His combat exploits had brought him honor and covered him with ribbons and decorations: The Legion of Merit, the Silver Star, the Distinguished Flying Cross, and the Air Medal with four Oak Leaf Clusters. Strictly military, he was referred to as a "book soldier"—meaning that he did everything "by the book"—undeviatingly. This was not the kind of officer who would look kindly upon the shoving of a superior officer, no matter how slight the shove. As we will see, his presence on the court-martial board would be challenged. As an officer of the period recalled some forty-two years later: ". . . Hell no! We didn't want him. . . . That's why we got him offa there! . . ."

But for the 101, including Daniel "Chappie" James, Jr., the leaden skies had begun to clear. What they had done was later seen by some as prefiguring the civil rights protests of the sixties. If this hardy group of men could have read Frederick Douglass's letter to Gerrit Smith, the abolitionist, in 1849, they would have agreed that it exactly described what they had done:

The conflict has been exciting, agitating, all-absorbing, and for the time being putting all other tumults to silence. It must do this or it does nothing.

If there is no struggle, there is no progress. Those who profess to favor freedom, and yet depreciate agitation, are men who want crops without plowing up the ground. They want rain without thunder and lightning. They want the ocean without the awful roar of its many waters. This struggle may be a moral one; or it may be a physical one; or it may be both moral and physical; but it must be a struggle. Power concedes nothing without a demand . . .[60]

Chapter Fifteen
The Changing of the Guard

I

"The Boys Couldn't Wait!" announced the headlines in the 30 June 1945 issue of the *Pittsburgh Courier*. *"477th Bombs Tokyo (Make-Believe); Now They're Ready for the Real Thing!"*

Only one day had passed since Col. Benjamin O. Davis, Jr., had assumed command of the 477th Composite Group. It seemed certain now that it would see action in the Pacific. Suddenly came a new esprit de corps, and with it, a new idea: *Why not do a simulated bombing of Tokyo?* John H. Young III, the Washington correspondent of the *Courier,* was on site and smelled a story. Colonel Davis cleared the exercise and Lt. Daniel "Chappie" James, Jr., acting group operations officer, helped assign "a typical crew" to fly the next day's mission.

Friday dawned, and the crew assembled at base operations. With parachutes and flying gear, they went to the briefing room where, in the role he was to play countless times in the future, Chappie James briefed the crew on its "imaginary" mission.

"The target for today is Tokyo," James intoned. Advising the crew of flak and fighter opposition they could expect enroute to target, he then turned to the maps, pointing out the railway marshaling yards as primary target in the city's center. The secondary target, he advised, would be the harbor installations in the Nanoa Bay area. Initial point (IP) for bomb run was Tadami and post-assembly would be over Mount Bandia. He asked for questions. There were none. Captain Southall then briefed the crew on the type of bombs to be used, bombing altitude, and weather (good, with maximum visibility). It was a good morale builder, even though their starting point was Godman Field and their real target Berry Field at Nashville, Tennessee. It gave Chappie a chance to try his wings as a budding operations officer, the *Pittsburgh Courier* got a tantalizing story; and S. Sgt. Harold J. Beaulieu, the base photographer, had a chance to use his skills.

After the "Tokyo Strike," Davis found it necessary to hustle over to base operations to see Lieutenant James, flexing his command muscle, delivering a lecture "pointing up the necessity for keeping at least sixty percent of the aircraft in the air each day."

It is perhaps significant that, for all his innate intelligence, leadership potential, and popularity, Daniel "Chappie" James, Jr., was not chosen to be a member of the general court-martial detailed to try the three lieutenants. Nor was it a matter of rank, since his good friend, 1st Lt. James Y. Carter, with whom he had carpooled between Selfridge Field and Detroit, was a member of the court. Two other lieutenants were also involved. In point of fact, he was regarded as "just one of the boys," a "helluva pilot" and a long way down the command ladder by higher ranking black officers. Of promising quality, but really nothing special.

On 24 June 1945, First Air Force special orders detailed the newly arrived Col. Benjamin O. Davis, Jr., as ranking member and president of the court-martial board with seven captains (Knox, Wiley, Duren, Stanton, Yates, Kennedy, and Newsum), a Captain Harris as defense council, Captain Redden as trial judge advocate, and two lieutenants, one as assistant trial counsel (2d Lt. William T. Coleman, Jr., to later become transportation secretary). It was to be, save for the trial judge advocate (prosecutor) and court reporter, an all-black court; for as Fitzroy Newsum, a member of the court, recalls: "They wanted to portray that they were tried by their own."

It would not be fair to say that the then-Col. Benjamin O. Davis, Jr., didn't think very much of Lt. Daniel James, Jr., but it may not be very far off the mark to surmise that Davis probably had some reservations about him. When asked about Chappie in an interview, the retired Lieutenant General Davis said, "I really didn't know James that well. . . . First saw him as a student at Tuskegee Institute, where I was Professor of Military Air Science and Tactics. . . . Saw him, but did not know him . . . ."

And in response to pundits who speculated that Chappie and others had taught him how to shoot landings and fly the B-25 and was accepted by him as his *regular* copilot,[61] Davis rather forcibly asserted: "Not really. In 1945, while at Godman Field, I was invited to speak at Tuskegee. I flew down in a B-25, which happened to be James's B-25. . . . He flew with me . . . ."

"One of the boys," James could usually be found wherever there was excitement or furor, his humor sometimes overflowing in that deep voice of his to the tune of "Four-Leaf Clover":

Oh, I'm looking over
My old dog Rover
For fleas that I
Missed before . . . !

It was a throwback to his days at Tuskegee and Miss Lillie's school perhaps. "Chappie," they continued to say, "was always into *something*!" A bit of the rowdy resided in him, but always laced with humor and good cheer.

But much more than an incipient "rowdyism," humor and good cheer imbued Daniel "Chappie" James, Jr.'s, life at this stage. Although "just one of the boys" in the circumstances surrounding the imminent trials, he was always outspoken. It was a kind of down-to-earth outspokenness, directing his compatriot's attention to the need for quality and excellence. It was a matter of image, for Chappie believed that the image they portrayed as black officers and pilots was, in fact, representative of black Americans everywhere. On the other hand, he was regarded as dedicated to his new-found, sometimes seemingly elusive career, which at times seemed vague at the very least. It boasted no next step or way up to a next rung. For the moment, he believed that he and his fellow black officers had a mission, and that mission wasn't necessarily fighting white people, it was fighting the common enemy. He was a "man of vision," often heard to say that there was much more to do than sit around talking about the issues surrounding the officers' clubs. And for that, his popularity often suffered, since some officers entertained stronger points of view about ending racism in the military *now*, often regarding him as somehow "suspect." The consummate politician, however, he was never too small to apologize when he saw that his outspokenness had somehow offended. In spite of that, some officers tended to keep him at arm's length.

No matter, even as "just one of the boys," his good cheer and presence always served to help him bubble to the top of the mix.

Joe Louis, the reigning heavyweight champion of the day, came to Godman Field for an exhibition fight, and Chappie was right there! Before anybody knew it, Chappie was flying Louis to various army airfields as he gave more exhibition fights. He and Louis were to become friends. When other entertainers came to the field, Chappie would be there. He was totally in love with people—especially those who entertained, made music and song, and those of any athletic bent. They were wish-books to him, for they did things he loved to do. Sing and dance. Perform. Play music. Prove their athletic prowess. He could be counted on to be at squadron parties. Although recognized as one of the best pilots in the bombardment group, he came to Colonel Davis's attention from time to time because of these *social* events—and sometimes, in a most unwelcomed way.

As a case in point, there had been a wonderful squadron party in downtown Louisville, Kentucky. Frisby Carter, Daniel "Chappie" James, Jr., and others had enjoyed it immensely. They were in high spirits, and laughter abounded. It was perhaps therapeutic. Nobody talked a great deal about Marsden Thompson, Shirley Clinton, and Roger Terry, still in house arrest. Finally, it was time to go back to Godman Field and the grind.

It could have been Chappie who suggested that they stop enroute for a hamburger. People remember Chappie as a man who loved food. A man who, when he came to your house, would fling a cursory greeting as you opened the door, bustle past into your kitchen and, with a massive hand, tug open your refrigerator door asking, with an ingratiating smile: "What'cha got to eat?" The next question would be, "Where is it?" You'd share whatever you had because "that's the kinda guy he was!"

Daniel James, Jr., the tallest and biggest, led Frisby Carter and others cheerfully into the nearest Whitecastle hamburger joint. Maybe that's what caught the white sailor's eye. The big, black lieutenant, walking into this Whitecastle hamburger joint with gusto, leading a flock of black men as if he owned the place. Maybe this white sailor felt some strange, angry impulse deep inside his brain. For whatever reason, he sang out as white sailors from the South home on leave *could* in those days,

"Hi, boy!"

Well, Daniel James, Jr., took exception to being called a "boy," especially since he was a first lieutenant in the United States Air Corps! A "ruckus" started at once. Right there in the old Whitecastle hamburger joint, Chappie began to jerk the hapless sailor around from "pillar to post." The sailor *tried* to jerk Chappie around from post to pillar but found himself dangling in the air in the grasp of Daniel's massive fists, which set the unfortunate sailor upon the Whitecastle's serving counter. James's face moved within inches of the sailor's countenance.

"Boy?" Chappie roared, "Whaddya mean, boy?"

"Er—"

"You see these bars? *Boy?*"

"Well, er—"

"I want an apology from you right now, sailor!"

"Ughhh!" grunted the sailor.

"Are you gonna apologize or not? I am *not* a boy! You understand that? I am a first lieutenant in the United States Army Air Corps and you will respect that! Well?"

"Y-Yeah!"

"Yeah, what?"

"Y-Yes, sir!"

"You apologize?"

"Y-Yes, sir!"

At this point, the Whitecastle manager came crashing out asking James and company to leave the premises. Somebody else got the sailor out.

The crowd that had gathered like winter fog dispersed. Daniel James, Jr., straightened his tie and smoothed his uniform. Frisby Carter might have sworn gently. That would have been that, had they been back on Godman Field. But they weren't. They still had to get there.

The evening was all electric. Nobody knew why, but it was just that way.

Chappie and the flock walked to the corner to wait for the Godman Field bus. Had they wanted to, they could have crossed the street and waited for one of the jitney drivers to arrive in their old cars. The fare was cheap enough. They'd take a carload to the base for a dollar a head. But tonight, James and flock opted for the bus and, as they waited there at the head of the line, a white captain from Fort Knox and another white officer sauntered up. Steely glances and a pause later, they deposited themselves at the head of the line *in front* of Chappie and flock.

"Hey!" James began none too gently, *"we are in front of you!"*

"Nigger," replied the captain, *"You ain't out in front!"*

Daniel James, Jr., immediately removed the captain from his perch at the head of the line. The captain began to return the favor until, red-faced, he issued the ultimate challenge.

"If you," he huffed, arms akimbo, his eyes narrow, "take off those lieutenant bars, I'll take off these tracks, and we'll settle *this* right now!" The poor captain had no way of hearing Chappie's father's voice inside his head repeating the old refrain: *"If there's going to be a fight, you start it!"* The bars and the tracks came off. There was hell to pay. The Louisville police sirened up, broke up the fight, and locked Daniel James, Jr., Frisby Carter, and the white captain in the local jail. Next morning, they let Frisby and the white captain go, but kept Chappie in the lockup; for, as far as the Louisville police were concerned, Daniel James, Jr., *had* to have been the instigator, as big as he was. Later in the day: "Colonel Davis sent [Major Webb] down to pick Chappie up out of jail . . . put Chappie in house arrest at Godman. [There was] a quick hearing on it, but nothing much came of it. . . . The captain instigated the thing by saying, 'I'll take off my tracks if you take off your bars'—and he *never* should have said that to Chappie." Still, Daniel "Chappie" James, Jr., was perhaps lucky that Col. Benjamin O. Davis, Jr., *was* the new commander of the 477th Composite Group. It was the start of a new era. Morale picked up noticeably.

Colonel Davis had begun, within a few, short weeks, to change the 477th Composite Group from a gang into a disciplined unit. Suddenly, the salute was back. James T. Wiley, a member of the court-martial board, remembers: "Right after the arrests and after the return to Godman Field, the morale broke down completely and no black would salute a white person. . . . We just did not salute. We just walked down the road . . . just look at them and walk away. . . . Even Selway was not saluted, and he was the base commander. . . . It was just like a gang . . ."

Although many of the men didn't like some of the things Davis stood for, they respected him and his forward-thinking way. Under Colonel Selway, Chappie might well have been court-martialed for these altercations. About this time, James might have also taken note of the new commander, for: "From then on, we recognized that it was a mighty goddamned good thing if you were going to have an all-black outfit to have a first-class black commander . . . And it was a matter of pride to him—pride, pride, pride . . ."

It's only speculation now, but it could be that Chappie survived this particular set of altercations because of that very thing. That "goddamned pride," beating like a metronome in Benjamin O. Davis, Jr.'s, heart. Pride, pride, pride. It was a matter of achieving self-reliance within his own unit, evolving protection for it and his men when warranted.

And while Daniel James, Jr., thought on these things, flew his B-25, did his duty as temporary operations officer and bomber pilot, and continued to be the social lion, events moved towards the trials; the outcome of which would later affect him, his career, and entire life in ways he never imagined. "Jesus Bob" Selway, as he was fondly remembered, was just about history as far as commanding black troops was concerned. A new day was dawning.

II

It was 1 July 1945, the day the army air forces decided to make Col. Benjamin O. Davis, Jr., the first black commander of an army air base. Black troops massed in parade formation along the flight line on Godman Field, watching the lone transport approach the field, touch down, and taxi to a halt near the review stand. The propellors stopped, and the people who would make it happen deplaned. Aboard were Lt. Gen. Ira Eaker, acting chief of staff of the air force, Brig. Gen. Benjamin O. Davis, Sr., inspector general's office and father of Colonel B. O. Davis, Jr. Truman Gibson, black, bespectacled civilian aide to the secretary of war, resplendent in his wide 1940s-style hat, baggy-panted suit, shirt and tie, and Brig. Gen. Edward Glenn, First Air Force chief of staff were also aboard. Gen. Frank O'Driscoll Hunter, the catalyst for the entire affair, did not see fit to attend.

Colonel Selway, still the base commander, met and greeted them. As they deplaned, *Pittsburgh Courier* photographers recorded the historic meeting. It was a strange scenario. General B. O. Davis, Sr., stood in the foreground, while behind him, his son seemed to strain, reaching across a great, wide space to shake Colonel Selway's hand. Selway, in turn, looked as if his shoes had suddenly grown suction cups, arm extended, his body grotesquely leaning into a somehow inviolate, empty space where black and white seldom met. In the background, Truman Gibson smiled tentatively while General Eaker smiled approval.

The air sparkled as they walked to the review stand. Repetitive commands rippled down the tarmac. Four thousand pairs of heels staccatoed. Flags curled in the wind as a B-25 bomber parked behind the beribboned stand bore witness. Commands echoed in the air, and the troops came to parade rest as Colonel Selway approached the microphone to introduce General Eaker. Eaker's amplified voice boomed in the summer air, etching itself on the minds of the four thousand.

With Colonel Davis, they would see action in the Pacific by late summer or early fall. Davis would become the post commander as soon as Colonel Selway properly turned over all material and equipment to Davis. The 477th had been reconstituted a composite group, consisting of two B-25 squadrons and one P-47 squadron, which would be the famous 99th Pursuit Squadron, now being reactivated minus men and equipment after its triumphant European tour. That squadron, Eaker went on, would be expanded as additional personnel became available. More than that, Colonel Davis would select his own staff and "those among you who are ambitious, can go as far as your ability and performance will take you!" It was, Eaker continued, "on my personal recommendation and insistence that Colonel Davis take command of this group because of the work I saw him do overseas. I came back from overseas to find that there were no plans for the 477th to go into action. There had been objections to an overseas assignment of the group because of the lack of replacements." But the general asserted that he, Truman Gibson, and General Hanley had beaten the authorities down, formulating the idea of combining a fighter squadron with the 477th to form the composite group.

Eaker introduced General Davis, Sr., who spoke from scribbled notes held in his hand, reminding them that they were overtrained and now needed combat. Somebody booed softly in the ranks. Davis, Sr., also spoke, as did his son after him, of the necessity of operating as and being part of a team.

The four thousand came to attention as the band began to play. The parade commander bellowed, "Pass in review!"—his voice ricocheting across the wide flight line. It was the first time in the history of the army air forces that an all-black group had paraded without the presence of one white face in its ranks. The review party came to attention on the review stand.

"A remarkable picture is this!" marveled the cut line under the photograph published in the next issue of the *Pittsburgh Courier*. At attention, executing a hand salute, were General Eaker, Brigadier Davis, Sr., Truman Gibson, civilian aide to the secretary of war, his hat held over his heart, Colonel Selway, Brig. Edward Glenn and, surrounded as if by an aura, stood that mustachioed and "youthful West Pointer," Colonel B. O. Davis, Jr. It was a day of which every black man in the entire United States Army Air Forces would have been proud could they have been there.

Later, in the base theater, with Colonel Selway's white officers on one side and Davis's black officers on the other, General Eaker, in a voice filled with emotion, looked squarely at the black faces before him: "If anybody had told me this could happen in the United States—I would never have believed it! These people," he continued, gesturing towards Colonel Selway and company, "are relieved, and here is your new commander—Colonel Benjamin O. Davis, Jr.!"

He gained the admiration of every black officer in the house, including Daniel "Chappie" James, Jr. "And that," commented Lt. Col. Spann Watson, USAF (Retired) years later, "was when we *really* felt relief!"

General Eaker continued: "I would be . . . surprised if you men do not push on and make this unit one of which you and the Air Force can be proud!" He went on to tell them that even Gen. Douglas MacArthur had said he'd be glad to have the 477th in the Pacific.

Colonel Selway "sat red-faced" throughout the ceremonies, apparently disturbed that his command had been taken from him because of the overwhelmingly adverse criticism directed at him for enforcing the Jim Crow policies and practices handed down by his superior.

III

The trials of the three officers still in arrest in quarters were to begin the next day. Because Roger Terry's offenses were thought to have been the more serious, two trials were scheduled. Thompson and Clinton would be tried together on 2 July and Terry alone on 3 July in the one-story base headquarters building's courtroom.

Although Chappie James was not to be tried, did not sit on the court nor to anyone's knowledge even attend the trials, some recounting of them is in order if for no other reason than to illustrate the immense obstacles he and his fellow black officers of the time were required to live with and ultimately overcome. Lack of promotions was only the tip of the iceberg. The issue of racism was stultifying.

The record clearly shows, for example, that, at the army's highest legal and investigative levels, decisions and recommendations had been made that the three black officers *should not be court-martialed at all,* but given a much lighter form of discipline.

In the confidential draft memorandum referenced earlier for the army's judge advocate general (with the margin-noted initials "W. A. R."), it was clear that the judge advocate's and inspector general's men had thoroughly reviewed the case and the charges emanating from it. The reviews commented on the heart of the matter: "All three lieutenants are Negroes. . . . This office is informally advised by the office of the judge advocate that *all* Combat Crew Training personnel at the field are Negroes, there being no white trainees and *no Negro officers other than trainees.**. . . It thus appears that (as a practical matter), the only officers prohibited from entering that particular officers' club were Negro officers . . ."

The preceding paragraph was not entirely true, since a black surgeon and chaplain were also assigned and should not have been classified as trainees because of their accomplished professional status. They were so classified, it will be recalled, by General Hunter, who somewhat pedantically referred to them as "giving training," and therefore "trainees." But the comments did strike at the core of the situation. The draft memo went on to predict the probable outcome: "Trial by court-martial of these officers could, it is believed, raise a question of *racial discrimination,* since it appears that the only officers excluded from the officers' club in question were Negro officers. Particularly would this be so if these officers [should be] charged with violation of Article of War 64, a capital offense, such action would (probably) result in wide and probably unfavorable publicity . . ."

Then came the judge advocate's conclusion and recommendation, which, if honored by air corps authorities, would have made court-martial unnecessary: "Under these circumstances (I am) of the opinion that although these officers were (probably) guilty of infractions of discipline, *the long-range public interest does not [appear to] warrant a trial by court-martial on charges growing out of the incident described . . .*"

Even the inspector general's review, although concurring that certain offenses had been committed, *"recommended that no further action be taken in this case."* But to preserve military discipline and achieve a "deterrent effect," should such a thing happen again—*something* had to be done:

> It is therefore recommended that reply . . . be made to the Commanding General, Army Air Forces [Attention: Deputy Chief of Air Staff] through the Air Judge Advocate . . . substantially as follows: *In view of all the circumstances of this case . . . it is [my] opinion that these officers should not be tried by general court-martial for their alleged offense, but that disciplinary action [should] be taken against them under the provisions of Article of War 104.† Subsequent thereto, these officers, unless good administration or their further training . . . requires other- wise, [should] be transferred to some other station. . .*

* Italics added.
† Article of War 104 was a far less serious vehicle for punishment than those under which the three officers were actually tried.

These conclusions and recommendations were transmitted on 11 June 1945 to the deputy chief of the air staff. It seems that is as far as they got, and it is assumed that the fine hand of Gen. Frank O'D. Hunter may have found a convenient burial ground for them since he frequently participated in meetings with the then-deputy chief of air staff.

At any rate, buried they were, and by command of General Hunter, an all-black, general court-martial board was detailed, with Colonel B. O. Davis, Jr., president. Only the prosecutor and court reporter were white. General Hunter sought protection from the liberals. The black officers wanted to be tried by their own kind. Not long after the sun rose on the morning of 2 July 1945, the court was to convene, trying Lts. Marsden Thompson, Shirley Cinton, and on 3 July 1945, Roger C. Terry who had, the charge sheets read, "offered violence against a superior officer."[62]

Chapter Sixteen
Trial

I

E arly sunlight slanted through the windows of the spartan-like courtroom. At the far end the long table and eight wooden chairs on the elevated platform were empty. It was as if people had been there, had just left, and would be returning soon.

It was Monday, 2 July 1945. The clock edged towards seven-thirty in the morning. An American flag reposed in a corner stand lending color to the drab roomscape. The door squeaked open. The court reporter, John H. Goranflo of South 42d Street in Louisville, Kentucky, arrived to set up his paraphernalia. It was all in a day's work for Goranflo. Today, he would make $84.14, including mileage at 5¢ a mile, to transcribe the 36,523 words to be spoken that day at 20¢ per word.

A few minutes before eight, muffled voices were heard outside the courtroom as the defense counsels (Capt. Cassius A. Harris III, with special counsel as recommended by the NAACP, Mr. Theodore M. Berry of Cincinnati and Mr. Harold M. Tyler of Chicago) entered. The doors were flung wide, and helmeted, sidearmed, and brassarded military police ushered in the accused. Capt. James W. Redden, trial advocate and prosecutor was to arrive next (that "big, red-headed cracker with a big Adam's apple"). Redden was the only white participant in the coming trials except for Goranflo.

Seconds later, Col. Benjamin O. Davis, Jr., arrived outside, exchanging pleasantries with the other members of the court. Then with solemn demeanor, they entered the courtroom as everyone sprang to attention. They sat at the long table. The angular-faced law member (1st Lt. William R. Ming) and

Capt. John H. Durden sat on Davis's left. To his right sat the remainder of the court (Capt. George L. Knox, Capts. James T. Wiley, William T. Yates, Fitzroy Newsum, and the very light complexioned Charles R. Stanton).

The drama built. Adrenalin probably caused the hearts of the accused to beat faster. Their futures lay in the hands of the eight officers facing them, led by the fabled, black West Pointer, Davis, the only black colonel in the entire United States Army Air Corps.

Marsden Thompson and Shirley Clinton were to be tried this day. Marsden was twenty-eight; Clinton, twenty-five. Both were "ninety-day wonders," commissioned second lieutenants in April 1943, after attending officer's candidate school in Miami Beach, Florida, for three months. One day separated them in the period they had been nonflying officers. Thompson had been an adjutant, a supply officer and later, a mess officer. Clinton had also been a mess officer (after attending cooking and baking school at Fort Benning, Georgia, for a month) and had become a combat intelligence officer after additional schooling at Orlando Beach. Both had good records. Neither had been in trouble. Even Colonel Selway rated their performance as satisfactory.

But today, they were to be arraigned and tried for willfully disobeying a superior officer and offering physical violence against that officer in the execution of his office. And Thompson was charged with an additional count of willful disobedience, having "refused" to leave the officers' club when ordered. They had, the air corps said, "acted jointly and in pursuance of a common intent, being engaged in a disorder among persons subject to military law and, having been ordered into arrest . . . did refuse and obey" the officer giving the command ordering them into arrest.

The trial began as Redden took center stage to ask the accused who was to be their counsel. They chose the NAACP-appointed T. M. Berry and Harold Tyler, placing them squarely in the forefront of the defense. Both Redden and Berry sought the advantage through the artifice of the peremptory challenge "by either side against any member of the court." Davis replied that there was no challenge.

The challenge game was far from over, however. "The prosecution," Redden said, "has no challenge for cause, but desires to preemptorily challenge Captain Stanton!" The reason for Redden's challenge of Stanton can only be surmised, although observers have noted that it was probably because Stanton was a very light complexioned black (so light that one "almost couldn't tell Stanton was black . . . he was just as white as the next guy"). Perhaps Redden thought that Stanton's mixed heritage would cause him to favor the accused. (Little did Redden know that certain of the black officers shared his distrust of this black man "as white as the next white guy.") As Stanton withdrew, Redden extended the right of challenge to Mr. Berry, the primary defense attorney. Berry was to send shock waves through the court.

"Neither of the accused desires to challenge any member of the court for cause,'' Berry began, ''but peremptorily challenges Colonel Benjamin O. Davis, Jr!''

Shock waves or no, the accused officers had very good reasons for the challenge. Terry, the officer to be tried the following day, provides the retrospective. It was that ''West Point background. *He* was the top guy; the ranking guy. *He* was a military ramrod with that West Point background . . . they didn't want anybody like that!'' More to the point, Terry continues:

And why *not?* [Davis] was the Army's man, that's the way we felt! He hadn't been there, he was over in Europe . . . we didn't know what [his] hierarchy was coming in with! By the time the court-martial went down, they hadn't been there three weeks. They weren't there when we were at Freeman Field! They came in when they set up the court-martial, but they weren't there when [we] had all of the confrontation with the Army!

In the heat of the moment, the fears as expressed by Terry may very well have been valid. But another theory exists, and that is that since becoming commander of Godman Field, Davis could not properly have held that post and also been the president of the court-martial board trying men of whom he was now the theoretical accuser. Memory dimmed, perhaps, by the passage of years, Davis himself remembers convening the court-martial and withdrawing, but does not ''remember the reason I gave.'' No matter, the trial moved apace as Capt. George L. Knox became president of the court-martial board.

''How do you plead?'' asked Redden.

''Not guilty to all charges and specifications!'' answered the defense.

The first witness, 1st Lt. Joseph D. Rogers, was called.

II

The court was thunderstruck after Rogers was sworn in as a witness, then refused to salute the president of the court-martial board as was customary. As Knox prepared to return the expected salute, Rogers made a slight, oblique movement, snapping a salute to the American flag in the corner. The court was chagrined at the flaunting of military courtesy with racial overtone.

''Er—ah, Lieutenant,'' growled Knox, ''it *is* customary that you salute the court!''

Chastised and a bit red-faced, Rogers saluted. Redden began.

''State your name, rank, organization and station.''

''Joseph D. Rogers, First Lieutenant, attached to Headquarters Section, 1550th Service Unit, Fort Knox, Kentucky.''

"Do you know the accused in this case?"

"Yes, sir."

"Is he in the military service?"

"Yes, sir."

Through continued questioning, Redden determined that Rogers was assigned duties as assistant provost marshal on Freeman Field on the fifth of April 1945, and that, on that date he was specifically assigned duties at the Freeman Field officer's club. Further, Rogers indicated that he went on duty that evening "about eight o'clock" on the orders of Major Baumgardner.

"What were your orders with regard to that duty assignment at officers' club and mess number one?" Redden wanted to know. Rogers minced no words.

"To keep nonmembers and trainee personnel out of officers' club number two!"

Any mention of Major Baumgardner was a bad rap for the prosecution, since he had recently been relieved as incompetent, making any statements or actions ordered by him suspect. Redden swiftly changed his line of questioning, determining that Rogers did in fact know the number of the building in which the club was located; that he did wear a military police brassard as evidence of his authority, and that an "unusual incident" did occur that evening in that a group of officers he recognized as "trainee personnel" came to the door of the club about ten past ten that evening. Rogers wrapped it up by saying that after he recognized them as nonmembers, and told them they couldn't enter, they came in anyhow, even after he gave them a direct order not to do so.

"Are any of the officers of that group present in court?" twanged Redden.

"Yes, sir."

"Will you point them out and name them?"

Rogers's arm pointed like a setter. "Lieutenant Clinton and Lieutenant Thompson!"

The questioning returned to the night of 5 April. "Well," Rogers harumphed, "I was standing in the door and Lieutenant Thompson and Lieutenant Clinton who were in front of the group—I understand later there were 19 officers in that group—they pushed me aside and the whole group entered the club!"

Redden assumed a stance of great empathy. "Demonstrate to the court just how you were pushed—how you were brushed or how you were pushed?"

Rogers explained, "I was standing in the door—the door on my right was half open. I had my arm braced both for the wooden door and the screen door, and they opened the screen door and just walked into it and pushed me back!"

Was there any comment, Redden wanted to know. Rogers remembered that Thompson said something.

"What did *he* say?"

"After I told him if he entered the building he would be placed under arrest, he said something like, 'Let me get inside and get arrested then!' "

On cross-examination, Mr. Berry wondered about Rogers's inexperience as a military police officer and went immediately for the jugular.

"On April 5th, Lieutenant Rogers, how long had you been serving as an assistant provost marshal?"

"From about March 5th—somewhere along in there."

"Approximately *one month?*"

"Approximately one month."

Berry also established that the night of the incident was the very first time Rogers had been ordered to police the officers' club, and had him reiterate that he had done it on Major Baumgardner's orders. The next question made Redden fidget.

"Can you state, in exact or near exact words, the entire order given you by Major Baumgardner as to the reason for being assigned to club number two?"

Redden exploded. *"I object to that!* There's no reason for the provost marshal to state a reason for giving an order—if he gives an order, that's the order and it is not up to a subordinate to question it!"

"Sustained!" said the law officer.

Berry rephrased the question.

"The best that I can remember, he told me to go to the club and keep trainee personnel and nonmembers out of the club. I was to give them—tell them—give them an order not to enter and if they did enter to place them under arrest."

The next series of questions from Berry were critical, for with them, he established that Rogers's assigned targets for the evening were the men from the operational training units, but that he wasn't given any kind of order as to how to identify them as such.

"How many groups of officers alleged to have been trainees or alleged to have entered the club wrongfully came to the club that night?"

"I object to that!," Redden exploded. "The witness has testified as to only *one* group on direct examination!" Berry defended his question by patiently explaining that he was only testing Rogers's memory.

"Overruled!"

"Three!" Rogers answered and probably knew at once that he had stepped onto thin ice as Berry promptly delivered a Sunday punch.

"As a matter of fact, Lieutenant, *were there not four groups?*"

"I object to the prompting of the witness!" Redden twanged.

"Overruled!"

Rogers elected a circuitous route by replying, "there were *not* four groups who entered—more than three groups came to the door, but only three groups entered!''

Berry then changed directions. Now he tested Rogers's ability to recall elements of time and, pointedly, how it was he recognized the accused as "trainees" in the first place. Reading from a previous sworn statement signed by Rogers, he established that Rogers had said that the black officers and flight officers appeared at the officers' club "about 2145 hours" (9:45 P.M.).

"Then," Berry rasped, "your testimony as 10:10 P.M. is in error?"

"It is," Rogers admitted, knowing that he had stubbed his toe. There was probably a small gleam in Berry's eye. Rogers probably squirmed a bit. His chair grew warmer as Berry undoubtedly stared at him intently.

"Now, you have testified that, as the men approached the door, you *recognized them as trainees—how did you recognize them as trainees?*"

"From my own judgment!" Now came the first shattering of Rogers's testimony, and he began to doubt himself. "I might be wrong," he stuttered, "I imagine they were trainees because most of them were *wearing pilot wings*. Either men of the pilot group or the CCTS. . . .'' he trailed off.

"Who wore pilots' wings, do you know?'' shot Berry. It was getting uncomfortable for Rogers. His memory forsook him. He couldn't remember whether Clinton and Thompson wore wings. He couldn't remember if he asked them whether they were trainees. He couldn't remember whether he'd talked with any of the men at the door. He couldn't remember if he'd had a conversation with Thompson. He couldn't remember whether he'd told them that the club was reserved for base personnel when they entered. Rogers fled like a swallow going south for the winter, and still Berry continued to press like a cold, slashing storm.

"Didn't Lieutenant Clinton state that 'I am attached to base personnel'?"

"I don't remember that if he did—"

"What *did* you say?"

Rogers remembered that he'd told them to stop. After they'd stopped he told them they weren't to use the building, and if they insisted, they would be placed under arrest.

"If they *insisted*—they would be placed under arrest?"

"Yes, sir!"

"Did they say anything?"

"Not that I remember—not then—"

"When was anything said?''

"After I had given them an order [Lieutenant] Thompson said something to the effect—'Get out of my way and let me get in and get arrested!' ''

Further testimony from Rogers revealed that at no time were the officers required to identify themselves, and he seized Thompson by his right overcoat arm as the rest of the officers swarmed about him and into the club.

"Your witness!"

On redirect, Redden reestablished that Rogers was there at the door of the club on official business in the execution of his office, had ordered the accused not to enter, and that Thompson and Clinton were present when the order was given and did not obey. Rogers was then subjected to lengthy, detailed examination, as to whether or not he had a gun.

"I believe you testified you were armed?"

"That is right, yes, sir."

"Will you describe to the court what you mean by that statement?"

"I was wearing a gun!"

"Side arms?"

"Side arms."

"Attached to your web belt?"

"Yes, sir."

"And your pistol was in plain sight?"

"Yes, sir."

"Was your brassard in plain sight?"

"It was."

"You had been ordered to keep nonmembers out of the club, hadn't you?"

"I had been ordered to keep them out of the building and if they entered to put them under arrest."

"Were you given orders—were you given any orders with respect to using force?"

"I was not."

The question had burned in many a breast since that fateful evening. What *would* have happened had Rogers pulled the gun and threatened to shoot? Fitzroy Newsum, a member of the court, provides this retrospective: "It was [that bit] of native intelligence that said, 'this is a useless situation. Don't do anything stupid!' If he had used that gun, he would have been overpowered."

III

Such was the flavor of the trial. Redden went for the throats of the accused and strenuously objected when his line of questioning seemed at risk. Berry hammered like a boxer at inconsistencies of the witnesses and their credibility, pounding Redden on points of military law at every opportunity. Ming, the law officer, steadfastly overruled the prosecution's objections. Captain Chiappe dodged questions as to his real status—a "supervisor" or a "trainee," since he was commander of most of the men on trial.

The next witnesses of note introduced by Redden were Maj. Andrew White, the club officer, and finally, Colonel Selway, himself. Both unabashedly saluted the American flag and needed to be reminded of military tradition and courtesy before they would salute Captain Knox. White conveniently forgot his conversation with black officers early in the confrontation in which he'd said: "Let's be frank, fellows, the club is not open to colored officers!" Like the proverbial greased pig, White slipped in his own grease several times on issues concerning how he *knew* the black officers were not members of the club. Knowing that race could not be the admitted issue, Berry mercilessly pounded him about identification methods he could have used to make such a decision: their names, their eligibility for membership, or unit to which assigned. White allowed that he knew about Army Regulation 210-10, and paragraph 19 in particular, outlawing segregated officers' clubs, but ordered the black officers out of the club in spite of that knowledge. And finally, White allowed himself to be cornered in an untenable situation, and Berry verbally hogtied him.

"Did you know Captain Chiappe?" [squadron commander of most of the black officers involved.]

"I do."

"Was Captain Chiappe a member of the club?"

"He was." Every black person there knew White had fibbed. Berry pressed on, then verbally skewered him.

"Isn't it a fact, Major, *that on the said day, 5 April 1945, that these men entered the club and were placed under arrest by you and that Captain Chiappe arrived on the post at the same time?"*

Redden objected. Berry calmly suggested that perhaps Chiappe had simply been a "guest?" Ming overruled the objection as White finally admitted that he didn't know when Chiappe took out membership. Berry then shot his testimony full of holes by forcefully reminding him that Chiappe's status was essentially the same as that of the officers he had placed under arrest for entering a club to which they did not belong because they were not members, since he was the commanding officer of the *training* squadron which "disqualified" the black officers for membership. Furthermore, Berry postulated after much objection and bickering over points of military law, that the order Rogers and White gave the black officers to leave the club "was illegal since it was a violation of an Army Regulation (and) the purpose of the order was to discriminate."

Selway blustered, was evasive and often openly hostile. He frequently demanded that the court recognize his point of view: "As long as it is a matter of record in here I think these questions are objectionable, irrelevant and immaterial. I think this entire line of questioning is irrelevant, but since the Court has ruled otherwise I will say I received telephone instructions from General Hunter on numerous occasions concerning assignment and use of facilities on that station. I had no letter order from him. . . ."

Whatever recollections he had of Base Regulation 85-2 were "vague." The original letter order restricting use of the club for the black officers belonged to his predecessor, not him. In effect, all of it was hearsay, because none of it was "through [his] own knowledge," and furthermore, "I was never present when any person was denied [entry]."

A parade of witnesses for the defense followed (2d Lts. Robert Payton, Coleman Young, Clifton Garrett; Flight Officer Howard Story; Lts. Thompson and Clinton, at their own request).

The court found Thompson and Clinton not guilty of all charges and specifications after one hour and forty-five minutes of deliberation.

But the nightmare began all over again the next day for twenty-four-year-old 2d Lt. Roger C. Terry in a new trial. Redden's opening statement, according to Terry, promised death for "disobedience of an order before witnesses in time of war." Additionally, Terry had "offered violence" against a superior officer by pushing him as he entered the club. His trial was not much different from that of Thompson and Clinton. Many of the witnesses were the same. Colonel Selway was rigid, dispassionate, and sometimes hostile. Goranflo, the court reporter, transcribed 19,271 words, collecting $49.64 including mileage. The court deliberated and found Terry not guilty of willful disobedience, but guilty of violation of the sixty-fourth Article of War because he offered violence against a superior officer in the execution of his office, pushing him aside by physical force. He was directed to forfeit fifty dollars of his pay for a period of three months.

General Hunter, First Air Force commander, viewed the outcomes with jaundiced eye. His endorsement to the trials read, in part: "In the foregoing case[s] . . . the sentence[s], although grossly inadequate, is approved and will be duly executed."

"It was," James T. Wiley, a member of the court recalled some forty-three years later, "a sort of mock trial. Here we were, an all-black court. We were looking for reasons not to do anything. I believe Colonel Davis had the same attitude. If there was a way out, he would have been for it." And if there is salvation for Colonel Selway, Fitzroy Newsum, another member of the court, provides it:

> It's hard to call him a hostile witness. [Ask] hostile to whom? It was *his* regime and tactics that were on trial . . . so of necessity, he had to be very hostile. . . . *He* was the one being . . . defied. He was simply [the organization man] . . . He was carrying out the orders. As such, he would not have learned anything. All [he knew] was rigidity . . . do

as we tell you . . . apply the segregation system. He never learned anything. There was no way in the world he'd back off his position . . .''

"Mock trial" or not, it was a major event affecting the career of Chappie
James and his fellow Tuskegee airmen. A new reality had been achieved for
them all here at Godman Field. Many people believe that each human triumph
is somehow reflected in the cellular knowledge of the entire species.[63] Perhaps
this was the real focal point of this intense drama, and out of it James's full
thrust towards his own unique reality was yet to come.

Chapter Seventeen
Healing

I

Few Americans who were alive then would ever forget 6 August 1945, the day America dropped an atomic bomb on Hiroshima, Japan. One bomb decimated the midsection of the city. Thousands died in nanoseconds, while others lingered interminably, living to tell the story through cruelly seared lips.

One bomb, they said, probably saved a million American lives. But still, eighty thousand dead in a flash was no laughing matter. When Japan sued for peace on 14 August 1945, the long eyes and sighs turned into sighs of relief. It was over. No more death and dying. The war had gone away.

More than the war had gone away for the black officers and enlisted men on Godman Field. Not only had the infamous Colonel Selway gone, but so had all his white officers. Colonel Davis wasted no time in replacing them with his own, allegedly within thirty minutes of assuming command. Activities on the base reverted to peacetime status. Emphasis was placed on military conduct, aircraft maintenance, and reorganization.

Even the base newspaper, the *Godman Field Beacon,* had a new look. Showcasing better layout and accurate proofing, it contained more features and local news. Venereal disease rates continued to fall sharply in the face of the Davis-installed VD Control Committee. Stringent control measures were the order of the day. Some said that the improved morale presaged the decline.

The shortage of guest housing remained as acute as it was under Selway. No relief was in sight. The government had no reason to fund such additions during times of peace. Although nearby Fort Knox had plenty of officer housing, its post commander was anything but amenable to Davis's request to use it, having been more than cooperative when Colonel Selway had the power. When Colonel Davis called First Air Force headquarters, the Fort Knox post commander said: "I don't know whether you are familiar with Fort Knox . . . but this is an old cavalry post . . . we have four general officers living here . . . and by God, they just don't want a bunch of coons moving in next door to them . . ."[64]

Even General Eaker, for all his recent candor and rhetoric, backed down when confronted by the same post commander, saying that he couldn't understand why the army air forces were entitled to any quarters at Fort Knox.

Religious life picked up on the station. Average attendance nudged 300 on Sundays at the base chapel as court-martial rates plummeted. Chappie James was in his element. Back on the football field again with the Godman Field Bombers, he wore number fifty-five. He was big Chappie James on the line, and because of his presence, the team was considered a potential powerhouse that couldn't miss. The team's coach was Lt. Archie Harris, a nationally known athlete, lately of Indiana University. Major Webb, the newly appointed coordinator of base athletics, punched up the publicity by offering season tickets to the winner of the "name the team" contest conducted some time before.

With Chappie an integral part of the team, the Godman Field Bombers rumbled against Camp LeJeune, North Carolina, kicked sand in the faces of the Lincoln University eleven in Jefferson City, Missouri, and dueled with Lane College in Jackson, Tennessee. Shaw University at Louisville fared no better, and the Bombers wiped out the white marker lines as they took on Wilberforce's team in Xenia, Ohio. Down in Tyler, Texas, observers say they shook the ground, and even the alligators took note when they clashed with Southern University in Baton Rouge.

Chappie and the team were full of hope at the beginning of the season as the Bombers destroyed all opposition in their first three games, drubbing opponents twelve to zero, thirty-nine to seven, and thirty-three to zero. By Christmas, however, the victory roll aborted as the base newspaper mourned the outcome: "Bomber Bowl Bid Dropped—J. C. Smith University Named in Cotton-Tobacco Bowl!" Chappie and his fellow warriors now packed their football togs in moth balls as the season ended.

It was Christmas and Colonel Davis's message in the base newspaper was proof that things had changed immensely:

SEASONS GREETINGS from the Commanding Officer . . . Christmas of 1945 is for most of us different. . . . War is over—no longer are we training for movement overseas, or at a Port of Embarkation awaiting shipment by dull, grey transport to distant theaters of operations. We have left victoriously the fields of battle where we spent last Christmas dreaming of our own firesides. . . . Mrs. Davis joins me in wishing

each one of you and your loved ones a joyous Yuletide and the best that
the world can offer during the coming New Year . . .

It was a far cry from Colonel Selway's message of the year before, exhorting
all to "bend that throttle of energy."

Chappie James and his fellow officers probably chortled at a bit of doggerel
written by a Pfc. Boyd L. McCoy and printed in the *Beacon* during this first
Christmas without the tentacles of racism reaching out in an immediate fashion:

Dear Santa, please come by my barracks tonight
Bring me a white piece of paper with discharge in sight.
Don't worry about the new suit or the dress
Just bring that piece of paper—and I'll *get* the rest!

II

There was much to remember beside the changing of the guard and improved
morale as 1946 began. Many men had begun to really communicate one with
the other. Beginning at the Camp Atterbury Support Base and later at Godman,
there sprang up a "GI Town Hall." The barracks "bull session" evolved into
meaningful exchange; no subject was sacrosanct. A first sergeant led a discussion
of the book *Freedom Road*. Pfc. Frank Hutchinson asked, "Is the Woman's
Place in the Home?" Was World War II the Negroes war, too? Was it important
that blacks organize?

GI Town Hall fell into disarray as the reorganization continued, but as 1946
dawned, perhaps somewhere in the minds of those who had attended Town
Hall, the voice of Cpl. Charles Evans still rang as he had led the discussion,
"Reconversion and the Negro," quoting Pierre van Passen to close his presentation: "A day will surely come when man, having grown tired of walking alone,
will turn to his brother. On the day when we shall have learned to feel the
sorrows and the joys, the suffering and the hope of others as our very own;
that world order of love and justice for which the Universe, and of which the
planets in the stillest night are the splendid but imperfect symbol shall have
come nearer. . . . On that day alone the brotherhood of man will have become
a reality . . ."[65]

Thus the problems Chappie James and all the rest had encountered and
were still encountering, must somehow have begun to be bearable. Even Colonel
Davis, faced with shifting sets of mission alternatives since V-J Day; a base
with very poor recreational facilities for his men with no improvements in

sight; inadequate housing for dependents; a severely mismanaged air corps supply system on base at his arrival; and units to command, which, by their very nature, were considered "peculiar,"—might have taken heart at the quote, if he had heard it. That majestic statement of hope may have inspired his 1945 response to an interviewer's query as to whether Negro troops respond favorably or unfavorably to command by Negro officers. One might have wondered, in those days, whether he believed his own answer at the time.

It was a difficult question, he hedged. There were variables. Generally, though, he thought that *black troops did respond favorably to black command.* But the limitations of the times rode hard upon his shoulders. The variable existed. "In certain sections of the country, the authority of the white man is traditionally supreme and Negroes thus are conditioned early in life to recognize that fact. It logically follows, therefore, that Negro military units which are largely representative of those sections of the country would, probably, respond favorably to command by white officers . . ."[66]

It was a tightrope upon which the colonel gingerly walked. Today, someone noted, it might be called "weasel wording—talking out of both sides of one's mouth." For really, what *was* the truth when it came to exercising command authority over black troops? Or was the answer really that black troops, like white troops, served best under *competent commanders,* regardless of their color?

That may be where he was headed, but at barely thirty-four years of age, it was perhaps pressure enough to be the highest ranking black officer in the United States Army other than his father, saddled with the job of proving that the men of his race whom he commanded were as good as any other. It was perhaps the politic thing to say, and for that he can now be forgiven. For nobody who really knew him could say that his heart was not really in the right place. Alan Gropman, in *Blacks in the Army Air Forces During World War II,* observed: ". . . B. O. Davis, Jr. [as Commander of the 477th], advocated integration, but called for a gradual approach out of fear of white reaction."

Davis selected competent, tried-and-true subordinate operational commanders unlike the swift replacement of officers administering the base. Maj. William A. Campbell he assigned to be commander of the reborn 99th Pursuit Squadron. Campbell was a veteran of 106 aerial combat missions over Europe. He held the Distinguished Flying Cross with nine Oak Leaf Clusters, earned while escorting fighter strikes into the heart of Germany with the 332d Fighter Group. He appointed Maj. Vance Marchbanks as surgeon. Marchbanks would become a general one day.

Davis's "gradualism" did not sit well with younger officers like Daniel James, Jr., champing at the bit for recognition. They waited, without promotions, for yet another five years. One day, Chappie would understand and would remember that: "General Davis had a job to do, and if he hadn't held . . .

tight rein . . . that unit would have been taken away from him . . ." And if then-Colonel Davis had not held a tight rein over Chappie (and the rest), the odds are that Chappie never would have survived his own expansive temperament to become a four-star general. Headstrong, irreverent, and mischievous, he always looked for ways to circumvent the rules.

It was part of Chappie's charm underneath a wonderful, gentle exterior. At least he had the guts to be an "original" within an aura of military rules and often-boring regulation.

III

As early as January 1946, rumor circulated about an impending move for the black bomber and fighter squadrons. At the time, Colonel Davis could not say whether it were true. It was well known, however, that Godman Field would be too small to house the great numbers of men the air force was sending, especially after Tuskegee closed later that year. There was simply no other place to send the blacks who wanted to remain in the air force. Everyone waited. Something was in the wind. Still, Colonel Davis had received no official word. So they trained and flew, maintaining proficiency. At the same time, more experienced men were lost to postwar discharges. Airplane inventory dwindled because of accidents and aging, until by the middle of February, the P-47 inventory had been reduced by almost two percent, the enlisted population dwindled by forty-one percent, while the officer corps increased almost ten percent.

By late February 1946, rumor became fact. They *would* be moving to Lockbourne Army Air Base in Columbus, Ohio. In one respect, the air force had done them proud. Lockbourne was an air base with adequate hangar space, good runways, and excellent housing. On the other hand, the air force simply reaffirmed its position on segregation, assigning an entire base to what was later to be dubbed, "Ben Davis's Air Force," and the "Spookwaffe." The air force knew that this many blacks simply weren't welcome anywhere else. Tactical Air Command, to which their unit had been assigned, had already complained that it was being assigned too many blacks.

The planned assignment of the units to Columbus, Ohio, hit the city like a bomb, inspiring the editor of the *Columbus Citizen,* to decry their coming. "The 477th," he said, was "a bunch of troublemakers." They were simply "American servants," fighting for the country. He intimated that he could stop the move if he wanted to, because "this is still a white man's country!"

In spite of the opposition, planning for the move continued as morale picked up. People, including Daniel James, Jr., felt better because Godman Field *was* dilapidated and old. Moving into Lockbourne was like moving into the Hilton. Colonel Davis maintained a level head in the face of euphoria, ordering his men to stay away from Lockbourne prior to the actual move, to prevent possible incidents. The black people of Columbus, Ohio, knew they were coming, and were out in force to greet them on 13 March 1946, when the unit moved to the new base, flying over Columbus at eighteen thousand feet in flights of four so as to not "alarm the people."

But down there on the ground around the runway, the black populace knew their boys were in town. They turned out by the hundreds. The black pilots gave their civilian friends a show of flying skill, executing what must have seemed awesome, four-point barrel rolls and graceful chandelles before landing with a roar of engines and propellor blades glinting in the sun.

Once in place, the unit suffered because of personnel shortages caused by the continuing, high separation rate. It became necessary to consider long-range planning, involving the use of regular army people in key positions so as to achieve stability. They were forced to rely heavily on the results of on-the-job training to ensure continued proficiency. Now that the unit was assigned to Tactical Air Command, its mission was defined as "demobilization and recruitment; cooperation with and assistance to other tactical units and continued training through on-the-job training [so as] to broaden military experience of both officer and enlisted men and permit accomplishment of administrative and technical training needed for peace-time operations."

That was pretty dry stuff for an aspiring junior officer like Daniel "Chappie" James, Jr., still chafing at the paucity of promotions and at his inability to find quarters for his family right away at Lockbourne, even though quarters existed. A wait was necessary, and he and Dorothy took a one-room apartment, leaving nine-month-old Spike with his grandmother in Tuskegee. It took several months before they were assigned quarters, finally bringing Spike home to Lockbourne. His homecoming triggered high emotion in the household. Looking back, Dorothy remembers the bittersweetness of those days: "When we got Danny back, he didn't know his daddy at all. He only knew a picture as daddy, and this giant with the deep voice frightened him terribly. *Come to me, I'm your father!* . . . Danny would cry, and I'd cry, too! It really broke my heart!"

In spite of these setbacks and small personal trauma, Chappie gained a great deal of satisfaction with his reputation for being a daredevil pilot and a person of great ambition, who was always pushing forward. When others despaired and decried what seemed to be a "Sargasso Sea" effect in which recommendations for promotions were routinely returned from higher headquarters, festooned with reasons why they *could not* happen, Chappie affirmed his intent to remain in the air force and one day become a general officer. He was a party-goer, greatly admired by the opposite sex. As a result, people gathered around him, some clinging like metal filings to a magnet. Again, he played football against Ohio colleges, shone as a basketballer, and led parades with the same intensity and élan he led flight formations. He wanted tremendously to be recognized.

Although James recognized Benjamin Davis, Jr.'s, success and ability as a career officer, he partially blamed him for his slow advancement. In return, Davis had reason to wonder if Chappie would ever really become a soldier. The two were of different stripe. James's nature was effusive and outgoing; Davis was taciturn, conservative, and, above all, proper. As one Captain Williams, Davis's weather officer at the time, remembers:

> Chappie was one of the fellows. B. O. was the son of one of the first black generals. He was at West Point, [where] he had to put up with the goddamn four years of silent treatment. He was the only colonel on the base at Lockbourne. Most colonels hobnob with other colonels. He had nobody. He had a very tight circle of friends; three or four lieutenant colonels. [He was] a lonely man. One word [from him] could cut!

Williams goes on to illustrate by recalling how a weather briefing he was giving then-Colonel Davis was interrupted by an unfortunate captain who happened to wander by in civilian clothes while on base.

"Captain!" Colonel Davis growled, "You *speed* to your quarters! I never want to see you on this base again in civilian clothes!"

"The cat turned *white!*" Williams fondly remembers.

"Okay, Captain Williams," Davis calmly continued, "proceed with the weather briefing!"

James marked time, continuing to fly the B-25, even though he disliked the duty, becoming the instrument-check pilot for the aircraft. The fighter pilot in him seethed with frustration. In spite of that fighter pilot need to exist on the edge; to savor danger, there was a gentleness about him some might categorize as benign vulnerability, which endeared him to people who knew him.

There were the times that Jim Mason and Bob Wilson, both maintenance inspectors in the air inspector's office, would drop by Chappie's house. Good friends, they felt comfortable doing this at any time of the day or night. Chappie wouldn't be gentle with them for disturbing his privacy. He'd cuss them out, but he'd listen to their plaints for an "extra bottle of booze, or some money to buy some booze." It was a camaraderie, a "one-of-the-fellows" routine. But there was a time, they recall, that their unannounced visits would not be welcomed. It was a time sacrosanct in Chappie's world, when he'd come home after a flight or just before leaving the house to fly. At either time, Chappie would spend at least "fifteen minutes with Dorothy." They would watch as "he and Dorothy would sit down and court. He'd just hug her—just like they were courting, rather than being married."

"He would not talk to us until that time was up. And we'd have to wait. So, while we were waiting, Jim Mason would find his booze in his cabinet, and we'd drink up his booze! Ha! Ha!" Their success at this endeavor was short-lived for, "from then on, he'd lock the door, so we couldn't get in!"

In spite of his gentleness and tender attitudes towards his family, however, he remained, as biographer James R. McGovern, in *Black Eagle*, observed, "a hard charger," and this was to bring him into sometimes unsettling confrontations with his commander, the usually taciturn Col. Benjamin Oliver Davis, Jr.

IV

All was not playtime for the black pilots and airmen at Lockbourne. In November 1946, the 477th Composite Group flew to Southern California in support of Sixth Army in joint army-navy amphibious war games. Attached to Twelfth Air Force, its mission was to provide air cover and tactical air support.

As Colonel Davis and his deputy watched from the Blythe Air Base tower, Captain C. Y. Williams led thirteen B-25s of the 617th Bombardment Squadron, while Maj. William Campbell shepherded ten P-47s of the 99th Fighter Squadron into the blue California skies on a first-strike mission. On "X"-Day, the P-47s were airborne at dawn, set to perform escort duty for the 47th Bomb Group and fly cover for their own bombers to target, softening the resistance for land forces to retake San Clemente island from the enemy, as ten thousand 2d Infantry troops landed. That afternoon, the 99th Fighter Squadron patrolled above China Point on the southeastern tip of San Clemente. On the twenty-fourth, they helped attack the airstrip at Camp Pendleton, theoretically destroying many aircraft on the ground. On "D"-Day, twenty-four aircraft from the group supported the Normandy-like invasion of Aliso Canyon near Oceanside, California. P-47s rendezvoused over March Field with the 62d Troop Carrier Wing, providing cover for the transports, strafing the target area at low level, knocking out twelve tanks, strafing vehicles and gun positions, then attacking the Pendleton airstrip and beach areas as the B-25s, in attack formation, bombed the area, disrupting supply and communications lines. Major General Old lauded the effort. It was a "can-do" mission, and one that should have begun to dispel questions about the abilities of this "unique" unit. Back at Lockbourne, the base newspaper, *The Lantern,* told the story in a two-page spread in its 26 December 1946 issue.

It was a tribute to them all, including Daniel James, Jr. It attested to the command skills of Colonel Davis as well as flight leaders Williams and Campbell. The air force was slowly changing. Even the color of its uniforms presaged change, as enlisted men and WACs arrived at Lockbourne to preview the proposed new, blue uniforms.

Colonel Davis was proud. His 1946 Christmas message to his men read in part:

> Our organizational structure is well-defined. . . . Our corps of civilian personnel . . . is filling an important place in our operation. . . . On the base and in the community of Columbus, our daily relations have . . . shed a feeling of good-will and cooperativeness. We have been able to present the air forces and the army to the civilian population in a highly creditable light. This has been due in the very largest part to the bearing and soldierly character of officers and men alike . . .

The colonel did not leave it there. "Much has been done. Much yet remains to be done in 1947. We must continue to work and *to shape ourselves to a finished unit in the peacetime Army of the United States.* I have firm faith that all of you . . . will do your part to make Lockbourne the best Army Air Base in the United States."

In April 1947, the 617th Bombardment Squadron and the 99th Fighter participated in more war games, this time at Fort Benning, Georgia. Again, Major Campbell "led his Thunderbolts in screaming dives, leaving smoke and debris, strafing the target area with 50 calibre ammunition and 5-inch rockets." Two thousand spectators gasped with awe at the skill of the black pilots.

After other exercises in Georgia later in the year, the 477th Composite Group was deactivated in mid-1947, to be replaced by what was ultimately to become the 332d Fighter Wing, consisting of three fighter squadrons, the famous 99th, 100th, and 301st. Although some discontent resulted from this action as B-25 pilots were retrained to fly fighters, the move was probably welcomed by Daniel James, Jr., since fighters were his first love. Unfortunately, some twenty-five officers (navigator-bombardiers) were taken off flying status by 1 July 1947.

From time to time, enforcing the exemplary bearing and soldierly character of his officers and men would sorely try Colonel Davis's patience as they took part in war games and air indoctrination courses at Fort Benning, with maneuvers at Myrtle Beach, South Carolina, during their checkout period. Perhaps he might have wondered if he had not been premature in his congratulations. Not often, but on occasion, it would be Daniel James, Jr., the "hard-charger," center stage his attention, bringing him erect in his commander's chair.

For it was at Myrtle Beach that Daniel James, Jr., became a bit miffed at a fellow officer who insisted upon a bit of horseplay in the showers in quarters.

According to then-Capt. Archie Williams, weather officer: "We were all set to come home. I had briefed them on the weather. We got in the shower. . . . We started popping towels and tearing T-shirts. Next thing you know, Chappie and this other officer were duking it out! We stopped it, but [the word] got back to Colonel Davis. When we got back to Lockbourne, they were on the carpet."

Chappie and the other officer sat meekly outside the colonel's door, awaiting the ultimate upbraiding. It was a tense time. Suddenly, the colonel's door opened, and the clear voice of doom could be heard.

"Send those officers in to me! Send 'em in!" Davis commanded as he closed the door. The two officers stood tall, just as the colonel's door opened again. The sergeant outside Davis's door gestured them towards the colonel's office and—

"I don't want to see 'em—send 'em back out again!"

Captain Williams remembers that "old Chappie and this other cat were bitin' their fingernails! 'B. O.' just wanted to scare the pee out of them!"

"Send 'em in!"

"No, I don't wanta see 'em anymore!"

Finally, Colonel Davis did see them and gave them a royal chewing out, not least because their subordinates knew they "were officers—(why), in *front* of all these *enlisted men!*"

That encounter would have been enough to cause the average first lieutenant to settle down for a long time, but Chappie "was a free spirit! . . . that's Chappie! As he said, 'balls to the wall, man! Go for it!' "

And *that* is what he was doing that same summer at Eglin Field in Florida, checking out in the P-47, bringing it around for a landing too fast and high on a short runway, the hot thermals floating him up and up, like a feather. Pilots standing near the runway gasped. There was no way James could make it! If he kept floating high, he'd crash. The man in the tower was having fits.

"Take it around! Take it around! Try another time!"

"Don't worry," crackled Daniel's voice over the radio, "I can handle it!"

At the midpoint of the runway, his ship was still aloft.

"Don't try it! Take it around!" yelled the man in the tower. The fire trucks stormed out and down the line.

By now, even Chappie could see that he would run out of runway, but he came in anyway, sailing madly into the red sand dunes at the end of the runway, the plane upending, coming to rest upside down, wheels spinning, with James still in the cockpit, "just hanging there," held in place by the harness.

Pilots and maintenance men ran to the airplane. They found a sheepish Daniel James, Jr.

"I thought I could make it," he grinned.

A guy named Frank Keene found a piece of barbed wire and grounded the aircraft in order to drain off static electricity, preventing an errant spark and explosion. Chappie could be heard doing his usual cussing.

"Hey, Chappie!" somebody said, "with all the gasoline running out of this thing, instead 'a *cussin'*, you better start *prayin'*!"

He finally realized what was happening and calmed down a bit. Somebody brought a light crane, lifted the airplane, and they were able to get him out. Later, Chappie remarked that he "saw his entire life pass in front of him." Some wit responded that, as "bad" as he'd been, there was *no way* he could have seen *his* life pass in front of him in such a short period of time!

V

Maybe they were right. It wasn't long before 1st Lt. Daniel "Chappie" James, Jr., was on the carpet again. Col. Benjamin O. Davis, Jr., ramrod-straight in his chair behind a clear, polished desk, regarded him with frigid calm. Lieutenant James stood tall. Not a muscle twitched.

"James," the colonel grated, "a farmer has just called this base! A mink rancher!"

The colonel's thin moustache danced on his upper lip. The voice stung.

"And it seems that a bunch of P-40s came across—a flight of four—and buzzed his mink ranch and his mink; they were in foal at the time, dropped their young mink and ate 'em!"

Later, James would remark in retrospective good humor, "Now mink do that sometime, I found out—that's how they solve the welfare problem!"

The colonel would not be put off.

"Now I *know* who did it! And the way I know who did it, I just went down and looked at the schedule!"

"He just wants me to know how smart he is," James thought.

"I saw that you and that bunch of juvenile delinquents you run around with were up there and I know that *you* scared the farmer's mink! Now, I'm going to give you a choice. You can either have an Article 104 or a court-martial. Which do you want?"

"I'll take some of the 104, Colonel!"

"Okay, baby, you got it! I'm fining you $50 a month for six months! Do you have anything to say?"

"No, sir!" said James. He saluted and walked out, making straight for the hut he and his friend, Jim Mason, shared. Mason had some explaining to do. He was there, laid back in exquisite comfort as Chappie charged in. Mason looked at James quixotically.

"Hey, baby! I hear you been up there talkin' to the man!''

"Mostly listening. Now listen, Jim, you owe me a hundred and a half, babe! Because I know I was nowhere near that mink ranch! And I looked at the schedule, too, and I know *who else* was up there—and *you* did it!'' James boomed, pointing a beefy, accusing finger.

"Well, hell—why didn't you tell him?'' Mason sat up on his bunk.

"Hell, how in the hell could I tell him, when at the same time I was out there over Lake Huron turning over sailboats?''

It was James's way. Loyal to his friends. Thinking all the time. Knowing when it was better to stick up for a friend than to tell what really happened and make a bad situation worse. He had to do things for himself. People would know he existed, that he was talented, and had positive contributions to offer the country, the air force, and the world. It was not enough to be one of the better pilots and more dependable athletes around.

The days of dance, song, and performance learned in Miss Lillie's school permeated his soul. Bill Ellis, of Los Angeles, a fellow pilot of the period, remembers that: "He was one of the biggest hams you ever saw in your life. If you had a piano and a stage and a group of people, he wants to sing *somebody* a song! [And] he could sing—he had more than a modicum of talent—always willing to go on stage.''

Enter 2d Lt. Alvin J. Downing, an extremely talented musician, assigned to Lockbourne in February 1947, from Tuskegee Air Field in Alabama. Assigned the chore of special services officer, Downing quickly put forth the idea of organizing talent shows. The talent available in each squadron was taped, a show presented after the regular Friday movies, and an award given to the squadron with the best show. So successful were these that a larger, three-hour show was organized, using the best talent from all the squadrons. They called it "Operation Enjoyment.''

Suddenly, James was in his element, becoming producer, master of ceremonies, and sometimes singer. Enlisted men and officers, men and women alike, comprised the cast. Ellis continues: "I really think this was . . . the beginning of the saga of Chappie as far as this particular phase of his career was concerned.''

It was perhaps providential that in August 1948, on the night one of the biggest shows was being presented, a C-47 landed at Lockbourne to refuel. A Californian, Lt. Col. Joseph F. Goetz, was on board. Goetz, well-connected in the entertainment industry, and USAF chief of special services entertainment, upon seeing how spiffy and well-run the base was ("B. O. ran a tight ship.''), prevailed upon the all-white crew to remain overnight and fly out the next day.

They found no movie at the base theater. The talent show was in progress. Goetz was delighted and amazed. He is reported to have remarked, probably to Colonel Davis, that his command "had been thinking of putting a show together for the Air Force, and here *is* one! Let's take *this* one and develop it!''

Goetz sold the concept to the air force and not long after, the entire cast, including James and Al Downing as music director, were ordered to Langley Field, Virginia, Tactical Air Command headquarters. There, Goetz used his show business acumen and expertise to polish the routines. Dancers were choreographed and the jokes honed. Scripts were written. The music was more precisely orchestrated and 1st Lt. Daniel "Chappie" James, Jr., was chosen master of ceremonies.

Ninety days later, a new show emerged like a butterfly from its chrysalis. It sparkled, bubbling over with a special kind of joy and happiness. Joe Goetz dubbed the new show—"Operation Happiness!"

After a dress rehearsal at Langley Field, the show returned to Lockbourne for its November premiere.

"It was absolutely delightful! Just like chalk and cheese!" Bill Ellis remembers. And it was. The effusive, commanding presence of Chappie James as master of ceremonies, delighted spectators with his welcoming, jokes, and songs sung in his deep, melodic voice. Al Downing and a counterpart pianist, on twin pianos, titillated the audience with improvisations on "Tea for Two."

The WAC chorus line, exposed shapely, sepia legs as they kicked high and in rhythm with Rockette-like precision. A magician confounded the senses. Comedians tickled the funny bone, and the orchestra backed it all with that fat, round, big-band sound, its soloists shining intermittently, like morning stars.

VI

As Operation Happiness was launched, other important events were occurring in the labyrinths of the United States government and the air force. Although it did not change the status of the 332d Fighter Group, the air force was declared an autonomous service. The wing continued to be plagued by manpower shortages, and in some instances, could not use men assigned them in the specialties they had been trained in.

In Washington, Truman and his aides pondered the possible effects of the Negro vote on the coming 1948 election and what the Democratic party, and Truman himself, could do to ensure it. The air force itself was pondering the effects of segregation on its existence as an effective force. Its deputy chief of staff for personnel, along with the McCloy Committee, continued to sling barbs at segregation, calling it a waste of manpower. Stuart Symington, secretary of the air force, went on record during 1947 as pro-desegregation, stating that "blacks should be able to enter the Air Force whenever they could on their merits." This new direction, lauded by black leaders and media, was met by a formidable phalanx of resistance from high-ranking military officers. It would be, some thought, too radical a change. It would start a string of riots. There would be disruption. There would be desertions. Even during World War II and the formation of the wartime 332d, a famous air force general had thought integration was a mistake and even then, "they rushed into it too fast [and] almost ruined the Services." And the next air force chief of staff, Lt. Gen. Hoyt S. Vandenberg, ascending to the office in 1948, had stated as early as 1945 in a memorandum to General Arnold his largely anti-integration stance. Colored troops, he noted, would be grouped in lower and/or minimum qualifying scores; due to the lower average intelligence of the Negro, his elimination rate in pilot training would be higher than the whites. "Notwithstanding the claims that all people are created equal," he wrote, "the vast majority of whites insist on racial segregation. To avoid incidents and to provide for harmony . . . both for white and colored, segregation is essential."

This was true, he reasoned, "because of the Negro's lower average intelligence, lack of leadership, poor health, high attrition rates in training and resultant excessive cost of training . . . [which] cannot be justified."

It was high irony. Shortly after becoming air force chief of staff, it would be Vandenberg's assignment to carry out President Truman's Executive Order 9981, requiring equal treatment in the armed forces.

The order, some have noted, was at least as important as the Emancipation Proclamation. Designed primarily to reap benefits politically both for the president and the Democratic party, it was earthshaking, nevertheless:

> It is essential that there be maintained in the Armed Services of the United States the highest standards of democracy, with equality of treatment and opportunity for all persons in the Armed Services without regard to race. . . . There shall be created in the National Military Establishment an advisory committee to be known as the President's Committee on Equality of Treatment and Opportunity in the Armed Services . . . the committee is authorized . . . to examine into the rules, procedures, and practices of the Armed Services . . . to determine in what respect such rules, procedures and practices may be altered or improved with a view to carrying out the policy of this order.

On 28 July, a reporter took the proverbial bull by the horns.

"Mr. President," he wanted to know, "does equality of treatment and opportunity mean an eventual end to segregation?"

"Yes."

VII

Operation Happiness was a great success everywhere it played. From the first free performance at Memorial Hall in Columbus, Ohio, it was a fitting response to the editor of the *Columbus Citizen,* who snubbed the blacks upon their arrival and dubbed them "a bunch of troublemakers." Things had changed, as the *Citizen* now allowed that "Columbus has come to feel a kinship for the Lockbourne outfit."

Through fourteen performances before six air base communities, audiences were delighted, bestowing applause on the show and the master of ceremonies. The show was outstanding in all respects—from The Flying Band to soloists Bill Chatman, Pfc. Nicholson, Verline Jones, and the enchanting, winsome Evelyn Matthews, who captivated audiences with "I'll Close My Eyes," or "I've Got It Bad and That Ain't Good," backed up by the Airman's Quartet. From the "Remote Control" comedy set, in which two zoot-suited gentlemen part with their cash for a remote-controlled dollie, then argue as to who gets which half—to the Jitterbug Drill Team. From the "Samba Spotlight" number to the vivacious Sgt. Rebecca Gilbert in her dance routine, wearing "top hat, white tie and dancing tights."

But the real star was Chappie James. Chappie was using Operation Happiness as a vehicle to become known throughout the air force. At every base, he sought out the base commander, the generals, and anybody else with any authority. They may not have known anybody else in the show except in passing— but *they remembered Daniel James,*—"that big fella."

Even then-Colonel Davis had jumped on the bandwagon: "I must have seen Daniel James more during Operation Happiness than at any time during his career . . ." Praise and plaudits were everywhere:

. . . Lieutenant Daniel James MC'd the show with wit and finesse . . .
Lieutenant Daniel James . . . was tops as Master of Ceremonies and did much to add to this superb entertainment with his [singing].

Only one reviewer found Chappie's performance lacking. Said he: ". . . Lieutenant Daniel (Chappie) James, the Master of Ceremonies, although lacking the poise of a professional em cee, kept the action moving at a rapid clip . . ."

It is difficult to believe, someone has noted, that the Operation Happiness program blurb about James was not *written by* James. He undoubtedly had input. Under a picture of James, the master of ceremonies, belting out "Run Joe," it read: "A dynamic stage-master, 'Chappie' . . . is a towering 6 foot

4 inch, 230 pounds. He has . . . logged more than 3,000 hours of flying time in fighter and bomber aircraft and holds a Green Card certifying that he meets the USAF's rigid standards for flying under weather conditions. Enthusiastic reviewers have hailed the MC pilot . . . as a near-professional sensation . . ."

Miss Lillie's words were ringing loud and clear in James's head. Here was the door to opportunity. His "bags were packed," and he had wasted no time getting about the business of charging in.

The door was to open wider.

A fringe benefit James enjoyed during Operation Happiness was the use of a P-47 fighter assigned him for the duration of the tour. Everything ran like clockwork until the show at Mitchel Field in New York. There, his P-47 malfunctioned ("my jug was broke"), and he hopped a ride to his next stop in Washington, D.C., on a C-54.

The new chief of staff, Gen. Hoyt Vandenberg, was aboard. The door of opportunity burst open. James charged in. He had a chance to talk with the general.

"This," James remembers, "is when I got a deep insight of the man."

"What," General Vandenberg wanted to know, "do you think of the plans we have for integrating the services?"

There is no official record of what James actually replied. People have speculated that it's a pretty good bet he indicated that the ending of racism and segregation in the air force was the only way to fly. He may have expounded a bit on the theories of excellence his mother taught him, indicating that, in his view, excellence should be the determining factor for success in any career, even the United States Air Force. He may have mentioned his own edict for Operation Happiness: The show will not play to a segregated audience. He may have noted that it worked.

Whatever James said was listened to with great care by General Vandenberg. He was touched. So was Chappie: "We talked generally, and when we finished, he left, and I remember he walked off the plane and then came back to shake my hand. I will never forget that. Not just that gesture, but how really interested he was. There were other military leaders who obviously were not interested in the conversation at all—they couldn't have cared less."

It was a rare, soulful, conversation between a black first lieutenant and the chief of staff of the United States Air Force. It was one of those electric moments in which the already great and the about-to-be-great meet, and each persuades the other of a need to change the world.

For not many years before, General Vandenberg had come out against the concept of integration. His words were heeded, and used by subordinate commanders as a kind of unofficial air force doctrine. But this day, he was somehow changed. James was changed. So would the United States Air Force be changed within the contexts of R. Buckminster Fuller's "Technology and the Human Environment": "We are not going to be able to operate our spaceship Earth successfully nor for much longer unless we see it as a whole spaceship and our fate as common. It has to be everybody or nobody."[67]

Chapter Eighteen
Everybody

I

Daniel James, Jr., continued his role as the spark plug of "Operation Happiness" during 1947 and 1948. He made a name for himself as accomplished master of ceremonies, singer, and a supporter of civil rights, continuing to refuse separate performances of the show for blacks and whites in southern cities near air force bases.

With President Truman's 1948 Executive Order 9981, air force officers, such as Lt. Gen. Idwal H. Edwards, air force deputy chief of staff for personnel, looked critically at the ultimate effects of segregation. Establishing roadblocks for blacks, it denied them opportunities at higher levels in the air force. Most importantly, segregation was unwieldly and inefficient, leading to duplication in training and utilization of specialist personnel. Combat situations would produce unacceptable problems and turmoil. In the black units, replacement pipelines would be inadequate due to lack of qualified personnel.

Stuart Symington, secretary of the air force, was the primary agent in making the president's executive order real. A persuasive, focused person, he met with General Edwards and Eugene Zuckert, assistant air force secretary.

"I want this integration thing carried out as the President has ordered! He has ordered this to happen and it's going to happen because it is right and because the President said so!"

More than one protesting air force general stood aghast at the sudden policy shift.

"Stop [your] double-talk," Symington growled, "and act! If you don't agree with the policy, then you ought to resign now . . . we don't want to do it halfway. It [is] the right thing to do morally . . . legally . . . [and] right to do militarily.''

General Edwards expanded on the subject: "The Air Force has adopted a policy of integration under which Negro officers and airmen may be assigned to any duty in any Air Force unit or activity in accordance with the qualifications of the individual and needs of the service.''

"The needs," the general explained, "were efficiency, economy and effective manpower." Even General Vandenberg, it was noted, "was opposed to forcing [actions that would prove] debilitating and destructive to the organization as a whole.''

How much of General Vandenberg's new policies on racism were attributable to his chance meeting with Daniel James, Jr., will never be known. But a change had occurred, and, once General Vandenberg was ordered to integrate, and a plan to accomplish it had been drawn up, the action moved with alacrity. His orders were backed by the president with Lieutenant General Edwards leading the way.

While Colonel B. O. Davis's "Air Force" would be wiped out by the new scheme, the black pilots and airmen were on the brink of a new day in which their pride would no longer be tainted by their being labelled inferior, nor would they ever again be accused of being "protected" behind a shield of segregation.

But integration of black airmen into the mainstream air force was not universally accepted by all black officers at Lockbourne. They protested to the NAACP and anyone else who would listen. The dissenters were the officer underclass, "the little people, captains, first lieutenants and the first three graders" of the enlisted ranks. The integration game would affect them more than any other group, they thought. "If," they said, "the Air Force's real purpose is a democratic service, this plan won't succeed because it would ultimately eliminate . . . Negroes from the Air Force" and would do it such that "it will be a rousing success . . .''

They had seen the 12 February 1949 issue of the *Army-Navy Journal* claiming that the shift would result in the assigning of top-flight officers to commands. This, they thought, sounded good, but was totally unrealistic. They weren't "gullible enough to believe," they went on, "that a black squadron commander with the rank of Major . . . would be assigned [as] the Commander of a white fighter squadron. . . . That's pretty good, but we don't believe it and neither does the Air Force!''

By the time five years had passed, they projected, only forty or fifty black officers would still be in the air force. They based their point of view on the air force's miserable record of promoting qualified black officers. It was "an exercise in deceit," an attempt to "block an ungodly number of people out of hard-earned money.''

But there *was* a way out, they thought:

- Keep the 332nd Fighter Wing intact as a non-Negro unit, remembering that the Wing has many vacancies because of the high discharge rate,
- Assign white personnel to fill the vacancies. . . . This should *not* be construed to mean [that] Negro officers [would] hold staff positions throughout the base but would ensure their use in positions in which they were qualified . . . a better deal than [having] Negro officers scattered throughout the Air Force in small proportion,
- Assign personnel according to qualifications and performance of duties assigned, instead of the "Screening Board" machine which tends to hold cliques and gives way to eliminating qualified officer and enlisted personnel, not because of not being able to qualify, but because of personality conflicts and party politics . . . the greatest evil in the organization. . . .[68]

Perhaps these officers saw Colonel Davis and his "management team" of higher-ranking black officers as something of a clique. However, whatever the real driving force behind the mini-rebellion, it was too little and much too late. The air force received its directives and acted "with remarkable speed and resolution."

On 13 May 1949, Maj. Edward C. Gleed, Colonel Davis's second in command, and Maj. Thomas J. Money traveled to the Pentagon as representatives of the 332d. They were briefed on the guidelines of the new Air Force Letter (AFL) 35–3, directing implementation of an integrated air force.

The following day, two officers from Air Training Command (ATC) and a team of noncommissioned officers arrived at Lockbourne to give tests, establish a screening board, and interview all airmen on station. Led by Lt. Colonel Thomas M. Noonan, Continental Air Defense Command (ConAD), the Screening Board was to:

- Determine which officers and airmen were qualified for immediate assignment in their assigned Military Occupational Specialties (MOS),
- [Identify] officers and airmen requiring, or desiring additional training,
- [Identify] personnel to be retrained in the duty being performed at the time of screening.

At the same time, similar screening boards were being convened at air force installations across the United States as instructions were issued by local commanders.

The new secretary of defense, Louis A. Johnson, approved the equality of treatment and opportunity policy. Air Force Letter 35–3 was given the widest distribution.

All airmen on Lockbourne were administered a written, three-part examination, the net scores of which indicated fields in which they would perform best. After the tests were scored, and a personnel counselor interviewed the airmen, one of the predetermined recommendations was made regarding their futures in the air force.

Officer screening was another matter. As Maj. Thomas Money, the recorder of the redistribution board, remembers, "they had more information about the officers, [so] the total process required with the airmen wasn't necessary." And too, Colonel Davis, as president of the redistribution board, had a vested interest in the outcome. According to Alan Gropman in *The Air Force Integrates: 1945–1964,* Davis meant to nominate only his best pilots and those most likely to succeed. Quoting Gen. Idwal Edwards's approximation of Davis's intent, Gropman wrote: "He [Davis] intends to recommend Negroes for assignment to white units only in those cases where the individual is, first, of such temperament, judgment and common sense that he can get along smoothly as an individual in a white unit, and secondly, that his ability is such to warrant respect of personnel of the unit to which he is transferred."

The technical training of each officer was carefully considered, as were their present and past performance in duty assignments and their stated career preferences. Recommendations were made to Air Force headquarters, and these formed the basis for final assignments.

At one o'clock on 17 May, the officer interviews began and were completed by 23 May 1949. One hundred and sixty-eight were screened out of an assigned 242. The balance were due for release because of a reduction-in-force in progress, placed on detached service to other stations, or were army officers on duty with the air force.

Assignments were worldwide. Six traveled to Alaska. Thirty were assigned to the Far Eastern Air Forces (FEAF). One went to Okinawa, and twenty-two flew to the Old World, for duty with the United States Air Forces in Europe (USAFE). The remaining officers were scattered across the United States, most going to northern, central, or western states.

The officer underclass, disgruntled about the selection process, were correct in one assumption: *not one black officer was assigned to a position where he or she would have command of white troops.*

Neither that nor the selection process deterred Chappie James, however. It opened bright vistas for him to know that, at last, he would be a fighter pilot in an equal opportunity setting. Until now, he was seriously disillusioned, about to resign from the air force and go home to Florida. Integration was the opportunity he had yearned for—a chance to prove himself as a pilot and leader of men. For the moment, he alone saw himself doing these things. For most of his fellow officers, he was too closely identified with Operation Happiness. Maj. Thomas J. Money, USAF (Retired) remembers: "We all liked Chappie . . .

(he was) a very jolly fellow . . . in charge of the Operation Happiness entertainment group. We thought that he was quite a good entertainer, singer, dancer and what-not. I guess we never thought that Chappie had the leadership qualities then that he displayed at a later date . . .'' He would later see his proclivity towards the entertainment field as one more obstacle he had to overcome, but for now: "This was the chance I'd been waiting for, really, and I must admit I let my own personal desires for progress take great precedence in deciding what path I would follow.''

The air force completed integration of its forces within a year, at least three years before the army addressed the issue. For better or for worse, the air force was committed to integration, light years ahead of the American public.

II

Although Chappie James was elated that integration had finally come, he wore no rose-colored glasses. In his heart, he knew that the vestiges of racism would not disappear overnight. In spite of that, the immediate goal beckoned— "get with an integrated outfit and prove that [he] was one of the best fighter pilots around!''

In September 1949, he went to Clark Field and the 12th Fighter-Bomber Squadron, 18th Fighter Wing, in the Philippines. Sixty-five miles north of Manila, its tropical, lush greenery seemed deceptively peaceful. The *Hukbong Magpapalayang Bayan,* communist rebels, called ''Huks,'' were in full rebellion, attempting to force the government to break up large estates and give the land to poor farmers. Gunfire pierced the nights near Clark Field, sometimes overwhelming the sound of aircraft engines and causing occasional American casualties when airmen mistakenly wandered into forbidden areas.

By late January 1950, Dorothy and the children were on their way to the Philippines by ship. On the base, Chappie bragged a lot to his buddies about his pretty wife. So insistent and proud had he been that a delegation was there to greet the family when they arrived on a February day. Dorothy had been seasick throughout the voyage. Danice suffered the effects of seasickness, too. Only Spike weathered the trip with no side effects. It probably wasn't funny at the time, but Chappie later fondly recalled the sight of his ''pretty wife'' when she came down the gangplank.

"You never saw,'' he chuckled, ''such a bedraggled creature as my 'pretty wife' in all your born days!''

It was Friday when the family arrived in Manila, riding a bus to Clark Field. Danice, Chappie's little daughter, sat on his lap watching the tropical greenery flash past as the bus wended its tortuous way. Wonderment welled in young eyes at the destruction evident from the bus windows.

"Daddy, why are the bridges broken?"

"Those are from explosives," Chappie explained in his fatherly way, "it was part of the war."

And that was not all. There were shell holes and bomb craters all over.

They settled into comfortable officers' quarters, laid out in circles. The living on Clark Air Base was easy; the surroundings, lush. For the first time in any of their lives, they found themselves living in pure luxury, even to having servants in and around their quarters. There was a little Filipino girl to look after the house. Her younger brother became the "yard boy"—looking after the grounds. Tropical greenery surrounded them in an exotic cacophony of color; wild orchids, fuschia, and hibiscus hedges. Orange and banana trees abounded.

The white officers and their wives knew the Jameses were coming, but nobody baked them a cake. The presence of black fighter pilots made adrenalin flow, especially among southern families.

Said one wife: "I'll be damned if I will ever have a nigger in my house!"

But Chappie James would begin to change that. The beer was free at the officers' club Friday nights. Why not begin there? He went down alone. It was a strange amalgam: "I will never forget," Chappie remembers, "the first night I walked into the officers' club . . . everything stopped with the music. The band got quiet . . ." Whispered conversation filled the air. Heads turned in concert to stare, as one officer, another wife, turned to nudge others in a parody on *Guess Who's Coming to Dinner?* Nobody spoke to Chappie or even approached him. After awhile, the small combo recovered and started to play again. As far as Chappie was concerned, that was the best thing happening as he nodded his head to the beat. At the end of the piece, the saxophonist jumped off the platform and came over to Chappie.

"Hey, Mop!" he began in the "hep" language of the day, "My name's Taylor, what's yours?"

"I'm Dan James."

"Do you blow, man?"

"No, but I'm a mighty good listener!"

The saxophone player's name was Spud Taylor. A first lieutenant like Chappie, the two took an instant liking to each other.

"Call me Spud!"

"Okay!"

"Try to get the Twelfth," he confided, "that's my outfit!"

A new friend who loved music, fronting an entire band! A new arrival in the person of Chappie James, master of ceremonies, song and dance! It was "another way to realize my goal of [competing] on an equal basis, [for] if they were going to hinder me with racism I was going to overcome through the power of excellence . . . my Mother taught me long ago!''

Chappie didn't drag his feet. Determined to be the best, he ranked second in bombing accuracy, giving the best performance average in rocketry (five fired, five hits). He became one of the better top ground-gunners in the group. It became chancy to bet against him when competing for most hits. In sports, he was a basketball star, sinking thirty points in his first game; he was first baseman on the softball team and an effusive builder of team spirit. Go by the tennis courts, and he was there. Plan a round of golf, and the odds were he'd be there. From time to time, one could see Chappie's run-down jeep whizzing through the housing area, loaded with his fellow officers' children—just giving them a lift. Go to the officers' club, and he was onstage smiling, singing with his new friend's band, cementing the friendship, and delighting his squadron mates. In point of fact, Spud Taylor and he were ''almost like brothers.'' James R. McGovern, in his book, *Black Eagle: General Daniel ''Chappie'' James, Jr.*, quotes Col. Frank Buzze, a member of Chappie's squadron: ''After a month or so it would have taken an incredible bigot to dislike Chappie James.''

Chappie's zeal did not go unnoticed or unrewarded. Col. Harry Moreland, squadron operations officer, recognizing talent and excellence when he saw it, made Chappie a flight leader. Through the excellence his mother drilled into him, Chappie thus began eroding the taboo against assignment of black officers to command white airmen.

It was obvious that he wanted to be simply one of the boys. To a certain extent, he became that, with more than a modicum of respect thrown in. But as he suspected when he first received his new assignment, the vestiges of racism didn't easily fall away.

Racism's pall descended on his family. Danice, his kindergarten-aged daughter, found herself constantly beleaguered by white school children at the bus stops on the corner near their quarters.

''You're a stupid!'' spat the children.

''What's a stupid?''

''You're the stupid————, my Mommy said so!''

They'd walk to the other side of the street, leaving her isolated and hurt. She'd follow. They'd recross the street. Spud Taylor's wife Hazelle, watched the scenario from her house, went to the corner, and confronted the offending children.

''Every time she crosses over, you run back. Why do you do that to her?''

''Well, uh, er, she's got a lunchbox and we don't have one,'' explained the obvious leader of the pack after some deliberation.

''I don't think that's the reason. I gave her the lunch box and I will give you all one. Then will you—?''

''No, we are not going to stand with her because she is a nigger!''

"Now who told you that?"

"My daddy and mommy did, they told me that she is a nigger."

Spud Taylor heard about it, went over, and had a little talk with the daddies and mommies. Things got better for Danice. At school, the teachers were extremely nice and understanding. It was the kind of thing Spud Taylor did constantly for Chappie James, running interference among the racists for his newfound friend. Later, Chappie would discover the extent of Spud's interventions in his behalf.

At home, Chappie assuaged his daughter's hurt. By now, it was an old routine Danice would never forget. Holding her on his knee, bouncing her up and down to the rhythm of the song he'd sing to her:

> Oh, I wanta be—
> A friend of yours!
> [they'd each point to the other]
> Oh, just a little bit more . . .
> I wanta be your honey bun
> Cloudy or sunny . . .
> Just a little bit more!

And there were the air force parades to help her forget. Watching Chappie march by, his polished shoes glistening in the Philippine sun. Waiting, for the most delicious part of all there in the crowd after the parade, when Chappie would find his family, amble over, and pick her up. "So much warmth, and so safe!"

It was part of a lesson Chappie taught his children. Never be a browbeater. Don't linger on hardship. Never stop and take issue with anybody along the way who wanted to steer things in the wrong direction. If there's something to get done, go ahead and do it. He passed his mother's teachings along to his own children. Chappie never forgot and neither would they.

Near tragedy of a different kind struck Chappie James. Just after taking off in a two-seater T-33 in the spring of 1950, he and his fellow pilot flamed out when only fifty feet off the runway. Restart was impossible. They pancaked, sliding to a sickening stop in a nearby rice paddy. Time was critical; jet fuel could blow any second. Chappie couldn't open the canopy; the controls were up front with the unconscious pilot. It was Chappie's size and build that saved them. He reared like a bull against the plexiglass canopy, loosening the pins and flinging it away in the nick of time. Flames seared the aircraft's skin as Chappie jumped out of the plane, pulling the over two-hundred-pound pilot out, dragging him to safety as the plane burned furiously.

It was no small feat. No single man, the air force thought, could bend the

locking devices holding such a canopy. Chappie was burned severely and frac-
tured a vertebrae in his back. He was placed in the hospital for several weeks.
Early on, Spud Taylor came to visit. The visit was ill-timed as far as the
medical staff were concerned. Spud was fierce as the nurse on duty blocked
his way.

"You can't go in there! He's in shock!"

"Little girl, you can't stop me," growled Spud, pushing his way past her.
Providentially, Chappie awakened. Spud stood there for a moment, staring at
his friend. A smile crossed his face.

"Man, I saw you! Just trying to be spectacular!" The two old friends chuckled.

Chappie had profited from his experience on Alcaniz Street. In the wreck
of the plane, he fought fear through meaningful action as he had done when
bullies threatened to beat him and steal the fifteen cents his mother had given
him to buy a loaf of bread.

They awarded him the Distinguished Service Medal for valor.

Recuperating at home, he lay flat on the floor from time to time, easing
the back pain. Danice would watch and wonder why he did such a thing.

War loomed in Asia as the North Koreans invaded South Korea on 25 June
1950, driving United Nations forces into a perimeter around Pusan, confronting
them with ninety thousand soldiers of the North Korean People's Army. America
was committed. So was the 18th Fighter-Bomber Wing and Chappie's 12th
Fighter-Bomber Squadron. At a briefing, the pilots were given the news. They
were needed to provide tactical support for United Nations ground forces in
Korea.

The squadron left Chappie behind as his injuries healed. In August 1950,
he joined them, while Dorothy and the children returned to the United States.
It was to be a dirty, mean little war, calling up, as war does, every fiber of
individual dedication and courage. The 12th Fighter-Bomber Squadron flung
itself into the fray. Some were to die. And this time, everybody went to fight.

III

When North Korea began the invasion of South Korea, America was unpre-
pared for total conventional warfare. It was a time of reduced air force funding.
American strategic thinking centered on the possession of nuclear-strike capabilities countering the Soviet atomic threat.

It was an air force shrunk from two hundred combat wings at the end of
World War II to only forty-three. Combat-tested fighter squadrons had been

disbanded, their airplanes junked, deteriorating in huge military storage parks. During the four months after September 1945, over one million airmen were discharged. Reserves were released from active duty. Even Lt. Gen. Ira C. Eaker, former commander of Eighth Air Force, admitted that not one operational group existed that was ready to defend the United States.

Evaluation of the North Korean threat showed that it could be countered by air-to-ground combat. In the Far East, conversion to fighter-jet aircraft had just begun. Considering the extent of the threat, the air force switched its strategy. Chappie James, Jr. recalled, "we switched [to the] P-51 [Mustang] . . . it was more adaptable to flying fields and conditions under which we fought."

The war began for Chappie in hot August at a field called K-2, at Taegu. Spud Taylor was there; so was a softball team member from Chappie's months in the Philippines, Howard C. Johnson. And there was old Ted Baader, dubbed "Mother" (because he delighted in looking out for the rest of them). It was natural for Chappie and Spud to fly each other's wing, so close was their friendship. But it didn't end there. Taylor and Johnson asked the squadron commander to assign Chappie to their flight. With Baader in tow, they became known as the "ferocious four," flying determined, close-support fighter sweeps. They alternated the role of flight leader among them and repaired to the Pusdan Hospital club at week's end to swizzle beer.

Many of Chappie's youthful dreams came true. More than just a pilot, he became a fighter pilot living on the edge in real combat where danger was ever-present. He became what he later delighted in calling himself: *a warrior,*[69] experienced in combat, symbolized by a black panther insignia on his flight helmet. *He* was the "first black panther," he later asserted in an aside directed to the Black Panthers of a coming era, [and] "the difference is, this Black Panther fights *for* his country!"

The advancing North Koreans threatened forward airfields, making it necessary to move the P-51 squadrons temporarily to Japan. By September, they were back at a base code-named K-9, alternately moving to K-34 at Pyonyang, K-13 at Suwon Air Base, to K-10, Chinae Air Base, back to K-34, and again to K-13 as the battle hopped around the Korean landscape.

Chappie's combat life moved at an unrelenting pace. With the actual battle-fields only fifteen minutes away at times, he flew five to eight missions a day, delivering the Mustang's ordnance of bullets, rockets, bombs, and napalm in devastating, low-level close support sorties and interdiction raids. Strafing at tree-top level, the "furious four" helped break up North Korean attacks before they began, destroying trains, the vaunted Russian T-34 tanks, and enemy supply lines.

During September 1950, General MacArthur unleashed his brilliant Inchon end run while the Eighth Army broke out of the Pusan Perimeter. As the Eighth Army advanced, 12th Fighter casualties mounted. By October 1950, four pilots of twenty-six assigned were listed as missing in action. More casualties were to come. If these losses bothered Chappie James, it didn't show. On 15 October 1950, he sat in the catbird's seat as flight leader, his call sign becoming "Black Leader"; his flight, "Black Flight." It was a mission in close support of ground forces near Namchonjom, Korea. Black Leader and his flight of four executed the attack a few yards in front of friendly troops. Directed by friendly artillery-spotter shells, Chappie called the strike, rolling in on enemy positions in a series of devastating attacks with napalm, rockets, and machine-gun fire through dense haze, smoke, and barrages of antiaircraft and automatic weapons fire. Again and again he called the strike until all ammunition was expended. The record reflects that Chappie himself accounted for over one hundred North Korean dead. It was a distinguished display of airmanship, and the Distinguished Flying Cross joined Chappie's other medals.

Chappie was promoted to captain on 31 October 1950, but was one of the last to hear about it. He was on a rest-and-recreation trip to Tokyo. CMSgt. James H. Edmondson of Sacramento, California, ran into Chappie on a Japanese train. He and his friends had seen the announcement of Chappie's promotion in the *Air Force Times,* and were immensely proud.

"Hello, *Captain!"* they chimed.

"Waddya mean, *Captain?* Hell, I'm the oldest first lieutenant sporting wings you've ever seen!"

They showed him the *Air Force Times* announcement. He beamed.

"Captain James! Well, whaddya think about *that?* Well, we'd better have a little nip on that!" he laughed, reaching into his little go-to-hell bag, pulling out a small bottle of booze.

"We *all* had a little drink!" Edmonson recalls.

*   *   *

It was early November, and cold snow had come, turning the rough concrete of the runways into icy hazard. On 1 November after a build-up across the Yalu River, the Chinese intervened in the war, slamming into North Korea with a quarter of a million troops. Combat flying became harder, with enemy troops hiding themselves and their equipment in ravines, draws, and under bridges along major routes. And now, with the Chinese, came the communist MiGs, flying high, diving out of the sun, making a pass at American fighters, then climbing away into the sun. The Eighth Army was in disarray, retreating and fighting a series of holding actions as they went. Mission priorities shifted.

It was maximum effort, close air support of ground elements now under heavy attack.

The "ferocious four" were there, Spud Taylor flying leader, as they covered an American parachute drop to effect the release of American prisoners. Antiaircraft fire downed Spud a good ten miles behind enemy lines. Chappie became leader and immediately put an "aircap"* over the spot Spud crashed, covering him with their machine guns. They could see that he was out of the airplane, crawling into a ravine, his leg apparently broken. Chappie radioed for a helicopter. There were none, for all were on alert to protect General MacArthur's latest tour of the battlefield. Frustrated, Chappie flew to the helicopter base, leaving the remaining P-51s to continue the aircap.

Fighter pilots say that the feeling of seeing your buddy blown out of the sky is indescribable. While flying to the helicopter base, Chappie must have felt it. But the trip was to no avail. The army found Spud the next day, his body raked with bullets.

Chappie had nightmares for a long time, going into deep depression over the loss of his closest friend. The strain of combat began to show, bringing him close to breakdown, not unlike the death of his snow-white dog, Honey Rags, back in Pensacola when he was a teenager. One night not long after, in the little tent officers' club down on the line, pilots sat around commiserating about Spud's death, about what a shame it was. Chappie was relatively silent. His "power of excellence" had taken him far, but this he could do nothing about. It was beyond his reach. Perhaps he wondered what he would say to Spud's wife when next he saw her, and if he did, he knew it would never be enough. Spud was dead, and words would never bring him back. He turned in his chair and slowly began to sing "My Buddy":

> . . . Nights are long
> Since you went away . . .
> I think about you
> all through the day . . .
> My Buddy . . .

They say he sang the whole song, then got up and walked out. Maj. Charles Hauver of Poughkeepsie, New York, recalls the aftermath of the story as he heard it: "The club was very still . . . it was like a parting gesture for a comrade . . . a beautiful remembrance . . . it chokes me up every time I think about it."

* Air cap: combat air patrol in air over downed pilot.

IV

Concerned that Chappie's depression might adversely affect his flying ability, his commander gave him authorization for rest and recreation in Japan. Returning, he flew a stint as a spotter in the little, vulnerable T-6 over the winter Korean landscape of grey snow and mud. His name was drawn to serve as a forward air controller (FAC). Going up on the line, he spent thirty days with the ground troops, calling in air force strikes to support them in battle. It was hazardous, hard duty. Their jeep was chock full of communications gear, its whip antenna undulating in the winter air, sitting high atop frozen hills to increase radio transmission range. The very sight of the jeep parked in the open was a gift to the North Korean troops. As Chappie remembered: "Got about three jeeps shot from under me. Mostly mortar fire. They could stick a mortar shell in your back pocket. And they would just search for that antenna, and when they saw it, they'd start shooting . . . shelling . . . trying to knock it out . . ."

Chappie and his FAC team would take the communications lines and go down into a ravine to call in the air strikes, thus avoiding instant death from mortar fire riding the Korean hills. It was freezing cold, and, on more than one occasion, he kept up his own and others' morale by singing spirituals down at the bottom of the icy ravines. Many grizzled Korean veterans remembered Chappie's stentorian, booming renditions of "Ol' Man River" rising from the frigid ravines and foxholes while mortar shells and bombs burst all around.

Later, assigned to jets, Chappie performed unarmed reconnaissance over North Korea. During this period he ran into minor difficulty with the base commander at Taegu as he taxied an F-80 into a revetment area. Turning the jet around, the engine poofed great clouds of dust into the commander's face. Remembered as "one of the terrified Turks of Taegu" (from his panic-stricken behavior when the North Koreans got too close), he became very upset. Growling, he stormed over to Chappie's airplane where he still sat in the cockpit.

"You do that again, I'll kick the [stuffing] out of you!" he screamed.

Chappie regarded him for a moment, then answered very deliberately.

"I'll go along with everything you say, sir, except the last!"

And then, "Chappie unfolded out of the cockpit to his whole six-feet-four, two hundred thirty pounds—and *that* diminished the threat right there!"

Luck almost ran out a few weeks later. Flying close air support, he'd lined up for a high-speed pass against gun emplacements, as he'd done myriads of times. That vertical dive at more than seven hundred miles an hour, then climbing quickly to forty-three thousand feet was a "milk run" he used to say. But this time, the North Korean gunners got him. "When the big stuff hits you it's like being slugged, and you can no longer hold onto your mount or [get it] to do your bidding.''[70] And so, at seven thousand feet, no longer able to control the jet, he punched out, parachuting down behind enemy lines. It was his lucky day, and he would later delight in telling the outcome of the war story: "Damned if a Marine tank crew didn't pick me up and rescue me!"

He was back at base before dusk, got another airplane and went on yet another mission. And perhaps, later in the dark, Korean night in the tent-covered officers' club where the beer foamed and flowed, they sang an old fighter pilot song in celebration.

By the end of December 1950, Chappie completed his 100 combat missions. Korea and first combat were over. They sent him back to Clark Air Base in the Philippines, where he helped train pilots on their way to the war and deliver some of the first jet fighters to the Chinese on Formosa. And through it all, his faithful Dottie wrote to him every day. They were newsy, loving letters. He remembered them later, long after the Korean furor had passed: "Unless you've been out there, you can't realize how much it means to have a wife like her behind you . . . her letters were the one thing that helped me when Spud was killed."

He had achieved his ultimate goal, becoming "one of the better fighter pilots around," acquitting himself admirably in a slashing air war. Perhaps there were those who still had reservations about him because of the color of his skin. For these, the message born of the mayhem of Korea was: "Over a few beers, I've even had white guys say they like me, but you can keep all those others. . . . They respect me. They've seen me roll in on that target when the flak was heavy, just like they did, and come scooting out the other side. They respect me."[71] And *that* acquisition was perhaps the grandest of all.[72]

General James's mother, Lillie Anna James, and great-granddaughter Mildred Cecilia Hunter. (Courtesy of Gloria Hunter.)

Officers' mess, Godman Field, Kentucky. (Courtesy of Harold Beaulieu.)

Maj. Gen. Frank O'Driscoll Hunter and Col. Robert Selway. (U.S. Air Force photograph—Office of Air Force History.)

Lt. Daniel James, Jr., and visiting entertainers at Godman Field. (Courtesy of Harold Beaulieu.)

477th Bombardment Group (M) on parade. (Courtesy of Harold Beaulieu.)

Col. Benjamin O. Davis, Jr., in summer uniform. (Courtesy of Harold Beaulieu.)

Lt. Daniel "Chappie" James, Jr., as master of ceremonies for the variety show, Operation Happiness. (Courtesy of Harold Beaulieu.)

Colonel James and his "guy in back," 1st Lt. Bob C. Evans, preparing for combat takeoff. (Official U.S. Air Force photograph.)

Celebrating the end of a successful mission. Cols. Robin Olds and Chappie
James at Ubon Royal Air Base, Thailand. (Courtesy of Tuskegee University archives.)

General James at work aboard an executive aircraft. (Courtesy of Tuskegee University archives.)

Receiving a gift from a Pensacola friend. (Courtesy of Hank Basham.)

General and Mrs. James being presented by Pensacola friends. (Courtesy of Hank Basham.)

First star. Dorothy James looks proudly on. (Courtesy of Dorothy James.)

Visiting with M. Sgt. James J. Griffis, Outstanding Noncommissioned Officer of the Year, at the Air Force Academy awards banquet. (Courtesy of the Air Force Academy.)

Second star. Major General James is pinned with his new rank by his son Daniel III and his wife, Dorothy, as Secretary of Defense Melvin R. Laird assists. (Official Department of Defense photograph.)

Third star. Lieutenant General James is congratulated by Secretary of Defense James R. Schlesinger. (Official Department of Defense photograph.)

The James family. From left: Frank Berry, Jr.; daughter Danice; sons Spud and Daniel, the latter holding granddaughter Jamie; Chappie holding grandson Frank W. Berry III. (Courtesy of Dorothy James.)

Proud father with sons Daniel James III (left) and Spud. (Courtesy of Dorothy W. James.)

Singing along with Sammy Davis, Jr. Concert at the Air Force Academy field house. (Courtesy Roy J. C. Johnson.)

General James retires. Gen. David C. Jones looks on in the background. (Official U.S. Air Force photograph by M. Sgt. Yuen-Gi Yea.)

Mass of the Resurrection for General James at the Shrine of the Immaculate Conception, Washington, D.C. (Courtesy of the *Washington Post*.)

Honor guard stands by as pallbearers carry General James's casket. (Official U.S. Air Force photograph.)

President Reagan and Dr. Benjamin F. Payton, president of Tuskegee University, undrape building marker at the dedication of the General Chappie James Aerospace Center. (Courtesy of Tuskegee University archives.)

Dr. Payton dedicates the permanent exhibit of the last F-4C Phantom jet flown by General James in Southeast Asia. (Photograph by Frank Lee. Courtesy of Tuskegee University archives.)

Henry P. Bowman, national president of the Tuskegee Airmen, makes presentation to Tuskegee University president Payton. (Frank Lee photograph, courtesy of Tuskegee University archives.)

President Reagan receives plaudits of the commencement crowd prior to departure. (Courtesy of Tuskegee University archives.)

Alcaniz Street monument to Chappie James in Pensacola, Florida. (Photograph by the author.)

Chapter Nineteen
Seasoning

I

Over seventy and crippled by arthritis, Arthur James (unrelated), an old first sergeant who used to look after then-2d Lt. Daniel James, Jr., back in those days, talked about how his men regarded Chappie: "When we enlisted guys used to get together, we'd always say that if Chappie ever gets a chance to be a high-ranking officer, he'll be one of the best. He was never the kind of officer who looked down on you. He looked straight at you and he always listened to what you had to say. And he expected you to look straight back."

It was 1951, and the prophecy was no fluke. James was to wear the silver oak leaves of a lieutenant colonel within five years, the exact length of time he had remained a lieutenant in the segregated air force. The door of opportunity not only opened, but remained ajar. "The ending of segregation, and war," James remembered, was "fortunate for me as an aspiring young officer, because it gave me a chance to practice my skills under the toughest of conditions . . . to the ultimate."

As a young American black of his era, James was lucky to have a mother like Lillie Anna James guiding his early life. An astute educator, Mrs. James was undoubtedly aware that young, black men like her son had but three primary ways of reacting to the oppression they faced as adults. They could move towards the greater society, against it, or away from it. Movement against society intensified societal oppression. Moving away from it caused hopelessness and paranoia. The trick was to *move towards* society and help to integrate it.

The air force now provided an integrated society although it was far from perfect so soon after desegregation.

Almost immediately, Chappie faced employment discrimination, operating to keep him away from the job for which he had been trained. Assigned to the 27th Fighter-Interceptor Squadron at Griffiss Air Force Base, New York, in May 1951, as a jet fighter pilot flying the F-86, he encountered a movement to remove him from the unit because of his race:

> . . . I could never prove it was because they wanted to keep it all white. That was the word I got from the guys who were there. [The] Operations Officer, when he saw that I was black, is supposed to have said: "We'll find some way to get rid of this guy!" So he very cleverly had me . . . go to all-weather school down in Florida, which qualified me for a different airplane than they had. It turned out to be a blessing in disguise . . .

Although the 27th Fighter operations officer attained his goal of bouncing James out of squadron, the act was indeed providential. The gods smiled on James again as the squadron drew duty in Iceland. An American-Icelandic agreement existed forbidding assignment of blacks to that country. Returning from all-weather school, James's assignment took him to the 58th Fighter-Interceptor Squadron at Otis Air Force Base, Massachusetts, where he became a flight leader and finally, an operations officer. His fortunes changed dramatically: "My career really took off because I ran into guys who really didn't care what color you were."

He began to attract attention and move out from the crowd because he "got to be known as a helluva combat fighter pilot—his speciality." People like Maj. Curtis N. "Rusty" Metcalf, 58th Fighter commander, Col. Grover Wilcox and Oliver G. Cellini were impressed with this tall, black officer. According to *Ebony Magazine,* James was regarded by Colonel Cellini, the 4707th Wing commander at Otis, as something of a protege, and he saw great potential in James as a flier and commander. By 1952, the gold oak leaves of a major graced James's epaulets and, in April 1953, he became the first black air force officer commanding an integrated fighter squadron in the continental United States. Of 400 men assigned to the 437th Fighter-Interceptor Squadron, only Chappie and Lt. Ernest Carigwell were black. Chappie became the darling of the media, always neat, hair closely cropped and moustache faultless. *Color* magazine wanted pictures of him with his men. He let the country know what he considered the basis of his success: "The most important person in my squadron is the lowest-ranking airman, because if they're unhappy, then they will not perform and you will not have a squadron. . . . My door is always open. You don't have to go through the chain of command to see me. . . . [Come and say] . . . 'Sir, I have a problem!' "

Chappie blossomed, becoming a booming-voiced giant of a man, standing six foot, four inches, weighing close to 250 pounds—the biggest jet fighter pilot in the world! His new job matched his size, for the 437th Fighter was an important link in defense of America's air space, protecting the billions invested in industry throughout the New York-New England area and the millions of people living there.

It was time to get the family up from Tuskegee. He had established himself and was making a viable contribution to the air force mission when discrimination again raised its ugly head. A Massachusetts landlord on Cape Cod refused to rent him a home for his family. It took firm self-control to deal with the turn-down. Said he later: "That's a very sore spot—a very sore spot!" But he contained his anger (with great effort, it seems), found another house, and overcame the racial obstacle through "sheer personal effort."

Then-Lt. Charles Hauver, assigned to an adjacent squadron, remembers Chappie at this time: "I didn't know Chappie personally then. I was just a little lieutenant in another squadron . . . just an R/O [radar observer] in the back seat. I used to see this big, black man over there running things. I was impressed." He was everywhere. With his engineering crews, listening to their status reports. Chatting with his alert pilots in the billets where they ate and slept. Meeting with the full squadron of four hundred at least once each week. "Skipper," they called him. He always cared, always seemed relaxed and confident. In return, they rewarded him with outstanding performance. Fastest turnaround in an annual air defense exercise of all squadrons on the eastern seaboard; winning over all neighboring squadrons in rocketry. Venereal disease rates were down, absence without leave (AWOL), practically nil.

Said Colonel Cellini, the wing commander: "[Chappie is] our outstanding pilot, a born leader and a *good guy*. Discipline and efficiency are high in his squadron, maybe because he never expects his boys to do anything he can't do himself—and *better!*"

A third child was born to the Jameses here at Otis. Another son, the child was named "Spud," after Chappie's good friend, Spud Taylor. Spike was already eight years old. For the first time, Chappie was there all during the pregnancy.

"It was wonderful," Dorothy remembers, "I'd had the other two alone, but this time, Dan was there all the time, worrying and fussing over me."

He was something of a pest at the hospital when the time came. Nervous. Fidgety. Pacing. Pushy. Injecting himself into the procedure.

"Now," a frustrated doctor finally boomed, "I don't tell *you* how to fly planes! And don't *you* tell *me* how to deliver babies!"

Dorothy wanted a girl; Chappie wanted another boy. And he was not beyond a bit of bribery, as if Dottie could control it.

"Get me a boy, honey," he cooed, "and I'll buy you a mink!"

Whether Dorothy ever got the mink is not documented, but she did deliver another boy. He brought her yellow roses and a note that said: "You're the greatest!"

But moving toward the greater society when traveling on leave with his family across the wide American landscape in the early 1950s was another matter. Out there, not many had begun to "understand each other as complete human beings," especially when the other person's skin was black. Not many could understand the need to tear down the "constraints of segregated role relationships." It was an artificial barrier, but a very real problem when the James family was forced to drive long and protracted distances because there were no public accommodations for blacks.

Driving nonstop to Montgomery, visiting a favorite aunt in Columbia, South Carolina, and then returning home to Pensacola, Chappie had a way of making the miles fly by. He'd regale Dottie and the children with tales of his days at Tuskegee and his old football friends: "Meatball" Stewart, "Red Hot" Moore, Uncle "Red," the quarterback from Louisiana, who played both center and tackle; and "Fat Albert," the center. These old heroes became like a second family to the James children.

There were poignant moments, too. Like the time they'd stopped in a small southern town near a wide playground on which a solitary black child played. The child's solitude and absence of adult supervision bothered Chappie's young daughter, Danice.

"Mommy?"

"Yes?"

"Can't we adopt her? She doesn't have a Mommy or a Daddy like us!"

Exchanging glances, Dottie and Chappie were very quiet for a moment.

"Danice," Dottie began, "even though you don't see her Mommy and Daddy, she has one, I'm sure. She may be just working, you know. How would you feel, if someone just—*adopted* you without checking? She has a Mommy and Daddy, I'm sure!"

Although Dorothy usually left "air force business" to her husband, sometimes she'd wonder about his inner motivations. She knew he loved football and golf, that he liked to be out in the fresh, open air. But there was the flying thing, the fighter pilot in him. One private moment, she asked about flying.

"How does it feel?"

"It's wonderful! It's a feeling I can't describe. It's so wonderful, you feel like—you're close to God!"

And maybe that's why, back at Otis, he loved to fire up the F-94C he'd dubbed "Chappie's Chariot," to fly off into the wild blue yonder, often dropping in on his old hometown pals down in Pensacola. He'd let them know he was in town with the same mischievous flair he used when he had been an instructor pilot at Tuskegee Institute, threatening to land his plane atop the library building. But now, there was a new, huge, bellicose, whining jet-engined sound, putting the folks around Belmont and DeVillers streets on notice that Chappie was back.

The low-flying jet fighter shook the timbers of the frame houses, and set their windows rattling while everyone looked up, eardrums vibrating, at this marvel of human technology. Chappie's hometown friends knew the sign. He needed a ride home from Sherman Field.

Old friends, the late Maurice Lucky and Richard Morris, would jump into one of Lucky's laundry trucks or Morris's hearses and rush out to the field to get him. Down Barrancas Avenue or Pace Boulevard they'd go whizzing, driving across the drawbridge guarding Bayou Chico hard by Sanders Beach. Sailing down Barrancas, past what was old Fort Barrancas, now the Pensacola Country Club where Chappie was to sometimes play golf, and where, once upon a sunlit, Florida day, they thought he was a groundskeeper instead of a patron. On down Navy Boulevard perhaps, or Gulf Beach Highway to find Chappie beaming there at Forest Sherman Field.

Once settled, Chappie, Lucky, and Maurice would be off on the town. For a moment in time, the old friends would be together again, "partners in crime," as niece Gloria Hunter remembers. Deonice Lucky, Maurice's wife, recalls her husband's rhetoric at such times: "*He* said he was going fishing. . . . I don't know *where* they'd go!"

One place Deonice did know they went was to old J. P. Newton's Sugar Bowl down on Belmont Street, where the local "happenings" were for black folks. Had it existed during the years of prohibition, it would have been called a speakeasy. Instead, J. P. Newton, black, handsome, mustachioed entrepreneur, dubbed it the Sugar Bowl, later adding a disco called the Bunny Club.

One entered the place either through the Bunny Club off DeVillers Street or through the Sugar Bowl on Belmont Street. The Sugar Bowl, primarily one long bar, extended the length of a long room, with high-backed, side-armed, fancy barstools positioned so closely patrons got that "canned sardine" feeling of absolute togetherness. Behind the bar, liquor bottles winked seductively. Jukebox music seared the smoke-filled room. Barflies and waitresses constantly plunked coins into the nickelodeons spaced along the bar. Facing the customers, these machines looked like electronic rodents with wide teeth, on which were printed titles of popular black music of the day.

It is a place created by J. P. Newton to make money and serve as a platform for his personal edicts. For "J. P." has a conscience of sorts. It is as if somewhere in his heart of hearts, he feels for the customers who while away hours there, dancing to exhaustion, perhaps, or maybe taking a blithesome, dusky filly off to bed. "J. P." is concerned about his patrons, and admonishes them with prominently displayed signs announcing his "Newtonian" philosophies of life. Somehow, his patrons appear heedless of his exhortations.

"No Loitering," proclaims a sign outside the building, but the customers loiter anyway: on the hoods of cars, against the cars, and on the street. On the building outside near the corner, a large sign pontificates:

A Message to Young Brothers and
Sisters. STOP using violence.
REGISTER to VOTE. That's your legal weapon!
—J. P. Newton

And just inside the front door, another sign entreats, *"Respect Yourself. If You Are Caught Fighting, Using or Selling or Even With Drugs, that will be Your Last Night in the Club." Signed J. P. Newton, Owner/Manager.* Just over the door, another sign instructs: *"Don't Stand in the Doorway."* Behind the bar, facing the customers at the bar, a sign yells:

NO SLEEPING ON THE BAR OR IN
THE CLUB!
—The Management

Gentle signs remind that the Bunny Club and the Sugar Bowl exist to make a profit, for both the owner and the government. *"Sales Tax Included in Our Prices,"* whispers a sign by the cash register.

In 1988, the signs still existed, but there is a strange melancholy about the Sugar Bowl. It seems a throwback to another decade, when black hopes somehow shone brighter and seemed more urgent. The composition of the crowd seems changed from the glory days of Chappie, Maurice, and Lucky. An assemblage of ghosts seem to sit on the fancy barstools.

For Chappie, it was a place to reconfirm blackness with black friends from the hometown. To laugh, spin tall tales, relax, have a nip, and let down the hair. Sometimes, far into the night, Gloria Hunter would get a call from Chappie, looking for a place to bed down for what remained of an evening. (They jokingly called her "Holy Glo," because "you can't do *nothin'* 'round 'Holy Glo!' ") All this, of course, would not interfere with a visit to see his Mother and her school. He'd stop by the school in uniform and thrill the youngsters with good talk and sage advice. He'd thrill his mother, too. Gloria remembers: "It was one of the few times I ever saw her quiet. She was *so* proud! She'd just sit and listen."

Then the fun and frolic would be over and it was back to his newly integrated world at Otis. Always a showman, his takeoff would be something to see, especially if he had landed at Maxwell Air Force Base in Montgomery on an official trip. "He'd take off," "Chief" Alfred Anderson recalls, and "then you'd see him go straight up and up, through a hole in the clouds and we'd watch until we couldn't see him anymore!"

II

Chappie's public-speaking abilities surfaced at Otis. With the arrival of the new F-94C and its loud afterburner, it fell to him to address the people of Falmouth, Massachusetts, explain the aircraft's characteristics and why it made the noise it did, and assuage their alarm. He spoke so well that invitations as guest speaker poured in from Lion's Clubs, schools, even the Massachusetts Institute of Technology (MIT). And whenever he spoke, he'd always sing a favorite spiritual—"Joshua Fit the Battle of Jerico."

In 1954, the Massachusetts Junior Chamber of Commerce awarded him its Young Man of the Year award. Pleased at the positive responses to his speaking ability, he'd crow a bit to Dorothy when he came home:

"Oh, they liked my speech!"

Dorothy would smile knowingly, because she knew he was so talented.

"—And the spiritual!" he'd finish, a broad smile wreathing his face.

In subsequent speeches, civilian defense would often be his topic. After hearing him speak, members of the Rotary Club in Harwich, Massachusetts, wrote: "Well might we be proud and feel a sense of security and confidence when we have a man of his caliber in positions of trust and leadership [over] our boys."

At home, he relaxed and played with his family. He got a kick out of his son Dannie's toy airport and model planes. Dannie idolized his father and wanted to be a flyer, like him.

The James's home was often a stopover for celebrities Chappie had befriended. Since Chappie had met Joe Louis while at Godman Field and ferried him around the country for exhibition fights, the friendship stuck. The great Joe Louis came calling, absolutely striking Danice dumb with amazement that he liked ketchup on his eggs! ("How gross!")

Active in youth groups, Chappie spoke to youngsters in the schools and made Danice's world even brighter by agreeing to be part of the PTA talent show at her school. Students were to bring a parent, first telling what that parent could do. Her father would sing. And he did, performing his favorite spiritual, "Joshua Fit the Battle." People loved it. But not all members of the James family thought a great deal of Chappie's need to sing spirituals. From Florida came word from his brother, Tony, that he ought to "cut the spirituals and the song and dance routines!" "It was a hurting, cutting thing" to Chappie, Danice remembers. But that was part of him, and he never abandoned it. He seemed to have a built-in instinct for knowing what the public would buy, what it seemed to want and like. The response validated his convictions, as his experiences with Operation Happiness had proven.

In August 1955, he became the commander of the 60th Fighter-Interceptor

Squadron, also based at Otis Air Force Base. As he took over command of the 60th Fighter-Interceptor Squadron, civil rights issues burned brightly in the South, until on 1 December 1955, Mrs. Rosa Parks made herself comfortable on a segregated bus in the seat of her choice in Montgomery, Alabama. Her refusal to move to the back of the bus signaled the beginning of the Montgomery Improvement Association, headed by Dr. Martin Luther King, Jr., mounting a one hundred percent-effective boycott against the Jim Crow bus system. It was an event Chappie noted, as did most black Americans, but he busied himself with his duties while making friends with southern neighbors like Lt. and Mrs. Bendel McDonald of Louisiana. He would be physically near the center of the civil rights revolution sooner than he thought.

In April 1956, with the approval of Col. Leon Gray, new wing commander, Chappie was promoted to lieutenant colonel. As required by the selection board, he was alerted for attendance at the air force Air Command and Staff School at Maxwell Air Force Base in Montgomery, Alabama. The family was elated, for the assignment indicated that the air force saw great promise in Chappie James and his innate leadership abilities. Dorothy thought "they'd done it backwards, he'd commanded first and *then* they sent him to Air Command and Staff School!"

No matter, the family packed and, in two cars, a 1952 Cadillac and a new, red Thunderbird, drove to Atlanta in tandem. Spud rode with Dottie while Spike and Danice switched off riding with Chappie in his pride and joy—the red Thunderbird. They reached Tuskegee around midnight, and there Dorothy's father greeted them with a hot dinner of corn muffins, okra, corn on the cob, and pig ears.

They settled in at Tuskegee while Chappie attended school on Maxwell Air Force Base, living in the BOQ. Dorothy was particularly happy, because she could spend rare moments with her father.

Command and Staff School was no picnic. It was nine months of intensive study and analysis. There were courses in weaponry and warfare, languages and religious history, and the international roles of countries that could be potential enemies of the United States. He needed every possible moment for study, and the light in his BOQ room burned late into the night.

Civil rights agitation was in full swing. "People were marching," Dorothy remembers. Chappie elected to remain on base rather than risk involvement in Montgomery. As a military man, he felt it was important to his career to remain aloof. Although he tried to avoid it, the ugliness of racism caught up with him in the most unexpected way.

On weekends, Chappie would drive down from Montgomery to relax with his family in Tuskegee. A distance of only forty miles or so, it was usually uneventful. One weekend, however, he made a minor mistake. Instead of buying gasoline for the car on Maxwell Air Force Base, he decided to stop for gas at an off-base gas station outside Montgomery. He probably never thought about it, but tempers flared in Montgomery.

With a frown Chappie hardly noticed, the service station attendant filled his car with gas. He listened absentmindedly to the little "ding" the pumps made in those days as the gasoline slithered through the hose and the dials spun round with the number of gallons pumped and the price. His mind probably centered on seeing his family in less than an hour. In uniform, he responded to the attendant's announcement of the money owed, removed it from his wallet, and paid his bill.

Then it happened.

With hard, beady little eyes set in a face filled with hate, the service station attendant spat on Chappie James. Like a dormant volcano, Chappie seemed to keep things inside him most of the time. This time, it must have been one of the hardest things he ever did, to keep from knocking this small, mean little man underneath some nearby car. But he did. He brushed the spittle away and drove home to his wife. She knew: "The minute . . . he walked in, the kids ran up, and I could tell—his face—something was wrong!"

He didn't want to talk about it in front of the children, but later, he told her. She remembered the expression on his face most of all and her heart seemed to bleed. "I've always said," she later remarked, "that young thug didn't realize how *lucky* he was! Here was a man who volunteered for everything and fought for his country and to have *that* happen to him! [That thug] was the luckiest man in the world. Chappie drove home to me and I could tell how upset and hurt . . . *that* hurt!"

The year 1956 contained more personal trauma for Chappie. It was the year he lost the greatest idol of his life. His mother, Lillie Anna, died of a heart attack complicated by high blood pressure. Chappie did not cry upon the passing of the human being who gave him life and the ethical principles by which he guided that life. Gloria Hunter, his niece, explains: "Chappie was never one to show lots of emotion. I don't remember any tears. After all, he was a big air force officer and he couldn't stand around and bawl. But I know it affected him . . ."

The images coursing through his mind when they lay his mother to rest in Saint Michael's Cemetery probably came in great profusion and no logical order. He remembered that his mother was a Christian, who believed unalterably in the power of prayer. He remembered how, every New Year's Eve, everyone around her was asked to kneel and pray. How later in life when she was so beset by physical problems that she could no longer kneel, she stood over them all and prayed with them nonetheless. He remembered the family prayer meetings sparked by her each day and for at least ten minutes on Sunday. His mother's unstinting devotion, sitting up all night with him and his siblings when they were ill, if that's what it took. How his mother "wore her body out'' giving of herself, not only for him, his brothers and sisters, but every black child in Pensacola who attended her private school between 1900 and 1956. Synthesizing perhaps her greatest lesson of all: *Education is the thing; stay in there and fight for what one is able to do, then succeed at doing it.* Hearing how she died (''she came out of school Friday and died Sunday morning at home''), they were sad moments for Chappie. As his niece, Gloria Hunter, commented, ''He must have loved her . . . 'cause he never stopped talking about her as long as he lived.''

III

In July 1957, the Pentagon beckoned. The Pentagon, its limestone face gleaming on the west bank of the Potomac River, boasted five concentric rings of office spaces connected by ten corridors, reminding one of the spokes of a wheel. Sprawled across twenty-nine acres, it possessed over three million square feet of walled space, its corridors stretching seventeen and a half miles with offices containing over forty-five thousand telephones, surrounded by parking lots accommodating almost ten thousand vehicles. In this imposing structure, a man's importance is supposed to be measured by the number of windows in his office. Chappie James had no windows and was so far down in the dungeon he had to call the gate guards to find out if the sun was shining!

Even though he disliked the place (according to Robin Olds, one of his commanders-to-be who was also stationed there, ''he hated it''), he understood the importance of the assignment. He had considered the Air Command and Staff School a way to improve his professional military education. A member of the air staff, he took to his duties with relish. Problem solving. Assessing staffing problems. Reviewing problems related to airplanes and air force operations. He regarded it an opportunity to really practice not making a profession of being black, a trap his mother had warned him to avoid. Whenever anyone used ''blackness'' as the driving force behind a problem, he spoke out against it, demanding that the regulations be followed.

It was a new opportunity to learn and to hone his skills as an effective air force officer. He was convinced that constant study, under others and by himself, inside *and* outside an airplane, was the high road to success. Later in his career, he was to observe that the reason some black officers didn't progress was due to inertia: ''Some guys stalled out as Majors and Lieutenant Colonels because they stayed in the cockpit too long. Can't put [them] on [the] air staff. Never took care of [their] *military education* [which taught] them how to *be* staff officers.''

So involved was he in what he was about, he'd sometimes forget promises made to his family.

He'd promised his daughter, it seems, that she could date at age sixteen. The time had arrived. A student at Sacred Heart Academy, she'd met a young man who caught her fancy through her brother. It was important, however, as things were in those times, that he first meet her father.

"Mother, I'd like to bring Julian home to meet Dad!"

"Oh, you want *me* to tell him?"

The evening quickly slipped by. Dinner time arrived. The conversations were good-natured but cursory. Danice pushed her mother.

"Did you mention it?"

Embarrassed silence followed. Chappie read the question marks forming on their faces.

"Oh yeah, what?" he boomed.

"Dan, Danice is sixteen now," Dorothy patiently explained, "and you said she could date—maybe let a boy visit here—here at the house!"

"House?" he shouted in his deep voice. "What? I never said such a thing!"

"Daddy! Daddy! You *did!* You *did!*" Danice reminded, pushing back the tears, and leaving the table in utter consternation to fly upstairs to her room.

Through the walls and closed door of her bedroom she could hear her mother and father still discussing the issue, punctuated with a few sentences about Chappie's golf plans. And then, "But Dan, you did!" Muffled words. "I'm afraid you did."

Dorothy and Danice won the round. Julian was to take her to the football game and meet Chappie after. It sounded simple, but Chappie was the type of individual who could outmaneuver the average person. His curiosity about this Julian knew no bounds. And that is how Danice and her friend caught sight of a red Thunderbird flashing past as they walked along the street. The brakes screeched and the driver jumped out, slamming the door behind him. It was Chappie. Julian braced for the worse, his body at rigid attention as her father approached.

Danice knew her father well. She knew he went primarily on feel and evaluation of situations before he got into them. She watched the evaluation of Julian going on as her father came closer. Julian was darned near as big as Chappie, much bigger than he had originally thought. Now they were face-to-face, eyeball to eyeball.

"Well!" Chappie effused, "Hello, young man!"

"H-Hello, sir!"

"I'm Colonel James!"

"Y-Y-Yes, sir!"

"Walking with my daughter, I see!"

And suddenly, things were all right. Someone has said that, for all of Chappie's assertiveness, strength and determination, he never came from the mental perspective of "I win; you lose." Underneath, he was very sweet and affectionate, especially in familial relationships. Julian saw both the aggressiveness and the sweetness in those few seconds, but both were only facets of his love and concern for his daughter.

Chappie stayed at the Pentagon's Air Defense Division, DCS/operations,* until June 1960. In July, he was ordered to the 81st Tactical Fighter Wing, Royal Air Force Station, Bentwaters, England, as assistant director and later director of operations.

Wherever he had gone, he did his best to eliminate prejudice in both military and civilians by his own personal dignity, ability and humor. At Otis, he counteracted prejudice through public service, in youth work, and speeches while delivering pep talks to high school football teams. Largely responsible for integrating the golf courses in the vicinity of Otis, he spoke out against institutionalized racism at every opportunity.

During the move, the children's bikes were stolen and his precious record collection was plundered. "He was *hot* about that!"—and well he should have been, for he loved music and the jazz greats. His record collection was star-studded. "There was," Danice remembers,

> Frank Sinatra, Nat "King" Cole, Peggy Lee. [We'd] always hear music in the background. Used to watch Mother and Father dance. [There was] Lifeline, Cannonball Adderly, MJQ [Modern Jazz Quartet], Dizzy Gillespie, Thelonius Monk. [He] loved the rhythm of the Bossa Nova, the drums and bongos. [There was] Cal Tjader, Billie Williams, Ella Fitzgerald [and] Sarah Vaughn, Joe Williams, Sammy Davis, Jr., Count Basie, [and] Miles Davis. He knew many of them . . . (he) played golf with Sammy Davis, Jr.

It hurt that someone would rob his magic mountain of music, but it had to be taken in stride. There was a job to do, a new time and place to demonstrate the power of excellence. It worked. He was to be almost revered: "Everyone liked him. He was like John F. Kennedy; nobody wanted to find fault with him. . . ."

There were reasons this was so.[73]

---

* Deputy Chief of Staff for Operations

Chapter Twenty
Synthesis

I

As Chappie James began his tour of duty with the 81st Tactical Fighter Wing at Bentwaters, England, America was on the verge of what was to be its most dizzying decade of the century. Some have called that decade "a vast cultural laboratory," where experimentation seemed to be the order of the day. New kinds of musical sounds, stagecraft, and writing erupted. The split screen appeared in the movies and, on television, black people began to play leading roles, instead of the traditional, stereotyped parts that they had been confined to in the past. The new Pop culture was to ingest America in one vast gulp. It was "Hey Jude" and Paul McCartney; *2001—A Space Odyssey* and Stanley Kubrick. Sly and the Family Stone caused people to wonder if James Brown was really the "King of Soul."

"Negro" was out. "Black" was in. People who had barely spoken before began to touch each other. It would probably be unfair to say that Rosa Parks's interrupted bus ride, the resultant bus boycott and continuing demonstrations began it all. In retrospect, these things made people aware of the power of effort across class lines. A full-blown revolution without cannon fire, it was an authentic mass movement, which in the end not only united many different elements of the black culture but many elements of other American cultures as well.

Although the air force was now an integrated service, its members were still part of America. Integration of its ranks caused a trauma, the effect of which remained. Class upheavals within America could not help but have an impact on the air force.

Because of his media attention as "America's first black commander of an integrated fighter squadron," his loudly proclaimed promotions, speeches and steadfastness in "singing spirituals" as part of his public appearances, Chappie James was already being looked upon by the more rebellious factions of the revolution as an "Uncle Tom," who was being "rewarded" because "he does and says what the white people want him to say." Indeed, "Uncle Tomism" has been defined as "aggressive meekness, i.e., self-effacing humility (and) . . . sometimes the 'meek' Negro can . . . snatch victory from defeat . . . [for] while deluding whites, he is also telling in the manner [taught by] Christianity as the 'core of morality' [that] the meek shall inherit the earth; suffering will be rewarded and the final victory will be achieved in heaven."[74]

Was it "Uncle Tomism" for example, to follow the guidance of his mother in the face of racial harassment while a cadet at Tuskegee; to take it on the chin as it were, in order to get what he wanted—a commission as a lieutenant in the army air corps? Was it "Uncle Tomism" to seek the conservative approach when the black officer "firebrands" sought to integrate officers' clubs and theaters at Selfridge, Godman, and Freeman Fields? Was it "Tomism" to do his bit by flying dispatches out to the media about his fellow officers' plight rather than shove his way into an officers' club, thus avoiding protracted confinement?

Hardly. But the accusation did bother him. Later in his career, he was to define it as one of the "obstacles other than racism," which dogged his heels. The other was his "reputation for flamboyance," evident even at this stage of his career, when he was being written about in the papers much more than officers of his peer group. He could easily substitute "charisma" for "flamboyance" in his mind and feel alright about it, but "Tomism" really irritated him, especially the later charges that he actively "looked for publicity—and that's how he gets all those favors!" In the coming days, he would bristle when the "Tomism" charge came from other blacks who said: "Oh Man! You *know* Chappie is a token Nigger! They're not gonna give him anything with authority—any great authority!"

His voice was to fill with emotion in response, because he thought that "with one statement, they have wiped out all of the blood, sweat and tears that I've put into this, and all of the tough years, and all of the preparation, and all of the desire and drive that I have been able to demonstrate to my supervisors. . . . And they say 'they just gave it to him because they made him a token black!' Well, there's no such thing as a 'token' four-star General. . . . They don't give stars to anybody in this business . . ."

It was prophetic, for Chappie James possessed a very strong *desire to succeed*. With a very active intellect, he could assert himself in quite productive, original ways, backing it all with his personal strength and talent. At Bentwaters, these attributes came together in a synthesis which resulted in a complete casting off of the inferior role of ["Black"] . . . the cessation of all of the debilities traditionally placed upon black skin by American society . . . the stilling of self-hatred . . . an end to claims of white superiority; to dire poverty, to the social conditions permitting inflated rates of disease and inadequate medical care, low intelligence scores, heightened crime rates . . . the right to participate fully in American society with the dollars and dignity of other Americans . . .[75]

At Bentwaters, Chappie sought no sympathy, curried no favor, but simply stood tall among men. Already in his early forties, he had begun to mellow. Since he wore his hair extremely short, his face appeared fuller. His nose flared a bit more; his weight, a solid 250 pounds. The beginnings of a furrowed brow lined his forehead. Like a seasoned oak, his footballer's neck remained, the slightest hint of a double chin appearing as the first "old man" lines began to deepen from nose to mouth. The proud, neatly trimmed moustache survived, while that small cluster of razor bumps black men sometimes get rode the left quadrant of his chin. His appearance was even more impressive and massive.

Given to dramatic movement and articulate speech, and able to inspire men, Chappie's massive size added to his style. He strove to present a "colorless" persona, bereft of race and skin tone. His approach fostered outstanding morale. The result was that his compatriots noticed his character first, not his color. He was the embodiment *par excellence,* of another of Lillie Anna James's teachings. He was to growl it in future speeches, stirring his audiences to the quick: "If they say you're dirty, make sure you're clean! If they say you steal, make sure you don't! If they say you're dumb, make sure you're smart! If they say you're scared, make sure you're brave, my son!"

He brought those teachings to the 81st Tactical Fighter Wing. Avoid separatism. Throwing the idea of reverse racism into the garbage can, by beating racism's jibes to the punch, spotlighting them himself through good-natured joshing, including the white-hot, slanted "nigger" and "honkie" labels.

Around the 81st Tactical Fighter, he often referred to himself as the "BNIC" (Big Nigger in Charge).[76] If someone complained because he failed to get back to them on an issue, he'd flippantly respond with, "I'm sorry, but I haven't revised my Honkie list lately!" Or if he couldn't bring someone up on his mental screen because he'd forgotten their name, he'd moan, "Oh, all you white guys look alike to me!" Thus, he defused racist remarks before they blossomed.

Beyond that, he was an ideal ground commander, employing skills learned as a fighter squadron commander at Otis Air Force Base, Massachusetts. He cared, "going that extra mile" to help members of his command when they needed it. Concerned about the human beings that were in his charge, he inspected the food they were to eat and was there to greet them on the flight line when they returned from late-night flights. He was learning the lesson of not being overly judgmental or caustic if someone made an honest mistake. However, nobody could call him easy if there was a "repeat offender" whose action placed unit efficiency in jeopardy.

To their chagrin, black airmen learned about the Chappie James brand of fairness across the board. Airmen of color who thought the hue of their skins gave them an inside track were rudely disappointed. He'd look them straight in the eye, commenting: "You've got the talent! Stop complaining and do something to help yourself!"

A master politician, he wisely formed coalitions with other officers in the wing who could support him both militarily and socially. James McGovern calls this group of perhaps fifteen officers "Chappie's family." Intrinsically, McGovern notes, these officers accepted Chappie as "The Chief," the leader to whom they were loyal. In return, he was equally loyal, committing to them "decent duty, advancement and social graces." Camaraderie transcended race.

Socially, Chappie loved to party as fighter pilots do. He and his special "family" were leaders of the social scene at the officers' club. He relished his "deep-dish olive pies" (martinis) as much as the rest, but never mixed duty with social events. Using the air force catch-phrase all officers and airmen have heard at one time or another, he was not beneath reminding them: "He who hoots with the owl at night cannot fly with the eagle in the morning!"

But when it *was* time to party, he was at his best. A time to be witty, to dance and sing. To sing, when the deep-dish olive pies ran free and strong, the old air force pilot's songs—"Air Force 101," sung to the tune of the "Wabash Cannonball," perhaps.

As a night grew mellower, so would the songs, their words containing a mellow kind of risqueness.

And even though the idea of white women dancing with black men still left a bitter taste in the mouths of some purists, he danced with the Englishwomen who flocked to the fighter pilot parties. And sometimes he'd dance with the *same one* more than once! According to McGovern, "eyebrows would be raised." And why not, he thought, for "the fact that they were white did not matter." It was "within his right to enjoy the permissive moral climate of Bentwaters!" It was "who you were," and "not the color of your skin."

Ralph Maglione (a major at the time, he would retire as a two-star general) was a member of Chappie's "family." The two of them often did routines at the officer's club: good-humored routines that helped them to laugh at themselves and bear the burden of racism more easily.

Political activism would have compromised his chances with the air force and generated questionable results. Following his mother's teachings, he was in complete agreement with Dr. Alfred J. Morrow of the American Jewish Congress: "The conclusion is inescapable. The policy of equal treatment without regard to race, color, religion or national origin cannot be implemented within the framework of racial segregation. Equal treatment and segregation are mutually incompatible. Efforts to accomplish both are certain to result in failure. *Segregation must go, and the sooner the better.*"[77]

Chappie James simply preferred to operate as if segregation and racism didn't exist. He believed in the tenet and lived it, resolving to *act equal* at all times.

After stints as assistant director of operations and director of operations of the wing, then commander of the 92d Tactical Fighter Squadron, he became deputy commander for operations for the 81st Tactical Fighter Wing, under Col. Robin Olds as commander, an old friend from his Pentagon days. The two of them made a good team, although marked differences existed in their command styles and personalities.

Robin Olds, like Benjamin O. Davis, Jr., was the son of a general and came from a distinguished background which was enhanced by his marriage to film star Ella Raines. Graduated from West Point in 1943, he was selected an All-American tackle the year before. By 1972, he would be a triple ace, having shot down seventeen enemy aircraft during the Second World War and Vietnam. Even the names he conferred on the fighters he flew were sassy. "Scat I," he called his P-38 Lightning during first combat, cycling through "Scat VII," a P-51 Mustang, at the end of the war. In all, he was credited with 107 combat missions, 24.5 victories, 13 aircraft shot down and 11.5 airplanes destroyed on the ground. He was wing man on the air force's first acrobatic team.

Chappie James came from the Alcaniz Street ghetto of Pensacola, Florida, struggling against the odds, bulling his way through a cadet program for black pilots when nobody wanted black pilots. But he, too, was battle-tested in Korea, flying over one hundred combat strikes, killing over one hundred enemy troops on a single mission, the Distinguished Flying Cross emblazoning his chest. He'd called his fighters by other names. "Be Happy with Chappie," announced his P-47 Jug used in Operation Happiness. "Chappie's Chariot" was the name of his F-94C up at Otis.

Both were warriors, but important differences existed in their approach to command. According to McGovern, leadership for Olds began at the flightline. Relationships with his men "could leave them a bit uneasy," as Olds himself sometimes appeared to be somewhat detached and "tentative." In contrast, James is described as a "great ground commander," who, "like a great football coach lecturing his team at halftime," made his pilots "chomp at the bit" to fire the next rocket or drop the next bomb. However, an affinity seemed to exist between them, even though they did not always do things the same way.

The combination clicked in spite of the differences. Each complemented the other, as evidenced by the proud wing they built together. The unit won the Daedalion Trophy in 1963 for outstanding maintenance management capability (Chappie had made a *friend* of the maintenance officer—not always an easy thing to do). The Daedalion, highest maintenance trophy to be won air force-wide, set the 81st Tactical Fighter Wing apart, for the 81st was the first organization in the United States Air Forces in Europe (USAFE) command to win it. The wing won the American ambassador's Anglo-American Community Relations Award for five consecutive years and the National Safety Council Award of Merit for four consecutive years.

Upon receiving the second consecutive Outstanding Unit citation from Major General R. W. Puryear, Third Air Force commander, Robin Olds was moved to say: "I have asked myself countless times what motivates these young men to give so much for such a sustained period. It cannot be a personal recognition . . . it has to be dedication . . . dedication."

An observer has noted that perhaps at least part of it may have come from his "expert ground commander," then-Lt. Col. Daniel "Chappie" James, Jr., one of the ablest and most dedicated officers in his command.

II

The family settled in nicely at Bentwaters, the children comfortably enrolled in high school. Danice graduated, returning to the United States to attend college, while Daniel III, president of the student council, graduated later. Englishmen treated them well, one Stanley Pierson surprising them with a pair of tickets to that year's Wimbledon.

Beyond the alerts emanating from the Cuban crisis and the assassination of President Kennedy, "it was," Dorothy James remembers, "very nice—no wars!" Although Chappie tried ignoring racism, events in 1963 simply could not escape notice. He tried to take Dr. King's civil rights demonstrations in stride. It took Police Safety Commissioner Bull Conner's police dogs and firehoses in Birmingham, Alabama, to get his undivided attention as it did all segments of black America. Although it was a demonstration against "the most thoroughly segregated city in the United States," the Birmingham march was billed as a peaceful statement of humankind. The flashing television images shocked the nation. Outraged, Chappie seriously thought of resigning his commission by the time of the Selma march.

Other events were brewing in Tallahassee, Florida, which would emotionally pull him further into the revolution's seething cauldron. His daughter was arrested for taking part in a Congress of Racial Equality (CORE) demonstration in downtown Tallahassee. Aimed at desegregation of a theater, the students were given so many minutes to disperse. Failing to do so, all were summarily arrested and marched to a makeshift jail in a sweltering police car garage. CORE leaders entreated them to stay calm as police tried to incite violence through intimidation, moving them to an even more unsavory place. "It was like a dungeon," Danice remembers, "hot and full of gas fumes," on the bottom floor of the garage.

"Hold your heads up! Keep your heads up!" cried the CORE leaders. Pride was to be maintained at all costs. The situation grew more desperate by the minute. On their knees, they crept over congealing oil on the concrete floor. They tried laughing to minimize despair. It did no good. The police booked them anyway. They were fingerprinted and photographed as their captors chuckled.

"Color—*black!*"—"Eyes—*black!*"

"Excuse *me*," retorted Danice defiantly, "they're *brown!*"

She used her right to make a phone call advising her father's sister, Aunt Lillian, in Pensacola of her plight, seeking help and support. She received a tongue-lashing instead. "We are *ashamed* of you! You're there in school! *James* is a proud name! [Think of] Uncle Tony! It's a *disgrace* to the James family!"

The demonstrators were moved into the jail proper, their heads high, their captors laughing all the way. Chappie and Dorothy were called. Chappie called Danice immediately, his emotions in turmoil. She got the call at 4:00 A.M., Tallahassee time, a civil rights lawyer interceding.

Tears were already streaming from Danice's eyes. What could she expect from her Father? "Baby, this is your Daddy! If I was there, I would have done the same thing! We're *proud* of you! Go for it! Hang in! You're a *true James!* My daughter! Daddy loves you. *Don't worry about your Aunt and Uncle!*"

Now the tears really streamed. Daddy understood. It was a basic difference between the generations of the James family, Danice later realized. "A difference between the older Aunt Lillian, her younger father and mother" and now, herself. In one respect, Aunt Lillian was right—the James family *was* a proud family—but at this time of swirling change and high emotion, one part of it had not yet caught up with the other.

As Chappie's tour of duty at Bentwaters drew to a close, the story goes that Robin Olds, concerned about the racism James might encounter driving across the United States, suggested that he might consider flying rather than driving. The spirit of the revolution grasped him. "I intend," he heatedly replied, "to drive this damn car [Jaguar] anywhere I want to go!"

III

In September 1964, Chappie received "another Deputy Commander invitation." It was a reassignment to Davis-Monthan Air Force Base, Arizona, and the 4453d Combat Crew Training Wing, the first air force organization to get the F-4 Phantom jet fighter. Chappie was first the director of operations and training and later, deputy commander for operations. On 15 November he moved within a single step of his first general's star as he was promoted to full colonel.

It was a proud moment. A lieutenant colonel over eight years (April 1956), he now stepped into the elite circle of eagles. He could barely wait to get home and tell his wife.

"Dottie, I've been promoted to colonel!"

He waited expectantly, almost breathlessly, for the congratulations he knew were coming. Smiles and laughter. A big hug. A kiss. It was almost the way it was when he was promoted to lieutenant colonel. That time, she didn't jump and grab him. She simply turned and almost wanly smiled.

"What's wrong?" he demanded.

"All I'm wondering is," Dorothy began in measured tone, "what took them so long?" They grabbed each other and hugged in ecstatic joy.

"Then," Dorothy remembers, "he understood!" She was as happy now.

Chappie was imposing enough as an officer of any rank, but as a full colonel, the image was awesome. There's a story around about the day in the base theater he briefed a group of newly arrived young officers, a budding astronaut among them. It was a day nobody wanted to be near the stage or the speaker, lolling many rows back in the gloomy space. Suddenly, there was the awesome sight of huge Colonel James. They'd heard about him, and now they were meeting him.

"Good morning, gentlemen! I'm Colonel James!"

There were a few "Good mornings," as the colonel eyeballed them.

"Gentlemen!" came the roar, "If you wanna be *fighter* pilots, you've gotta sit in the front seat!"

The analogy was too positive to miss. The F-4 was a two-seater aircraft in which the pilot *always* sat in the front. There was, they say, a clatter and clamor as the young officers moved into the front rows with greatest alacrity, almost as one man.

As the man said, "Chappie could outmaneuver the average person!" But even he could be stymied from time to time.

IV

Although good at outmaneuvering others, Chappie learned that there were times when *he* could be outmaneuvered, and oftentimes it was fortunate that it happened that way. This did not concern the planning and training of the F-4 combat crews that were his charge, but his home life. Retrospectively, one suspects he knew that he was being outfoxed and welcomed it, for his family and children were his soft spot.

His daughter, Danice, was now making her way in the world as a TWA airline hostess. Flying, after all, was in the family blood. Young, vivacious Danice was filled with effervescence and worldliness, which led her, on occasion, to participate in the social whirl around Davis-Monthan Air Base. One particular night she was destined to meet the most important person in her life next to her father. She'd attended a party that evening with an air police lieutenant. Sitting alone across the room was one Frank Berry, an air force flight surgeon. Rumor had it that he'd just split up with a young lady, also at the party, who had plopped down on the other side of the room, obviously hurt and very bored. One of Danice's sorority sisters egged her on.

"That's Dr. Berry," she whispered excitedly, "one of the most eligible bachelors in Tucson!"

Danice was unimpressed.

"He doesn't turn me on!"

"Oh, but you have to meet him! He's just home from Vietnam!"

Frank Berry spotted Danice too. Her sorority sister continued to spur her on. Frank stood by the watercooler, punch in hand. In between sets, he asked her to dance. She finally accepted.

"Oh, Miss TWA, eh?"

The music swayed. Extremely thin, tall, bespectacled, and dark, Frank Berry was filled with few surprises. They danced in a momentary silence they both knew wouldn't last. Perhaps she was expecting the usual line spouted by many young air force officers. Instead, Frank Berry floored her with a bit of homespun practicality.

"Well? Can you cook?"

"What?"

A bit of an insult at first, it stopped her in her tracks. It *was* different. So different, it seemed a bit wonderful.

"Y-Yes—"

"What can you cook?"

"Chicken—potato salad!"

"Sounds *great!* Maybe we can go on a picnic sometimes!?!"

"I guess—so."

But the customs of the James family, the old way of doing things, constrained the budding romance. It would not be easy for Frank Berry. He had to meet her mom and dad. He didn't know who her parents were. After all, Frank's air force career had been Strategic Air Command-oriented. He had never met Chappie or heard of him, and Chappie was the director of operations!

Frank asked for, but did not get, her telephone number. She'd heard about

Frank and decided not to be just another one on his hit list. Resourceful, Frank simply looked it up on the base telephone directory and began to call almost daily.

She was never available. Her mother would field the calls.

"Oh, I'm sorry, but Danice is still sleeping!"

One fateful day she told Chappie about her new would-be lover, a doctor from the hospital. Chappie bristled.

"There's only one black physician at the hospital, and he's married with a family!"

At breakfast a few mornings later, it was on his mind.

"Where were you last night? [I've] seen very little of you!"

"Oh?"

"Frank?"

"He asked if I could cook! Do you know him?"

"Yes, dammit, and he's married! What's he doing talking to you?"

Chappie didn't take kindly to hospital doctors anyway. These people could keep him from flying through some medical invention, like the doctor back at Walterboro who wanted to put strange things on his records just because he'd gotten a wee bit tipsy. Or at Lockbourne, when they'd groused at him because of his weight, and only waivers saved the day. Chappie had a "conversation" with the black physician, this Dr. Anderson. He was abrupt. Dr. Anderson was shook up, to put it mildly.

But Frank Berry would not be outmaneuvered. He kept calling. Half-asleep one morning, Danice could hear her mother running interference over the telephone.

"Well, just a minute—let me see!"

A knock on the bedroom door.

"Danice?"

"Uh-hmmm?"

"It's Dr. Berry!"

"Uh-hmmm!"

"Danice," Dorothy went on exasperately, "this young man has been *very* persistent! You owe him an explanation!"

She struggled to the telephone.

"Danice?"

"Yes?"

"Well? I've got the chicken?"

Silence.

"Come and fix it?"

That brought Danice awake. Her brown eyes widened into startled orbs.

"What *are* you talking—come fix your chicken—*you're* married! *You've got a lotta nerve!*"

"Married? But I'm not married!"

"But my dad said—"

"He may have been talking about my friend, Anderson. How about a movie? How about tonight?"

"But you've got to meet my parents first!"

V

It was one of those hot, sultry Arizona evenings after work in the military housing area. Cocktails on the patio, flat-topped coolers whirring. Pitchers of martinis being mixed. Cool glasses to the lips. Everybody heard Frank coming to visit; come to spark the director of operations' daughter. The muffler of his baby-blue Olds rattled on the street. Even so, the denizens of the tranquil street were only slightly disturbed as the martinis abounded.

Directly in front of the James's house sat Chappie's beautiful, grey Jaguar. There was *just* enough room in front of it to park another car. The Olds hic-coughed, then coughed, as Frank eased it into reverse for the parallel park. Maybe it was some cruel witch; some errant reflex that took over Berry's accelerator foot, but the baby blue Olds leapt backwards in an unusual burst of speed, to crash into the front of the beautiful, grey Jaguar sitting at the curb like a work of art.

The entire street went silent. Did this little flight surgeon, this driver of the chronically coughing baby-blue Oldsmobile without a muffler—*know* whose car he had just tried to savage? If he didn't know, he was damned certain to find out in one hot, little minute, the neighbors thought.

Eyes were riveted on Chappie as he rose like some strange Sphinx; half-man, half-bird, all air force full colonel.

"Hurry now," soothed Dorothy, "don't fuss at him. He's a little late!"

Years passed as Chappie ambled out. Not much damage to the car. Only the bumpers had collided.

"Frank," Chappie breathed, "everything okay?"

The entire street breathed again, to the tune of tinkling ice cubes and sparkling, familial conversations. The match had begun.

After a tour in Vietnam, Frank dated Danice for a year. Frank came by one evening to talk to Chappie. Dorothy thought that "he had that certain look!" She and Danice knew something was about to happen. "Maybe *this* is it!"

Frank and Chappie talked in the den.

"Well, sir, I'd like to take that daughter off your hands!"

Chappie regarded Frank for a long moment.

"Well, I'm not losing a daughter—I'm gaining a son!"

It was a family thing. A sweet outmaneuver. This was completely different from the job back at the base, where the job was training fighter pilots to be combat-ready, Vietnam-style: aircraft versus aircraft, pilot against pilot. Teaching types of combat missions. Channeling the energies of the combat fighter pilot, honing them until their attitudes agree with Ernest Hemingway's quote in Walter J. Boyne's book, *Phantom in Combat:* "You love a lot of things if you live around them, but there isn't any woman and there isn't any home, not any before, nor any after, that is as lovely as a great airplane. And men who love them are faithful to them even though they leave them for others. A man has only one virginity to lose to fighters, and if it's a lovely plane he loses it to, there his heart will ever be."

Chappie taught the fighter pilot jocks roll-away maneuvers, the standard high yo-yo, the barrel roll attack; how to approach a defender at high angle-off and long-range, using the barrel roll to reduce that angle-off without energy loss. He taught them to fight in the F-4 Phantom; to control its massive energy in hostile surroundings. With his students he experienced sickening G-loads that pushed down their helmets, ripped away oxygen masks, inflated their G-suits, and dug their equipment into already tender ribs. Chappie taught them to concentrate on instruments while staying relatively calm, their breathing belying stressed innards. He knew the limits of mock battle and steeled his students against the day they would see a buddy blow up or go spiraling down to oblivion, capture, or death. He checked that they lived up to their billing as fighter pilots, about whom the studies say: "[They] are by nature independent doers who want always to be in control . . . risk-takers, but don't want to hazard others or be hazarded. . . . [They] have . . . certain characteristics: aggressiveness, confidence, self-discipline, dedication, awareness, and instinct to hunt and kill, courage, fast reactions."[78]

This is what Chappie James did and what he loved. This was the place to maneuver and outmaneuver. It was his nature, and he was good. Home was tenderness, his records and music, his little dog, his wife and family and good food.

But by 1966, other skies began to beckon, the skies over rolling terrain with strange-sounding names. Ubon. Udorn. Thailand. Da Nang and Phuc Yen, Cat Bai and Hanoi.

Vietnam.

Vietnam, the Southeast Asia conflagration that had raged since the French involvement in the late forties. President Eisenhower had committed U.S. involvement to "assist so Vietnam and other free countries of Southeast Asia [could resist] Communist aggression." President Kennedy in turn had committed aid and advisors. In August 1964, the North Vietnamese attacked the U.S.

Navy destroyer *Maddox* in the Gulf of Tonkin, and two days later, the U.S. Navy destroyer *Turner Joy* and the *Maddox* again. U.S. guns growled, attacking North Vietnamese patrol boat bases while China deployed MiG 15/17 jet fighters to Hanoi's Phuc Yen airfield. The first U.S. air strikes descended on North Vietnam in 1965—"a demonstration," by President Johnson, "of America's determination to retaliate against military targets so that Hanoi would understand that it was not immune from attack."

Vietnam became a hot shooting war and big news at elite fighter bases across the United States Air Force. It was Chappie James's cup of tea. A chance to practice his skills; to become a warrior again, because he was, as he concluded after Korea, "a helluva combat fighter pilot!"

And that is why, he later remarked in an interview, he was ready to fight when his friend, Col. Robin Olds, assigned to command the 8th Tactical Fighter Wing at Ubon Royal Thai Air Base in Thailand, dropped by Davis-Monthan in mid-1966, and said: "Last time I saw you, you were ten pounds overweight— if you lose it and want to fight, come on!"

Oddly, although Dorothy James verifies the fact that Colonel Olds did visit Davis-Monthan in 1966, the retired Olds himself does not agree that he had anything to do with James's assignment to Southeast Asia. Says he, when asked if he asked Chappie to join his command in Vietnam: "No, he was assigned— probably by his own contacts."

Perhaps memory played tricks on both James and Olds. The point is moot now, for the fact remains that Chappie James received orders to report to Olds's 8th Tactical Fighter Wing, and he champed at the bit to go. Dorothy knew he *had* to go and she stood away to wait yet again in silent separation.

From the point of view of a career fighter pilot like Chappie James, Jr., it might have been an exhilarating challenge. But in terms of military strategy, national political implication and U.S. foreign relations, it was not. It was, instead, a conflict which went counter to U.S. military strategy, itself based upon superior force and general nuclear war. It was the antithesis of Robert W. Ginsburgh's observation in *U.S. Military Strategy in the Sixties*. He wrote:

We may, in fact, be entering an era reminiscent of the 18th Century, in which outbreak of conflict is so dangerous that victories are won or lost by maneuvering of forces up to the point of, but without the climax of, a battle . . . In an age of maneuver, we would expect implicit or tacit agreement . . . on the rules of the game. The crisis would have to be managed in such a way as to allow the "loser" an acceptable way out . . . that there is some gain for him in not fighting.[79]

Vietnam did not follow that pattern at all.

A test of Chappie James's skills in combat began in December 1966. The

8th Tactical Fighter Wing was his vehicle. And maybe now he'd be singing those old fighter pilot songs again, like the one he always said he'd written back in the 92d Tac at Bentwaters fashioned after the old 99th Pursuit Squadron song. It had been written down in Tuskegee, Alabama, and sung when the squadron swept into battle in North Africa. Chappie had been too new, too inexperienced a cadet to join their ranks then. Perhaps, inside his head, it became, as he was enroute to Thailand, the 8th Tactical Fighter Wing fight song:

> Contact, joy-stick back
> Roaring through the blue.
> We are the men of the great 8th Tac tried and true
> We are the heroes of the night
> To hell with the Commie's might
>
> Bold Phantoms defenders of the right
> Drink a toast all Phantoms
> To those daring men
> May they always win the battle
> Live to fight again
> For we are rulers of the blue
> A righteous wrecking crew
> Fight! Fight! Fight! Fight
> The fighting 8th Tac!
> Hey!

Chapter Twenty-One
Sawadi!

I

Thailand means "land of the free." To have a cool heart is the ultimate ideal of the Thai people. A contented land, it is a place of tranquility in life and daily affairs, for "there is rice in the fields, fish in the water." This Thailand to which Chappie James had come to help fight America's latest war was also friendly country, where "Sawadi!"—the universal, spoken "hello" of the Thai's hung gently in the air.

Ubon Royal Thai Air Force Base, the home of the 8th Tactical Fighter Wing "Wolfpack," sat in the center of Ubon Ratchathani, province number sixty-seven, in the northeastern sector of the country. It was a population center totalling some 15.2 million. When the tropical southwest monsoons come in the rainy seasons of May, June, and July, lasting into October, the world goes topsy-turvy as monstrous leader clouds build, and thunder rumbles. Down in the capital of Bangkok, they turn on the lights at noon, as the atmosphere seems to take a huge, breathless pause, followed by a great wind arching through the treetops like the swells of an angry sea. Over in Vietnam they called it *Crachin*, and the rain comes suddenly without preambled showers, cascading ferociously. But Chappie arrived at Ubon in the middle of the December-January dry season, a time when rain is nonexistent, and temperatures soar.

Temperature and humidity were not the only uncomfortable things at Ubon when Chappie arrived. The North Vietnamese air defense complexes were slowly but surely being upgraded, taking an increased toll of U.S. Air Force aircraft. At low altitudes, North Vietnamese automatic weapon and small caliber antiaircraft fire proliferated, forcing USAF pilots to sacrifice the element of surprise in favor of increased safety, dive-bombing targets from higher altitudes. By the spring of 1965, enemy defense capabilities ensured successful attack by MiG-17 fighters on F-105 aircraft attacking a bridge. In July 1965, the SA-2, surface-to-air, Soviet-built missile was introduced and put in place around Hai-phong and Hanoi, bringing down one F-4C Phantom Jet and seriously damaging the other three in an attack formation of four on the first day of its use. Increasing MiG interceptions during September-December 1966 caused 55.73 percent of 192 strike aircraft to jettison their ordnance.

With improved ground-control methodology, the enemy was better able to coordinate his fighters, affecting American mission accuracy and operational capability. Even so, the 8th Tactical Fighter Wing, under Col. Robin Olds (now assisted by Col. Chappie James), claimed an enviable battle record. During a 180-day period in 1966, his Wolfpack downed twenty-four MiGs while only losing twelve fighters.

New tactics evolved pending solution of the problem. In lieu of the old tactics, Brigadier General Olds recalls that his fighters would: "Go in at 5-minute intervals between flights, each flight navigating individually . . . at 4500–5000 feet . . . corkscrewing . . . as hard as [they] could . . . once [across] the mountains . . . and into the SAM and gun defenses . . ."

Under these conditions, navigation was very difficult, negatively affecting target identification, acquisition, and attack. It was a matter of getting in, navigating, dodging the surface-to-air missiles, and keeping out of the small-arms fire. Once acquiring target, it was hitting: ". . . .(After) burners and pop up, up, up you go and roll over the top . . . try to . . . line up on . . . . . . target . . . bomb . . . get the hell out of there!"

Evolution of tactics to avoid the "flying telephone poles," (the surface-to-air SAM missiles) was quite another matter, because: "A SAM . . . was locked on. . . . You had to play with him . . . had to force the missile down and . . . at the last moment . . . pull and hope he wouldn't make the corner [which] puts you [into] small-arms fire. . . . Below 4,500 (feet) the concentration of small-arms fire was murderous."

While Chappie James was getting his "Southeast Asia legs" as deputy commander for operations, taking over some of the mundane matters of wing administration, the F-105 strike wings were getting their first allotments of newly arrived electronic countermeasures jamming-pods, which afforded them self-protection against enemy radar detection. According to Brig. Gen. Robin Olds, although there weren't enough for everybody, their receipt was the "single most important impact on the whole sphere of tactics." They afforded a departure from old tactics of "a five-minute [attack] trail in which a flight would be on its own, in trail," a dangerous maneuver at best, enabling enemy gunners to improve kill ratios.

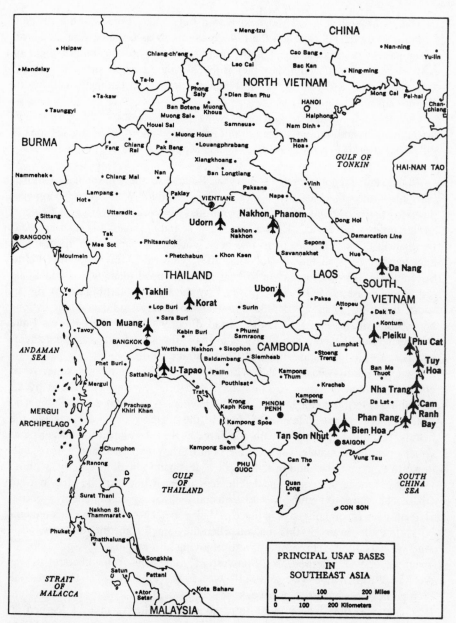

from *Aces and Aerial Victories: The USAF in Southeast Asia, 1965–73.* Office of Air Force History, Headquarters USAF, 1976.

The ECM pods formed the nexus of a bold plan. Borrow the electronic jamming pods, install them on the F-4 Phantoms so as to make sure the North Vietnamese would come up to fight, thinking they were attacking a flight of F-105 crews against whom they had enjoyed a modicum of success. Instead, they would face a sky full of F-4C Phantoms, armed to the teeth with air-to-air missiles.

Colonel Olds sat down with other wing officers in the "tactics shop" in the back room and discussed the possibilities. They were "blue-sky sessions," full of "what if" postulates and "what would we do if" problem statements.

At an ambassador's cocktail party at Baguio in the Philippines, Colonel Olds mentioned the blue-sky tactics to Gen. William W. "Spike" Momyer, Seventh Air Force commander. An operational general, Momyer knew fighters, fighter pilots, and tactics. He was the ideal sounding board for such an idea. In essence, the preliminary plans had been worked out. Their fulfillment might help handle the MiG threat. Not long after, General Momyer called Olds to Seventh Air Force headquarters to hear the developed plan, which had as its ultimate purpose a MiG sweep, planned by the 8th Tactical Fighter Wing. In short, the F-4C Phantoms would simulate the timing, radio communications and speeds of the F-105 "Thuds"; head directly towards the enemy's Phuc Yen airfield and Hanoi. The idea was to make the MiG fighters commit themselves, take the lure, come up, and "have a nice battle."

General Momyer tasked Olds with devising the exact tactics, time, force composition and told him to come back and brief Seventh Air Force by 22 December 1966. Planning went into high gear. A Captain J. B. Stone and Colonel Olds spent eighteen-hour days in the "back room" working out the details, coordinating with Seventh Air Force as they developed the master plan. Other operational matters went by the board. They requested and got a stand-down to tune up radars and missiles. All of this had to be done quietly, without generating undue suspicion and excitement in the wing. But the airmen were smart. They knew something was up, especially since they were suddenly working sixteen- to eighteen-hour days in place of their usual ten-hour stints. Olds remembers, "they'll always do this for you when they smell something in the wind." And he was right. The airmen were enjoying the enigma. T. Sgt. John T. Trammel, USAF (Retired), of Shrevesport, Louisiana, remembers: "It was the best outfit morale-wise and skill-wise I was ever in . . . That was the high point of my career. Not because it was a war, but because I never thought I'd be in an outfit where there were so many skilled people. I learned so much." Chappie James's talents as a morale booster were already evident, and the airmen noticed: "Robin and Chappie contributed to that, definitely. I don't think you could have gotten that feeling with any other two people. The chemistry between the two of them was something to behold."

II

Meanwhile, Chappie James went about his business of being a fighter pilot, taking his share of missions over the Ho Chi Minh Trail and, on a less frequent basis, into the infamous Route Package VI.* Route Package VI was the most heavily defended area, until that time, in the history of active air combat. It was roughly the size of the state of Massachusetts. Although he flew most missions, including that of aircap,** Chappie only flew seventy-eight combat missions during his entire tour of duty in the arena. He averaged six or seven combat sorties a month as opposed to the air force credo that eighteen to twenty missions per month were necessary to maintain proficiency in the newest fighters. Chappie, in fact, "didn't fly much," according to retired Brig. Gen. Robin Olds, the wing commander. Further, according to Olds, the impending *Bolo* MiG sweep was "about the *only* mission he flew in Route Package VI."

There were solid reasons for Chappie James's reduced flying schedule as opposed to Robin Olds, for example, who "would have spent 24 hours a day in the cockpit if he had his way." Though Olds loved to fly, he was also practical, understanding that someone had to handle the "ground stuff"—the personnel problems, the paperwork, and other factors involved in administering a combat air force base and wing manned by some four thousand servicemen. Ground command and troop management, it will be recalled, was Chappie James's particular cup of tea, and he did it with his usual flair for excellence.

Chappie also recognized that a reduced flying schedule meant reduced proficiency in handling the extremely complicated F-4 and its myriad systems. Linked to his advancing age (late forties), he realized that: "The less you fly, the more it takes to get your proficiency back in a combat situation . . . and that's a quick way to the graveyard . . .''

But he loved the missions he did fly, broadcasting his personal slogan: *"Yea, though I fly through the valley of death, I shall fear no evil. For I am the meanest muthah in the valley!"* And when he roared up to launch his F-4 Phantom with 1st Lt. Bob C. Evans, his GIB (guy-in-the-back-seat), he always

---

*ROUTE PACKAGE VI: Beginning at the demilitarized zone, North Vietnam was divided into two parts: VI A (air force) and VI B (navy). The air force had three areas of attack and the navy, four. Consensus was that the air force had a much larger, more hazardous area to cover than did the navy task force.[80]
**AIRCAP: Air Combat Patrol. Usually used with a prefix, i.e., ResCAP (protecting helicopters performing rescue duties or other orbiting aircraft); LowCAP (protecting low-altitude fighter operations) and MiGCAP, which needs no further explanation. Could also include close air support missions (CAS).

wore his special helmet with the replica of a black panther emblazoned across the front of it.

The legend of Chappie James continued to form at Ubon. He was a high-ranking officer to whom you could talk, no matter who you were. An officer who was accessible and would help you if he could, while maintaining a sense of humor. M. Sgt. Herbert C. Harper, an armament technician, remembers how Colonel James picked him up in his staff car one day as he was walking to the flight line and had him hop into the back seat. Harper chuckled at the memory of a black full colonel driving a staff car with a white master sergeant in the back seat!

And one day during the yearly dry-season water festival, when the Thai custom was to toss water on anyone and anybody in homage to the rain gods so as to ensure water for the last planting, as Chappie drove slowly past the airmen's and noncommissioned officers' clubs, three or four airmen ran out to the car, jerked upon the door and dumped a bucket of water on him. Chappie got out of the car, but instead of chewing them out royally (as he could have easily done), he smilingly derided them while shaking a cautionary, beefy finger at them as the howling airmen retreated.

But no matter what Robin Olds seems to remember about Chappie's flying Route Package VI, it is obvious that he flew that perilous route more than once. One does not easily forget going "Downtown" to Hanoi on that aerial highway labeled VI, humming the Petula Clark tune under the breath, down the same flight paths at the same hour today that a flight did the day before. They knew you were coming and, down there on the ground, a spotter could see the black smoke contrails of the F-4C engines long before you arrived. He'd blow a bugle or ring a bell signalling your coming. A thousand rifles would point skyward, hoping you'd descend low enough, come within range. And up ahead, the antiaircraft shell bursts awaited in all their multicolored glory, all white and blue and orangey-black. The big guns were waiting, too, coughing up "big, black puffs . . . like ragged, six-foot-tall rectangular boxes" that hung in the air like medieval kites, searching for your very soul. And there were the SAMS (surface-to-air missiles), sporting a 349-pound, high-explosive warhead.[81] The enemy hoped for undercast so he couldn't be seen before blowing you out of the sky.

One day, during the dry time, antiaircraft fire got Chappie James. The experience deepened his belief in the brotherhood of man and made the foolishness about skin color so much hogwash. Coming out of the hell of Hanoi after a raid, his F-4 Phantom sported fifty-six holes. He radioed his second element leader, a white guy from Louisiana, where everybody is supposed to be prejudiced.

"Bill, you ought to take the lead, baby, and you all get back to the tanker because I don't think I'm going to make it! I'm going to try to get as close to the Red River as I can before we park this thing!"

They could hear the Vietnamese vectoring their MiGs toward them.

He waited for a response. There was none, but glancing down from his cockpit, he could see the other elements of his flight sweeping back and forth around him, their throttles all the way back to stay with him. He had one engine going, the other shot to pieces. He looked again, and his pilots were still zinging back and forth over his F-4, escorting him and giving him protection.

"Bill!" he radioed again, "Get them outta here! Get them on down there! You've got to get to that tanker, and you're burning up precious fuel here now! Get them going!" he ordered.

"You know, Mac," he heard through his intercom, "I don't hear a damn thing. I think my radio is out!"

"Me too, Bill," came the reply. "I can't hear either!"

Out across the limpid, blue sky, a KC-135 tanker crew heard them and, as Chappie later recalled, "they were a bunch of white fellows, too!"

The tanker commander turned his multimillion-dollar machine towards the troubled flight. They achieved rendezvous, and the F-4s began to hook up, so low on fuel they "must have been on fumes." They staggered the refueling. No one guy got a full load. Instead, each stuck the boom and took just enough to hang there in the sky. They cycled through that way, "and the tanker took us all the way back home."

In retrospect, Chappie noted, it was a lesson. "We (really) don't hate each other after all . . . it's really not necessary . . . and we can't afford it—which is more important!"

Not long after, Chappie flew a strike in the area of the North Vietnamese airbase, Phuc Yen. Their sharpshooters shot up his airplane very badly. There was simply no way to make it back to his home base at Ubon in Thailand, so he set the ship down at the emergency strip at Udorn. Sixteen holes adorned the fuselage. It was a miracle that he had made it, he thought (although such damage from shrapnel was commonplace).

While he was sitting around talking with other pilots about his apparent good luck, an American journalist approached him for an interview.

"What do you think about all the civil rights problems going on back home, Colonel?"

"What're you talking about?"

"Well, about the tenor of things. They're changing, you know. Why, there's Stokely Carmichael and Rap Brown—"

"Not interested!"

"Well, H. Rap Brown said—"

"Look, friend, I'm really not very interested in all of that, really. See, I consider myself darned lucky to have been able to land my airplane at this emergency strip in one piece, y'know? And I'm busy looking over the airplane and thanking God for allowing me to get close enough to home base to get back there! And I really don't have any comments, okay?"

When he got over to Udorn base, they told him that Sammy Davis, Jr., was there. Singing. Performing over at Club Two. He went over and found Sammy leading the troops, singing "We Shall Overcome." The experience made him respect Sammy Davis, Jr., because just being in-country, in an area fraught with possible death and danger set him apart from the run of entertainers. Chappie never forgot it and would remind Sammy of the encounter years later.

The presence of the writer may have been the catalyst which caused Chappie to make a trans-Pacific telephone call to Dorothy in the United States. Maybe the connection was bad, but Dorothy remembers that he was almost screaming.

"Dottie, I'm all right! I'm all right! Can you hear me?"

"Yes!"

"I'm okay! I love you! I'm all right!"

Perhaps it had been the reporter. Maybe he was afraid of how the media might have twisted his near miss with death, if they had in fact written about it. But he wanted to set the record straight with Dorothy.

For all of his usual good nature, Chappie was zeroed in on the need for excellence in every facet of his performance. He could show intense displeasure when achievement of that goal was thwarted. He was a team player, and expected those around him to play the same game. The armament technicians found out how deeply this conviction was felt one day when Chappie found it necessary to abort a mission because of a weapons release malfunction. He landed early with a full bomb load. Frustrated and angry, he taxied towards the weapons maintenance shack, a wooden frame building next to the flight line with a tent draped over it. Opposite the weapons maintenance abode, he swung the F-4 around. The jet wash blew the canvas tent off the hapless shack. Not much more needed to be said. He vented his ire and frustration in a unique but pointed way. The armament people didn't know what the problem was, but the problem was isolated in short order.

But when teamwork was evident, James was more than pleased with Robin, their pilots and himself:

Well, what was really happening was that we were running the s——— outta that outfit, you see? And the kids were having a great time . . . they were leaning on that desk next morning wanting to know *what time do we take off to go North?* A lot of them were dragging their feet when they started getting shot down—but not in *our* outfit! Kids would come—it's the first time I'd ever seen kids who were *not* on schedule at all . . . that would come to the briefing anyway and say, *Hey, you guys feelin' all right? If you're not, I'll take your place!*

Chappie and Robin Olds had instilled in their pilots that the place to be, if they were going to be over there in the war zone, was up north, prosecuting the war. In return, they gave them something back. "At the slightest excuse, we'd have a big parade; we'd have a torchlight parade down the middle of the street because one guy just finished his 100th mission. A guy'd get shot down and get picked up by the helicopters, [and] we'd have a big torchlight parade; and up at the bar . . . having a good time!''

After any big mission, it was a cinch that "Black Man and Robin" (after Batman and Robin, popular cartoon characters of the period), as Colonels James and Olds were called behind their backs, would be at the individual clubs, issuing a "well done!" and "thanks!" The scenario was predictable. Colonel Olds would look at the bartender.

"What're these guys drinking?"

"Beer!"

"Set 'em up! Let it roll—and I'll get the tab later!"

Chappie would echo the sentiment.

"Yeah! Set it up!"

"We'd all sit there," Technical Sergeant Trammel remembers, "and have a couple of beers. I suppose later the colonels paid for it!"

That's the kind of wing Olds and James ran. High profile. High morale. From afar, some people had the gall to call them "a couple of showboats!" But it got the job done. Excitement ran high as planning proceeded for the coming fighter sweep up north, deep into the enemy's sanctuary.

III

Code-named *Operation Bolo,* the planning for Colonel Olds's answer to the MiG problem moved ahead. Because the air force was restricted from attacking the enemy fighters on the ground for political reasons, this plan to force the MiGs into an air battle on the United States' terms held special allure. The ultimate objective was to deceive and lure the MiG air defense force into a reactive posture and, once they were airborne, seek them out, engage, pursue, and destroy them.

The plan required that the attacking F-4C force would have to appear on the enemy's radar as a normal F-105 strike force. The attacking force would follow normal strike force composition, the usual F-4C MiGCap and F-4 counter-force with the usual F-105 "Wild Weasel" Iron Hand* flights. The precise route the usual strike force used was to be followed.

*WILD WEASEL: The F-105 Thunderchief (nicknamed the "Thud") aircraft. Used to suppress enemy guiding radars and surface-to-air missile sites. First in and last out of an air strike, they were known by the mission name of "Wild Weasels," after the small carnivore adept at sniffing out and destroying vermin. Iron Hand was another code name for these type flights.

The final touch in this mimicry was the procurement and installation of the electronic countermeasures pods, designed to foil antiaircraft defenses. Not only did they require procurement and installation, but the crews had to be trained in their use. Since there weren't enough at Ubon to do the job, pods had to be "borrowed" from nearby bases at Takhli and Korat. "If," Colonel Olds commented, "we were going to look like [F-105] Thuds, we had to carry what the Thuds [were] carrying." Ground crews jerked the pods off the F-105 fighters as their pilots growled in the background.

"What's happening?"

"We don't know, but they're going to Ubon!"

There were control boxes to be installed, and pods to be modified for the F-4s. Wiring needed adjusting. Stateside air materiel areas dispatched electronics experts to help. It seemed that the entire air force joined in to support the coming mission. Flying formations had to be modified, repositioning wing men so as to maximize the counter-measures-barrage-effectiveness of the pods.

Code names were assigned to the enemy airfields. Gia Lam became "Burbank"; Phuc Yen, "Frisco." Kep became "Chicago"; Cat Bai, hard by Haiphong, became "Miami." The delta between Haiphong and Hanoi was suddenly "Texas," while the real estate north of Hanoi became the "Dakotas," and "Canada" and "Greenland." MiG launch and orbit points were identified as maintenance crews brought thirty-three fighters from Ubon up to the mark for the mission. Tanker rendezvous times were intricately and carefully worked out. Intelligence reports concerning previous MiG attack points were reviewed, as were the probable length of time MiG aircraft could remain airborne after five minutes of air-to-air combat. And how long could the F-4C fight and come home safely? How many airfields should be covered?

There would be an east and west force. Their code names would echo those of American automobiles. From the west, seven F-4C flights from the "Wolfpack" at Ubon would lead off. They would get the enemy when he was airborne, sweep his orbit areas, and cover two of his airfields. Five F-4C flights from Da Nang Air Base in Vietnam would arrive from the east and cover two additional airfields, blocking egress and ingress from nearby Chinese airfields. And the sky would be filled with support aircraft. KC-135 tankers, arcing out to refueling tracks. EB-66 aircraft, tasked as orbiting electronic/early warning radar stations. Twenty-four F-105 "Wild Weasel" flights, to suppress enemy surface-to-air missile capabilities and antiaircraft flak. Other F-104 fighters, to protect the counter-air forces as they aimed for home after the engagement.

It was to look like a usual daily, unescorted F-105 strike; imitating the F-105's refueling rendezvous tracks, approach routes, altitudes, and airspeeds.

Eighth Tactical Fighter Wing pilots were briefed for days. They had to learn new procedures because of the size of the strike and review basic air-to-air tactics. The most important precept of all was pounded into their heads: "Never, never try to out-turn the more agile Mig!"

General Momyer approved the overall strike plan on 22 December 1967. Seventh Air Force suggested that Olds send Col. Chappie James over to lead the fighter strike force from Da Nang, but Robin Olds thought better of the idea. "I thought about that and I thought about that," he said to General Momyer, "[but] I just can't do it . . . because he'd be very, very unwelcome. The guys could hack it. It's their wing. They've got a good piece of this mission and I just don't want to do that."

The usual Christmas and New Year bombing-halt went into effect, during which the North Vietnamese built up their forces, presaging a big push after New Year. But a United States surprise awaited them.

Operation Bolo was set for 2 January 1967. Satellite pictures showed foul weather ahead. At mission time it was fifteen hundred feet overcast with cloud cover to seven thousand feet, predicted to go to seven thousand feet with broken clouds. After a one-hour delay, the order to execute came down from Seventh Air Force headquarters.

And somewhere, several hundred miles up in North Vietnam, a group of North Vietnamese fighter pilots had but a short time to live.

Chapter Twenty-Two
Battle Cry

I

There was probably no way Chappie James would have consented to be left out of the impending *Bolo* MiG strike. The need to be part of it struck deep into his psyche, activating his fierce sense of pride. His administrative duties kept him on the ground far too much. It was a matter, too, of maintaining the continued respect of his pilots. He agonized over it to the point of depression.

"I know what some of them are saying," he confided to a close friend, "they think Chappie James hasn't got guts. How can you be a leader out here and command respect without flying with them?" Friendly assurances to the contrary were unacceptable to him. Administrative-type officers assigned to a wing headquarters who seldom or never flew were none-too-affectionately called "Wing Weenies" by fighter pilots.[82] In fact, Chappie James himself might have sung that old fighter pilot song about these people:

> Oh, there are no fighter pilots up in Wing
> Oh, there are no fighter pilots up in Wing
> The place is full of brass
> Sitting around on their fat a——
> Oh, there are no fighter pilots up in Wing!

And a fighter pilot James most certainly was, administrative duties be hanged. So he led the second flight behind Robin Olds in what became the largest, most successful American fighter victory in the Vietnam War. And too, since

229

he was not sent to command the participating fighter elements from Da Nang as Seventh Air Force had suggested, he was tagged by Robin Olds to be the "take-over command" in the event Olds was shot down.

Early on 2 January 1967, the banshee-yells of jet engines filled the Southeast Asia air. The east force, seven flights of four F-4C Phantom jets, fired up at Ubon, the flights code-named after American automobiles. "Olds," "Ford," "Rambler," they were called; "Plymouth," "Vesta," "Tempest," and "Lincoln." Col. Robin Olds rode up front as flight leader of his namesake flight. Chappie James rode second up front as flight leader of "Ford" flight. Crew chiefs checked aircraft systems. The slow roll began toward runways' ends, while arming crews removed red safety clips from the rockets slung underneath.

The west force, five flights of F-4C Phantoms from the 366th Tactical Fighter Wing at Da Nang Air Base in South Vietnam, repeated the systems-check-arming routine. Earlier, in the soft predawn light, twenty-five KC-135 refueling tankers had hastened toward refueling tracks. Iron Hand F-105 aircraft cleared the runway and flew towards assigned surface-to-air (SAM) and flak suppression targets. F-104 pilots prepared to protect counter-air forces when they departed the battle-zone-to-be.

Jet engines roared a thunderous battle cry twenty-five minutes after the hour as the first wave of "Ford," "Olds," and "Rambler" flights launched from opposite ends of the runway at five-minute intervals. At fifty-five minutes after the hour, the second wave, "Vespa," "Plymouth," "Lincoln," and "Tempest" flights sprang upon the air, their exhausts roaring. James, Olds, and other flight leaders orbited to rendezvous with the three other planes in their flights, taking final headings toward North Vietnam, while the F-4C Phantoms from Da Nang leapt into the air.

Coordinates for linkups with circling KC-135 tankers crackled over Thailand. The Phantoms moved gingerly up to the gas pumps in the sky, holding gently, keeping speed and heading constant until, with a metallic, traumatic contact, the tanker booms connected. The added fuel was lifeblood, for every minute over target required every possible ounce for maximum performance. Breaking away and re-forming, "Olds" and "Ford" flights flashed towards North Vietnam at over six hundred miles per hour. "Tempest" flight lead had aborted, joined by its number two plane because of fuel receptacle problems. Later, its remaining aircraft decided not to penetrate the battle zone. Only six of seven flights from Ubon were left.

Heavy overcast hampered visibility as the F-4C Phantoms winged their way into the vicinity of Hanoi. "Olds" flight, first to enter the battle zone, encountered no MiG interceptors as was usual in the routine F-105 Thunderchief flights they were simulating.

"They haven't shot at me yet," Olds observed, "Let's keep going."

They went further in, down Thud Ridge. Olds's guy-in-back sat glued to

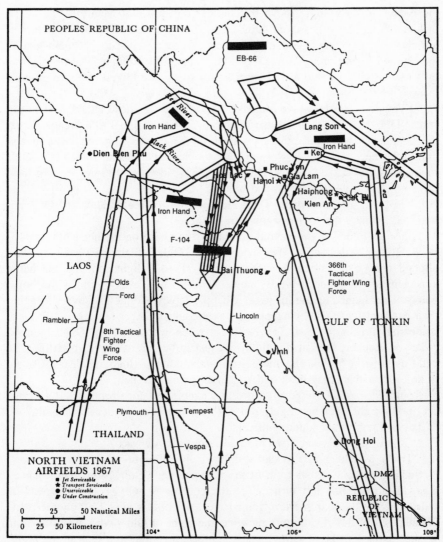

Battle Plan - Operation Bolo (Approximate)
January 2, 1967

the radar. Still nothing. Above the clouds, the day was beautiful, the sky a brilliant blue. They heard no MiG calls. They passed right over Phuc Yen airfield just as planned. Olds flight swooped down, "just to get them mad," then turned over Hanoi and back to Phuc Yen. Still nothing. The respite was brief. As "Olds" made a 180-degree turn to the northwest, his guy-in-back came alive:

"I've got a paint! Twelve o'clock!" The bogie was dead ahead and closing fast. "Olds" flight started down after him, when Colonel Olds realized that the bogie was low and either below or in the clouds, coming head-on and going like hell. The MiGs were up! Rather than charge into the clouds, Olds took his flight back up, across Phuc Yen, then did a fast 180-degree turn back down to Phuc Yen. It was cat and mouse.

"I'm going to catch them when they pop out of the undercast," Olds announced, "that's the way it's going to work!"

James's "Ford" flight entered the battle zone hard on the heels of "Olds." With all the maneuvering they had done, "Olds" flight had used up their allotted time over target, as "Olds" and "Ford" flights entered the battle zone almost simultaneously. By now, "Olds" flight was getting good bogie paints. They looked up in time to see Chappie James's flight flash over, dropping their external fuel tanks. Chappie was exuberant for other reasons: "I had just made my turn at the Son Tay reservoir when we picked up Olds flight on radar (no Rockets Free at this time) but just to be sure we don't blast him, he calls out on the radio: 'no more free shots, gang!' (loud 'n clear!) Couple minutes after that, they flash underneath us going like hell!"

Robin was on the verge of chewing Chappie out for dropping his external fuel tanks right over his flight. But before Robin could open his mouth, one of James's wing men sounded the alarm:

"Olds lead, you've got two MiG-21s right on your ass!"

"That's a helluva way to start a fight!" Olds thought.

Suddenly, MiG-21s shot out of the clouds from all directions. Olds slanted away in an extreme left turn to see the cavernous nose scoop of a MiG-21 closing. Only the extreme turn fouled the MiG pilot's aim. Still another MiG zoomed out of the clouds, turning wide and right of Olds, who went after him at once as he left the first MiG to his number three and four men in the flight. Targeting the MiG, Olds instructed his back-seat man to lock onto that great big rascal of a Sparrow radar-guided missile. Immediately, the high-pitched tone signifying lock-on was heard in his headphones. Olds fired two Sparrows at the MiG, but they broke lock and strayed. The MiG began a steep dive in evasive action as Olds fired a pair of heat-seeker Sidewinders, only to miss. Another MiG popped from the clouds to his right, turning wide to the left. In afterburner, Old's F-4C streaked into a high-speed, cantilevered climb behind the turning MiG. Foxlike, he was on him, hanging there, "half upside down,"

Olds was to later recount. He was the "snake in the grass," waiting for the North Vietnamese pilot to complete his turn. Waiting, and stalking, waiting and rolling in on him until, thirty-five hundred feet behind the MiG, he had him in the crosshairs, puffing away two Sidewinders. The event seared itself into Olds's mind: "That was a beautiful sight . . . that little thing jumped off the rails, cocked over at an angle . . . and you could just see it arc right up!"

Olds watched the progress of the Sidewinder in surreal fascination. "It's going to hit!" he yelled. "It's going to hit! It's going to hit! And, *plow!*"

The Sidewinder exploded in a vermillion flash on the MiG's right wing. "The whole thing," Olds remembers, "torn completely off at the roots and the rest of the MiG tumbling forward, end over end, then falls lurching and spinning into the clouds below!"

Full battle had been joined.

"Look out, Walt, he's at your seven and firing!" Olds heard over his headset.

"I got one! I got one!" someone screamed.

"Lead, there is one more closing at five—fast—break right—now!"

"Ras, he overshot—get him—ah, beautiful—tremendous!"

"Rambler lead, there they are—two o'clock—two of 'em—slightly low."

"Okay, attacking!"

"Rambler, look out, one coming in from three o'clock—break!—break!"

The North Vietnamese pilots were in a state of shock. Expecting to find the usual F-105 Thunderchiefs, they probably thought it was going to be a day of easy pickings, but instead, they found themselves in a fight for their lives, with the powerful, energy-filled F-4C Phantoms. The battle swirled.

"Rambler three here—I've got two MiGs, three miles at twelve. Engaging. Four, take the one on the right."

"Look at that! Look at that! He's ejecting!"

"Olds, this is Ford. Four SAMs coming up at your six o'clock. Don't break, they're not guiding!"

It was Chappie James.

"Olds lead, this is Ford. I'm right behind you, Chief. Don't worry, I'm covering your tail!"

But James had troubles of his own:

I thought I'd better look, so I whip quick like into a roll to the right and sure enough there sat the prettiest '21' you ever saw, in near perfect firing position on Ole Donnelly (my number 4). I immediately called for a hard right break for three and four, figuring the MiG would go with them and this would put me in perfect position to have him. For some stupid reason, when Bull broke his element right (and I'm breaking right harder 'n hell) that MiG broke left and came canopy-to-canopy with me (near midaired us). I started a barrel roll for separation as he started to accelerate and fired a Sidewinder at him, but (too many Gs) it missed him. He yanked that "21" around so hard he near stalled out and slid right down in front of Raspberry (my number 2) who was inside the turn and near line abreast with me. I called to "Ras" to "take him"; and he said "got him!" In the meantime these other two MiGs have swung around and overshot us and I snapped off two Sidewinders at them (just to keep them honest). Bull and Don (3 and 4) take off after them and I continue on around (and straight down by now) on Ras's wing after the other guy. The MiG pulled out just above the cloud tops and started a tight left, slightly climbing, turn. I remember thinking at the time, "We're too close and too many Gs" when Ole Ras went into a big ole barrel roll and settled right back into perfect position (range wise). I think the MiG driver must have thought that we had overshot and was wondering where we were, as "Ras" promptly let fly one Sidewinder which knocked his tail off. The MiG pitched up sharply and burst into a big fireball . . . lovely!

Rambler flight entered the battle zone as James's "Ford" flight exited. Chappie's personal mission report continues:

We immediately swung around to see if there was any gravy left for us in the "Olds" flight first, which we could see and hear going right next to us but they had just polished off the last one (they got three) and we had to scuffle and talk like mad to keep them from taking a shot at us. It was about this time the Charlies on the ground started lobbing SAMs up at us so we pulled the perfect appropriate maneuver at that time, namely GET THE HELL OUTA HERE!

As "Rambler" flight came in, two MiGs were sighted after one orbit at two and three o'clock low. "Rambler" lead launched two missiles, one hitting and destroying the MiG. A MiG-21 then slid between "Rambler" lead and the number two ship. Both executed a defensive split, breaking up, left and down. "Rambler" two came out of the maneuver behind Rambler four, turned inside the MiGs, firing a pair of missiles for another kill. Meanwhile, "Rambler" four fired and detonated a missile in the tailpipe of a fleeing MiG, resulting in an explosion and fireball. "Rambler" four, after a wide, looping G-turn, again positioned and locked on an enemy ship, firing four missiles, detonating high and to the right of the escaping MiG for a probable kill. A parachute was noted in the area.

"Lincoln" and "Vespa" flights were the last to enter the battle zone, but no further enemy aircraft were sighted.

It was refueling time for the run home. In order to go into afterburner to evade surface-to-air missiles and MiGs or to ensure adequate reserve for possible traffic delay because of a barrier engagement or battle-damaged aircraft, air refueling was a requisite. To miss a refueling track could be critical, as experience had shown. Flameout could occur. A mere six feet separating aircraft from a refueling boom could be tragic. At the moment of the second refueling, James and other flight members might have remembered Capt. Richard Penn and Lieutenant Finzer, who ran out of fuel less than six feet from an aerial tanker's boom. "You're almost there," Captain Penn remembered, "and then suddenly there is nothing you can do but punch out [eject]." Penn and Finzer had been on an early morning mission north of Hanoi when their Phantom jet took anti-aircraft hits. The fuel indicator suddenly went to zero. They called for a tanker and asked for navy search-and-rescue guidance as they headed for the Gulf of Tonkin. For a frantic twenty-five minutes, they tried to rendezvous with a KC-135 tanker. Suddenly, there it was, right in front of them, but then flameout occurred, twenty seconds away. They had no alternative. Punch out. Now. A navy helicopter from the U.S.S. *King* picked up Finzer and, twenty minutes later, Captain Penn.

"Post-strike refueling," remembers Colonel Olds, "is a necessity. If you play your cards right and pray hard, you can get to the tanker." It is the ultimate game of Russian roulette. Olds remembers plugging in one day "with 800 pounds [of fuel] left—about eight minutes of flying time."

After the refueling, in that marvelous, floating way fighter aircraft have of detaching the boom and pitching away gracefully into space, James and company headed down home to Ubon. To Ubon, where ground crews and officers waited in anticipation and excited conversation. Indeed, it seemed that the whole base was on the flight line to see what had happened.

Like sudden thunder, the lead elements of the attack forces were in the air above them, as if from nowhere, roaring across the base in traditional victory rolls. Going around, the first ship touched down to taxi past the wing command center. The pilot raised his hands, clasping them overhead as a signal of mission success.

They clapped, cheered, roared, and yelled in approbation.

Still the returning Phantoms fired across the base, circling, then zooming in to land like darts thrown by some smiling war god. They came in as the ground crew counted the return of their charges. "That's two," they breathed, "that's three . . . now four!" It was a whispered prayer, blossoming into yells. "That's five . . . and six . . . and seven!"

Now the last plane landed and a wild yell went up. *"All safe!"* The waiting crowd erupted in a maniacal, roaring cheer.

The 8th Tactical Fighter Wing was an "ace" wing already, but how many kills had there been? One had only to watch the demeanor of the pilots walking in from their planes. A smile and a little nod bespoke a MiG gone to its happy hunting ground. The kill count began. One, two, and three. Four and five and six, then *seven!* What? Was this possible?

It was magnificent joy and absolute ecstasy to have been a member of the first "double ace" wing in all of Southeast Asia, without the loss of a single aircraft! Robin Olds was hoisted up and carried from the flight line like a victorious football coach. When they put him down, he said: "It's a great day for the wing. You maintenance men did it. This is your day. I'm proud of all of you!"

After debriefing, he added: "I feel pretty good. I'm proud of this wing and grateful to 7th and 13th Air Force for making this mission possible. This is a great day for the entire Air Force!"

What of Chappie James, a flight leader in this ferocious dogfight which, by some accounts, lasted for fifteen minutes before the MiG-21 force retired from the area? What of James on this, the United States' first overwhelming aerial fighter victory of the Vietnam War?

James's missiles had been errant shots through no fault of his own. It was simply the way the battle had flowed. And back at the officers' club, some were saying that Capt. Everett T. Raspberry, James's wingman, had actually saved his life with the barrel roll maneuver. According to James R. McGovern, in his book, *Black Eagle:* "The story spreading around the club . . . was accepted with friendly grins."

The pilots were in all the clubs that night, telling and retelling the story of the battle. Of tactics. Of bravery and skill. Beer flowed. Hands executed those barrel rolls again, and mouths recreated the sounds of lock-on while fingers fired Sidewinders and Sparrow missiles.

And what of James, who, at the last minute had been denied the chance to lead the fighter elements out of Da Nang on this magnificent strike? The strike elements who, according to Robin Olds, "never figured in the battle." A force which, except for one flight, "just milled about and never came in—unfortunate because, according to electronic intelligence, Vietnamese MiG-17s were orbiting right where number 5 flight should have been—and that's pretty sad."

It was the clouds that had bugged them, Colonel Olds later said. "They just did not decide to fly their mission above clouds, and I can understand their reluctance . . . because old number three flight here headed right down there, over the clouds in SAM Valley—Jesus!—that takes guts!" And further, said those pilots in debriefing, they never got an "execute order" even though, according to General Momyer in his book *Air Power in Three Wars,* they made "repeated attempts to get into their assigned areas."

Perhaps the point is meaningless now, but it is worth the speculation to wonder what would have happened with those flights if Chappie James had commanded them. This Chappie James, who later said:

In combat, it's a matter of seeing that stuff coming up off the ground at you and having to fly through it with never entertaining a thought of not (doing it). . . . A guy asked me in a press conference once, "Well, why didn't it ever occur to you sometime—why don't you just fly on past that target and come on back and say my bomb racks didn't work or something happened—I couldn't get my gunsight to work and then come on back and be safe?"—*That thought never entered your mind, if you've got any PRIDE! Too damned proud—I'd rather die than see the rest of these guys go wheeling in there. And you're damned right I'm going in there. . . . I'm the leader! I'm on the point! Do you think I'm gonna turn around and go back home? Hell, I'd rather blow myself up!* (And *that* never entered my mind, either!)

Quite possibly it would have been a different day. Maybe America would have lost some pilots that day, but maybe not. One thing is for sure. There would have been no "milling about." There would have been no "waiting for an order to execute" because Chappie believed the same as Robin Olds: "They got their execute *before* they took off—this is your frag order. Fly it. Execute it." Perhaps the enemy kill ratio would have been even higher, because as Chappie James loved to say of himself: "I am a warrior. I make no pleas for pity for that. I'm proud of that. I am a fighting man. And I fight for my country. She's mine and anybody who wants to take issue with her and he comes across me and he's against us, gets a bloody nose!"

Perhaps James completed a personal mission report because he didn't win the kewpie doll that day. And although aerial dogfights at supersonic speeds involving missiles capable of blowing men and machine instantly into oblivion were a fighter pilot's workaday world, perhaps James spoke for many of his fellow airmen who also missed the kewpie doll that day when he said: "First of all, it is so darn great to be back in a combat situation and this is a real going thing we've got here. I was in the BMF (stands for 'Big MiG Fight'). Although I didn't get one, I'm very proud of the fact that I was part of the whole operation."

II

In March 1967, William McAdoo and William Kirk, two old comrades-in-arms who served with Chappie at Davis-Monthan and Bentwaters, arrived at Ubon. Typically, Chappie felt it necessary to introduce them to combat. This he did with the usual Chappie James flair, leading the flight after scheduling his friends for their first combat. Chappie was especially impressed with Bill McAdoo and Bill Kirk (to be USAFE commander one day) and "the young John Moore." Kirk, Chappie thought, "was a winner from the day he stepped into an airplane," and would "go to a weapons range and play grab-ass with you in the sky any day you wanted." Knowing that in combat it's the best team that wins, he loaded his commander's (Robin Olds) flight with McAdoo, Kirk, and Moore because "with a team like that somebody's going to hit the deck and it won't be us!" He worried sometimes about the younger fighter pilots not so easy to type, because "you can never tell a fighter pilot until that first tracer crosses the windshield . . . until those golf balls start coming up off the ground—that's when the guys better with a piece of chalk and a stick are better off out of a cockpit!"

Chappie is remembered at Ubon in much the same way he was remembered at other air force bases. Always maintaining an enthusiastic and large following, working hard, and playing hard. Singing, always singing at the officers' club. Singing popular songs and old favorites. Singing the ever-present fighter pilot songs he loved at the bar. It was he and Olds who, as a matter of protocol, met the congressmen, dignitaries, royalty, and generals who visited Ubon.

Among these was his old commander from the days of Godman Field, Kentucky, and Lockbourne Army Air Base in Ohio, now-Lt. Gen. Benjamin O. Davis, Jr., still the air force's only black general. Lieutenant General Davis now commanded Thirteenth Air Force, one of the major commands under which the 8th Tactical Fighter Wing operated. General Davis remembers the visit and more: "[I] next saw [Chappie] in Ubon, Thailand, at the 8th Tactical Fighter Wing. Visited with him and Colonel Olds. [It] was a pleasant visit. He later visited me at Clark Air Force Base [Philippines]. My wife and I had him to lunch."

Davis may have had a small bone to pick with both Olds and James, since he had issued directives prohibiting victory rolls at the end of combat flights. To airmen of the wing, aware of both the directive and the fact that Colonel Olds, as the commander, continued the rolls in spite of it, it seemed that "Olds disobeyed constantly." Since, as director of operations, Chappie's job was to reflect the style of the commander, it may have looked as if both colonels were disobeying the Davis directive.

In their view, however, there was good reason to continue the victory rolls. It wasn't just "ass-shining" and show-off, but a valid and necessary fighter pilot training tool. According to Olds, the U.S. pilots assigned to them "arrive here bright-eyed and bushy-tailed and extremely naive. . . . It took considerable . . . blackboard skull practice and . . . application of practice. . . . After coming home from a long mission we had . . . enough fuel to append 5-10 minutes of practical tactics. We always do it. . . . I never let them rest . . . practice every moment."

The odds are that Davis probably understood; at least the tradition of victory rolls and practice tactics continued until Olds's tour of duty was over. It was part of a bigger picture of constant teaching so as to apply the lessons learned in combat: "Certainly if nothing else, some hard-headed fighter pilots . . . in the 8TFW have learned that you simply cannot turn with a MiG. You just can't do it. . . . You can't flit about the sky . . . with impunity . . . just because you've got a more modern aircraft. (The bitter lesson is) . . . the (enemy's) going to nail you . . . the first mistake you make . . . and the first mistake is . . . trying to turn with them . . ."

Chappie James undoubtedly subscribed to these theorems, not only because Olds was the commander, but also because his job involved scheduling and planning flight missions; making certain that pilots, planes and weapons were on line to make them happen. Also, he was a chief proponent of the United States' presence in Vietnam. That attitude helped minimize disconsolate attitudes among his own men about the war's futility, and especially those inflamed by demagoguery about the Vietnam War from certain black leaders in the United States.

By the summer of 1967, the media was full of such declarations. Chappie could not be still in the face of it.

There was H. Rap Brown, virtually unknown until then, inciting would-be black militants to near frenzy as they stood in the aisles where he was to speak, grabbing at his hands as he approached the speaker's platform.

"Rap, baby, Rap!" they chided. "Run it down, Rap, run it down!"

H. Rap Brown would oblige with language designed to incite.

"When the honkey asks what he can do for me, I tell him that he can give me some guns!"

And there was Stokely Carmichael, intimating that blacks were ready to fight at home but not in Vietnam, a Cuban magazine quoting him thusly: "If the people in the United States had been armed, they would have taken good care of President Johnson!"

"This thing got to me," Chappie exploded, "the lawlessness, rioting; men like Stokely Carmichael acting as if they speak for the Negro people. They aren't, and set civil rights back 100 years!"

Chappie made it clear that "thousands of Negroes are fighting here [in Vietnam]." He worried about the time when these fighting men would find it necessary to live down the trouble Stokely "and other idiots like him have built." It was a matter now of "speaking out firmly against them and [against] violence."

He was right on several counts. The extremists *were* setting the civil rights movement back, and they did not speak for the majority of blacks.

Jay Gould, in the *New York Times,* writing of the emotional involvement men like Carmichael and Brown incite on television, thus setting back the issue of civil rights, noted: "Reading the remarks of Mr. Brown and Mr. Carmichael can hardly compare with seeing them on television and watching the gestures and intonations of speech that punctuate their imprecations . . .''

Across the country, other blacks wrote letters to editors divorcing themselves from inclusion in the extremists' diatribes: "Mr. Carmichael represents me neither here in the United States nor on the island of Cuba. I find his delusion . . . that he is representing any Negro outside . . . the criminal or totally ignorant and impressionable . . . laughable . . .''

Chappie declared himself "an American first, and a black second," as did most black military men of the era. The black panther emblem he had proudly worn on his fighter pilot's helmet could no longer be used. It stood for an ideology which he could not embrace because Chappie James loved his country more than he loved himself. Any person or group anywhere that would discredit or otherwise attack the United States of America automatically lost respectability in his estimation.

He continued to chafe at the news of growing dissidence at home. Casting about for an acceptable way to react, he wrote an essay and entered it in the Freedom Foundation Contest of 1967. His old friend, William McAdoo, was moved as he read the essay before submission. Titled "Freedom—My Heritage, My Responsibility," it won the George Washington Medal for 1967. The title succinctly stated his point of view on the value of freedom. In the essay he put forth his belief that the country's strength was couched in its unity; that therein lay the innate talents of "free men blessed and ordained with the rights of freedom working to provide, enjoy and grow." And anyone trying to disrupt that unity by any means actually drives "wedges of fear and discontent" between people.

"I am," he wrote, "a Negro and therefore I am subject to their constant harangue. They say: 'You, James, are a member of a minority—you are a black man. . . . You should be disgusted with this American society. . . . You can only progress as far in any field that you choose before somebody puts his foot on your neck for no other reason than you are black. . . . You are a second-class citizen.' ''

But Chappie had the answer, and that lay in what he saw as his American heritage of freedom: "I am a citizen of the United States of America," he proudly proclaimed. "I am not a second-class citizen and no man here is unless he thinks like one, reasons like one or performs like one. . . . Today's world . . . situation requires strong men to stand up and be counted—no matter what their personal grievances are. Our greatest weapon is one we have always possessed—our heritage of freedom—our unity as a nation."

Reprinted in the *Stars and Stripes,* the essay may have had a positive effect on the morale of American fighting men. It is the kind of Chappie James utterance that prompts men like air force CMSgt. James O. Helms, still on active duty in 1988, to say: "Colonel Chappie James was and still is one of my war heroes," and Chappie's old friend, Col. William McAdoo, USAF

(Retired), to comment: "I think one of the strongest things he did was his faith in the American way of life. He would express it differently perhaps than a lot of us would. I think he had a very strong belief in the American way of life."

III

The war ground on, and sometimes the job as director of operations almost made Chappie pull out his hair, as on one Friday when one of his fighter pilots decided to "push" a comrade's wounded F-4C Phantom home to rescue point and safety, while Chappie monitored the whole thing on the ground.

Part of a four-plane flight sent to strike the huge Thai Nguyen steel works north of Hanoi, one ship, piloted by Capt. Earl D. Aman of New London, Texas, with Capt. Robert W. Houghton of Monicello, Utah, in the back seat, was hit as it rolled into the target. The plane shuddered. A second F-4C, piloted by Capt. John R. Pardo of Hearne, Texas, with Lt. Stephen A. Wayne as his guy-in-back, was also hit but not as critically as Aman's ship. Both ships were losing fuel, but Aman's airplane was losing it especially rapidly. Chappie James winced.

"The flight leader," he recalled later, "asked for a tanker, but it was obvious no tanker could get there in time."

One of Aman's engines flamed out. Awestruck, James continued the story.

"Pardo saw that his buddy was going to go down in enemy territory and so he decided a little push would get him to a rescue point."

Pardo radioed Aman to jettison his drag chute, so he could put the nose of his F-4C against Aman's fighter's tail. That done, he found that the jet wash repeatedly threw him off, and Aman's tailgate constantly flapped, making the "push" attempt impossible.

"It was like trying to stick wet spaghetti up a tiger's tail," James remembered.

Suddenly, Aman's second engine stopped working; his stabilizer was shot, and the ship bucked wildly. Not to be outdone, Pardo had a flash of brilliance. He'd connect with Aman's tail hook—the arresting tailhook used by carrier planes and by the air force as a safety device.

"Lower your tail hook," Pardo ordered.

As the tail hook descended and locked into place through the exertion of hydraulic and pneumatic pressures at 900 pounds per square inch, Pardo nosed the windscreen of his fighter up against the hook as he flew directly underneath Aman's airplane.

"He had to do it gently," James fumed. "Like pushing another fellow's car without scratching your bumper!"

It worked. They reached the rescue point. Both crews eventually punched out and were rescued by Jolly Green Giant rescue helicopters. Another hairy day in the life of Chappie James, director of operations.

"It was a great act of courage and flying skill," he later admitted, growing a bit testy perhaps as he added, "I don't expect it to become standard operating procedure. In fact, *I don't ever want it to happen again!*"

There was more to it than just the danger involved. It went to the possible loss of a wingman and the trauma attached to that. Col. Dick Jonas, USAF (Retired), remembers that in *The Dick Jonas Songbook,* Vol. I: "In a flight of four fighters . . . he is the youngest, least experienced, low man on the totem pole, fourth in command . . . precarious, his life expectancy shortest of the four. . . . I love him. . . . He is my brother . . . when he went down, I wept unashamedly. . . . The years can never heal the hurt nor dry the eye of any fighter pilot who returned home without his wingman."

Chappie James was no exception. As a fighter pilot, he shared the feeling. And that is why they gathered nights around the officers' club bar to sing *Blue Four,* the song Dick Jonas wrote:

> There's a fireball down there on the hillside
> And I think maybe we've lost a friend
> But we'll keep on flyin'
> And we'll keep on dyin'
> For duty and honor never end.
>
> There's an upended glass on the table
> Down in front of a lone empty chair
> Yesterday we were with him
> Today God be with him
> Wherever he is in your care.
>
> They were four when they took off this morning
> And their duty was there in the sky
> Only three ships returning
> Blue Four ain't returning
> To Blue Four, then, hold your glasses high.
>
> There's a fireball down there on the hillside
> And I think maybe we've lost a friend
> But we'll keep on flyin'
> And we'll keep on dyin'
> For duty and honor never end.

December 1967 beckoned and not long before Christmas, the Australian contingent based on Ubon decided to fill the American airmen's club with foam from one of their crash trucks. Just for fun and the hell of it.

"We'll show you Yanks a bloody white Christmas!" they roared. The prank was taken in good spirits as the Aussies cleaned up their mess.

Near the end of the year, Robin Olds's replacement arrived. Olds returned to the United States after over 150 combat missions, to be promoted to brigadier general in 1968 and become the commandant at the Air Force Academy, a post he was to hold until January 1971. Since he arrived at Ubon after Robin Olds did, Chappie's rotation date had yet to arrive.

Olds would not soon be forgotten. The man had hero status, for some of those he left behind remembered flying Robin's wing as together they flashed across the Red River, zooming down Thud Ridge "so close to the ground you had to look up to see the treetops." He was the kind of commander they wrote songs about and sang them lustily when the booze ran free and strong:

> We flew in the Wolf Pack with Robin Olds
> Some of us ain't coming back
> In a Foxtrot-four called the Phantom II
> We flew with the Red River Rats.
>
> Robin came over to Ubon
> An ace with 22 kills
> He led the 8th Wing to victory
> In the skies over Hanoi's hills.
>
> The 435th and the Nite Owls, too
> The Nickel and the 433rd
> Went with Robin thru the jaws of Hell
> Leading the Wolf Pack herd.
>
> Smoking along to the firewall
> 25 feet off the deck
> Move over, Hanoi Hanna
> Robin's gonna break your back.
>
> Bandits! Bandits! over Thud Ridge
> Mig Ridge and Haiphong, too
> No sweat, sir, Robin Olds is there
> And behind him is the Wolf Pack crew.

The new 8th Tactical Fighter Wing commander was no Robin Olds. Things began to change, and Chappie found himself sometimes going against the grain as he sought to continue some of the morale boosters Robin and he had condoned. One, of course, was the meeting of a pilot completing his one hundredth combat mission on the line after he taxied in, celebrating with a huge bottle of champagne in hand. Chappie busied himself going up the ladder to the cockpit as soon as the F-4C Phantom halted, the pilot wearing a broad smile. The new commander was also there.

"Colonel," growled the new boss, "did you read my memorandum prohibiting the consuming of alcoholic beverages on the flightline?"

Chappie stopped but didn't answer. Several airmen stood nearby watching the scenario. Chappie took another step up the ladder towards the waiting major. The new commander repeated his question. They say Chappie paused, looked at the new colonel. A bit of derision rode his voice as he delivered the coup de grace.

"———you, Colonel!" he roared, pulling the cork out of the champagne bottle with his teeth as the bubbly stuff sprang foaming into the Thai air.

Nearby airmen were thunderstruck. They were, in fact, mortified, but with a tremendous admiration.

"Did you hear that?"

"Did Colonel James really say what I thought I heard him say?"

"Yeah, boy, he surely did!"

An airman who witnessed the scene remembers that: "It was one of those things where [Chappie] could do that to another colonel and you still respected him because you *didn't* respect the guy he was talking to. It didn't hurt [our] respect for Chappie at all . . . [for] he was a *team player* . . ."

Orders assigning Colonel James to Eglin Air Force Base, Florida, arrived. Only fifty miles from Pensacola, he no doubt looked forward to it, since it was almost like going home again. Time to be with the old family again. To see his sister and brother. Spend time with his family, who had patiently waited while he went away to war. It was a chance to hobnob with old chums again and revisit old haunts.

White House administration had not missed his public utterances about the Vietnam War, his participation in and support of it. Both the *New York Times* and *Time* magazine had run pieces about his upfront denunciations of home-grown extremists.

As a result, President Lyndon Johnson gave Col. Chappie James a hero's greeting at the White House in mid-December 1967, soon after he returned to the United States. The summons netted James the "Johnsonian knee-to-knee talk," the ceremonial handshaking before photographers' flash bulbs and a personal introduction afterwards. The president seemed proud of "the progress the services have made, advancing people on their merit without regard to color." In return, James avowed that American air power was effectively minimizing the ability of North Vietnam to fight. As Chappie usually did when he found himself center stage, he warmed to the subject of the fighter pilot's world. He told Johnson that they call Hanoi and the adjacent Phuc Yen airbase "Downtown"; that his pilots adapted that from the vintage song, "You should be nervous tonight because tomorrow you got to go downtown." It was a joke begun in the bachelor officer quarters, and the next thing you knew, they were humming the tune rolling onto the runways headed for combat. He talked of the surface-to-air missiles, the SAMs, those "terrible weapons that cause . . . a lot of headaches." Of high unit morale, of which he was justly proud because "my fighter pilots have always had a great morale. It is the greatest fraternity in the world."

Vietnam had hardened him to steel. Robin Olds and the 8th Tactical Fighter Wing "Wolfpack" expanded his knowledge and capabilities as a professional air force combat officer, allowing him to move past simple theory into the practical arena where people died. He had survived. And most of all, he was now viewed by the American power structure as a political asset, worthy of special consideration. As one officer later observed, there were miles for Chappie to go now. The right place and the right time were quickly approaching.

Chapter Twenty-Three
Respite

I

It was 4 April 1968, and Martin Luther King, Jr., leaned over a balcony at the Lorraine Motel in Memphis, to be greeted by the sharp bark of rifle fire, a bullet tearing into his neck and ending his life sixty minutes later.

The killing spawned outrage among blacks. Chappie and Dorothy watched as the news flashed garishly across the television screen. Shock and disbelief chilled the air; there was an unnatural silence. Chappie wept. The doorbell rang and Dorothy remembers: "Our air force neighbors were the most beautiful thing. All white. The president of the officers' wives club . . . her husband was a colonel . . . another officers' wife was a nurse . . . we all wept. . . . They came in, and some of them were crying, too. That was so beautiful. I'll never forget that. 'We're so sorry,' they said, 'we're so upset . . .' "

Chappie James returned to the United States in December 1967, one step ahead of the coming of 1968, the year America shuddered. Lance Morrow, in *Time* magazine, says it was a time when American "history cracked open; bats came flapping out, dark surprises . . . tragedies and horrific entertainment; deaths of heroes, uprisings, suppressions, the end of dreams." And for one dreadful moment, it may have seemed to Chappie that King's death was perhaps the end of a dream. He had supported Martin Luther King's ideologies and applauded the civil rights movement. Through them, he had envisioned great hope and ultimate progress for America. But almost immediately, violence, the thing he hated and denounced the most, began to overtake his beloved America. Riots swept Washington, D.C., Baltimore, Chicago, Kansas City, and ultimately, 125 cities across the land; places like Watts, Detroit, and Newark. One night, Bobby Kennedy addressed blacks whose souls were filled with tears and grief from the back of a truck in Indianapolis:

"Those of you who are black can be filled with hatred, with bitterness and a desire for revenge," he said. "We can move forward toward further polarization, or we can make an effort, as Dr. King did, to understand, to reconcile ourselves and to love."

Maybe that night Chappie remembered his vow to love and care, taken that cold and freezing night not too long before when he had driven through the main gate of Eglin Air Force Base past the shivering sentries, and how he had gone to get them coffee, easing their tour of duty. If so, perhaps the flashback helped him gear up for his scheduled speech in Atlanta the next day to Air Force Association officers about racial problems, and somehow go beyond the color of another's skin. According to James McGovern, quoting one of Chappie's friends, "the atmosphere in the hotel was very tense as Chappie got up to deliver his speech." But it was not hatred of which he spoke, it was his continuing "faith in excellence." It was not polarization; it was faith in the system. It was not revenge, but faith in the future. It was a variation on an old Chappie James theme:

They say, "You should be disgusted with this American society—this so-called democracy. You are black and here somebody is always going to remind you of that. You can only progress so far in any field that you choose before somebody puts his feet on your neck for no other reason than . . . you are a second-class citizen and you should be disgusted with the treatment you get here."

I say, hell, I'm not disgusted—I'm a citizen of the United States of America and I'm no second-class citizen either and no man here is, unless he thinks like one and reasons like one and performs like one. This is my country and I believe in her and I believe in her flag and I'll defend her and I'll fight for her and I'll serve her and I'll contribute to her welfare whenever and however I can.

If she has any ills, I'll stand by her until in God's given time, through her wisdom and her consideration for the welfare of the entire nation, she will put them right.

It was the day they brought Martin Luther King's body home. The media reported what Chappie said, and people noticed. Perhaps, as William A. Coughlin reported in the *Los Angeles Times*, "it may have been more than coincidence that there were no riots in Atlanta on that weekend when they blazed so fiercely elsewhere." Coughlin also noted that it was "quite a speech for a black man in Atlanta to make" the day after King's assassination. But like King, Chappie believed in America and her systems; he believed that in the long run, those systems used correctly would help solve many problems minorities suffer within the country. He was not exempt from racism's barbs. From that gas station attendant who spat on him while he was attending the Air Command and Staff School, to other attendants who delighted in calling him "boy" even though he wore the uniform of a full colonel in the United States Air Force. From the gate guard at Otis Air Force Base in Massachusetts who branded him "a goddamned nigger," to the pale young lady who pulled her car in front of his in a Fort Walton Beach, Florida, gas station to exclaim: "I'm late for my appointment with my hair dresser and besides, nigger, I don't have to explain all this to you!"

Pensacola itself also showed its racism to James from time to time. When he was beset by a racial incident in his hometown, it hurt more than anything that could occur elsewhere. A military Catholic priest sent two Italian exchange pilots over to see him because they felt that Pensacola had been less than friendly to them as visitors. The thought was that Chappie, already a full colonel, and his family might be able to steer them to areas in which a fuller social agenda might be realized. Everyone met at his sister Lillian's house, including his niece and her husband, Gloria and Cecil Hunter. They talked about places in town they could go and probably not encounter racial problems. Cecil Hunter casually mentioned the Torch Club on Navy Boulevard, but had serious reservations as to whether or not Chappie would be welcome there. Dark and swarthy, with black, curly hair, the Italian pilots could easily be mistaken for black. Used to integrated living with the Air Force, and the privileges accorded his elevated rank of colonel, Chappie could not imagine that he would be refused service, given the changing nature of the American scene, especially in his hometown of Pensacola.

"Oh," he said with great confidence, "I can go anyplace!"

Gloria tried valiantly to persuade him otherwise.

"Dan, they're *not* going to let you in!"

"Oh, *hell* yeah!" he responded, "they're going to let *me* in!"

Dressed in full uniform, he swapped shirts with one of the Italian pilots, left his jacket at his sister's home, and the three of them went to the Torch Club. The owner of the club approached their table immediately.

"I can serve these two Italian pilots, but I can't serve *you!*"

They say Chappie immediately began letting the club owner know just who in the hell he was. A full colonel in the United States Air Force, and all that. The owner eyed him for a mini-second.

"Hey," he exploded, "I don't care *who* you are, you're *still* a nigger to me!"

It devastated Chappie. The famous James temper undoubtedly flared, but he couldn't do anything physical. He was, after all, a full colonel in the air force. Gloria Hunter recalls the aftermath: "When he came back, Dan's eyes were glassy. He said, 'You told me, but I didn't believe it!' [The authorities] never did anything . . . they never put the place off limits. And it just died away . . . and it's still down there."

II

Perhaps because of the well-publicized welcome by President Johnson and obvious approval by the administration, Chappie James's personal star began to ascend. For approximately a year, he was in demand for speaking engagements across the country. He spoke with fervor to "a variety of audiences, including service clubs, church organizations, Air Force dinners, Boy Scouts, school assemblies, and graduations"; to national service organizations, Armed Forces Day celebrations, and a plethora of corporate conferences. On 30 May 1968, he appeared on the "Mike Douglas Show" and a television talk show out of Chicago. The fourteenth of March 1968 became a Chappie James Appreciation Day in Pensacola, and he became the honorary parade marshal on Independence Day in Bridgeport, Connecticut. In mid-1969, the Florida Jaycees presented him their first Outstanding American Award.

Response to his speeches and presentations was positive from every area of the country. Letters from the public, addressed to his superiors, and hosts of television shows on which he appeared spoke of his words as if they were fresh, March winds. They heard him when he spoke of the "need to man the ramparts of freedom." They nodded in agreement when he "chastised those who divide our nation by their demonstrations, riots and taking into their own hands the laws of the nation." They valued his "polished and well-organized speeches." It was, they said, "a pleasure to hear a man who can talk about his love for our flag and nation without embarrassment." And almost to a man, they thought him "a source of inspiration to our youth and a source of inspiration to all America." They wanted him to come back to speak again and again, if that were possible.

In spite of the glowing accolades, racism dogged his heels. He saw a possible assignment as wing commander at Myrtle Beach, South Carolina, go skittering away when "influential citizens" of that area protested. The job of wing commander would have certainly been a step up in his career, since he had been the number two man on several occasions. It would have also been a first, since no black officer in the *integrated* air force had ever commanded a wing within the continental United States. More disappointment waited around the corner. In 1969, he was passed over for promotion to brigadier general.

It was not as if James had not looked to his own career, and done all those things expected of him to earn advancement. He had, in fact worked industriously to achieve it, through his exemplary performance as an Air Force officer and alliances with powerful political friends.

He courted the good offices of an old Tuskegee friend during his cadet days, Congressman Charles C. Diggs, Jr., of Michigan. Diggs approached other members of the House in Chappie's behalf; L. Mendel Rivers of South Carolina; Robert Sikes from Pensacola. They found that Colonel James was "among only 300 who were receiving final consideration from a pool of 7,000 other colonels for the seventy-seven openings for general." Chappie did not simply rely on Congressman Diggs, he tried opening some doors himself by writing both Rivers and Sikes, congratulating them whenever they stood tall for military appropriations. He would tell the air force airmen, he assured them, about "great lawmakers" like them "who understand the need for the capability of our military element." And whenever they called for staunch American response in the face of any unprovoked attack, he would endorse their position. "We have spoken softly long enough," he wrote Rivers, according to James R. McGovern, "we have the big stick. I think it is high time we use it."

Knowing of James's eloquence at the speaker's podium they both responded by inviting him to speak about Vietnam and patriotism. In the final analysis, James could count all three men as friends and supporters.

If James could not be promoted at this point in his career, it did not affect his confidence. He knew that the hard work he put in on Eglin Air Force Base counted. He knew that his speeches across the country counted. And most importantly, he knew he was making an impact on the young and very young people of the land, a segment of the population he cherished and for whom he held great hope. He made inroads, in his way, on the stultifying racism still rampant in parts of the country, and he wanted black children in particular to know that American futures existed for them, too. James McGovern quotes one J. Allen Ball, a high school teacher, who wrote:

> We would like for you to send an autographed picture of yourself and any other material dealing with the Negro's role in Vietnam. We would also like for you to write an open letter to our student body as to the role they can play in the world community or on any subject you may like to discuss. We hope this will not be an imposition on your limited time, but any reply from you would be a source of inspiration to our youth as your fame and image has been a source of inspiration to all Americans.

If for a moment, delay in promotions bothered Chappie, a letter like that one probably took the edge off and was dear to his heart. As late as 1986, old and grizzled Tuskegee Airmen acquaintances of his observed: "If Chappie walked into a room full of adults and there were children there, Chappie would find and talk to the children long before he would talk to the adults."

It isn't documented whether or not he ever got around to writing the open letter the high school teacher asked for, but based on Chappie's love affair with youth, it's a pretty good bet that he did.

III

Thirty-six hours away by fighter jet and strategically astride the great Mediterranean Sea, Libya grabbed the attention of the international community. Although not many people knew very much about him at that point, a man called Muammar Khadafy was on the rise there. The United States, Britain, and France each had expensive agreements with Libya. The United States Bases Agreement, signed in 1954, had obligated the country to pay millions for the privilege of maintaining its sprawling Wheelus Air Base there. The costs had steadily escalated over the years until now, additional agreements to give "sympathetic consideration to Libyan requirements of additional aid," threatened to exceed forty million dollars.

As early as 1955 and 1956, Libyan tendencies seemed to indicate a drawing away from the Western orbit. In order to achieve her goal of complete independence, despite obvious dependence on foreign aid, she decided to establish diplomatic relations with Russia. This shocked the Western powers, none of whom had been informed that such negotiations were in progress.

Hope for a stable government lay in King Idris, known to the Western bloc as a "wise and devoted monarch." The thought was that, as long as he lived, prospects were great that rule in the Libyan kingdom would be "polished, benevolent and statesmanlike."

King Idris and his queen, Fatima, were vacationing on the Marmara Coast of Turkey on the morning of 1 September 1969. On sprawling Wheelus Field, the American flying training base, it was business as usual. The millions invested by America were evident amid the noisy takeoff of huge transport airplanes and the screaming formation of jet fighters periodically rotated from Europe for bombing and gunnery training missions. C-47s droned; helicopters hovered.

The day before, three Libyan armored car battalions had received permission for a night exercise. As dawn blossomed, instead of conducting the maneuvers they had gotten permission to perform, battalion officers and noncommissioned officers drove into Tripoli. There, they quickly struck and disarmed the police and British-staffed defense force. The television and radio buildings were captured, and commanders with the ability to interfere were seized.

A new voice rode the airwaves. Ex-Lt. Muammar Khadafy spoke to the country:

> In the name of God, the Compassionate, the Merciful, O great Libyan people! To execute your free will, to realize your precious aspirations, truly to answer your repeated call demanding change and purification, urging work and initiative, and eager for revolution and assault, your armed forces have destroyed the reactionary, backward, and decadent regime . . . with one blow from your heroic army, the idols collapsed and the graven images shattered . . .

The Americans on Wheelus Field were hardly awake. Some were only having breakfast and knew nothing of what had transpired during the darkness.

Khadafy went on: "From now on, Libya is deemed a free, sovereign republic under the name of the Libyan Arab Republic, ascending with God's help to exalted heights . . . extend your hands, forget your rancors, stand together against the enemy of the Arab nation, the enemy of Islam."

An orderly advised the American commander on Wheelus that the "BBC was reporting a revolution of some kind in Libya." American military personnel were immediately restricted to the base. Telephone lines to the American embassy sizzled. Intelligence busied itself translating Khadafy's speech while his soldiers established road blocks, enforcing a new curfew the next day, and completing the military takeover. Across the wide reaches of the Mediterranean, Soviet warships conducted naval exercises as they had been doing for the preceding two weeks.

Colonel Groom, the American commander of Wheelus at the time Khadafy struck, was to return to the United States, and a new commander was needed. Daniel "Chappie" James, Jr., became the obvious choice because, as Jerry Friedheim, then of the Defense Department, points out: "We knew he was there, and could provide another dimension. . . . He was not just a warrior, but he also had a little bit of the diplomat on the rough edges of the warrior. He had a way of working with people. And he could handle difficult people, and of course, Khadafy [would be] one of the most difficult . . . ."

IV

Assignment to command the USAF all-weather base at Wheelus was a dream come true for Chappie James. He had looked forward for years to eventually having his own wing. It was a challenge accepted without reservations. He learned of the pending assignment in March 1969, reported in July, was scheduled to assume command in October. To the surprise of many in the wide hierarchy of the United States government, even southern lawmakers, like L. Mendel Rivers, enthusiastically endorsed his assignment.

For all of its remaining racial dissidence, Florida would miss him. He had made such an impact on his native Escambia County, attitudes regarding race were changing as his career blossomed. This was especially true after Martin Luther King and the civil rights revolution. Escambia County's attitude grew more liberal as Chappie grew. He made it a point to be part of the community and its activities: "Be it Pony League, Little League, a church dedication, NAACP drive, unless it was utterly impossible, Chappie would come. He would help out just about any cause . . . he never forgot Pensacola."

More than anything, he wanted tranquility between the races in Pensacola. Howard Mitchell, a Pensacola car dealer and civic leader, recalls Chappie's concern for his community:

> I think the biggest impact he had on our community was when they asked him to go to Libya and try to settle that difference. He came by my office. . . . I was chairman of the Racial Committee. He said: "Mr. Mitchell, if there is any trouble with any dissident blacks who are not right, you call the Pentagon, tell them who you are and ask to speak to me in Libya and I'll get in a jet myself and I'll be here in 36 hours. If there is anybody doing anything wrong in Pensacola, I'll . . . throw them in Pensacola Bay."[83]

It was a speech that, if they could have heard it, probably would not have especially endeared many of the black populace of Pensacola to Chappie. It would have, perhaps, added more fuel to the fires that labeled him "Oreo Cookie" and a mere tool of the white establishment. But Chappie had gone beyond petulancy in matters of race. America and its betterment mattered. Its unity mattered, and anyone, black or white, who would threaten that would have to be dealt with in his view.

Other matters took center stage. American interests in Libya were paramount, since the entire government watched the sudden rise of Khadafy. And too, the welfare of military dependents and school children in particular was at issue.

A strong man was needed to counter the Libyan nationalistic and pan-Islamic pressures now generated by Col. Muammar Khadafy. Daniel "Chappie" James, Jr., was America's response to the challenge. The two colonels would collide sooner than anybody thought.

Chapter Twenty-Four
Showdown at the Tripoli Gate

I

It wasn't long before Colonel Khadafy tested the mettle of the new American commander. On 18 October 1969, Khadafy dispatched a column of Libyan halftracks which literally ran through the American gate guards, precipitating a major confrontation. Not only did they overrun the main gate, they ran the column of halftracks right through the housing area of the base at full speed. Chappie James was called to the main gate, where he shut the gate barrier down after quickly assessing the situation. Col. Muammar Khadafy himself stood a few yards beyond it, a fancy gun and holster hugging his hips. Khadafy stood there, wide-legged, his hand resting on his gun as he stared down Chappie James.

It was a page from the Old West, a parody of the shootout at the O.K. Corral, except that this was the main gate of Wheelus Air Force Base, astride the road leading to Tripoli, about fifty miles away. Chappie faced him down, his .45 glinting the Libyan sun.

"Move your hand away from that gun!" Chappie growled. Khadafy regarded him, a slight smile probably tracing his face as he dropped his gun hand. But Chappie James was as serious as death. Later, he recalled: "I told him to move his hand away. If he had pulled that gun, he never would have cleared his holster! They never sent any more halftracks."[84]

Chappie suffered no illusions as to his mission at Wheelus. He was the State Department's agent, and the ball was in that agency's court.* The primary

255

job was to wait for a series of decisions he knew was forthcoming. While he waited, he was to be responsible for the safety of five thousand Americans, including about twenty-five hundred dependents living inside Wheelus Air Force Base. As long as the American flag flew over the base, the whole thing was his responsibility. It would not be easy.

This was not the first time Libya demanded that foreign countries give up their bases there. In spite of assurances from King Idris, the political elements in the country had threatened American bases as early as 1964 and, in 1967, the mutterings about Wheelus grew to a crescendo. Mobs threatened to march on the base. The American commander scrambled his fighters. Over six thousand military dependents were airlifted to Europe. Temporary but guarded calm resulted, and the dependents were returned. However, increased profits from the sale of Libyan oil caused these elements of government to scoff at the need for continued dependence on American military assistance. America adopted a strategy of moderation. It would modernize Wheelus and represent it as an element of the Libyan defense. It would train Libyan pilots at American facilities and Wheelus-linked Libyan employees in data processing skills. American military authorities would minimize contacts between their personnel and the general population and control overflights of its aircraft, restricting them to desert-bound gunnery and bombing ranges.

All of this came to nothing. The Americans on Wheelus found themselves under nighttime Libyan curfew the day after the coup, cutting them off from their compatriots living on the economy, including those at the American embassy in nearby Tripoli. Colonel Groom, the Wheelus commander Chappie James replaced (James was a liaison officer from July until assuming command in September), immediately armed his fighters, strung barbed wire at the gates, and erected barriers, augmenting these defensive measures with sentry dogs and increased vigilance.

Colonel Khadafy moved pieces in the chess game he was playing with the Americans. American fighters were to be grounded. The Base Rights Agreement would be terminated. Port facilities providing food and supplies for the base were to be closed. It was clearly an undisguised attempt to make the base inoperative. It was a Libyan determination to assert "Libyan independence and sovereignty, neither of which were considered compatible with the presence on Libyan territory of foreign bases and military elements." It was a demand

---

* The Department of State is responsible for the conduct of relations between the United States and other countries and international agencies, recommending policies the U.S. should follow. It also negotiates treaties and agreements. Since the issue here revolved around a U.S.-Libyan agreement, it was therefore necessary for Colonel James to coordinate his operations through the State Department's ambassador assigned to the area.

for rapid withdrawal of military forces presently in Libya. This not only included the air base, but all Tripoli port detachments, the military assistance advisory group, connected areas outside the Wheelus perimeter, range training areas, certain communications sites, and water wells operating in support of the base. The crown prince relinquished the throne and all governmental authority, announcing his support of the new republic's government. Several Libyan army vehicles drove onto the base, transited it, and exited through the west gate. Personnel living on Wheelus were ordered to remain on base until further notice, while surveillance flights of the base perimeters were undertaken. On the third of September, Sixteenth Air Force headquarters issued orders restricting fighter transit of Wheelus for "fear of creating an atmosphere of noncooperation."

It was a tense time when Chappie James assumed command of Wheelus Air Base on 22 September 1968. Both colonels were superpatriots. Both were aggressive and unbending. And before the showdown at the Tripoli gate, Colonel Khadafy had an early opportunity to severely criticize Chappie's performance as he "held him accountable for either complicity or neglect" in the now-famous "Jew-in-the-box" incident.

On 23 September, the day after Chappie assumed command, Dan DeCarlo, supervisor of Wheelus Air Base dependent schools, set in motion his plot to provide secret transportation for "a Libyan Jew who feared for his safety under the revolutionary government." He had previously requested permission from Chappie to take musical band instruments requiring repair to Malta aboard a C-54 transport. Chappie denied the request, telling DeCarlo that he was not to go with the instruments, and he would send a military representative along to see to the repair of the musical instruments. But DeCarlo would not be denied, remaining determined to somehow spirit his friend from the country. In his view, something had to be done to help him. Memories of how the Germans treated the Jews during World War II haunted him. Bringing his friend, one Alphonse Pagani, Volkswagen distributor for Libya, to his home, DeCarlo decided to pack him in a huge box and manifest it aboard the C-54 as part of the shipment of musical instruments. Crating his friend, suitcases and all, in a huge, wooden tuba box, DeCarlo persuaded two airmen to help him transport it to the air terminal, where crew members helped load the box into the waiting aircraft. The airmen later recalled that the box weighed between 200 and 250 pounds and that it "felt like water," when they loaded it aboard the C-54. Attached to the manifest were apparent authorizations used by DeCarlo to travel to Malta along with the box.

Arriving in Malta, DeCarlo rented a Maltese truck with driver to transport his illicit cargo. On the way into the city, he suggested that the driver take a walk while he checked out the instruments. According to James R. McGovern, Chappie later recalled that "DeCarlo became concerned whether his friend

was getting enough air, and proceeded to crow-bar a light opening in the box."
Looking about, DeCarlo realized that the Maltese driver saw him open the
box, and was walking towards him. Professor DeCarlo, shot with adrenalin,
completely opened the box, releasing his friend, who jumped out of the truck
and ran into a nearby wooded area, suitcases in hand. The C-54 crew and
Professor DeCarlo were detained, accused of smuggling an unknown alien into
Malta.

It was clearly something Chappie James did not need. All hell broke loose
on Wheelus. Khadafy's government was mad. That James had allowed this to
happen was illustrative of the fact that the base perpetuated colonialism in
Libya and raised suspicions whether the United States government, through
Wheelus, might offer assistance and sanctuary to Libya's enemies. Khadafy's
men insisted on the right to inspect everything leaving Wheelus. James immediately advised Sixteenth Air Force of his order to all Wheelus personnel: "No
one, repeat, no one, except military, dependents and DOD [Department of
Defense]-sponsored personnel would travel on USAF aircraft in and out of
Wheelus."

Meanwhile, Professor DeCarlo's wife had the following unsigned statement
left behind by DeCarlo ("if something went wrong") delivered to Chappie:

> I am about to undertake something which to me may be the most important
> contribution I could make to my fellow-man. I realize the responsibilities
> and the consequences in the event I am caught. However, I am willing
> to risk all to help. For the first time in my life, I can see the result of
> hate, fear and war. Now I know what it means to be fearful of one's
> life; to run and hide; to be concerned that one may not see their loved
> ones again. To be afraid to the point of taking your own life before
> being caught by a people whose only hatred of an individual is because
> he is a Jew and not because he has done something wrong. . . . I cannot
> shirk . . . my responsibility as a human . . . as an American to help
> this individual. I realize, if caught, the embarrassment it may cause my
> country and family—but to me, the joy of helping someone is worth it.
> . . . No one knew about this plan except my wife . . . not one military
> man at Wheelus . . . nor my friends. I did not receive help . . . it is
> my sole responsibility. . . . Please let it be known that I would have
> helped an Arab or anyone else under the circumstances. I am not doing
> this for money . . . nor for personal glory but for the sake of a person
> whose only crime was being born a Jew.

The statement might have touched Chappie James, born as he was in Pensacola's ghetto, suffering racial slurs and innuendoes simply because he had been
born black. No matter how he may have felt, however, James pressed on as
what he was, the American commander of an American base on foreign soil.

He did not give an inch against the Libyan demands for immediate authority to inspect incoming and outgoing cargoes, and all mail coming into Wheelus. His attitude was the same when Khadafy's men announced their intention to post their own guards at the gates of Wheelus Air Base. But after high-level talks with Joseph Palmer, the American ambassador charged with negotiations with the new government, James was obliged to acquiesce, since the U.S. official position was one of agreement ''in an effort to initiate amicable talks on the future of the base and American oil holdings in Libya.'' The American approach seemed aimed at playing down the incident. The Office of Special Investigations (OSI) would investigate. The Libyan government would be advised as soon as the aircraft returned. A small news article appeared regarding a ''mystery man in a box in an aircraft from Wheelus.''

To add insult to injury, on 25 September, radio reports out of Tripoli contributed to more confusion: ''Libyan technicians have taken over the control tower at U.S. Wheelus Air base because . . . the Libyan government was angered by the reported escape of a Libyan Jew who stowed away in a plane which took off from the base.''

Chappie's telephone rang. It was a General Simler, who wanted to know what in the dickens was going on.

''Are there any Libyans in Wheelus Tower? Are there any Libyan customs officials on Wheelus?''

After checking, Chappie responded:

''Libyan personnel were in tower on training basis before coup. Afterwards, they were pulled out and sent to their own tower at Tripoli. There are none in the tower now!''

At three o'clock that afternoon, ten armed Libyans were on base, inspecting all cargo being removed from a recently arrived C-130. The Sixteenth Air Force vice commander cautioned James to use ''a cool head, refer to the American ambassador and inform the Libyan Foreign Minister that the U.S. was willing to have increased observation and inspection, but that this did not mean armed guards tearing apart flight packages.'' Chappie reminded the Libyans of Base Rights Agreement clauses which exempted Wheelus from search and seizure. Meanwhile, Dan DeCarlo was fined one hundred pounds (about $240) and released, his future career hanging in the balance.

Chappie met with Ambassador Palmer that evening.

''Mr. Ambassador, I'd like to return my aircraft, its crew and passengers from Malta—but not DeCarlo. I'll send for him later if directed to do so.''

Ambassador Palmer had reservations.

''If we attempt to return the aircraft and DeCarlo tried to return with it and we refused, could we be accused by the Libyan government of deliberately blocking efforts to gain custody of DeCarlo?''

The airplane would stay at Malta for the time being.

The Libyan foreign minister joined the meeting. He was advised of the

"Jew-in-the-box" incident, of extra security measures installed at Wheelus, and was assured that the United States would cooperate in order to prevent recurrence. The Libyan foreign minister remained feisty.

"Incidents of this kind are very obviously damaging to Libyan-United States relationships!"

"Agree!" responded the ambassador. "In releasing information to the Libyan people, please emphasize no involvement by U.S. military or officials. DeCarlo acted alone—in direct opposition to the intent and purposes of United States and civilian authorities!"

The seven-thirty Libyan news announced: "U.S. Ambassador Palmer advised yesterday that embassy and base knew nothing about smuggling of a Jew in a box by American teacher at base named Daniel DeCarlo."

James was obviously eager to rid himself of the matter. He finally requested a replacement for DeCarlo. Except for some problems dealing with transportation arrangement delays for DeCarlo's wife, still on Wheelus, the matter was laid to rest. Other more important issues were at hand.

II

Chappie James agreed with his air force superiors when they called for a tougher stance against Khadafy. The issue remained United States insistence on its full rights under the base agreement with the Libyan government, meaning that it would not prematurely withdraw its base until the original agreement expired. The base was an important training tool for NATO fighter pilots. During inclement European weather, their wings rotated to Libya for gunnery and bombing practice. There was "no comparable U.S. base," and, as Chappie had pointed out, retention of Wheelus was urgent. In fact, on 21 October, James advised Libyan Captain Al Gaidi and another Khadafy officer that F-100 flights would be resumed and rescheduled. Khadafy's officers doubted the wisdom of Chappie's decision.

"You should get permission from the Libyan government through the American government," they cautioned.

"I'm not seeking permission," James testily replied, "as this was already provided by agreement and I need only keep you informed of all flights that are to take place on a given day!"

The Libyan officers expressed great concern that Khadafy's new government might become angry about these flights. It might, they thought, worsen relations. After advising the ambassador of his intentions, Chappie determined that the flights should go on with a twenty-four-hour delay to check Libyan reaction.

James felt strongly about his actions, since flying had stopped after the coup. Training was still a requirement for the F-100 aircraft stationed at Wheelus, and besides, a muscle-flexing exercise could do no harm. It apparently galled Chappie James to be in a position where he could not take the strong stand he desired. Certain observers have opined that Chappie's point of view was "what America needed, and if Chappie's advice had been followed, we would still have Wheelus!"[85]

Finally, on 25 October, with ambassadorial concurrence, James's flights were belatedly launched. Two F-100 fighters took off for a test training flight. After that, Chappie authorized a flight of four each day, routing them over the water. Khadafy's people questioned them, but James stuck to his guns. The flights would continue. Khadafy gave in and authorized the flights. It was a round for Chappie.

One confrontation would be settled only to see another erupt. About nine-thirty in the evening, an urgent call summoned Chappie to the main gate of Wheelus. The Libyan guards there were incensed that a Captain Wilson had passed a car through the gate without submitting it to search when the occupants grew hostile.

"Colonel James," Captain Wilson explained, "I have been attempting to have my people search a vehicle driven by a Libyan Air Force officer and that officer refused to have his vehicle searched!"

An argument ensued, Captain Wilson explained. One of the Libyan officers had threatened to shoot him.

"Did you threaten to shoot?" Chappie bristled. The Libyan guards dropped their eyes.

"Yes," the Libyans replied, "but we meant that we would shoot at a vehicle that refused to stop! We did not actually mean we would shoot Captain Wilson and other American personnel!"

Chappie stood tall as only he could. They say he never blinked an eye.

"It's bad to threaten to shoot at all or to use the word shooting at the main gate because of misinterpretations!" he asserted. "If you fire on any of our people," he very deliberately continued, "we will be forced to return the fire. This will cause a major confrontation I am sure no one wants to happen."

For the moment, Chappie considered all of it a misunderstanding. Perhaps a smoke screen for an excuse to delay resumption of flying training.

At the ambassador's three o'clock meeting the next day, the issue came up again after desultory discussions about DeCarlo, who still had failed to return, and what, if anything, the U.S. could do to get him to return. The Libyan foreign minister cleared his throat and delivered a stinging complaint about the Wheelus commander and his behavior at the main gate.

"It was a confrontation, Mr. Ambassador, with my Libyan guards. The Commander threatened 'to fill their country with soldiers!' "

"I am certain Mr. Foreign Minister," placated Ambassador Palmer, "that this is not true." He went on to refer to Chappie's record for fairness and cooperation. Why, "the foreign minister *himself* had previously commented on the exemplary administration of Colonel James!"

"I was also surprised," confessed the foreign minister, "but I have to believe in the integrity of my soldiers, too!"

The showdown at the Tripoli Gate was finally laid to rest.

III

Muammar Khadafy continued to pressure the American government to withdraw its forces from Libya. Although this went against the grain of the air force and Colonel James, who continued to protest withdrawal, the American government finally agreed to remove military elements from the country, even though it meant that it would do so "more than seventeen months before the expiration of its rights agreement." The thinking appeared to be that ultimately, negotiations on Wheelus with the new government could never reach solution. At least, perhaps, quick evacuation might provide points of agreement with the new Libyan government, thus preventing "nationalization of American oil interests."

Khadafy's stance on these issues was rock-ribbed. All American forces must leave. The Libyan people must achieve their freedom. Wheelus was a "base for aggression under NATO." America's imperialistic interests were evidenced by American involvement in Vietnam. On the recommendation of the ambassador, an agreement was finally signed between both countries calling for evacuation not later than 30 June 1970.

The next moves were placed squarely in Chappie James's lap. Decisions needed to be made regarding the disposition of Wheelus Air Base property. It became immediately apparent that neither side agreed on the issue. Khadafy's people seemed to think that the base should be left almost intact, leaving generators, hospital equipment, radars, and navigational equipment in place. The Americans, on the other hand, sought to sell only its property that could not be used at other American installations. Chappie walked a tightrope, attempting to placate the Libyans on some issues, agreeing to give them time to retain certain property "as long as possible" before removal so as to replace them. He promised training assistance to the Libyans so that their people would have the skill to use certain equipment. Khadafy's people grew stiff-necked at these offers, especially when in the final analysis, it appeared that the Americans planned to remove all of their property that was not "nailed down." The Libyans rejected outright Colonel James's offer of assistance in contracting for aerodrome, maintenance, and communications services. Also refused was his offer to ask USAF for authority to release radar equipment, although James recommended purchase of newer equipment. It did no good when James explained to Khadafy's representatives certain radars were needed at an American air base in Spain. They insisted that it be left. A Colonel Ferjani and other young colonels drove to the main gate of the base, demanding to see Colonel James about the radar and generator equipment. He invited the Libyan officers on base and to his home in order to discuss the issue.

Tension was high as the Libyans entered the James living room. More serious confrontation was narrowly averted when Chappie noticed, as the Libyan officers sat down, that their driver walked into his living room to sit with a submachine gun cradled in his lap as conversation was about to begin. It was too much for Chappie to accept, especially in his own house. He stood, glowering at the senior officers in the Libyan party.

"I'm going to count to three," he growled, "and if that S.O.B. is not out of my living room by that time, I will physically throw him out!"

Whether the countdown to three actually began isn't known, but Chappie's response when asked if the carrier of the submachine gun removed himself when Chappie reared up to his full six feet four inches left no doubt about the outcome.

"Yes, and he was pretty quick about it!"

Colonel Ferjani's truculence kept the meeting on the edge of confrontation, as he continued to insist that all generators must remain. He grew angrier when James told him that some installed hospital equipment would be removed and asserted his authority to control Libyan-sponsored news media access to Wheelus, asserting his right to control access to USAF areas. Ferjani had a grab bag of complaints. Ambassador Palmer, he asserted, had assured them that the control tower would be given them. Chappie disagreed. Ferjani complained about U.S. policy by which needed equipment would be moved; about navigation facilities which would be taken away since "the USAF can easily procure this equipment, and it should be left in place for us!" Later, Chappie summed it up:

They wanted us to just walk away from the base and leave it intact. And I was trying to get as much of the high-value equipment out of there that we needed back home or that they didn't want to buy. We didn't mind selling the stuff. We were selling it for much less than it [was worth]. I was hoping that we could come to some sort of diplomatic solution and that we could get a new agreement with them. Because that's the first thing they said: "We're going to alter all of the agreements that have been made by the King . . . including the military base." Immediately, they changed their mind!

Closure involved two concurrent mission phases: negotiations for property transfer or sale, and evacuation of personnel and those assets not sold or left to the Libyans.

According to James R. McGovern, in *Black Eagle,* Melvin Laird, then-secretary of defense, stayed in close contact with Chappie James during these negotiations. Laird "made it clear that he wanted the equipment important to the United States to be moved out of Wheelus as quickly as possible, especially in light of ugly incidents surrounding the recent discussions."

The "ugly incidents" even reached out to touch Dorothy James, Chappie's wife, as she passed through the main gate one day. Dorothy's way, of course, in dealing with air force business was to leave all that up to her air force husband. But on this day, she could not ignore the threat by the Libyan guards.

"I was almost killed!" Dorothy remembers. A Libyan guard threatened to shoot through, then searched the car in which she rode. She sat aghast as a Libyan guard deliberately aimed his gun at her. Retrospectively, Dorothy was glad that Chappie was there to lean on: "It was *not* a bloodless coup! Khadafy killed people! [But] Chappie walked tall—threw out his chest. Khadafy didn't know what we had on that base. Guns and stuff. [Khadafy had] guards around him. . . . Chappie would not respect him."

On 24 December Colonel James and Ambassador Palmer appeared on live TV to inform Wheelus and Tripoli Americans linked to the USAF of base plans for evacuation. The Wheelus Aero Club, riding club, hobby shops, and all recreational facilities were closed. Suddenly, huge air force cargo planes landed at Wheelus Air Base under cover of darkness. Valuable American equipment was loaded aboard, and the planes were gone before dawn streaked the Libyan skies the next morning. The Libyans were handcuffed. Chappie moved his operations along strictly on schedule. Dependent travel was stopped and fighter planes assigned to Wheelus were flown to England one startlingly bright desert morning. It was an emotional moment for Chappie as the fighter pilots prepared for their last flight out of Wheelus. A strange melancholy tinged his voice as he was about to send them out to their ships:

Ever stop to think of the guys who flew out of here—aces like Jabara, Everest, Olds and Garrison—guys like Robbie Risner and Swede Larson, who are in the Hanoi Hilton now but who honed their tiger teeth many times over the sands of El Uotia?

Well, to hell with it! This isn't the end of it all. Just the beginning of a new chapter. Streaking through some other sky, some other time, to do what we have to do to maintain the professionalism required of our business. . . . It's the beginning of a new era, a new place to do our thing that might be a little more difficult than El Uotia was. The real estate will probably be more limited, the run-in lines will probably be harder to see, the safety section of the briefing will be longer and more detailed because the error potential will be substantially increased.

This is when the over-worked word "professional" that precedes the term "fighter pilot" gains true meaning. Those of us who answer the challenge prove that it does have meaning in the way we meet it.

In other skies, on smaller ranges, fighter jockeys of the Air Force will still hone their teeth and stand ready at any time to meet the requirements as air policemen for the greatest power on earth.[86]

Transfer of facilities of the 7272d Flying Training Wing to the Libyans began on 15 January 1970, and the Wheelus base newspaper, the *Tripoli Trotter,* in existence since November 1953, distributed its last issue on 30 January 1970.

Chappie James had shown that he was indeed an outstanding performer in his handling of the Libyan crisis. The Pentagon was watching, and the secretary of defense, Melvin Laird, gave him due recognition about the time nominations were being made to augment the general officer corps in the military for 1970. Chappie James's nomination to brigadier general was cleared by President Nixon as James was relieved of his command on 25 March 1970. The Senate approved the nomination, and the promotion was to be effective in July. It was no empty gesture. As Jerry Friedheim, of the secretary of defense's office remembers: "It was clear that Colonel James was somebody that was going to be available for other duties. And a lot of people began to roll around in their minds what kinds of things he could do. . . . He certainly showed that he could perform in a [higher] arena. . . . It was evident that that job was going to be abolished along with Wheelus Air Force Base."

As Chappie James had counseled his fighter pilots as they took off on their last flight out of Libya, it wasn't "the end of it all," but "just the beginning of a new chapter" in his career as Melvin Laird decided to have him assigned to the Pentagon to hold a position in the office of the secretary of defense. The position, deputy assistant secretary of defense (public affairs), now allowed the Department of Defense to effectively utilize Chappie's ability to sway public opinion in favor of the military with his considerable speaking abilities. It called upon his demonstrated ability in areas of diplomacy, enabling him to deal effectively with the other armed services, public groups, and the media. These job requirements easily earmarked the position as one to be held by a general officer.

It was a time of consolidation for Daniel James, Jr. Although it had taken twenty-seven years from the time he had been expelled from Tuskegee Institute, he finally received his college degree from the school. Many courses later taken on his own were accepted by the school for credit. The degree graced his records one year before his nomination for general, and completed the necessary qualifications.

If Korea and Vietnam had hardened him, Khadafy and Libya honed abilities linked to diplomacy and the art of negotiation, attributes he would sorely need in the coming years. And there were fond memories of Libya which lingered, some slightly bittersweet. Always, there was someone upon whom he had left an indelible impression, like the airman who walked up to Dorothy James in another time and another place.

"Hello, Mrs. James! Do you remember me?"

"No."

"I came to your house and put up your Christmas tree lights there in Libya."

"Oh?" Mrs. James replied, brightening.

"Were you nervous over there?" the airman asked concernedly.

"Yes, I was, weren't you?"

"No, ma'am! We knew Chappie stood up to Khadafy and saved many American lives!"

Chapter Twenty-Five
Star Track

I

Although James's nomination to brigadier general elated his friends and supporters, more than a little grousing about the promotion circulated among higher-ranking air force officers. Charges flew about, indicating that James received the promotion because he was black. According to James R. McGovern, in his book, *Black Eagle*, a group of disgruntled "white colonels argued that Chappie would have remained a colonel if it were not for the determination of the Department of Defense to put a new face on its higher officer corps." Further, it was seen as an attempt by the military to seek belated social acceptance by actually *lowering* its standards so as to "reward blacks with top positions." While some white colonels may have shared that view, there were also some generals who decried Chappie's promotion. Within a few years, Chappie would enjoy future promotions, and, according to an observer, the "petty jealousies" of certain of the starred ranks actually facilitated subsequent promotions, since, after his promotion, none of these gentlemen would admit to having positions within their commands that Chappie could fill. Therefore, he was kept aboard the Department of Defense ship as appropriate jobs were created justifying the promotions that were to come. Perhaps the color of his skin did have something to do with his promotion, but that is seen in the final analysis as a minor thing, since he more than filled the bill from a qualifications point of view when related to the job he was selected to do for the secretary of defense. "There is," remarked old friend William McAdoo, "a time and place for everything. The system used him, and it may have been unfair to him at the time, but he also used the system."

There were also insinuations that he had been selected to replace Gen. Benjamin O. Davis, Jr., as the only black general in the air force. But Chappie scotched these intimations by pointing out that it was ability and hard work that did it. He admitted that he was fortunate, and that: ". . . I feel like I worked for it and deserve it. . . . I did a lot of hard work and I had a lot of support from friends [to include] successful completion of command schools, my Vietnam service and recent work [in Libya] . . ."

Of course, friends and supporters were lavish in their congratulations upon his nomination to brigadier. Perhaps the most cherished of all came from Brig. Gen. Robin Olds, who wrote:

No need to tell you how delighted I am with your nomination to Brigadier. And it goes without saying that the promotion selection was based on a record of accomplishments. . . . I am really happy for you and Dottie. It has been a long, hard pull for you both, with tears and heartaches along the way. The recognition is past due and richly deserved. All I can say is that I am proud, damned proud of you both.

General H. M. Wade, chief of staff, Supreme Allied Powers, Europe, advised Chappie against continuation of the "fighter pilot" mentality, writing:

I am sure that you will realize, that is when you come down off Cloud 9, that you now belong to a select group within the Air Force and the things that you do will be closely observed by all of those who serve with you. Some things will come easy and others will be harder, but you have my confidence and I know that you will do your utmost to uphold the high standards by which the Air Force operates.

If, by the observation, General Wade referred to Chappie's reputation for flamboyance, his frequent coverage by the media and his musical diversions, he may have been surprised to know that the attitude was one Chappie privately decried and considered an obstacle to overcome. "No pun intended," he later intoned,

but I'm a colorful kind of guy! Many people may see it as that [flamboyant; notoriety] . . . but this guy happens to be a free spirit, but he still gets his job done and he's very serious when it comes time for duty. . . . I'm the target of some remarks . . . from my peers . . . [but] Chappie James would like to be another General like the rest of you, when it comes to the kinds of assignments he gets; with the way he is treated and looked upon by his peers; by the way he does his job. . . . Chappie James wants to be different. Not different, but *better* than anybody else . . .

That was the attitude with which Chappie approached his new Pentagon assignment. And this time, his offices had two windows. He could look through the massive, gold drapes and see his grey Jaguar parked nearby, a far cry from his first Pentagon tour, when he never knew what the weather was outside. In view of the increased anti-Vietnam War sentiment sweeping the country, Melvin Laird, secretary of defense, wasted no time telling Chappie what was expected: "Chappie, we are abandoning the campuses to the dissidents in this country! All of the people who are anti-establishment are getting their time on the rostrums of our high schools and in our college auditoriums . . . and it's mainly because we haven't seen fit to go, as many times as we've been invited . . ."

It was shortly after 30 April 1970, when South Vietnamese and American forces swept into Cambodia on the side of the Cambodian army to do battle against the Khmer Rouge and North Vietnamese. The American public was outraged. Antiwar demonstrations spawned. The military action, some say, indirectly led to massive student demonstrations on college campuses, approximately 760 closing down or threatening to do so. On the campus of Kent State University in Ohio, the ROTC building was burned. The Ohio State National Guard was called out. And on 4 May, in what was one of the more bizarre American confrontations during the twentieth century, twenty-eight National Guardsmen fired their weapons at demonstrating students. When the firing stopped, thirteen bodies lay like rag dolls over the grass and the parking lot. Four were dead and nine seriously wounded. It was a time, wrote James A. Michener in *Kent State: What Happened and Why,* "this nation stumbled to the edge of a precipice." Some National Guardsmen, it was observed, mercifully "pointed their weapons skyward, thus avoiding a [worse] slaughter."

It was not that the United States government did not want out of Vietnam. Secret talks had begun with Le Duc Tho in Paris as early as February of that year. Clearly, the war was a gross mistake. But withdrawal seemed to be a matter of honor and strategy. Henry Kissinger, in *American Foreign Policy,* wrote:

> Much of the bitter debate in the United States about the war in Vietnam has been conducted in terms of the categories of 1961 and 1962. Unquestionably, the failure to analyze adequately the geopolitical importance of Vietnam then contributed to the current dilemma. But the commitment of five hundred thousand Americans has settled the issue of Vietnam. For what is involved now is confidence in American promises . . . other nations can gear their actions to ours only if they can count on our steadiness.

The week after the Kent State shootings, the Defense Department decided to talk back, giving the government's view. The hope, in Chappie James's words, was to "enunciate an understanding from us, why we were doing what we were doing, and where we were coming from." It was to be a battle for the young minds of the country.

So Chappie was sent out to begin it. He was to find that the reception wasn't very warm. One of his first assignments was to speak to the graduating class at the largest high school in Pensacola, Florida. His mood wasn't really charged. He was still a bit depressed, having just spoken that morning to a group of MIA and prisoner of war wives and relatives. There had been questions he couldn't answer and answers his sources could not pry from the Vietnamese which would have made his job easier. On his way to the school, he cast about for a properly formulated speech for these young people. He knew that graduation was a new plateau for them and that, at best, they would be in a mood to only tolerate a guest speaker, no matter who it was. It was a time, he thought, to be witty, but profound; informative, but short, so they could "go party and get Dad's car home without a scratch."

Suddenly, an idea hit him. The valedictorian and salutatorian might provide the clues he needed for an address. That was it. He'd cue on the remarks of the "Val" and "Sal"—and take it from there.

Ensconced on the platform, he waited in anticipation. The class president was first, leading an original responsive reading. About their hopes and fears. Of how they planned to meet the challenges facing them in their newfound freedom. Chappie's smugness was short-lived, because the words escaping the class president's mouth smacked of defeatism and gloomy outlook, bringing Chappie erect in his seat. "Our world," the class president droned,

> is dark. We live in a dark world—
> The road of life is bumpy and rough
> And we're forced to travel this road.
>> The sea of life is stormy—
> We're on this sea and our boat is rocking and leaky.
>> I sat here a few short months ago
>> With some young men
>> Who have since gone away—
> To a strange land to fight a strange war
> In which many of them don't believe.
>> And far too many of them won't be returning at all—
> I live in constant fear for myself
> Of being atomized before my time
>> By some strange weapon of war
>> Man has made to annihilate man
> The population is exploding—

The environment is being polluted
Two-thirds of the world is hungry.

"My God!" Chappie thought, "how deep do we dive before we get outta the *pit?*"

But a little further down in the student's presentation, they began to sound the sentiment Chappie was looking for. They wanted everyone to know that they accepted the challenge to create constructive change in their time. They would do it themselves and they would do it within the scope of American law. They recognized, they said, that some of the existing laws had to be changed because some of them weren't responsive to the current needs of the citizenry. They realized that equal application of America's laws had to be improved, because the laws were not being equally applied. They promised to walk the halls of Justice themselves; some as elected representatives expressing the wishes of the constituency, because they knew that they could do that in America. And that, they concluded, is how they knew that today's gloomy days wouldn't last because they would act to make them lighter. Quoting a famous American president, they avowed: "The buck stops here!" And then they said: *"Look out, America! We've got it! Step aside!"*

A wide smile creased Chappie's face as he stood to speak, approaching the lectern with purpose. He thought: "How great! How grand!" One massive hand found its way into a pant's pocket, as was his style when he spoke: "My young friends," he began, "you have reason to have that faith. Because, you see, I found myself in a time when I didn't appreciate too much, once. When I grew up in this very same town . . . on the other end of Alcaniz Street." He told them of that dreary time when Alcaniz Street was a ghetto. Of what a miserable place it was to live, that part of Alcaniz Street on the other end of Blount Street where the white people lived. After a pause, he noted that if he could write a soliloquy to parallel theirs, it too would sound dark and gloomy. "It would say," he boomed:

my street is dark. I live on a dark street. My street is dark because my end of the street doesn't have any street lights. The street lights stop where the white folks start, four blocks up the street at Blount. My road is bumpy and rough, because my end of the road doesn't have any pavement. The pavement stops where the white population resides, four blocks up the street at Blount. I'm dark. I'm Black. I was born that way. But there seems to be some people who take a weird delight in trying to impress me that, at least in their minds, this relegates me to a certain position in society that they call "my place." And I am to remember, they would reason, to stay in "my place," if I want to get along and they waste no time in always informing me that, at least in their minds, "my place" is always behind and below and disenfranchised of my white brother.

Chappie then launched into discourse which was to become almost his stock speech all over America. Of the Pensacola parks, the benches painted black and white; of the waiting rooms, labeled colored and white; of the busses, painted white and their signage directing colored to the rear. All of this, he avowed, created a severe inferiority complex within him, as he walked two and a half miles every day past three modern and beautiful schools to his "raggedy, ill-kept, substandard one for colored on the other side of town."

"Two-thirds of the world is hungry? *Hell! I'm hungry!* I was hungry for knowledge and understanding and a little bit of opportunity that was equal and just a little bit of brotherly love. That's all I was asking. But I was given to believe that [this] wasn't possible at that time by some people. But I was not without hope and faith."

It was all those things his parents had taught him. No giving up. No quitting. Negating that "altar of despair." Believing in the "power of excellence." Pass by people who use racial epithets, as his father instructed him to do. And, above all, let the bywords always be: *"Perform! Perform! Perform! Excel! Excel! Excel! Contribute! Contribute! Contribute!"* Because *that* was all he ever heard as a child, and that was all that he knew at that very minute, that very point in time.

On 8 May 1970, he spoke to MIA and prisoner of war wives, media and relatives in the Pentagon briefing room. At fifty, wisps of grey crept into the curly, black hair, neatly cut and shaped in the popular "natural" style black men wore in those days. The eyes were piercing behind black, horn-rimmed, government-issue eyeglasses he sometimes wore. The heavily jowled face seemed determinedly set with concern, twin frown lines between the eyebrows. His stentorian voice penetrated the air: "Progress is painfully slow . . . we are joined together the nation and world in our efforts to make all people aware of the desperate plight of our men. [We] seek support of all people, in and out of government. [Our] goal: the release of the U.S. servicemen held prisoners of war or listed as MIA in Southeast Asia."

But it was not simply the government's problem: "It's *your* problem, too. Currently only about 450 of the 1500 men are, with varying degrees of certainty, believed to be prisoners of war. However, I must hasten to point out that the determination has been made without any official confirmation by the enemy."

At all times, Chappie conducted these briefings in real world terms, without any icing on the cake:

A few of these men we list, identified as prisoners, because of letters
. . . others [by] propaganda photographs or heard on broadcasts from
Radio Hanoi. . . . There remain more than 1,000 who are missing in
action. At this time, there is absolutely no way of knowing whether any
of these men are dead or alive. . . . We will be ceaseless in our determination to do all that is possible to obtain for these men and their families
the rights . . . due them.

And there were the statistics; always the statistics. "Of total missing, captured,
almost 800 downed in North Vietnam, 400 lost in South Vietnam and nearly
200 in Laos."

That night, he was in Gainesville, Florida, at the University of Florida. When
he arrived, a big protest rally was in progress in front of the administration
building. The students booed him. They blocked traffic. Strings of firecrackers
were discharged. The hostility was open and present. The only friends Chappie
thought he had were members of the ROTC, and most of them refused to
wear their uniforms because they feared for their safety as they walked across
the campus. And when he began to speak, not all students were happy with
his responses, one blurting out his disappointment and frustration.

"How can a black man like yourself support the intolerable racist war in
Vietnam?"

James burned him.

"Look, friend, I have been black for fifty years, which is more than you
will ever be, and I know what I believe in!"

There were plausible reasons for American presence in Vietnam, he expounded. Some say his presence on that campus helped water down the tense
atmosphere and prevent a strike planned the following week. As usual, the
hecklers were there. To needle and rabble-rouse, to ask the sharp-pointed questions. For a moment, Chappie may have silenced them with a spiritual, "Joshua
Fought the Battle," or "Motherless Child," or "You Must Come in the Door."
As often as not, the disgruntled ended up cheering him. In fact, several students
walked up to Chappie after his speech to say, "Look, I agree with everything
you said. I really appreciate your guts in coming out here and you do have
me thinking!" Even so, they had to get him off the campus in a special car
that night, such was the heat of the moment.

In El Paso, Texas, he not only stressed the importance of unity in America,
but found himself in the position of defending President Nixon's Cambodian
"incursion." On unity, he took the broad view: "Things are really tough in
America now . . . brother pitted against brother because of race, creed, color,
ideology or some other thing. . . . Those of us who have fought for it and
have kids over there . . . we're pretty concerned about it . . . and if you're
not concerned, you're part of the problem."

There was a new bottom line about war and the lack of patriotism which outlined Chappie's attitude towards these as a warrior:

As one philosopher once wrote: "War is an ugly thing; but it is not the ugliest of things. The decadent and decayed state of morals and patriotic feeling that is exemplified by some people in our country today relegates these people to a position that encourages our enemies. And they are only kept free by men and women who are stronger and braver than themselves." Machiavelli also stated that, "in war one must never remain neutral but must take a stand; otherwise the victor will count you among the vanquished and the vanquished will not find room for you in his cave!" Well, I'm not going to make any reservations in his damned cave! Because I'm going to see to it that *my* country stays free!

Defending Nixon's Cambodian invasion was a slightly different matter. Arnold L. Isaac, in *Without Hanoi: Defeat in Vietnam and Cambodia,* outlines the stance of the American people:

The Cambodian incursion . . . was the "single act by which the Nixon administration closed the trap on itself." Other aspects of the Vietnam war could be laid to "cleaning up someone else's mess" . . . but Cambodia belonged to Nixon and Kissinger. Americans could understand the need to withdraw their forces without humiliation and were willing to allow time for that to occur. But sending soldiers to fight in *another* Indochinese nation hardly seemed like the same thing . . .

Chappie's response was half-diplomacy, half-ghetto, and hard to refute: "This is a necessary move . . . we promised to bring the guys home, but we want to bring them home alive. It's the same as a ghetto fight. If a guy pulls a switchblade, you've got to do something about that switchblade . . . and *then* you walk away."

Perhaps the most emotional, personally heart-wrenching appearance Chappie made during this period occurred at Tennessee State University in Nashville. It was a black university, where students had burned the ROTC building to the ground, two hundred of them standing on a nearby hill watching the flames crackle through the structure. When Chappie spoke, it was right from the heart:

You didn't have the right to do that. You didn't have the right to destroy what you didn't build! You didn't build that, I did! I built it with sweat and blood and to prove that black men could be responsible pilots in the United States Air Force, and they deserve ROTC establishments on black campuses to produce these black officers, because that's where most of us came from. You didn't build it, you burned it down and you didn't have the right to do that! . . . Our business is the protection of this nation. . . . Those of us who fought for these buildings [are going to continue] to fight for them . . . We are not going to see them burned down. . . . And I mean that, baby!

"The time is now," he told them, "to get into the classroom and get knowledge!"

Around the twentieth day of May, he was in Fort Worth, addressing the Tarrant County Big Brother Annual Dinner at the Green Oaks Inn. Perhaps the emotional fires experienced at Tennessee State University remained banked in his heart, as he declared:

I've carried this country's "doubting Thomases" on my back through three wars and I didn't mind. . . . I do mind it when they start to destroy towns and institutions which I helped build . . . because then they get a little bit heavy. . . . Mutual distrust is ugly . . . no matter what its color. I came back from the war and I've found distrust here at home . . . hatred, distrust . . . raw, murderous hatred at home. You name your brand of hate and we've got it. . . . You name your brand of distrust and we've got it right here. You name your brand of turmoil, and you've got it right here on the shelf. You don't have to order it. I am a citizen of the United States of America and I'm not a second-class citizen. No one here is a second-class citizen until he thinks like one or performs like one . . . and if I stopped to challenge every man who called me a nigger, I wouldn't be a brigadier general today. I wouldn't have time. I'd still be on that corner, poor as a church mouse when I got back.

Chappie always unflinchingly looked his predominately white audiences in the eye. From time to time, he'd do an aside, acknowledging the presence of Capt. Walt Ellis, calling him "my coach," who "stays near the General's side to be sure he doesn't say things too outlandish!" Chappie was always aggressive, and even Captain Ellis's presence did not deter his answering touchy questions bordering on the political. Someone asked, for example, whether he favored resumption of bombing in North Vietnam.

"That's a political question!" asserted Ellis.

"That's okay!" James retorted, raising his hand. "I got him! If it's ordered," he allowed, "we'll resume bombing, but we're not pushing it!"

Chappie was like every other parent with a son or daughter in Vietnam, and he frequently mentioned his son, Daniel III, who "spots targets for troops!" His feverish speaking calendar took him into summer, when he praised the American Legion for its patriotic stance, telling them that "people who give up on America are giving up on society." And then it was the deep baritone voice singing "Joshua Fit the Battle of Jericho" once again. "The walls of Jericho," he told them, "represented bigotry and symbolizes understanding" and that "he is against militant stands by blacks and [he considers] every opportunity open to Negro Americans."

Letters poured in to Secretary of Defense Melvin Laird. "Last night," one began, "It was my privilege to hear General Daniel "Chappie" James Jr., USAF, give a talk at the Tarrant County Big Brother Annual Dinner in Fort Worth, Texas. I liked *what* he said, *how* he said it . . . and I only wish *every* person in this country could hear him."

In September, he wowed the marines at Camp Pendelton in California. The focus was elimination of racial problems in the armed services. These problems, he said, are going to be solved "by people who consider themselves Americans and not Africans. It's up to you to keep the faith, baby!" The marines roared their approval. And as the applause subsided, he paused a moment, his face brightening.

"I want to tell you about another military man!" Again, that deep baritone shook the rafters with "Joshua fought the Battle of Jericho." He said that he liked the song because it had meaning for today. "Those trumpets bring down the walls with truth, justice and brotherhood for all people!" The marines gave him a two-minute ovation.

II

In addition to the antiwar dissidence on college campuses and correlated demonstrations across the country there were other issues as important. All of these issues, including competent response to antiwar demonstrations, affected the public image of the Defense Department. There were problems of media credibility and racial unrest in the military, and of proper liaison with the thousand-strong POW-MIA wives, the organized spouses of air force and navy officers shot down, missing in action, or in prison in Vietnam. Grieving deeply, these women were a force to be reckoned with, concerned as they were over the questionable treatment their husbands had received at the hands of their Vietnamese captors. And too, the quality of their lives and that of their children also suffered, as they struggled to make ends meet and raise their families as suddenly single parents.

The POW-MIA wives merited sympathy from their government and Secretary of Defense Melvin Laird made it axiomatic that government at least had to listen. The existence of that axiom made Chappie James a natural for the job. A civilian, it was thought, even though that person may have had some military service, couldn't do the job justice. It had to be someone from their own "family." Someone with good credentials, who understood how the families really felt and most of all, knew and understood how the men missing or in prisoner status felt. Chappie had flown with them. He knew what the prisoners would have expected him to do *vis-a-vis* their families, because he knew them like brothers.

Chappie met with and briefed the POW-MIA wives. It wasn't easy. He held a lot of hands and wiped a lot of tears. Beyond that, it sometimes could be terribly difficult, because there were times when he, as the government's agent, had to say, "No, I'm sorry, but we don't know any more!" And there were things of course, that Chappie knew as a person privy to the details of Laird's strategy of "Vietnamization" (withdrawal), that he simply could not discuss on a day-to-day, public basis. But he knew that talks were going on and that the situation would be resolved one way or the other. Laird, for example, had pressed for a timetable to shrink the United States forces in Vietnam to roughly 206,000 men by the end of 1971. Indeed, the very basis on which he had joined the Nixon cabinet was that he was convinced that the American people were "fed up with the war." And after a visit to Vietnam, Laird told the president that the electorate "would not be satisfied with less" than the eventual disengagement of American men from combat.

So Chappie knew that the families of the MIA-POW's were not going to be forgotten or abandoned. And yet, again there were times when he'd have to emphatically say, "No, I'm sorry, I don't know anymore about your loved one!" For this, he sometimes took more than a modicum of flak, even though he spent hours in attempts to mollify a complaining family. They sometimes shouted and hollered at him in utter frustration. They broke down and cried. Through it all, he tried valiantly to keep cool. Sometimes, it all became quite impossible as army wives, who perhaps thought that Chappie, as an air force officer, had little sympathy with the plight of their husbands, went around him to complain to what they perceived as higher authority. Times like these hurt, but he handled all of it better than most. As Jerry Friedheim, an assistant secretary of defense recalls: "One thing to remember is that the other services didn't have a Chappie James. They had some liaison officers, but they didn't have anybody as qualified as Chappie. . . . But it was inevitable that these kinds of things would happen . . . and Chappie understood."

Alternating these briefings with Daniel Z. Henkin and Jerry W. Friedheim, both from the public affairs office, Chappie still delivered speeches around the country as he had been doing in the past. The schedule was rigorous. There were times when Secretary Laird and he would go out as a team on speaking engagements. Chappie remembered that, on occasion, they'd turn the engagements "into a church meeting." His father a minister, Laird would switch focus at the last minute and deliver what amounted to an impromptu sermon. When he'd finish his "sermon," he'd call on General James to "sing a spiritual." Unabashed, James would haul his full six feet, four inches up, put his full

230 pounds into the act, and belt out "Joshua Fought the Battle of Jericho," moving his audience so that it called for two encores. The two of them were very good together, and became close, personal friends over the years. They managed to present a program of high patriotic philosophy, and when a speaking engagement was over, "everybody left knowing that these two guys may not *solve* the problem tomorrow, but they weren't bad guys to have *in charge of* the problem."

The Department of Defense was comfortable in its selection of Chappie James to do the job. The animosities and jealousies of the colonels and the generals simply didn't matter. They knew that there were a lot of people who got left out of the general officer selection process. Because of that, the selection process may have looked a bit arbitrary, and perhaps sometimes it was. But the comfort in selecting Chappie James lay in the philosophy that "people are picked *at the time* for *the job,* for general slots *are jobs,* and the idea is to pick somebody who can do *that* job." Jerry Friedheim remembers:

Anybody who goes back and looks at [Chappie's] record, and what he accomplished in a lot of different arenas, it's absolutely impossible to say he wasn't qualified. . . . He was the best person to do the things he was asked to do. It was clear to me that there were few general officers who could have done the things that he did in relation to the situation; and a lot of general officers who couldn't have done it at all. They wouldn't have had the patience to relate . . . plus his credibility as a warrior, which was absolutely superb.

And Chappie himself was quite comfortable doing what he was selected to do. In his Pentagon office, memories of his wild and crazy "salad days," which struck awe in his subordinates, stared down from a neat frame:

Yea though I fly thru
the Valley of Death
I shall fear no evil,
For I am the
"meanest muthuh"
in the valley.

On a corner of his desk his "Colonel" coffee mug still sat. No time to update the tag. Two bulletin boards were loaded down with appointments and schedules, many of which were speaking engagements with colleges, universities, other organizations, and families of prisoners of war. And sometimes, in between the furor and scramble of meeting with people assigned to the office of the secretary of defense, there was a moment to sit and philosophize with someone like Deputy Secretary Jerry Friedheim. To think of the Civilian Pilot Training Program and "Chief" Anderson, Tuskegee Institute and the Tuskegee Airmen. To remember the times of Godman and Freeman Fields, and that "officer club thing." "He didn't talk too much about it," Friedheim remembers, "but whenever he did, he'd turn it into a positive thing." He'd talk about how, in the next hour or so he was scheduled to leave for a talk somewhere, and "I'm going to tell them that things are changing; that they can do better and to never let things get them down!"

III

Chappie James took his message on positives straight to the Air Command and Staff College at Maxwell Air Force Base, Alabama, where career air force officers were training for their futures. Inviting questions after a presentation, he seized the opportunity to express points of view regarding racism in the military, a Department of Defense concern.

Beginning by making it perfectly clear he simply did not make a profession of being black, he avowed that there was not, in his view, time for that. And since he had been black for fifty-one years, he possessed enough experience to answer any questions they might pose on the subject.

Of immediate concern to the students was the issue of race problems in Vietnam and what was being done about them. It was a sore point with Chappie, for he had been criticized by the congressional Black Caucus on that score. He disagreed with the congressmen in principle about what he considered "wild charges of institutionalized racism in the services," emphatically denying its existence, saying that in the three years immediately passed, the services had made more progress than in their entire history. He was forced to admit, however, that individual, practicing bigots remained in the services, and the end result, of course, was that the services do reflect the problems existing on Main Street, U.S.A. The big difference, he explained, between the services and the tenor of the country, was that the air force at least had mounted a systematic attack on those problems.

Beginning with the secretary of defense, the air force attack displayed a real moral commitment to finding solutions. But be that as it may, "we are never" he asserted, "going to get it solved until air force commanders have the same kind of moral commitment." And such moral commitment does not mean finding solutions simply because "the regulations say there will be none of that," but because, *"in their hearts, they realize and know that racism is wrong."*

Enough of that kind of moral commitment did not exist, nor did it exist in other places, he lectured. Therefore, the services suffered accusations, fraggings and intimidation by persons who relished the spreading of hate. Beyond that, the air force "was also hurt by the guy who has been raising hell about everything, from haircuts to the soul handshake," things one shouldn't even bother about. From his personal point of view, how the troops shake hands simply didn't matter to him, as long as they can fight, because that is what the military was in Vietnam to do. Unfortunately, he suggested, the press was always on top of incidents such as these, and they make "every newspaper in the world." That kind of publicity adversely affects the morale of the young, black GI proudly leading his platoon through the jungle against the enemy. In spite of it all, he observed, they come home with ribbons and personal pride intact, but the media seldom wrote stories about that. And the pity, Chappie thought, is that Americans seldom hear about their white brothers who fight alongside, learning in the process to respect their minority compatriots a lot more than they did before they went over and saw them perform. Certainly the most poignant thing of all, Chappie observed, is that oftentimes, "they save each other's lives along the way."

The secretary of defense, in Chappie's day, was devoted to solving racial problems:

If we catch any practicing bigot, he is dead, professionally, in this service. We do not have any place for a commander who cannot be concerned about racism and have a commitment against it. Mr. Laird has stated there will be no more of that. And if we find them out, they will not command a latrine detail in this service, anymore, anywhere, I can promise you . . . that is going to help solve it . . .

The student officers also expressed concern over the low percentage of black officers in the air force of that time, and, particularly, they wanted action which would increase the chances of a black pilot's moving on to command positions. There was, Chappie pointed out, an effort being made to enhance minority recruiting. And despite what the militants were saying in the "outside world," he observed that lots of progress was being made in that arena. Even the president, in that era, was concerned about racial and minority affairs. Minority recruiting could be difficult, because the air force and the flying arms of the navy and marines cannot take just anybody. Of necessity, Chappie said, standards have to be kept high, but "we must make sure there is a vehicle for the young black and other minority members to be able to compete for these positions."

He described, in retrospect, a model program of the era touted by Admiral Zumwalt, who related how minority attendance was almost doubled at the Naval

Academy. The navy went out and found them, then recruited them: "The Navy told them it needed them, and offered them a $50,000 plus education in return for five years of their lives. You don't find too many, no matter what color they are, who are going to turn that down [and] if someone is dumb enough to reject that offer, we probably could not use him anyway . . . ."

So the way to minority involvement, Chappie believed, in the air force and other services was to go out and talk to potential recruits *in all areas of society*, not just in the lily-white areas anymore. It was going down to George Washington Carver High School, to find the young minority group member who has the ability but not the means.

Chappie pointed out that other solutions resided in the activation and utilization of human relations councils, equal opportunity councils on air force bases and other installations, along with "representatives of the other side [proponents of bigotry and racism]." Once the information is sifted, the logic went, and the purified word comes out and is sent to his people, commanders had better make sure that it has red, white and blue stamped all over it, and it amounts to equal opportunity for all: "If not, he gets fired, and we put in someone else who will make sure all his people get an equal break. . . ."

Chappie decried the distortions of the dissidents angry over the Vietnam War, who for the sake of "peace" effectively stepped on the pride and dignity of the armed services. "They have thrown a little mud on your uniform and mine," he told the student officers. "But," he cautioned, "our reaction cannot be anger and name-calling; it must be through established programs designed to counter such intrusions." It is, he said: "going out and talking to 'Reverend Jones' and 'Sister Smith' . . . getting them to talk about it from the pulpits . . . letting them know that we are not a bunch of killers. [And] when we find someone within our numbers who has gone astray and tarnished the uniform . . . we must show [that] we are big enough to take action against him."

And too, Chappie made it clear that the air force or any other of the services are not country clubs. "A viable fighting force must be maintained," he asserted with a fighter pilot's roar, "and to do that, discipline is of prime importance. Command must be understanding but firm. Without discipline, we become a mob." But at the same time, Chappie believed there are some things about which command can listen to young people in the service. For example, perhaps hair could be allowed to grow a little longer. Accommodate that by getting some bigger hats. There are simple things one can do:

Like keep cool when a man shakes another man's thumb and they beat each other's elbows, arms and thighs, doing the "soul shake." I do not care, as long as that man is standing tall when I call my formation. I do not care, as long as when I walk by he throws me a "Good morning, sir," and salutes, and I return the courtesy. We are not going to back away from that. I do not care, as long as he takes direction when I give it, without my having to explain . . . why. I do not have time for that over Hanoi at 30,000 feet. He had better learn that when he is back at the post.

Ultimately, an overall solution, Chappie thought, is to "maintain the mix that we have now." For an admixture of races helps take the primary brunt of officer procurement off the backs of the military academies, and is reason alone to continue to maintain a viable ROTC program so that: "We can keep the kind of integrated mix of races, religions, social strata and everything else, that makes it a truly democratic *American* military force—democratic to the point that we set. Realistically, that cannot be too permissive, or it would not be worth anything as a fighting force."

The crux of it, Chappie smiled, is that the air force and other services "must show our attractiveness to the young men that we want, then we will get the mixture we want." The ultimate purpose is not to worry about what percent of the force is going to be black or white, because that will seek its own level. In the long haul, the resultant force, he concluded, will not be all black or all white or all Mexican or Puerto Rican. And even if it were, he projected, his voice slightly rising: "I will tell you frankly—and I do not care what the papers say about dissention and all that—if they were the kind of people that the majority of blacks, Mexicans, and Puerto Ricans whom *I* know in this service are, we would not have a bad army anyhow . . . they love their country, just like you and I do."

Finally, a student asked for an air staff position on the personal problems of the top levels of air force management. The answer was easy for Chappie, who simply quoted his boss, Secretary of Defense Melvin Laird: "You know, one of the first things Mr. Laird told me when I came aboard, was to remember that my suit was purple—that I had to be concerned with all the services across the board . . ."

It was a bittersweet quote, for he had to admit that, "of course, when you wear this *blue* suit as long as I have and love it as I do, it is not easy to forget the color *all* of the time!"

Jerry Friedheim might have been proud, had he been there to hear what being a good listener during that timeless moment back in the Pentagon had wrought. The quote would have been frameable: "I'm going to tell them that things are changing; that they can do better and to never let things get them down!"

Brig. Gen. Daniel "Chappie" James, Jr., was on the star track. There were still miles to go, for the University of Pittsburgh beckoned, and that was one place they were going to "give him a fit!"

Chapter Twenty-Six
Galaxy

I

*K*ill 'im! Kill 'im! Kill 'im! How many villages did you napalm today? Kill 'im! Kill 'im!'' chanted the inflamed students at the University of Pittsburgh. They lay for Chappie around every corner. The chant grew more strident each time he left one building for another. *"Kill 'im! Kill 'im! Kill 'im! How many villages did you napalm today? Kill 'im! Kill 'im!''*

They trailed behind as Chappie and his party walked along the campus, jostling, walking backwards in front of them, aiding the rest of the crowd in their efforts to "take a shot at the military guy." After speaking to the ROTC contingent, Chappie walked to the nearby auditorium, honoring the request to speak to a group of concerned students.

Entering Stephen Foster Auditorium, Chappie saw that the place was peopled wall to wall. Although tension was high, it appeared that he would be able to speak in relative peace and calm, in spite of the hundreds of voices filling the space.

"Blang!'' went the doors at the rear of the auditorium, swinging wide to admit a raucous crowd shouting obscenities and waving signs that read "ROTC Off Campus!" Chappie and everyone else in the auditorium tensed, except the little girl who had invited Chappie to speak. Suddenly, she became a five-foot-two warrior standing in front of James's microphone, arms akimbo and eyes flashing.

"Wait a minute! Wait a minute!" she yelled, lasering her voice towards the intruders. "Goodness gracious! We invited him and we're going to hear what he has to say! If you can't stand in here and let him talk and then ask him questions and let him answer them, then *get outta here!* If you don't want to hear it, out! And if you want him, he's coming out that door and you catch him whenever he gets by you. But, *in here,* we're going to talk to him— *now!*"

ROTC protest signs wavered as shocked expressions clouded the faces of the intrusive students. Some turned and walked out. Others put down their signs, taking seats in the aisles. The grit of the slip of a girl surprised Chappie: "It shocked me. Really did. And that little girl was just as spunky as she could be. She faced 'em, by God! . . . She was only about five-foot-two and I couldn't tell you her name if my life depended on it. . . . They turned around and walked out. . . . That turned the whole, dad-gummed thing around!''

"We had a good exchange," James remembered. He wouldn't always agree with them, he said, but as usual, he began to lay out the government's position. The best strategy for peace is a good defense. Caving in on Vietnam sends a signal of American weakness. We want the war to stop but the president of the United States refuses to crawl to the peace table. "Nobody dislikes war more than warriors!" It was vintage Chappie James, and when he was through, the students gave him a standing ovation. Later, in the school cafeteria ("the mess hall," in Chappie's military parlance), he noted that the mood of the students there "seemed subdued." But, "Oh, they [gave me] a *fit* at the University of Pittsburgh!''

As menacing as the experience had been at the University of Pittsburgh, it was nothing compared to what awaited Chappie at the University of Wisconsin. James had not been scheduled to speak there, but took Secretary of Defense Laird's place because of a change of plans. Laird had been challenged by the leaders of the student protest movement to debate the merits of the war, and he was promised a large turnout if he appeared. But on the day Laird was to speak, he was required to appear before Senator Fulbright's committee "to explain something about the Laotian incursion.'' The University of Wisconsin was a veritable antiwar fortress. In the summer of 1970, student activists bombed the mathematics center "because it allegedly trafficked in war technology.'' When the word spread that Chappie James was to appear, protest leaders brought in Chicago Seven defendant Rennie Davis and Weatherman Linda Evans to speak. Law enforcement was everywhere. Even though the field house auditorium was heavily guarded, its windows were smashed with snowballs. Davis reveled in the fact that the mathematics center had been bombed, forecasting that: ". . . If the government doesn't stop the war, we are going to stop the government!''

Students, Davis went on, should "shake down" the faculty for large sums of money, buy old cars for use in coming demonstrations and block access to the Pentagon. On 26 January 1971, Chancellor H. Edwin Young put part of the campus off-limits. Two thousand protestors prepared to "march to the field house to demonstrate against General James."

Sub-zero temperatures greeted the dawn on 27 February, the day of Chappie's scheduled appearance. As Chappie's entourage approached the administration building, he saw fifty black crosses planted in the snow nearby. Myriad students wore peace symbols. The crowd was intensely hostile. The scene remained vivid in James's memory years later: "They'd made about two thousand snowballs to throw at Secretary Laird and they didn't waste them when I got there!"

Snowballs pelted Chappie's car by the hundreds, smashing against its windows, oozing icy fingerpaintings down the cold, clear glass. He could not help but wonder which snowball contained a brick or rock that would successfully smash the windows, showering him with shards of glass. Removing his sunglasses, he stoically rode it out, too proud to duck and much too proud to lie down on the floor of the car. Prior to his arrival, he had asked the protest leaders to reserve two tables for members of the Afro-American Club. Chappie was to pay for them (since it was to be a five-dollar-a-plate dinner). He wanted to make sure that the minority students had a chance to attend. If perhaps he wondered about that between the pelting snowballs, once inside the field house, he had his answer. The black students boycotted his speech. More than 750 people were there and not one, single black:

They did that [reserved the tables] . . . and they couldn't find anybody to come. Those tables were very visible. And then I got the word that they wanted me to know that they had boycotted it literally because they didn't agree with the things I was saying; [the things] I stood for. . . . If I wanted to talk to them . . . come down there. . . . If you've got the guts . . . come on down . . ."

The invitation temporarily went on the back burner. The atmosphere in the field house sizzled. As the university chancellor introduced Chappie, antiwar chants flayed the frigid air outside. Waitresses slipped messages into folded napkins decrying the nation's involvement in Indochina. Peace signs adorned their uniforms. The chancellor's voice droned, calling for the "most rapid withdrawal of our troops in Vietnam within the national interest." The brigadier's star sparkled as he rose to speak:

I've got the message! We got the message a long time ago, but we ask for your tolerance as we search for an early solution. The Nixon administration would like to get all combat forces out of Vietnam. We have met or beat every commitment to withdraw forces we have made. But the other side must show good faith. We cannot, for example, compromise the welfare of our prisoners, nor forget them.

And then he hit them with unique James dialogue: "It is fine . . . to speak of freedom now, *but unless the United States is a strong, united nation, there will be no place to be free in!"* In spite of their antiwar stances, James's expert ability to verbally put their flag before them, challenge their patriotism, and underline love of country paid off as the students interrupted his speech several times with applause. In spite of themselves, they stood as one man, delivering a standing ovation when Chappie finished his speech.

And now it was time to address the issue of the blacks who isolated themselves in their Student Union building. The Office of Special Investigation (OSI) for that region, assigned to protect Chappie, checked its location. They didn't like it. On a dead-end street, it had one way in and one way out.

"Sure, I'll go down there!" Chappie advised them.

"Look," said the OSI man in charge, "you can get down there and with these mobs that are swirling around town today, they can cut off that street there and then we'll have a heck of a time guaranteeing your protection! We don't want you to go down there!"

"What I'm going to do," Chappie announced, "is just get a Yellow Cab and go over to this Black Student's Union, and walk in there, and that's not going to tip off the crowd at all and I can talk to those students!"

"Sir," objected the OSI chief, "I can't let you do that. I'm responsible here! Anything happens to you, then my boss is going to have my tail! It's *my* responsibility to protect you, if I can!"

The argument between the two became heated. The OSI chief might well have saved his breath, because, as Chappie remembers, "I was going anyway!" In the end Chappie prevailed, looking the OSI chief straight in the eye.

"You can't stop me," he roared, "unless you lock me up, and you don't want to do that!"

The Yellow Cab stopped two blocks from the Student Union. Ellis and James walked down those blocks. Outside was Pete Greenberg, then the editor of *The Cardinal*, the most radical paper on the campus, trying futilely to gain entrance.

"What's the problem, Pete?"

"Well, they say they've decided that they don't want any honkey reporters in there!"

"Well, if they won't let you in, Pete, I'm not going in there!"

A Mr. Salter, in charge of the Student Union group, stood there belligerently. Chappie looked him in the eye.

"Mr. Salter," Chappie growled, "You know you people are talking about racism and this is *really* the only instance of racism that I've seen here since I've been on this campus! Now, if you can throw snowballs at me and shout derogatory remarks, none of which are based on race, they were based on this uniform and here you are denying a guy in here because he's white!"

Not only did Salter and company deny Greenberg entry, they also refused entry to a TV camera crew. They had to "go back and get an all-black crew, or they couldn't come in either!" The famous James temper probably came close to flaring.

"Now if *that's* it," Chappie shot, "then the deal's off. *I'm leaving!*" As they turned to leave, a voice lurched. It was probably Salter.

"Wait a minute!"

There was a hurried meeting inside. The door opened.

"Okay, come on in!"

It was not a truce by any means. In fact, the group seemed more hostile than any of the other students had been. Chappie was accused of selling out black people because he was a military person. Instead of championing the military, he should be striving to break up the military and become antiestablishment. Period. And how about the inequities inherent in the number of black men killed in Vietnam? What's your position regarding a race war in the United States?

"You've got to work within the system," Chappie responded as always. "It's slower but it is surer. Blacks don't get deferments that whites do for schooling and occupations, therefore their casualties are disproportionate in Vietnam."

"War in Vietnam is illegal!" flared one student.

"I don't feel it is illegal! I don't feel I have to lie for Laird or Department of Defense. If I ever felt that I had to, I will quit my job!"

"You are obviously a patriotic man. What can you say to convince us that we should be as patriotic?"

"I can only tell you the way that I feel. Although I admit that there are many things wrong with America, there are less things wrong with her than in any other country. I still feel the question of racism is soluble here, and I think it can be solved without polarizing back into black and white!"

Later, in an almost agonizing evaluation of the confrontation, the thing that seemed to bother Chappie the most was the fact that the black students "didn't arrive at their position through reasoning—it's all emotional." But in the final analysis, he felt that it represented a victory for him because he refused to let them make him mad. He walked out of there, "with [his] pride intact." He was grossly disappointed that none of the students, except Mr. Salter, came up to at least say, "Thanks!" Perhaps Mr. Salter said it for all the rest at the end, when he stood up to face Chappie.

"Well," he said, "the time you've spent with us has been very worthwhile. I think that you state your position well. I think it's laudable and I appreciate your coming down."

Chappie would never forget the stridency of their voices. Particularly those voices sure that racism was rampant in the military and that it was institutionally supported. The charge bothered him because he knew the air force was farther ahead than any other segment of American society in eliminating it. Viewing the TV clips that night, he thought he had clearly won.

"It was a great victory!" he remembered years later.

The next day, the *Madison Capitol Times* reported: "James Keeps Cool in Afro Center 'Hot Seat'."

II

During 1971, Chappie James continued his strenuous speaking schedule. Speaking at the Orlando Naval Training Center, he made it clear that his primary assignment was telling people about the plight of America's prisoners of war and those believed missing in action. There was no room for intolerance, but, he cautioned: "There will always be dissidents. You will have to carry the dissidents on your back and the heaviest load you are going to have to carry is those who oppose you and whose big, fat mouths are so uninformed."

In many respects, his Pentagon assignment and resulting exposure to the American public went a long way towards the ultimate maturing of Chappie James. He learned to accept that one cannot please everybody, even though barbs from some quarters hurt, and could bring up sudden defensiveness in him. "Some people," he remembered, "have called me a 'Tom.' But I didn't just walk in here; I fought every step of the way. I don't mind name-calling, since men like Whitney Young and Roy Wilkins have been called 'Toms,' and I'll take their company any time."

He learned about the possession of power and how best to use it. As far as Chappie was concerned, power was a force to be used positively and constructively. His mother had schooled him on that score decades before, and he used it now: "If you're at the top you don't have to plead the way you do if you're at the bottom. You can exert a helluva lot more pressure from the top with that authority than you can from the bottom with that torch, sign or brick . . . my motto is *build a nation, not tear it down!*"

Always a champion of the young, he took the opportunity to speak to thousands of them and made it clear that development of the young was not a matter of race: "There is a battle for the minds of the young, black and white. . . . I don't agree with the separatists. I think the black pride thing is the most beautiful thing I've seen in years, but we should not put it all together and keep it to ourselves."

He maintained a realistic perspective on the pursuit of the civil rights revolution, for while he supported its ultimate focus, it became clear to him that blacks could not survive an armed confrontation with whites. This undoubtedly formed the basis for his theory of "working within the system—excel, and then change things." And although he was constantly attacked for it, he frequently made his point of view known: "In a shootout, you're going to get shot down, because there's more firepower on the other side."

In speech after speech, he expanded on the theme, often smiling, left hand jammed into a pocket, the right often engaged in wide, perpendicular gestures; leaning in towards his audiences as he answered their penetrating questions. At Fort George C. Meade in Maryland, he told a gathering of the EEOC:[*]

> People who run things in this agency should be truly representative of the people of the United States. . . . Don't give up on society. Meet the challenge with ever-increasing determination to solve the problems. [You] have to stop sacrificing your lives running *against* authority and [advocating] force. We will lose that battle because we are a minority. But there are enough fair people who wish to see equality come to pass. I am not saying everything is right. Not all opportunities are open to our people. But there are more than 10 years ago, or five years ago. . . . Things are getting better. We are not all the way there yet, but we are getting there. There is always a market for excellence.

It was the same thing he'd counseled the high school students in Pensacola. Performance. Excellence. And beyond that, the logical results: *"Win!"* America was the thing that mattered:

> This is the greatest country in the world! We will help the United States maintain her position at the top! That is our job, every one of us. Stop finding so many ways to hate each other and get together; to ensure the unity that has always made people . . . gain respect as a nation. . . . Give all an equal chance. . . . Then, and only then, will we truly overcome.

The "Phil Donahue Show" afforded Chappie a nationwide audience in 1971. Donahue flung him a series of potent challenges, from probing James's feelings about those "12,000 kids they just busted," to the fact that the war had been in progress for ten years, with fifty-five thousand dead and forty thousand "perhaps on heroin" and still no way out of the war was apparent. From the fact that Chappie was "the first or second air force black man to become a general," and therefore a possible "token," to his "professional judgment of the [American] image around the world." From audience questions asking "how he, a black man, [could] justify to the black man to go someplace else to defend one's right that he doesn't enjoy at home," to the question from Donahue

[*]Equal Employment Opportunity Commission

wondering whether, since he had "sustained oppressed conditions, going to [fight] on another continent was a kind of misappropriated energy." It was a totally absorbing hour, given the concern around the country over the Vietnam situation.

As to the twelve thousand kids who were "busted by the government," Chappie understood their feelings but questioned their motives, "because I don't think it is necessary to try to stop the government or bring the government to a grinding halt [in order] to be heard in this nation." The war would stop if America persisted in "the direction that has already been set." He opined that "the road out of Vietnam has already been set by the government of the United States, and that some of the people yelling the loudest that it hasn't been set are people that really realize that it has and would like to take some credit for it when it happens, as it inevitably will." To the allusion that, since he was one of the few black men until that time to be a general officer, he might just possibly "feel token," Chappie replied that he did not; since tokenism "implies that somebody gave me something just to have a black man as a general, say we have got one, you see him sitting over there in the corner."

He went on to say that he considered himself a general of all the people under him; that he was not just a general of the black people, following his discourse with a precis of his past command responsibilities.

It was not the first time he had been labeled a "token." Jonathan Winters recalls seeing him at the Los Angeles Rams' training camp, where "this guy, McCutcheon, was attempting to put Chappie down by inference to his position as a 'token.' "

"How does it feel to be a token?" bellowed McCutcheon.

Jonathan Winters recalls that the room went awfully quiet all of a sudden. Chappie put his hands in his pockets, looked steadily at McCutcheon and delivered a bomb.

"When the wheels go up, McCutcheon, we all are tokens!"

As deftly, Chappie fielded the justification by one black to another to defend rights not enjoyed at home, saying: "We are not asking a man to go someplace else to fight for his rights. These men are going some place in upholding the foreign policy of the United States of America and, as citizens, with the heritage of being born an American citizen, comes the responsibility to contribute."

As to this "responsibility" being "misapplied energy" as Donahue suggested, it was "exactly like saying if you put a man on the moon, why doesn't this microphone work!"

The American public reacted to the appearance on the show with verve: "This man," Mrs. Constance M. Read of New Jersey wrote, "is forceful, articulate and intelligent. He is one of the most exciting spokesmen for administration policies I have ever heard. He makes me proud to be an American."

Nor were Chappie's efforts ignored by President Nixon. According to James

R. McGovern, the president "retained very positive impressions of Chappie's overall service on POW-MIA matters."

Chappie saw all his efforts on behalf of the prisoners of war pay off as the first group actually came home in February 1972. He arranged for their transportation, uniforms, hospitalization, and medical assistance. Not only was he there at Travis Air Force Base to greet the first plane load that came back, he went with the airplane that dropped them off across the country. Later, with Secretary of Defense Elliot L. Richardson, he visited all the various hospitals where they were taken and talked with them. It was, Chappie recalled, "a very rewarding experience."

That summer, his boss, the late Daniel Z. Henkin, recommended that James be promoted to major general "because of his unusual skills in the Defense Department." The air force growled at the idea. Many other officers had precedence over Chappie, it said. For some time, it looked as if the recommendation would simply be filed away. It took intense conferencing at the highest levels; but finally the review boards relented, and he became a major general on 1 August 1972.

III

It was about this time that Johnny Ford, the black mayor of Tuskegee, Alabama, first met Chappie James. James had come to Tuskegee for Homecoming at Tuskegee Institute. It was a thing he never missed if he could possibly make it. Johnny had been a little boy when Chappie went to school there, became the mayor of the town, and was acutely aware of the "legend" in the person of Chappie James, who visited the city in those days in his red Thunderbird. He'd drive over from Montgomery, and the town would turn hot. "Yeah," Johnny Ford remembers: "Chappie James, the baddest dude in town! Chappie was *always* bad! When Chappie hit town, I mean *everybody* knew it! We'd just turn out the whole town for him. He'd be the grand marshal in the parade. Had to have barbecue and fried fish—and we'd have parties! He really enjoyed himself!"

Fraternity brothers, the two of them became good, fast friends over the years, along with other friends like Percy Sutton and Basil Patterson. In fact, it was more than a personal friendship between two men; their families became friends. Johnny and Chappie would sit and talk for hours in that relaxed manner Chappie could assume. About football, and Chappie's days at Tuskegee, and how he enjoyed the game. "He also liked to sing," Johnny remembers, and "if he got to enjoying himself at a dinner party or something, you'd always be in for a treat of his singing." At times, Chappie would get into a really serious vein about his people. "He was very sensitive to the problems of African-Americans," Mayor Ford recalls, "because he had grown up very, very, poor. His background had given him firsthand experience with poverty in America and he talked about his aspirations. He wanted to be:

> in a position where he could do something to not only inspire people, but to just actually help improve the quality of life for our people. Create jobs, and better housing and better education for our children. And he was really for young, black kids staying in school, preparing themselves, so that they would be able to compete. So he was just tremendously committed to our race and felt that race should never be a barrier for us, but they should build on it and turn it into an opportunity for us."

It was now 1973, and in the Pentagon, Jerry Friedheim, encouraged by Secretary Richardson, asked Under Secretary John McLucas to promote Chappie to lieutenant general. The third star was perhaps an easier goal to realize since Chappie would now become a *principal deputy* and number-two man in public affairs. The job itself was now the qualifier, and promotion boards were out of the picture. The air force secretary indicated that he would "take it under consideration," adding that "the Air Force didn't pass out ranks to any but extraordinary airmen." Friedheim was ready for that one.

"Chappie is extraordinary in every respect," he enthused, "in his service to the Air Force and also his service to the Department of Defense and the entire government!"

The Daughters of the American Revolution found out just how special Chappie James was on a fine, spring evening in April, as he made the first speech ever by a black before that organization. It was, after all, the same organization that denied use of their hall to Marian Anderson, the famous black singer, some thirty-four years before. According to Nick Thimmesch, a reporter who was there, Chappie reminded one of a black icon standing there "amidst the ferns and orchids." The DAR ladies regarded him in awe, resplendent in their "elbow-length evening gloves, long gowns and sashes."

"I assess," Chappie began, "the progress that's very visible tonight as I stand here, and I don't have to explain that to you." America, to Chappie, was a veritable, shining jewel:

> I love her . . . if she is ill, I will hold her hand and bring her roses. When angry students tell me to go back to Africa, I tell them, "This is my home. I was born here, an American." When black militants cry for separatism, I told them I was once separate but equal, but I'm not going back under that blanket, no sir! When I came into this man's Air Force, I vowed I would become a general officer, and I am, as you see!

Thimmesch noted that "eyes went misty and old throats dry." The applause was so thunderous George Washington himself could not have commanded more if he had been crossing the Delaware in plain view of that gathering of the DAR. The organ roared the "Stars and Stripes." At attention, Chappie "stood in full salute for the 'Retiring of the Colors.' " As a footnote, Nick Thimmesch in the *Los Angeles Times* noted that later, several black ladies became members of the DAR who could not have been members before Chappie spoke.

Chappie James became a lieutenant general on 1 June 1973. Friedheim remembers that Chappie was always thrilled and pleased to be recognized. But he always wanted to give other people the credit. He came by Friedheim's office to thank him for his part in securing the promotion. Friedheim said: " '*We* didn't do it! *You* did it. Thank your Mother!' He worried that somebody was doing something special for him. He needed to know [that] what he was doing was important. He was doing a really unique job. He was a unique personality!" Together, they toasted Chappie's mother in Friedheim's office.

About a year later, General Brown, the air force chief of staff, called Chappie into his office.

"Chappie," he began, "you need some management experience to be competitive for promotion!"

This Chappie knew. He needed *top level* command experience in management, since the biggest organization he had commanded up until that time was a wing. Because of his unusual assignment in the Pentagon, he had missed command experience at the division and numbered air force levels. And he knew exactly what General Brown was intimating. But he also knew they would never promise him anything. He knew that there were only twelve four-star generals on active duty, and only four were "going home" (retiring). The competition would be fierce!

His assignment was to be vice commander, Military Airlift Command, at Scott Air Force Base in Illinois, under Gen. Paul K. Carlton.

"So go out there and do the best job you can," General Brown said, "and we'll see what happens!"

Leaving the Pentagon in August 1974, he became the vice commander of Military Airlift Command in September, the command some airmen in other air force commands (and especially Chappie's fighter pilot compatriots) sometimes disparagingly but lovingly referred to as the "Trash Haulers."

IV

While the experience in public affairs was invaluable, the assignment to Military Airlift Command quickly broadened Chappie's management skills. It wasn't just dealing with war, it covered areas of procurement, congressional contacts, and close involvement with navy and marine matters in addition to pure air force chores. As vice commander of Military Airlift Command (MAC), Chappie had to do "a hell of a lot of the nuts and bolts work of actually managing material," a new arena for him, because of the huge scope of the management task. While managing the largest command in the world, Chappie began overseeing huge movements of material and men, and the budgeting of millions.

The four-star commander of MAC, Gen. Paul K. Carlton, apparently was a firm believer in showing someone how to do something, then getting out of the way to let them do it. He spent considerable time giving him detailed guidance and then "just set [Chappie] out there and let [him] run it." Carlton busied himself with congressional negotiations and flying around the command monitoring its operations, since its scope was worldwide.

MAC completed several important airlifts, and then came the huge exodus from Vietnam. Chappie learned how to deal with the complex Military Airlift Command operational plans designed to move huge cargoes of men and equipment: "What they do is pull out the contingency plan for supporting [a country] if a big supply is called for by the State Department. . . . They'd come in with a requirement to [move] X number men and so many tons of material."

The requirement had to be broken down into appropriate size and bulk for transport aboard the famous C-141, or C-130, or C-5 cargo planes. The contingency plan spelled it out. Computations had to be made, determining how many ton-miles were involved, how many airplanes would be needed, and how many reservists would be needed for crew assignments. Chappie was at the helm, managing the Vietnam fleet. His pilots had his empathy, because that could be a difficult assignment since "it had the added attraction of being shot at while [they] were doing [the operation]."

Although Chappie hated flying big cargo ships ("it makes me sick"), he was as fiercely loyal to the command and its decisions as he had been to his fighter units. This was demonstrated when he heard that Senator Proxmire had suggested that Military Airlift Command should have 747-airplanes rather than the C-5s. He was uncomprising in his support of MAC's decision to use the C-5, later commenting:

> There is no airplane made today that can do the job for the military that the C-5 can because it's made for outsized loads. There's the front loading and the back loading. To get a tank in a 747, even if you modify it, so that you could open up the nose, you've got to get up such an angle that is so steep, then try to get it in there with some kind of device loader that's gonna jack it up to run it in there. While in a C-5, you load 'em up, drive 'em in there!

The air force was watching. General Carlton gave Chappie a "strong recommendation" based on his work as military airlift vice commander, and, when the command of North American Air Defense Command in Colorado Springs came open, the new secretary of defense James Schlesinger and Secretary of the Air Force McLucas decided after long deliberation and discussion that Chappie could handle the position. But the air force was not easily convinced. Chappie's star had risen because of work done in *public relations,* not in specific operational commands. However, he had commanded units in Air Defense Command after Korea, and perhaps that experience would help. It probably took, however, last minute, strong support from Deputy Secretary of Defense Clements before the air force finally "went along."

In some respects, James's imminent rise to four-star rank paralleled the ascent of Martin Luther King into the great civil rights revolution as a leader. If Rosa Parks had not, on that fateful day, refused to give up her seat on the Montgomery bus, Martin Luther King would undoubtedly have been a recognized and respected black minister, but perhaps not the celebrated leader of the great revolution that he became. It was a matter of timing and of events. Chappie recognized its importance:

> Timing [is] important, and it doesn't matter what color you are. Being lucky enough to get with supervisors who recognize . . . what your capabilities are. . . . [I've] been lucky in this regard . . . since segregation [was] broken up . . . and we were allowed equality . . . lucky enough to come into organizations where the Commander had accepted the end of the segregated business . . . [enough to say,] "To heck with it, everybody here is a man! Come in here and do a good job for us!"

The events of the late 1960s and early 1970s and the intensity of divergent public opinions over the Vietnam War, splitting the American constituency into shattered fragments was a stage made for his talents. A military officer of relatively high rank, a black man to boot, who loved his country and was patriotic to a fault, with unusual ability to persuade, could not help but begin the healing required to help hold the wounded country together. Without these particular circumstances, an observer has noted "it is unlikely Chappie James would have become a four-star general."

But regardless of what the nay-sayers speculated, Chappie James became a four-star general on 29 August 1975, the very first black one in the history of the United States of America. Some observers laid the promotion at the door of conservative Senator Barry Goldwater, since Chappie's diatribes against the dissidents and his theories on how equality should be attained by minorities were seen by many as "conservative." Senator Goldwater emphatically calls the insinuation completely unfounded:

I had nothing at all to do with Chappie getting his fourth star. In fact, no individual did. Chappie earned his fourth star in the same way that all officers earn their promotions. . . . He and I were good friends . . . we flew together . . . talked together a lot. . . . I enjoyed both [him] and his wife and family. But that was the extent of anything I might have to do relative to him. I've always been glad that he did get that fourth star.[87]

And that is undoubtedly the way Chappie James regarded the promotion himself. Nobody *gave* him anything, in his view:

And I've always tried to be [better] . . . and I have some personal standards of conduct that were applied as goals for me from the time I was born by my Mother. And I still try to live up to those standards of conduct. . . . The people who know me best know that. And the people who were most responsible for my promotions know that . . . and believe that. . . . P. K. Carlton knows. . . . Secretary Laird, who gave me my biggest break . . . knows.

There was "happiness and joy" in the James household when the news of promotion to four stars was received. Scheduled to take over command of North American Air Defense Command (NORAD) in ceremonies at 11:00 A.M., Friday, 29 August, Chappie had the stars pinned on his epaulets the day before at Scott Air Force Base headquarters in Illinois. "There was a special sparkle in his eyes when they pinned on the stars," his wife remembered. "It was almost as if he was saying with his eyes, 'You see? I told you I could do it!'"

Telepathically, Chappie probably also sent that message to all the junior officers with whom he had served at Godman, Freeman, and Lockbourne Fields, who had only smiled tolerantly in those days when he used to declare that he intended to make a career of the United States Air Force and, more than that, become a general officer.

General James would be replacing Gen. Lucius D. Clay, Jr., who was retiring from the air force after more than thirty-three years of service. The new responsibility was awesome, and included the Aerospace Defense Command, the United States' element of the joint United States–Canadian North American Air Defense Command, both headquartered in Colorado Springs, Colorado. Under his command would be some sixty-five thousand humans, assigned to elements of the United States Army, Navy, Air Force, and the Canadian Armed Forces.

Fifty-five years of age, now, and a veteran of thirty-two years service with combat flying in two of America's wars, he was to become the eighth commander in chief of North American Air Defense Command since its inception in 1957.

James had come to the mountain top; and he had gotten there through "all of the blood, sweat and tears that I've put into this, and all of the tough years, and all of the preparation, and all of the desire and drive that I have been able to demonstrate to my supervisors."

It was sweet, and ample vindication for all those who said: "They just gave it to him because they made him a *token black!*" Perhaps in the back of his mind that day, the words he was to later enunciate on that subject were forming: "Well, there's no such thing as a 'token' four-star General! . . . They don't *give* stars to *anybody* in this business—you *earn* 'em!"

The four stars took him to the top of Cheyenne Mountain and the windowless city the United States had carved deep inside it, behind "nuclear blast–resistant doors in a four and a half acre grid." They took him into an awe-inspiring, storied domain of fifteen buildings made of steel, constructed to float on monstrous springs that would cushion them against the terror of nuclear detonation, while protecting state-of-the-art computerized tracking systems capable of signaling the first alert of aerial or missile attacks against America.

And somewhere out across the great track of the country, some of the "doubting Thomases" he had gladly "carried on his back," busily searched through telephone books and called operators for this man's new telephone number. They were concerned, they said, because: "Did you know there's a black, four-star general that can push a button and start a war?"

Again and again they read their papers, clucked their tongues, and resolved to call this black man as soon as he was settled.

Chapter Twenty-Seven
Cheyenne Mountain

I

The road to the air force Cheyenne Mountain complex eased to the right off Colorado Highway 115, snaked upward through scattered stands of scrub oak, hardy and tough as the granite mountain itself in the Colorado Rockies. It was the winding road that General James's limousine traveled early every morning, climbing over one thousand feet, sampling the rarified Colorado air, plunging into a long tunnel bored through solid granite. Radio messages crackled. The commander in chief is arriving. Aides bustle. Over four thousand feet later, the car slowed to a stop outside steel doors, designed to withstand the assaults of thermonuclear blasts. The CINCNORAD got out smartly. The time could be as early as five o'clock in the morning, but usually it was somewhere between seven-thirty and eight o'clock. The general entered his blast-proof, windowless city, the eight stars glittering on massive shoulders. A big man, he seemed larger because of the sparkling stars. Over fifty now, he still looked like a football player, the neck thick, the figure almost triangular to the eye. He walked like a stallion. In that place, nobody cared much that he was a black man, with skin the color of the cocoa bean. America's survival as a nation rode on his shoulders. He was the man whose people detected possible air or missile attacks vectored towards the United States and Canada. The man who funnels that information to the president of the United States, the Canadian government, and Strategic Air Command for split-second decisions and probably formulation of a counterstrike. And if bomber strike force contrails invaded American airspace, it was he who scrambled his fighters to knock them out of the sky.

The electronic wizardry he commanded in that time was awesome. Twenty-seven computers received and processed radar data from Alaska, Canada, Greenland, and other places, including data from the Space Detection and Tracking System and orbiting satellites sporting infrared sensors for missile detection. On command, specific pieces of millions of bits of information could be displayed for battle-staff perusal. The same system tracks locations of foreign submarines, satellite pathways, and fishing trawlers lurking just outside the legal limits of the continental United States. Nobody understood his mission better than General James. Determine that a deliberate attack or an aerial strike on the North American continent is under way, and know that it isn't a mistake or an exercise. With only three minutes to decide and act, his definition of that era of detente between the United States and Russia was born of home-grown practicality. It was "a Mexican standoff," he said, where

> he's got a gun on you and you got a gun on him. He says: "Okay, you put down your gun and I'll put down mine." You say: "No, you put down yours and I'll put down mine." . . . All the people standing behind you, the American folks, say: "Trust him. He's a brother. Peace! He's gonna be all right. Put your gun down and he'll put his down." And the people behind him are saying: "Don't you put anything down! You keep it on him. Don't trust him!" For those who argue he will disarm if you do, my question is, suppose he doesn't? Suppose he says: "Okay now, stick 'em up, dummy!" You say: "But you said you were gonna put yours down!" He says: *"Well, hell, if you believe what I say you're crazy!"*

The day moved swiftly as he prepared for his daily, morning staff meeting. Reading the messages file. Reviewing the public information file put together by an aide, defense items identified, with annotations as to probable impact. Checking his interviews schedule, ensuring that he isn't "boxed in." Staff meeting at nine o'clock sharp. Multiple briefings on the state of the command. Airplanes. Sensors. Radar and satellites. People and personnel operations. Intelligence. What did the Russians and the Chinese do today, and what did they do in the last twenty-four hours? Back in his office, the American and Canadian vice commanders come in for an executive meeting. That done, he dictates a few letters. His secretary briefs him on the mail. And all day long, there are briefings and more briefings. Status of building and construction. Checking the budget and utilization of monies in budgets of five million to eight hundred million dollars. Determine the status of assets exceeding seven billion dollars. He pumps his staff, satisfying himself the command operations are on line and within budget. And how about the post exchange system and the hospitals?

The "technical guys" come in to brief about trouble with a satellite out in space with recommendations for action.

For two hours, he tears himself away from all of it, to play a game of squash or racquet ball with his Canadian vice commander and have a bowl of soup and a sandwich. No more than that, because weight is a problem with him. More briefings. Time for the public, cards in his briefcase tell him when he has to be where. It is six, maybe seven o'clock in the evening. The day winds down, and then: "I go home . . . listen to my music, play with my little pup, my little poodle dog, who thinks he's human . . . and spend some time with my wife and have a nice meal and that's part of my diet problem, 'cause all during the [busy day], I'm not hungry, but [at night] *I'm starved!* . . . I eat too much, then go to sleep."

"There was no doubt who was running his staff meetings," a participant remembers. At times the famous James temper could flare. A Canadian aide, Maj. Roy "J. C." Thompson, remembers the day someone reported trouble with the kitchen at one of the far northern NORAD sites. It was a critical item, since men stationed there literally had nothing other than excellent food to crow about as a morale factor. "No booze, no women, and now no decent food; no nothing." At first, Chappie didn't react too concernedly, but the problem resurfaced several staff meetings running. And on one particular day, seated at the end of the huge, egg-shaped, six-inch thick, war room conference table, Chappie heard the problem about the kitchen at the northern site come up again.

"What's wrong with the kitchen?"

Discussion of the problem went on for about a minute, when, like a sudden thunderstorm over Pike's Peak, Chappie brought his monstrous fist down on the thirty-foot-long conference table with such force that the end of it left the floor!

"Let's get this kitchen sorted out soon, or *you're* going to be up there cooking for the troops!"

The problem at the northern site concerning the kitchen never surfaced again. He was not above a bit of devilment, either, using the austere environment of the war room to silently enjoy himself. A stickler for promptness, he was almost never late for a staff meeting. As a consequence, all his generals, colonels, and other staff were always there and seated before he arrived. One fateful day, however, General James *did* run late. The staff dutifully waited. Col. James Randle, his chief of safety, through no fault of his own, was to be the fall guy. It seems that Randle was seated so that Chappie could see him immediately as he walked into the room. His aide bustled in.

"Gentlemen! General James!"

As Chappie rushed into the room, Randle absentmindedly "looked at his watch." James picked up the movement.

"Jim, what the hell you looking at your watch for?" he began, momentarily chatting with nearby officers about something else. Suddenly, he turned to his chief of staff.

"I think it's pretty goddamned *dumb* when the Chief of Safety checks up on me, don't you?" James spat.

Randle remembers that he "could have gone under the chair!" He never looked at his watch again in that conference room. In fact, "I took my watch *off* and left it on my desk!"

Obviously, when a four-star general says something like that without smiling, it *is* time to quickly regroup! However, there was nothing serious about it, such that it would affect Randle's record, but it was just the thought behind the whole scenario. James undoubtedly knew it, and probably chuckled silently the rest of the day. He had been full of devilishness, even at Tuskegee those years ago.

But James *was* extremely tough on his black officers. He wanted his black officers to be better than the white officers, so that nobody could ever point a finger at one of them and even insinuate that he was being "helped by the four-star." For all of that, however, he never made a difference overall when dealing with his officers, black or white. He was known for his great sensitivity to their problems. "But," an aide remembers, "none of his black guys *ever* made a mistake! . . . They got rewarded, but they had to work *harder* to get rewarded!"

Excuses were not part of the General James lexicon. Results were. Basically a very compassionate human, he could come unglued when people made excuses sugar-coated with reasons *why* something couldn't be done.

"Do it! Do it now!" was an expression heard on occasion. "Don't give me that it can't be done; don't tell me why it can't be done! Let's *go!*"

That kind of Jamesian temperament was aroused shortly after he became CINCNORAD, when he was beset by irate telephone calls from across the United States from people who seemed to be upset because he was the NORAD commander; expressing concerns about the "black man who could start a war." The volume of calls was so great it necessitated changing his personal telephone number to avoid them.

"It was very interesting," his wife remembers, "people did not know my husband's job. All those phone calls and they didn't know what NORAD meant!"

That was enough to rile James, but the media added to his consternation as he was interviewed by a group of reporters concerning the NORAD mission. A young lady reporter from a now-defunct Denver newspaper led the charge, placing undue emphasis on the tag line that "there is a black man in charge of the go-to-war unit!" General James stood up front of the group, explaining the NORAD system, what it does, and its capabilities. He specifically explained what he could and couldn't do. But the question came back over and over.

"Would you push the button? Would you start a war?"

"No," General James explained, "I wouldn't start a war. I don't have the capabilities to start a war. I don't have any way, any capability, any buttons to push to start a war. We don't launch anything out here. I do, however, talk to the national command authority and tell them what I've seen. They, in turn, can launch an offensive strike. I don't tell SAC. I don't have anything to do with SAC, I just tell SAC what I see. I simply tell the national command authority. However, I do have command over [defensive units] and if there are airplanes coming to drop bombs, yes, I do have a direct tie to that. I can stop that. I tell my people, 'protect yourself!' "

In spite of that quite complete explanation, the young lady reporter from Denver chose to "take a piece of this and a little piece of that," and published a "rather scathing article" about his ability to start a war. When the clipping showed up in his briefing book, James was more than just a little upset, lashing out in the next day's briefing, absolutely amazed that his headquarters had done nothing to catch the lady's intent, or at best, review what she wrote. He called the newspaper and unloaded. After that, however, his staff began protecting him. At least two staff members were to be in the room whenever he gave interviews. They say he finally realized it was important for his staff members to be present, now that he had seen what the media was capable of doing.

But regardless of the awesomeness of his new assignment, its inherent headaches and pressures, Chappie was extremely proud of what he had accomplished while remaining totally humble about it all. Someone wondered what he thought about this promotion that placed him in the same place as U. S. Grant and "Black Jack" Pershing. The down-to-earth attitude was piercing: "This promotion is important to me by the effect it will have on some kid on a hot sidewalk in some ghetto. . . . If my making an advancement can serve as some kind of spark to some black or other minority, it will be worth all the years, and the blood and sweat it took in getting there."

II

In spite of the dizzying schedule at NORAD headquarters, Chappie still had time to speak wherever and whenever he was invited. In 1975, he spoke to newly naturalized citizens in Pensacola. In Denver, he entreated a gathering of the NAACP to do everything they could to make America work together, because "that's the only way it can work. The NAACP," he said:

. . . gets 'em out of jail. Don't go back to that. We have already overcome that. Assess the progress. Youngsters assess it. [See] how far we've come, from Alcaniz Street to Cheyenne Mountain. I don't say "Please!"—I say, "Do it!" I am a leader of men; of Americans. . . . We are all Americans. My aide is my brother. Youth of America, get out there and get with it! Give your total attention to peace. *Equality doesn't mean anything if there's no togetherness . . . and then we'll truly overcome!* . . .

Making America better for everybody was almost an obsession with Chappie. "Cut out the hatred and cut out the bitterness," he used to say with fervor in scores of places around the nation. "Stop finding so many ways to hate each other!" And then:

Some people say, "General, you're preaching to the choir. We *know* all that." But sometimes, the choir ain't singing loud enough! . . . You gotta bring the other guy along! You just can't sit there and say, "I didn't throw the rock! I didn't light the torch! I didn't start the riot! I didn't light the torch! I didn't rock the school bus! I'm a citizen and I'm proud of it. I didn't call my brother honkey! I didn't call my brother nigger!" *Did you tell the dummy who did, he's wrong? Did you have the guts and the courage and the sense of involvement to do that, or did you just sit there and act like you didn't hear him? If you did, you're part of the problem I'm describing, my friend!* . . . Responsible involvement (equates) to unity of purpose. There are three main pillars of a lasting peace and they remain strength, partnership and willingness to negotiate. . . . And if we can do that, we will truly overcome!

As Mayor Johnny Ford of Tuskegee, Alabama, has noted, Chappie was an expert at taking the attention away from himself as a black man, and shifting it to the country. "He'd stand up," Ford remembers, "and you'd see this tall, black man—but when he started to talk . . . about opportunities, country, flag, motherhood—you never saw the man anymore—just the words. People loved it. He was so articulate—my country, right or wrong!"

He was a kind of Martin Luther King, Jr., in uniform who some called the "last great hope beyond King." Both James and King wanted the same things for black people in America. The methodology was different: ". . . Martin Luther King had a religious base, and his was a quest for equality through nonviolence. Chappie's was a quest for equality through . . . preparing ourselves educationally and competing in the system . . . Whereas Martin Luther King espoused through equality and requiring equality for our people through . . . protest, Chappie espoused equality for our people through competition. . . ."

Even when he went to Pensacola to relax, perhaps in Trader Jon's place, (a famous Pensacola landmark) he was figuratively on the speaker's platform, decrying the rhetoric of personages like Stokely Carmichael (". . . he says he will fight with guns . . . well, who has most of the guns?") and H. Rap Brown ("he's never been anything but a publicity seeker . . . 'we're going to kill them all!' How about that cat! 'Going to kill them all'!"). He treated street rioters with slashing scorn ("I think about ninety percent of them are professional cowards . . . they wouldn't fight if you ran right over them!"), and verbally stabbed at people who blindly followed the extremists ("most of these people . . . are like little children who get behind a parade and follow it along. . . . All they see is the tail, and don't even know what the parade is about!"). Chappie found satisfaction in what he perceived as changing white attitudes in the country ("whites are now realizing that Negroes aren't just somebody that likes fried chicken, gets drunk on Saturday, steals and wants to rape somebody.").

In spite of his great speaking ability and popularity, he often suspected that he wasn't doing enough. It bothered him because he thought that perhaps he was somehow actually contributing to the problem:

> I will be the first to admit the black enlisted man was not as well equipped to fight it [segregation and prejudice] . . . and . . . I didn't provide much assistance to him. . . . I was busy moving ahead with my career. . . . I did talk to those who came to me. When I could put in a word for them, I would and whenever I would walk into an NCO or an Airman's Club I would make it a point to go over and chat with them. But I didn't make myself available to them . . . to provide advice. I probably could have provided more help, but most of us were busy forging ahead at that time [after integration of the services]—trying to solidify our new-found gains. . . . We probably did not do as much for the young airman as [we] should have.

Some thought that he was also needed more by the black people in Pensacola. He was a super-hero to the whites in his hometown. They gave him parades and honors, for they saw him as ultimately a valuable community asset. But many black people in Pensacola felt a lack of closeness to Chappie, and that he was not giving them the messages they wanted to hear. Certain members of the James family felt the animosity and pain in that, but put it down to jealousy. It may have been that Chappie could not have done more because of the far distance he had come. Dr. Maurice D. Brooks, Ph.D., formerly of Colorado Springs, Colorado, notes that "Communities have over-arching goals and Chappie became isolated from these. [A] black man is supposed to help 1 other black men, because that's what the over-arching goal is all about. 'Ray for us and screw them!' [But Chappie] could not participate in that."

The messages, Dr. Brooks continues, that many of the black populace of Pensacola wanted to hear from Chappie were unrealistic in the real world. Chappie could not be incorporated into the group because he had already gone along a path which made it impossible for him to bridge the chasm. He could only say to them: "This is what you have to do—get along this path to where you want to go." Actualization of their goals and aspirations in terms of his assistance was unrealistic. Dr. Brooks concludes: "Chappie had disgressed from the group . . . he had traveled a hell of a distance; had very little commonality with the group anymore. He was on the outside and [therefore] isolated. . . . When he did inject himself into their society, he was a sojourner; a visitor in a foreign land. He was no longer a native of that country or that people . . . and he had done it by choice."

Chappie's worries as to whether he had done enough for black airmen or his people in Pensacola were minor compared to the warning flags his close associates began to fly about his physical condition in the face of such a harrowing schedule. The strain was apparent. "Mrs. James," his friends counseled Dorothy, "your husband is killing himself!"

III

Almost imperceptibly, the strain and stress of Chappie's inhuman schedule of being CINCNORAD/ADCOM,* his unbelievable commitment to multiple speaking engagements, and his need to help anyone he possibly could who came to him with requests for help, began to show. In Mississippi, he found a young, black, star athlete with a high grade point average. He interceded with congressional friends and got him an appointment to the Air Force Academy. Calls from old Tuskegee Airmen friends were received about their sons and problems they were experiencing in a particular service, and Chappie would make an attempt to help. He was a four-star general who loved people. And for this, he was revered. Although he did a lot of speaking, he always met his military commitments. He was always there at firepower demonstrations and all NORAD exercises and emergencies. There were people who didn't like him, but that would have happened with any four-star general. Some people didn't like his particular management style or the way he did things, or simply that he happened to be black. But others felt that that was their loss. For if they had known him, they would have loved him.

But something was beginning to happen to him. Some people thought it

---

* ADCOM: Air Defense Command.

might have been the high Colorado atmosphere and the thin air of the Rockies. Dorothy noticed it: "He used to look very, very tired. He was always under pressure. But he was always a perfectionist. He always worked and strived . . . that was a part of living for him. He was just exhausted. He'd say, 'Oh, I'm so tired,' and come in and try to rest. He loved sports . . . that was relaxing for him, watching football [on television]."

Even though lines of fatigue etched his face, he could and would not forget his beloved command and the people who made it run. As a consequence, he was always on the run; seeing them, talking to them, and letting them know their commander cared. An aide's distraught wife complained because she had not seen her husband for forty-three days because he was on the run with Chappie. He was at Tyndall Air Force Base in Florida, checking out in the F-106 fighter. In Canada, visiting with his Canadian counterparts, reveling in the pomp and circumstance, trooping the line, enjoying the seventeen-gun salute. It was a parade, and he loved parades ("every time they play the Ruffles and Flourish in the General's March, my old heart goes right up."). He did interviews on Canadian television, welcoming a chance to provide "lucid and objective explanation of this job as he saw it." He traveled across the wild, cold tracks of Alaska, his wife, Dorothy, in tow, come to inspect his troops.

Dorothy loved the Alaskan trip. Both Chappie and she were amazed and thrilled by the deference shown them by the Alaskans assigned to NORAD. It seems that the president and Dr. Kissinger had preceded them, and the air force people asked that they be allowed to keep the furniture they had rented in place when they heard they were coming "because our air force boss is coming!" Dorothy remembers that the people were warm and friendly. Their attitudes reminded her of the days of long ago, when "people didn't have to lock their doors." The Alcan highway and the ice fog amazed her. The Alaskan king crab whetted her appetite, while Chappie went into the barracks of the ordinary airmen and talked with them; letting them know he cared and that they were doing a good job. He spoke at a dining-in night and downtown at a civic club, taking Dorothy along into a space where women weren't usually allowed. "He was the only one who brought his wife!" she sparkled in retrospect. And for the first time ever seeing a Canadian mounted policeman, she found herself thinking immediately of *Sergeant Preston of the Yukon* and how, in her mind's eye, she'd "finally met him!" And there were the mukluks, parkas, and the northern lights, dazzling the Arctic sky, salmon ships and salmon baked, chips of Alaskan jade, and gifts for the wife of "the boss."

But those things were simply perks for a four-star general; nice things to have while he got his job done. On his speaking engagements in the larger United States, he spoke, as CINCNORAD, of the urgent need for undivided attention to national security, cautioning that the United States must not let its military power slip away because of the Vietnam debacle. To do so, he lectured, would encourage confrontation with "a superior enemy" bent upon "exploiting the country's weakness.'' In the preceding summer of 1976, he raised his voice against military cutbacks already proposed by the Democratic presidential candidate, Jimmy Carter. Carter's naval background failed to impress Chappie, who insisted that ''there were many things about defense he might not know about at this time.'' He was in the camp of Gerald Ford, still president at the time, publicly congratulating him on ''not cutting the defense budget.''

After Carter's election, when defense cutbacks in military spending were actualized, James continued to complain about them to others, including former President Ford, hitting the new president's stance on the B-1 bomber. Prudently, he avoided public attacks on his new commander in chief, but nonetheless continued to stump for a military that was prepared. President Ford remembers Chappie during this period:

> General ''Chappie'' James was a great favorite of mine over many years. I knew him while I was in the House of Representatives and greatly admired his outstanding Air Force career. He was a superb pilot and a highly respected leader of men. As President, I became better acquainted with ''Chappie'' and his career achievements and was highly pleased that I could recognize his abilities as Commander in Chief, North American Air Defense Command. Our contacts and friendship continued when I left the White House. *Our views coincided in opposing the Defense Department funding limitations of the Carter Administration.*[88]

That spring, Chappie had clearly stated his position before the Doolittle Chapter of the Air Force Association:

> Power is an international language. Nobody needs a translator. Nobody wants to be a partner of a weakling. . . . We are not weak yet, but we have moved away from a position of strength. . . . We have gone closer to a state of parity which we think is acceptable to the people of the United States. But the danger here is that as you approach parity it is hard to stop the pendulum from swinging past center, and then the balance of power shifts to those people who don't hear you at all. . . . Given the technology today, if that pendulum swings too far, there is no recovery. . . . It makes [for] the most deadly game we have ever engaged in.

The lines of stress and exhaustion deepened across Chappie's face. In vain, Dorothy repeatedly tried to get him to slow down or take a vacation. His homework spilled into the back seat of his chauffeured car as he crammed under the courtesy light in the back seat on the way to work. Not only was the new president not listening, the air force chief of staff, Gen. David C. Jones was perceived, according to James R. McGovern, in *Black Eagle,* to be sympathetic to the "bomber people." Under Jones's aegis, the bomber people took policy control of the air force, intent upon "restructuring and cutting back NORAD." The game plan called for giving more of NORAD's duties to Strategic and Tactical Air Commands, leaving North American Air Defense Command a mere shadow of its former command structure. A long and drawn-out controversy erupted between the two generals, with James, the fighter pilot, calling for an "enlargement of the number of fighter planes" under his operational control. Chappie even wrote Jones a classified letter in which he outlined his points of view concerning the matter, but it was not successful. It was a new kind of battle for Chappie, a kind that his old mentor, Lt. Gen. Benjamin O. Davis, Jr., understood well.

But being "cool" in this circumstance seemed to be more than difficult for Chappie. Instead of "coolness," it seemed to generate unwarranted pressures, tensions, and correlated medical problems for him. Weight. An active history of high blood pressure. The "workout in the gym" between General Jones and himself was an exercise General Jones was winning, hands down. To lose *anything* was against Chappie's grain. The name of the game was to perform, excel, and win—always. And clearly, in this instance, he could not have a hope of winning, since the chief of staff himself was set against his thesis for America's defense.

He continued to live life to the fullest. Parties, sporting events. And whenever the opportunity presented itself, he sang at the officers' club and even down at Tyndall Air Force Base in Florida when he visited. It was food in abundance, and always, his Tanqueray gin in moderation. But he seemed to realize that his star was no longer in the ascendant. And he spoke of what he might do in 1978, when he was due by law to retire. Of offers made him by "think tanks," and corporations, and whether or not he might consider going into politics. Of one thing he was sure, however; he would not run for elective office, but he'd be there to see that the people who did and were elected toed the mark:

Hell, you elect somebody and send them to Washington. Screw it, you haven't done your job then if you just say, "Well, hell, I sent the sonofabitch up there, he represents me." You *tell* him how to represent you! And you make damn sure he or she knows what you expect of them when they get up there . . . that they make the system work; that they make the system responsive to all of the people in this country and especially to you.

Maybe in his quieter moments now, he thought about his father when he used to play football, and how *he* used to make him mad:

He'd go to the ball games, you know, and he was betting everybody—"My son's going to run four or five touchdowns—how much you wanna bet?'' He's up in the stands doing all this—what he didn't realize was that I wasn't as fast as Charles was [his older brother—"Big Chappie"], and a lot of times I'd break into the open and get caught from behind. . . . Going in for half-time he'd say, "Good gracious alive! Man, what did you do? You got just about to the goal post, *and you fell down!*" Fell down, my ass, didn't you see that halfback undress me out there?

So in a way, the "bomber people," with their space-age dreams and missilery, had done the same thing to Chappie now, and it hurt. He had begun to think retirement, and coming up on the age of fifty-eight in 1978, wasn't the time to begin a new career, he thought. It was time to start letting "somebody else do it, like his boy . . . like his daughter—she'd be great!" Danice, he thought, "used to be like Barbara Jordan," and it was imperative for people his age to "get the hell outta the way and let the kids come on!" It was as if he already subconsciously saw some sunset coming.

In April 1977, he unintentionally miffed his cousin, Mabel Bates, living in Pensacola, since he simply couldn't attend the fortieth anniversary of his high school reunion because of prior commitments. Mabel had written a song for him to sing at the occasion, dedicated to Booker T. Washington High School, where they both graduated. Written to the tune of "Shenandoah," it was probably the only song especially written for him he never sang:

> Oh, Washington, we love thee dearly
> Whether near or far away
> Oh, Washington, our thoughts are with you
> On land or over sea
> Around the wide USA.
>
> Though many years have passed before us
> We are classmates loving ever
> We've had some real good years
> We'll cherish them forever.

He sent Mabel his regrets in a 20 April 1977 letter:

Dear Mickey:

As we discussed on the telephone yesterday, I had hoped to make our class reunion, and was looking forward to seeing the old gang again. Unfortunately, I have commitments in Washington, Illinois and Orlando during that same frame and won't be able to make it.

Please say hello to everyone and extend my regrets. I am enclosing a check in the amount of fifty dollars.

Sincerely,

/s/ Dan
Daniel James, Jr.
General, USAF

He pressed on, attending the first Red River Valley fighter pilot's reunion in May 1977, a banner stretched across the bar reminding everyone that "Happiness is Post-Strike Refueling!" On 19 August 1977, he was at Tuskegee for the ground-breaking of the General Daniel "Chappie" James Air and Industrial Museum at the site of the old Tuskegee Army Air Field. Addressing the Sixth Annual Convention of the Tuskegee Airmen, he asserted continuing faith in the South: "The South has led the way in curing the ills of segregation . . . once the South makes up its mind that certain things are wrong, it will quickly make up its mind to correct them."

Attending a Denver Bronco's football game in mid-September, he felt great discomfort. Working the next Monday, he still didn't feel well and went to the Air Force Academy hospital for examination. They almost released him the next day, but a report on enzyme levels showed he had experienced "a mild disabling coronary event." He was kept in the hospital for observation, and a liquid protein diet was prescribed, causing the loss of over twenty pounds in six weeks. While he was there, his daughter, Danice, and her husband, Frank Berry, visited. He felt in good spirits and seemed satisfied that Frank would take good care of Danice no matter what. As they left him, Danice remembers that she felt an overwhelming urge at the elevator to turn and look at her father. He sat smiling on the side of the bed, giving her a wink. As the elevator doors closed, a strange feeling it was the last time she'd ever see him alive overtook her. He left the hospital on Thursday, 3 November 1977.

IV

An aide met Chappie at the back door of the Chidlaw Building when he came back on line. It was something of a shock. The weight loss was immediately noticeable. The medication took his energy levels down further than anyone had ever seen them. That magnificent, stallion-like way he had of walking reduced itself to a shuffle. Once, after the heart attack, he visited Tyndall Air Force Base in Florida. A message from the doctors preceded him. He was to have a vegetable tray, no "soul" food and nothing high in cholesterol. Col. James Randle, base commander, met him at the T-39 airplane when he landed: "There are only three or four steps to get down out of the airplane and he had to be assisted as he got out . . . he was a completely different individual from the one I had known. . . . I felt sorry for him . . . he'd lost weight and he really looked bad."

Chappie never really "came back" after the heart attack. There were spurts of energy here and there, in between the medication, but never a full recovery. There was a reason to be happy, however. Old friend, Sammy Davis, Jr., was coming to give a show for Chappie at the Air Force Academy field house on 11 November 1977. It was show time again, and the show must go on. Chappie met Sammy when his airplane landed. Smiling effusively, the two old friends exchanged a soul handshake as Sammy came down the aircraft steps. Chappie looked resplendent in his air force blue, thunderbolts flashing on the visor of his cap. Sammy wore a beige coat, the belt hanging free, a dark, broad-brimmed hat on his head.

The morning of the show an aide asked Chappie if he should attempt "the appearance on the stage" along with Sammy Davis, Jr., because of his medical condition. The aide thought him pale and a bit shaky. Chappie smiled into a nearby mirror.

"You know, that white boy sees things *I* don't see!"

Chapter Twenty-Eight
Star Crossing

I

The Air Force Academy field house was packed; the show starring Sammy Davis, Jr., spectacular. Near the end of it, a piano player improvised in the background. Clad in dark blue trousers and an open-collared, red sports shirt, the cuffs rolled up a turn, golden pendant swinging from his neck, Sammy took center stage, delivering the kind of mellow, trademarked talking he is famous for. Crisp, meaningful. So masterful is he at the craft, he can control the emotions of his audience perfectly. "This is my first time coming to the academy," he was saying, "and I couldn't be prouder to be allowed the privilege of entertaining all of you, and I mean that from the bottom of my heart! It is a privilege . . . ." Applause erupted on "from the bottom of my heart" and took off on the second "it is a privilege." He was verbally off and running now. "Feeling different," he said, "from anybody else in this country—this marvelous, crazy, glorious, magnificent country" in which he was privileged to live. He never wanted to forget about the military, and he was proud to sing wherever he could "because of the ability the Man upstairs laid on me in this business I am proud enough to be in." He was "just a performer," but:

> I can only say that wherever I go, if there's some cats from home there . . . we always put out the good show; try to do something . . . it's the least we can do. That's no big thing, but it is nice, also, to be able to say to you in Japan or Germany or wherever that I have been here.

Hey, man! I'm glad and I'm proud of it. . . . And . . . I don't wanna be corny but I stand as an example of what this country can do—that I, without an education, without anything—just the Man upstairs smilin' on me . . . no other country in the world, man, could it happen in except America, and so when I say thank you for the privilege . . . [The field house applause overwhelmed.]

He took the audience on a magic spoof ride after it subsided:

I wanna let you cats know I was in the Air Corps for about six or eight weeks! [Derisive laughter.] I was! And—er—I signed up—and this was back in 1943, man. And I signed up and I took my first 6 weeks training at Lowry Field in Denver. And the cat found out that I didn't have no high school . . . never went to high school . . . in fact I never went to school, period. And they called me in. . . . I wanted to be an aerial gunner—that's what I wanted to be. I was little . . . you see they take the little cats, you know! [Laughter] the cats said, *"No!"* They sent me to Cheyenne, Wyoming, in the *infantry!* [Big applause.] And I couldn't wait, see, 'cause I was so *impressed* with it . . . I don't know how it is now, but in those days, man, to watch all them movies the cats in the Air Corps—*Zhoom - pah - boom! Ba-ba-boom! Boom!* And the cats up there . . . hats broken down, man, and you *know* there was none'a this "Yes, Sir!" . . . it's always *"Hi, friend!"* There I was on Pole Mountain in Wyoming, "Ah'm comin', Sarge!" *I'm the only cat that ever took an M-1 apart and had two pieces left over and put it back together— and it was working!* And the Sergeant looked at me and said: "How you *do* that?"

When the laughter and applause died down, Sammy got to the real reason he was there, which was because of the warm and lasting friendship between Chappie James and himself. He asked Chappie, he said, if he could come in on this final big show for him, and be able to do it in his bailiwick. He thanked everyone who helped him make it happen, even the academy commandant, in whose home he stayed, gratified that "nobody asked him to do windows!" Then he really got serious: "This particular song is very special to me. And I use it as a closing song because . . . it is special. And I dedicate it to my man, 'Chappie'—and I do it with all the love in my heart to him and his missus. . . . We have been friends for a long time, and I just love the man. I wish him every good blessing in the world!"

Cheering and clapping made the field house rafters shake; then a protracted silence.

"I'd like to do this special—'Mister Bojangles!' . . ."

The audience roared and cheered.

"All *r-i-g-h-t!*" someone yelled.

Applause inundated. The Davis magic began, with the spoken "Ca-chee!" and a finger pop. A "Ca-Chee!" alternated with a finger pop, until the rhythm pulsated and undulated.

"Ca-Chee! Pop! Ca-Chee! Pop! Ca-Chee!—"all melting into the piercing, down-home whistling Sammy prefaces the opening lyrics by, and suddenly he is no longer Sammy Davis, Jr., but Mr. Bojangles ("I knew a man who," in sotto-voce, "talked of life!"). And anybody who really knew about Chappie James's dog, *Honey Rags,* and how that dog really did "up and died—dog just up and died"—probably felt some kind of moistness in the eye, when Sammy wailed that part of the song. Nobody knows for sure, but perhaps the flashback happened in Chappie's head and heart while waiting backstage, because, like Mr. Bojangles, "after twenty years . . . he *probably* still grieves" about *Honey Rags.* The ending of the song felt and sounded special, like a real Sammy Davis, Jr., tribute to Chappie James. Plaintive, almost a plea to Chappie not to go away; not to disappear into any sort of "good-night." The audience sat mesmerized and spellbound. When it was over, Sammy tried whistling his way offstage.

"Good night! Thank you!" he waved.

"More! More!" roared the audience, while the piano music pulsed in the background, and applause dashed along at full tilt for a full fifty-five seconds.

The academy commandant introduced the cadet wing commander, who made a presentation to Sammy. The commandant then introduced General James, that "great American, patriot, a great Air Force leader, great supporter of the Air Force Academy, of the Air Force and the country . . . the commander in chief of NORAD—Chappie James!" Rushed banter went on between Chappie and Sammy as Chappie began:

"Just before I give you a few things here, I spoke to you this afternoon, just briefly, about how *together,* we could make it! A great act! And since I was about to be unemployed here, you see, and—er—I wasn't going to be busy. . . . Are you hearing me?"

The audience was titillated.

"I'm hearing ya!"

"And I thought that *we*—Man, we'd be dynamite! Oh, yeah, we'd—"

"You mean, working together?"

"Yeah. You could give up the singing altogether, I could take over that. You go on back to the hoofin' bit—you know. I'd stand over there and do the *smooth* things!"

"What kinda—"

"Wait just a minute—singing! Si-i-i-i-ing-ing!"

"Can't I at least have an audience?"

"Alright!"

The audience seemed caught up in this fantasy.

"Yeah! Yeah!" they roared. Chappie turned to Sammy.

"All superstars have a song. I notice you always look at George before you sing. You know, every time before you sing!"

"I never know when he gon' leave me!"

"Okay—"

"He gave me the go! 'Birth of the Blues!' I'll do the first part, you take a little bit of the second part and whatever's left over we'll send to Frank!"

The audience laughed, then settled back. Sammy and Chappie sizzled the "Birth of the Blues." And when it was over, the audience simply went crazy.

"How about that?" quipped Chappie, "I think I'll go into singing!"

"Get offa my stage!" Sammy said in mock frustration.

It was Chappie's time to turn the tribute tables on Sammy: "Sam does more than make people happy through music, he has been in some pretty unsafe spots, too." And he told about the time he'd landed short in Thailand because his plane had been shot up, and how Sammy was there at a forward base leading the troops in a song called "We Shall Overcome!"

". . . And I respected the hell out of you for being there. You paid some dues for me and I love you!"

"There's nothing more to say except I will try desperately to—you're choking me up—some more?"

"Yeah, we went by the Army PX the other day. . . . We ran a deal on 'em in a poker game. We got the right one now. They'll never know. We wanted to get you something that came from here that really was a part of this great organization. And this is a part of the granite that came out of the great, big mountain up there where we've got all of those millions—billions of dollars worth of sensors—"

"*I don't wanna know about it!*"

"We don't want anybody else to know—"

"We wanna know what *they're* doing!"

"I intend to do that, babe! That's a piece of your rock!"

Sammy laughed delightedly at the gift. It was the ultimate presentation from the NORAD Command. But for Sammy Davis, Jr., it was a bittersweet thing, as sweet as it all had been. It had probably been on his mind from the moment Chappie met him at the airplane. Later, he would say: "I couldn't put my finger on it, but I just had that gut feeling something was wrong!"

It was a thing you feel but don't talk about. The concern was real, for their friendship spanned decades, since they'd met backstage after a performance when Chappie was just a young officer. The friendship stuck. And now it had come to this, presentation of the ultimate gift from an ailing Chappie. This "piece of the rock," a souvenir of cut and polished granite rescued from the quarrying done pushing through the mountain as the complex was built. It was treasured, especially when Chappie presented it.

Few in the audience knew the import of Chappie's earlier remark, "since I was about to be unemployed here.'' Although he had to retire on 1 May 1978 by law, the heart attack seemed to make it feasible to opt for retirement as early as February of 1978 on medical disability. Additionally, media speculation was rife that he was being ''forced into retirement.'' The chief proponents of this were syndicated columnists Rowland Evans and Robert Novak, who alleged that this was being done because Chappie had voiced strong objection to reorganization of his command. These allegations were denied by James and the air force. In point of fact, James himself proposed his own resignation, accepting a limited duty assignment as special assistant to the chief of staff, and stepping down from the NORAD assignment.

In December, during the change of command ceremony at Peterson Field in Colorado Springs, both Chappie and Gen. David C. Jones, air force chief of staff, were to put to rest the rumors regarding the alleged controversy. ''Earlier this year,'' said General Jones in a short speech to the crowd, ''we initiated a study on the future of air defense. I consulted with Chappie many times and I knew his views . . . he didn't agree with some of the study actions . . . no decision had been made yet. Chappie has been controversial. It's one of the strengths of Chappie James. He has pushed the system. He's made the system change.'' Jones went on to say that he applauded James for that. ''There are those,'' he continued, ''who say that he's leaving because of our controversy. Well, if Chappie James left a job every time he disagreed with something or was controversial, he'd still be a second lieutenant!'' James's counsel was valued and Jones regarded him as a ''true American.'' And too, it was James himself who asked to step down because of his anticipated period of recuperation from his illness. General Jones ended his remarks by wishing Chappie and his wife ''smooth weather and strong tailwinds for many years to come!''

In turn, James was to allow that his command had recently had some tough times, but they'd handled them. And although the accomplishment of those things took courage and initiative, they didn't call for quitting. Instead, they called for ''going back through the channels; try to argue the point, in order to get the men and materiel needed to provide security for this country of ours.'' ''The bond of friendship,'' he asserted, ''that existed between General Jones and myself is as strong today, if not stronger, than it ever was!'' Lt. Gen. James Hill, soon to be promoted to four-star rank, was to assume command of Chappie's beloved NORAD.

II

Dining-ins were of special importance to Chappie. Not only did they give him a chance to sing a little ''five-foot, two—eyes of blue—nobody knows—

what she can do," to a relatively captive but enthusiastic audience, they afforded a chance to deliver a heartfelt "Thanks!" publicly to the key people in his command. Beyond that, it was also an opportunity to share philosophical points of view about his management style, concepts, and beliefs.

Not often in the annals of military history have four-star generals or their equivalents lectured their men on the attributes of pride *and* love quite to the level Chappie did. It was a thing, he used to say after a few Tanquerays, learned back in the old 477th Bombardment Wing, under Benjamin O. Davis, Jr.: "There was nothing plainer to all of us, [than the fact that] we loved each other. . . . And, Number 2, we had a lotta pride in what we were doing." Months before, he'd spoken of it at his change of command. About pride, and what he meant when he talked about love. "Because, if you've got those two things going for you, you can overcome a lot of other things. Love, respect— a lot of people term it a different way—but it all boils down to the same thing. It's a kind of thing that makes people not fail each other because they care. And that's what NORAD is going to be about as long as I command it!"

Pride and love, he postulated, equals guts, and all three equal respect. When an organization has those things, it's simply a good organization and "something that's going to be a winner because people are not going to let it be anything less." The existence of these things also engenders understanding, in Chappie's book. A case in point was a "tough guy," named old Dan Brookshire:

> A couple of his guys got into trouble and, by God, I was going to react in a certain way, but he came to me—I didn't necessarily agree with him—but I appreciated the way he came back to me and said "Whoa! It's my people, boss! And I figure you just got 'em wrong. And now, here is my side of the story. And this is the way I want it to go!" And I figured how grand and how great! This is what I need, *a Commander!* And then I said, "Okay, after I finish telling you what I've got to tell you"—that guy on top of the mountain, he did what he thought he should do at the time and that was fine.

James believed that a good commander should be able to walk very close to the line, perform, and still have the guts to speak up, while choosing his words carefully. It was a send-off for Dan Brookshire to a new assignment on Taiwan. Chappie called Dan to the stage.

"There's a piece of the rock, baby!"

Brookshire beamed; the audience applauded.

"Thank you very much, sir. I certainly do appreciate a piece of the rock. You know, I've watched people receive this for several years and now I'm finally getting one!"

And that was the crux of it. Not *everybody* got one. And when it was presented by General James, it really meant something. Brookshire, in the full text of his acceptance and farewell speech, mentioned Tom Clifford, his black officer replacement. Chappie picked up the comments Brookshire made about the size of the shoes he was going to have to fill, and went further with them: "I was going to introduce Tom on the end of this—and, however, we do have Tom Clifford here tonight—who's a young man who is replacing Dan Brookshire, and he realizes the size of the shoes he's stepping into. *All I can say to him is 'Have at it, and I'll say something good about you when you do something!'* "

The remark was greeted with gales of laughter by officers in attendance and much applause. Later, after presenting a piece of the rock to an army General Mullins, who was moving on because the Safeguard missile system was withdrawn, Chappie returned to the subject of Tom Clifford:

> We've chosen General Tom Clifford, who's been wearing the black hat we think a little too long, because, if you'll excuse the expression, we don't give a damn about black hats, you know! The thing about whether it's a black hat or a white hat . . . is—can he command? And I think he can. My right hand man . . . thinks he can. The Chief of Staff agrees . . . We've got Tom Clifford commanding one of our now most prestigious regions when Brookshire turns the reins over to him.

III

Planning for Chappie's retirement parade and ceremony moved apace. Over at Systems Command on Andrews Air Force Base in Washington, D.C., air force Col. Ralph Hodges was approached by his counterpart in rank, Col. Bob Reining. The two had known each other from ROTC days.

"Ralph, I have the honor of being Commandant of Parade for General James. I wonder if you'd like to participate?"

"Why sure! As what?"

"The Adjutant!"

"Well, boy! That's quite an honor!"

Parade practice began in earnest and, on the morning of 26 January 1978, the date he was scheduled to retire from active duty, General James accepted the invitation of President Jimmy Carter to come to the White House for a chat. They smiled, shook hands for the cameras, and the president saluted him as a "superb military officer in times of peace and war," and reminded his audience that Chappie had "shared an equal authority with him while at NORAD, including the responsibility for initiating an atomic attack."

Dorothy was in the hospital recovering from surgery. Her husband's retirement was something she certainly did not want to miss.

"You may go to your husband's retirement," her doctor allowed, "in a wheelchair with a nurse."

The retirement ceremonies began at two o'clock in the afternoon at Andrews Air Force Base. Ralph Hodges, the parade adjutant, remembers seeing General James, "sitting there, with heavy thoughts coursing through his mind; you could see it." Dorothy was there, too, sitting in her wheelchair, the attending nurse and the James family close by. Nonetheless, it was a Chappie James kind of show. The pomp and circumstance. The air force band firing on all pistons, bringing the guests to their feet during "Ruffles and Flourishes" and the "General's March." This was no ordinary man being honored, for Secretary of Defense Harold Brown was there; the air force chief of staff, Gen. David C. Jones, "four senior Chiefs of Staff and dignitaries of all stripes," were there. It looked as if Chappie was "looking back over the years in his mind," as an honor guard snapped to. The time came to troop the line. Colonel Reining, the parade commandant, went over to the review platform to get Chappie. They say at first, he "stumbled" a bit. The swagger wasn't there anymore. "He looked tired," Colonel Hodges remembers, but when he trooped the line, he seemed to recover a bit; "I didn't expect him to live." Chappie spoke to the assemblage, doing a comparative reminiscence of the time his mother pinned him thirty-five years before, saying, "Do well, my son" and that morning, when President Carter said: "Well done, Chappie!" Then:

If I could write the script for my life all over again, of how I wanted it to go; I don't know of anybody else who has, to a greater degree, been able to do precisely what he set out to do, and what he wanted to do and what he had the most fun doing and that he held the most sense of accomplishment in having done, than I have. The Air Force is the greatest place in the world for me, and if I had it to do all over again, I'd do it exactly the same way!

Some observers say that for an instant, the old energy-filled Chappie James returned to great applause and affection as he finished: "Thank God for the United States of America. Thank God for the United States Air Force to keep her free. And thank you for giving me this honor. And God bless all of you."

He saluted four times; to the front, to either side, to the rear—never forgetting the troops. There was a particular sadness as they rolled his general's flag, the four stars disappearing into its fabric while sliding into its case. "It looked," an observer noted, "ominous."

"Ominous" or not, to people who were there and those who saw fit to comment, the indominatable spirit of Chappie James was evident this day, in spite of his affliction. After the retirement ceremonies, it was on to the Andrews

Air Force Base officers' club for a reception and another four hours on his feet. Socializing. Smiling. Extremely animated conversations with old Tuskegee Airmen friends. The whole family was involved, his son Daniel III, remarking to Colonel Hodge, the parade adjutant, "Now I know who it was giving those orders out there!" But beyond that, the entire day had been a marathon. There was an interview with Tom Brokaw of the NBC "Today Show," where he again defended NORAD's capability against charges of "marginal effectiveness," saying that he was satisfied with the nation's air defense. Again, he warned against the "trend to cut down on our regular forces," emphasizing that America must "improve [its] technology as the threat increases [or] we'll reach a point in time when we'll be left behind." More interviews with the press, where he again denied that his retirement was a "force out." ("There is not and never has been any bad blood between the Chief of Staff of the Air Force and myself.") In his farewell news conference, he gave an impassioned endorsement to the armed forces for their racial policies: "The services have made more progress than any other segment in society. . . . There is less racism in the armed forces than in any segment of society."

It was quite a day for a man recuperating from a heart attack. And what were his immediate plans? They were not firm. He would not seek political office, but he did intend to open a Washington office so that he can "be close [enough] to the arena to hear the screams of the Christians and the roar of the lions!" That was Chappie's way of saying he intended to watch the political give and take in the nation's capital.

IV

Chappie leapt into civilian life with verve. He could afford to. There were political and corporate offers, a home waiting in Pensacola if that was his desire. Writers longed to pen his biography. A film production company made noises. And then there was his dream, of "campaigning for advocates of American defense," regardless of race, "who would pledge to work to improve opportunities for poor people." No matter how fervently his NORAD staff had pled with him to reduce his speaking schedule before he retired, he immediately scheduled several speeches and television shows in order to tout his views on defense and equal opportunity.

He found civilian life a bit tricky. There were no aides to look after the small things. No air force staff at his beck and call anymore. No chauffeurs. Suddenly on his own, he discovered he'd quite forgotten how to deal with a flat tire or that if you left your automobile lights on, your battery would run down, and the car would not start.

Scheduled to speak in Milwaukee and Colorado Springs, he visited Dottie, still in the hospital and fighting rheumatoid arthritis. He was playful and loving, kissing and embracing her, hoping she'd be feeling better upon his return.

It was Friday, 24 February 1978 when he arrived in Colorado Springs to address the American Trucking Association Convention at the Broadmoor Hotel. Several former aides and friends met him at the airport (Cato Reeves, David Swennes, Art Ragan, Clark Price). The foursome meant to get a rise out of their former boss, hiding "around the corner" after his airliner parked at the gate. Resplendent in a "three-piece, blue suit with a pale yellow plaid vest," Chappie looked askance when he saw nobody there to meet him. Of course, when they appeared, all was forgiven after a momentary lapse into "general's parlance," the command voice returning.

"Nobody can keep to a schedule anymore. Things have really gone downhill since I have left this place!"

In spite of the opening camaraderie, he was tired, had a headache, and didn't seem to be himself. To top it off, he'd forgotten the medication for his heart ailment. Colonel Price, an old friend since Bentwaters, drove him to Peterson Air Force Base, where he received the medication and then relaxed, dining with friends. Later that night, the nausea and chest pains returned. Chappie collapsed at 1:20 A.M. at the home of friends and was rushed to the Air Force Academy hospital. He was pronounced dead at 2:00 A.M., mountain standard time, Saturday, 25 February 1978—fourteen days after his fifty-eighth birthday.

News of Chappie's death hit hard. Former Canadian aide, Maj. "J. C." Thompson was in the post exchange.

"You know the boss died last night!" somebody said.

Thompson jumped in his car and drove straight to headquarters. That's where all the discussion would be, he thought. He was right. They were all gathered there, "trying to figure out what [they] had to do next." The body would be flown to Washington the next morning aboard an air force C-141 Starlifter.

In Washington, Col. Ralph Hodges, the parade adjutant, was out in his yard next morning.

"Hey!" his neighbor called, "you heard about General James?"

"Well, yes. I was just at his retirement."

"No, he's dead."

"*What?*"

And two generals, one a black man, William Earl Brown, Jr., called on Dorothy to tell her that her husband was dead.

"Oh, my God!" she instinctively responded, "Not my husband!"

In the Philippines, Chappie's daughter, Danice, and her husband had just returned home from a dinner-dance. They knew something was different the moment they walked in the door. Their Filipino maid met them.

"Mum! Sir! I must speak to you!"

Danice went into another room; Frank remained in the living room. It was very quiet. She could faintly hear "Sir! Sir!" The maid covered her face and ran out of the room. Danice stood there, holding herself as Frank came into the room, taking her by the shoulders.

"Danice," he almost whispered, "Your Dad died."

The shock of it was total and complete. Everything drained out of her. Pushing Frank away, she became suddenly irate, walking, walking—between the living room and bedroom.

"No! No!" she thought, "I can't believe it. He was indestructible! Rain wouldn't touch his shoulders!" And she remembered the bible verse: "Jesus wept."

On Sunday morning, approximately three hundred people came to memorial services on Peterson Air Force Base, Colorado, for Chappie. It was cold. They stood under overcast skies near the runway and the C-141 Starlifter, watching as a hearse slowly arrived carrying James's casket, draped with the American flag. The wide, back door opened as eight airmen, acting as pallbearers, eased the casket out under the watchful eye of their commander. A black airman stood at attention by the airplane's outboard engine, holding the general's flag. A Canadian bagpiper had a bad time of it, trying to play in the cold and control his emotions at the same time. Tears coursed down the cheeks of many. It wasn't a general leaving. It was a friend who had left, and a very popular one, at that.

"*Present Arms!*" bellowed the ceremony commander, as the eight pallbearers began their resolute shuffle toward the waiting C-141 under the weight of the casket. While the band played the "General's March," a public information technical sergeant named Mike Bergman recorded the scene: "Slowly, carefully, pallbearers dressed in blue—the blue of the United States Air Force, carry the casket containing the remains of General Chappie James, aboard an Air Force C-141 *Starlifter*—the final flight for America's first black four-star officer."

As the jet cleared the runway on Chappie's last flight, the sky suddenly brightened and Pike's Peak came into view across the Colorado countryside.

"Chappie would have wanted it that way," somebody whispered.

At Andrews Air Force Base, in Washington, another group of mourners were already gathering for the C-141's arrival with another airman honor guard. Danice and Frank were en route home now, driving straight to the airport to board an air force KC-135 tanker. Air force generals met them at every stop. Flags on all air force installations flew at half-mast. From somewhere, Danice seemed to gather new strength. It was, "if coming to terms with death is something Dad can do—then I can do it too!" She began the flight with a newspaper article about Chappie in her hand. She folded it gently, carrying it on her knee during the entire flight. The eyes were moist. She cried out inside:

"Daddy! Daddy!"

It was as if a giant star suddenly bolted its constellation—a kind of star crossing—leaving an unalterably changed universe.

Chapter Twenty-Nine
"This Is My Country"

I

The lone C-141 Starlifter made an almost forlorn pass across Andrews Air Force Base. Everything stopped, as if caught in sudden suspended animation. People knew Chappie James's body was aboard. A crowd, gathering for hours now, grew larger. That Chappie somehow touched the pulse of America was obvious. An honor guard, made up solely of Tuskegee Airmen, waited in the wings near the long, sleek hearse from an all-black funeral home in Washington, D.C. Heavy resignation silenced the crowd.

Out in Beverly Hills, Sammy Davis, Jr., had the answer to that thing he "felt" about chappie back at the Academy but on which he couldn't place his finger. And the day before, interviewing with the press and getting through the grief, he admitted it had not come as a complete surprise. The love Sammy felt for Chappie showed. "He was a great man. The Air Force could use a thousand more men like him. When he appeared on my television show, we received so much positive mail from all walks of life. The letters said that Chappie makes sense. He could talk to kids. He could also talk to both white and black military people."

It was perhaps a misty Davis that recalled James's love affair with singing, performing, and his real job with the air force: "I think he would rather have been a singer than a four-star general. . . . When he was with friends and family, he would have a good time, but when there was business to attend to, he took care of that. . . . He was a gracious man who will be sorely missed, and . . . we can't afford to lose any more men like Chappie."

The C-141 Starlifter touched down, taxiing to a stop. The rear ramp whined down. An air force honor guard of four white and four black airmen, service cap straps cinched to their chins, securing their headgear against the wind, brought the flag-draped casket out, shuffled in unison towards the waiting hearse. The honor guard commander saluted, while an airman steadied the general's flag—its four stars blowing straight in the wind. It was the same base where James landed as a lieutenant in 1945, bringing the news that 101 of his fellow black officers had been charged with mutiny and treason because they wanted to be served at the officers' club on Freeman Field at Seymour, Indiana.

On Monday, Pensacola Mayor Warren Briggs directed that the flag at the Pensacola City Hall fly at half-staff through Thursday. In the United States Senate a resolution was passed expressing sorrow and regret at the death of General James, while old friend Bob Sikes addressed the House:

> Mr. Speaker, I am certain the House is united in deep regret that General Daniel James, Jr., is dead. America will miss him as a great leader who eloquently used every opportunity to extol our country's greatness and its continuing promise . . . his friends . . . are saddened by the untimely loss of a wise and strong leader who, in his rise to greatness, never outgrew those whom he knew, liked and trusted. . . . Yes, Chappie James is dead. He was the first black American to hold four-star rank . . . he served with distinction . . . won many decorations . . . became Commander NORAD . . . he rose to greatness through sheer courage and determination.[89]

As funeral arrangements were being completed, Florida Governor Jim Williams ordered flags flown at half-staff at all state office buildings through Thursday in honor of James. That night, 1 March 1978, a requiem mass was scheduled at Catholic University's Shrine of the Immaculate Conception in Washington. It was to be the first time any military officer had lain in state in that beautiful and solemn place surrounded by Byzantine and Romanesque art and architecture.

Chappie used to say that he was no second-class citizen, and no other American was, either, unless he believed and acted that way. That his words were heard was evident in the wide spectrum of humanity that came to send him "home." It ranged from the front pews, where congressmen and members of the president's cabinet sat, to the center of the huge room where secretaries and civil servants mourned; from high-ranking military officers and ladies in mink stoles to John Doe Citizen and his lady. And at communion, a young lady clad in a full-length silver fox knelt next to an old man wearing a threadbare sweater, while an enlisted man knelt beside a two-star general.

On the program for the Mass of the Resurrection, a replica of command pilot's wings and a print of James's official air force portrait stared at the

mourners under the high, vaulting ceilings of the shrine. Maj. Gen. Thomas
E. Clifford, black commander of the 26th NORAD Region, read from Daniel
12:1–3:

> At that time Michael shall stand up, the great prince who stands watch
> over the sons of your people; and there shall be a time of trouble, such
> as never was since there was a nation, even to that time. And at that
> time your people shall be delivered, everyone who is found written in
> the book. . . . And many of those who sleep in the dust of the earth
> shall awake, some to everlasting life, some to shame and everlasting
> contempt. . . . Those who are wise shall shine like the brightness of
> the firmament, and those who turn many to righteousness like the stars
> forever and ever . . .

As second lector, Negro Maj. General Lucius Theus, the director of the air
force's accounting and finance, read from Romans 4:7–12:

> Blessed are those whose lawless deeds are forgiven, and whose sins are
> covered; blessed is the man to whom the Lord shall not impute sin.
> . . . And he received the sign of circumcision, a seal of the righteousness
> of the faith which he had while still uncircumcised, that he might be the
> father of all those who believe, though they are uncircumcised, that righ-
> teousness might be imputed to them also.

Chief of air force chaplains, Chap. Henry J. Meade put Chappie James's
life into real perspective: "His was a spectacular life . . . he was a man with
a message, and his life story is a thrilling account of one person's ability to
rise above all adversity and become an example of excellence. . . . Chappie
James cannot and will not be confined to the sacred soil of Arlington . . .
our twentieth-century prophet Daniel will continue to help society . . . to be
the bridge over troubled waters."

Not once did any speaker or lector in this star-studded tribute forget to
mention the catalyst that welded James into the dynamo he became—his mother,
Lillie Anna James, who helped send countless lawyers, doctors, teachers, and
her own precious "Dan" into the competitive world through her teachings.
Col. Ralph Hodges remembers that the Committal Hymn, sung by the choir
and the congregation brought tears to the eyes:

> Lord, guard and guide the men who fly
> Through the great spaces of the sky;
> Be with them traversing the air
> In darkening storms or sunshine fair.
>
> You who support with tender might
> The balanced birds in all their flight,

> Lord, of the tempered winds be near,
> That, having you, they know no fear.
>
> Aloft in solitudes of space,
> Uphold them with your saving grace,
> O God, protect the men who fly
> Through lonely ways beneath the sky.

Beyond that, the recessional hymn, also sung by the choir and the congregation evoked sadness. The "Battle Hymn of the Republic" searched out the highest rafters of the space. "It was something!" remembers an observer, "It was really something!" And through it all, the bravest spirit of all was Dottie James. A "paragon of stability," they say. "She appeared to be composed. She never broke."

At Peterson Field in Colorado Springs, ecumenical memorial services went on at the same time in the base chapel. At ten o'clock in the evening, Chappie's body lay in state in the shrine after the mass. About two thousand people came by to say good-bye that night as a color guard stood watch. Chappie was moved to the Old Post Chapel at Fort Meyers near Arlington National Cemetery after ten o'clock.

II

The second of March 1978 dawned clear and bright; overcoat, scarf, and gloves crisp. Five thousand stood in the wind-driven chill, the famous and the common together, as they waited for the casket to be put on the black caisson. Television's "Cannon" was there, standing under a tree.

"Hello, are you Mr. Cannon?" Colonel Hodges asked.

"Yes, I am, sir!"

The two exchanged glances. Hodges remembers that "Cannon" said something like: "It is a great man we honor today!" Hodges will never forget seeing "Cannon" there, standing under that tree, alone in his own thoughts. Colman Young, mayor of Detroit and Tuskegee Airman, was there, standing in front of Hodges' wife.

"Can you see?" Colman inquired of Hodges' wife, offering to make room.

In front of the five thousand, Senator Barry Goldwater (R-Ariz.), and a member of the Senate Armed Forces Committee gave fellow committee member John Tower of Texas a camaraderie-driven hug. Red lights flashing, fast-moving black cars without markings roared up. A green station wagon followed with a gentlemen "riding shotgun"—the delivery system for Vice President Mondale, Secret Service and all. And still the ten thousand waited in the penetrating cold, standing ten deep around the artillery caisson in front of the Old Post Chapel, waiting for the flag-draped casket to be hoisted aboard. In that utilitarian way horses have of moving their skin against the cold, shivering air, six beautiful, black, matched horses puffed steam through quivering nostrils, occasionally pawing the ground.

Once the funeral procession was under way, it became the most moving celebration of death America has to offer—the military burial. The solemn, cadenced movement to the gravesite; the eight members of the honor guard slowly walking alongside the caisson bearing the flag-draped coffin. The airmen marching alongside and behind, holding the general's flag aloft; the horse without rider. Some mourners drove their cars the four blocks to the Arlington gravesite; a thousand walked the snow-covered paths snaking between the marble markers. And as they stood and walked, they spoke of General James, of Chappie, the man, and what it was he had done. They called him "Black Panther," because he earned that name in combat, and they thought of him "as the pioneer who showed black people that one of the ways out of the jungle was the military." They gave him credit where credit was due: "It was Chappie James who made it possible for blacks in all branches of the service to be more than foot soldiers." The Honor Guard of the Tuskegee Airmen walked in a place of prominence in the funeral procession, confident that they, too, were part of what Chappie James had done, and that without them, none of what he had done might have happened as early as it came about. "You feel embarrassed," someone said, "if you don't honor him. He was a warrior; a patriot. Americans should have a sense of social embarrassment—here's a man who can stand up because he *gained all of his respect.*" And when his moment came, "he chose that moment to pull America around him!" He was a moment in history to some; a moment couched in a time of war and confused feelings, and now people should feel ashamed of themselves for having treated him the way that they did! "If you served with him, you felt close to him," said a retired air force colonel.

At the gravesite, Dorothy James was flanked for a moment by Vice President Mondale on her right and by her son Daniel III, on her left. She sat down when Maj. Gen. Henry Meade presented the flag to her. The honor guard fired a twenty-one-gun salute to General James and, in the quiet that followed, blew taps. Tears threatened to overcome Dorothy James only three times— when they sang the "Battle Hymn of the Republic" at the Mass of the Resurrection, when General Meade presented her the flag, and when taps was played.

An observer noted that when the United States Air Force sent Chappie's body home in the C-141 Starlifter, that was the most humane thing he had ever seen this country do. But the country's humanity really showed when it selected a place in Arlington National Cemetery to bury him in Grave Number 4968–31, Section 2, at the corner of Grant and Roosevelt Drives. Chappie reposed just down the street from John F. Kennedy's eternal flame. Close by are the graves of Gens. Lewis Hershey and Omar Bradley. Adm. Bull Halsey and Pierre L'Enfante, designer of the city of Washington, aren't far away. But even closer is Gen. Benjamin Lacy Hunter, America's first black United States Army Reserve general. Most importantly, one of Chappie's benchmarks to excellence as a commander lay nearby—an enlisted man. "Keep them happy and you'll have a good outfit," he used to imply. And that is perhaps why the nearness of the grave belonging to Sgt. Peter Lisagor, United States Army, seemed to have a certain significance.

As mourners do when the burial ritual is over, the three thousand departed. Some people wished that President Jimmy Carter had seen fit to attend, but prior commitments took him elsewhere. The footsteps of the living crunched the March snow, leaving behind blazing bouquets of flowers, a coffin, and an open grave. The Pentagon gleamed across the Potomac. A passenger jetliner whined by, on its way to National Airport. And it was quiet and restful again. Dorothy noted wryly as Chappie lay in state in the Shrine of the Immaculate Conception: "He looked like he was at least getting some of the rest he so badly needed."

"I have no regrets," Dorothy said in interview after her return to the hospital for recuperation, "we both knew that after the first heart attack, you usually have another. In spite of trying to rest, exercise and diet, Chappie was always on the go. He gave his life." And across the country, the sentiment and accolades continued. People couldn't stop.

Gen. Ralph Maglione, an old friend and former leader of the air force flying Thunderbirds, suggested that sheer compassion may have killed Chappie: "I was deeply saddened. . . . I can't say I was terribly surprised, however. No wonder his heart only lasted 58 years—he used it so much! He was fiercely loyal up and down the chain of command. Loyalty, like his patriotism, was an image inbred, and he felt it as strongly as he felt love for his Mother."

"The nation again is mourning," said Mayor Johnny Ford of Tuskegee, Alabama. Melvin Laird, the man who gave Chappie his biggest break of all, said it very succinctly: "Chappie James was a man who gave his all for his country. He fought a tireless battle for the nation's strength and for equal opportunity for all."

The *Washington Post* editorialized:

There was a kind of rock-ribbed Americanism about General James—a patriotism and a sense of gratitude that some found incongruous in a man who in childhood had known poverty and segregation firsthand.

But there was really nothing incongruous about it. Chappie James simply possessed two qualities that nurtured his patriotism and powered his truly remarkable advancement to the top of the nation's military structure. An indomitable will to succeed and, with it, a profound sense of appreciation of the special opportunity his country offered him—whatever its flaws. There will be many tributes to General James, but we think none will more eloquently characterize him than the words he once used to describe himself. "I am," he said, "above everything else . . . an American."

III

It is August now, and the flowers left there in March are faded and long gone. An untypical, cool wind blows. The Pentagon gleams across the wide Potomac. Trees rustle; cicadas and crickets buzz and sing athwart the new wooden, black-chained stakes separating the hallowed knoll from the rest of the world. An Arlington National Cemetery blue and white, open, tour buggy, filled with vacationers of all nationalities, stops by the grave. The tour guide explains what the people see. The tall, large, grey tombstone, inscribed with four stars and a replica of command pilot's wings centered over:

Daniel "Chappie" James, Jr.

General

United States Air Force

February 11, 1920–Feb. 25, 1978

The tour buggy inches forward. The tour guide tells them what the back side of the tombstone says:

Daniel "Chappie" James, Jr.

". . . This is my country and

I believe in Her . . . I'll

Protect her against all enemies . . .

foreign and domestic . . ."

If the trees rustle loudly in the August wind in counterpoint to a silver jetliner rushing by, it may be possible to hear Daniel in the mind; music under, perhaps:

You see . . . this retreat into separatism . . . they are going back under the "separate but equal blanket!" We've got a statue in the middle of the campus at Tuskegee, where Booker T. Washington is standing there lifting a blanket from a black slave and it says something about "he lifted the blanket of ignorance from his people," and I like to think of that blanket as a blanket of ignorance exemplified in the separatism of today. They are trying to run back under that separate-but-equal blanket, and that's where a lot of racists still want them to go. They are becoming black racists. I was under that blanket once, and I always found it very separate, but never equal. They are going to find it the same way, and I don't want them to make that mistake all over again. . . . So I am concerned. I still think there are enough people smart enough not to retreat back that far. They may feel initially that separation is the answer . . . [but] when they come out of that business [they] don't want any part of separatism. From a point of racial pride, which I think is good, they gain all the knowledge that they can on their African heritage and put it in its proper perspective. They are not ashamed of their blackness, but by the same token they don't make a profession of being black. And I hope that we can proceed down that line . . . because that's the only way to fly!

Epilogue

I

Spring sparkled the air around Montgomery, Alabama, on the morning of 10 May 1987. The verdant countryside shimmered as a special urgency ripped the air on nearby Maxwell Air Force Base. Class "A" uniforms replaced normal fatigues, transforming air policemen tending the main gate. Strategically placed trucks blocked access to the base flightline. Armed guards rerouted traffic at key intersections. Marine helicopters used by the president of the United States were parked on the flight line. Local newscasters paced their crews. Officers and enlisted men preened. Air Force One, bearing Ronald Reagan, president of the United States, was due to land any minute, his destination black-run Tuskegee University at Tuskegee, Alabama, a little over forty miles away.

The pending visit by the president was a historic event. Except for a brief visit by the vice president in 1981, no chief executive of the United States had graced the university with his presence since Franklin Delano Roosevelt over forty years before. Today, Ronald Wilson Reagan was flying down from the nation's capital to deliver the 102d commencement address and dedicate the new General Daniel "Chappie" James Center for Aerospace Science and Health Education.

The center, named for its "distinguished graduate," America's first black four-star general, contained classrooms and technical laboratories, dedicated to excellence in aerospace science engineering. Army and air force ROTC programs would be better supported by the inclusion of a modern rifle range and additional classrooms, while a new memorial library and museum would house the archives chronicling the general's exploits. In special recognition of the roots of General James's evolution the new center included an outdoor plaza honoring the Tuskegee Airmen. A university arena/convocation center housing over five thousand became the building's core and centerpiece. A natatorium supported the university program of health and physical education, General James's major while at Tuskegee. And on permanent display outside the massive structure, sat the actual Phantom F-4C jet fighter last flown by General James during the Southeast Asian war, donated by the United States Air Force as a further honor to Chappie James. Another black general, Brig. Gen. Russell Davis, flew it there from Washington, D.C.

Rain sprinkled briefly but stopped as Air Force One taxied. President Reagan deplaned, conducted a few perfunctory conversations with official greeters and less than ten minutes later, boarded the waiting Marine One helicopter for the twenty to twenty-five minute flight to the Tuskegee University campus, two marine helicopters following in tandem.

The Tuskegee Airman Plaza became a focal point as its dedication ceremonies got under way. "Chief" Alfred Anderson, Henry Bowman, the national president of the Tuskegee Airmen, and Col. (Retired) Herbert Carter each address the huge audience, the overflow standing on long steps bordering the plaza and leading to the second level of the center. Later, the James family will attend the dedication of the F-4C Phantom jet last flown in Thailand by Chappie James, installed as a permanent monument.

Marine One lands outside, its huge props churning the air. The presidential limousine whisks the president and his party along the road toward the massive building. They are met by Benjamin Franklin Payton, Ph.D., L.L.D., L.H.D., D.H.L., president of Tuskegee University. Payton, an imposing black, bespectacled gentleman, clad in a dark, three-piece suit and possessed of a deep, mellow voice worthy of an operatic basso profundo, welcomes and ushers the president on campus. Alabama's foremost citizens, Governor Guy Hunt, Representative Bill Nichols, Senator Richard Shelby, and Senator Howell Heflin, participate in the unveiling ceremony of the Aerospace Science and Health Education building marker. President Reagan speaks of the patriotism exhibited by General James over a long and illustrious career. "He had four stars on his shoulder and fifty stars in his heart," he said, and issued a challenge to future university students: "Well, now, let his spirit hold the hand of these students and guide them through the challenges of higher education and through the frustrations of life. . . . I am most proud to dedicate this center in honor of a darned good pilot and a revered military officer and truly great American."

When the dedication was done, Presidents Payton and Reagan lifted the black tarpaulin from the stone marker. It was one of the proudest moments ever seen on the Tuskegee University campus. A reporter loudly asked a question about the ordering of contra aid at a time when Congress had banned such aid. Reagan refused a response, saying, "We're here for a different purpose, and let's just for a few moments, decide that there's enough controversy and we'll leave that in Washington for today!"

Inside the center, the media feverishly prepared to cover the speech soon to be delivered by President Reagan. Secret Service agents took their stations. Photographers camped out in front of the podium. Draped in academic gowns, both presidents and their entourages entered the convocation arena as the Tuskegee band played. The audience roared its approval, their applause engulfing the huge auditorium. Candidates for graduation filed in to the sound of "Pomp and Circumstance." Five thousand voices sang the national anthem as President Reagan stood erect, right hand across his heart. Dr. James Earl Massey, dean of the Tuskegee University Chapel said the invocation. President Reagan's head was bowed, his eyes closed, while Dorothy James fiddled momentarily with her academic hood, which seemed uncomfortable around her neck. The pace seemed to build after Senator Heflin, Congressman Nichols, and Governor Hunt officially welcomed the president to Alabama. Dr. Massey led the audience in a specially written Litany of Dedication. The responsive reading by the five thousand was awesome:

> With grateful thanks for the blessing of Almighty God and for the help of all who have made possible this new Center for Aerospace Science and Health Education;
> *We join in this service of dedication . . .*

> To honor the life and service of the late General Daniel "Chappie" James, Jr., exemplary alumnus, ardent patriot, and distinguished soldier who became the first black four-star general in this nation's armed forces;

> *We dedicate this General Daniel "Chappie" James Center for Aerospace Science and Health Education . . .*

> To memorialize a remarkable black American who by his courage, aggressiveness, vision and commitment brought honor to his Alma Mater, his family, his race, and his nation;

> *We dedicate this Center . . .*

> With appreciation for his example as one who rightly claimed equality of opportunity, and used his opportunities with unselfish concern to benefit his nation;

> *We dedicate this Center . . .*

In recognition of one whose strong trust in God and Country helped him become one of this nation's most respected citizens and highly trusted defenders of its freedom and stability;

We dedicate this Center . . .

Blessing and honor and power and glory be unto our God, and may peace be unto all who wisely use the facilities of this Center, from this day forward . . .

Amen and Amen . . .

No one present in the great hall that day will ever forget the performance of the Tuskegee University Concert Choir and Concert Band as they sang and played "America the Beautiful." Tympanies signalled the beginning of the piece as the band artfully stated the musical theme. President Reagan turned in his seat to hear and watch. The performance sent chills up and down the spine, and when it was over, the applause, whistles, and cheering ran rampant.

"All right!" they yelled, and "Yeah!"

Benjamin Franklin Payton proudly approached the lectern, his face beaming. "You have just heard," he said, "the best choir and band in the world!"

He stood proud and tall. The applause approving his last statement faded.

"Ladies and gentlemen, the fortieth President of the United States!"

To the surprise of many visitors in the great hall, the applause greeting Ronald Reagan, Republican president of the United States about to address an audience of five thousand black Americans, built to a crescendo.

"I guess," an observer in the audience smiled, "*we* even like this guy!"

President Reagan immediately grabbed the hearts of many in the audience: "This is a most fitting day for a graduation ceremony because it coincides with the day we give thanks to the individuals to whom we really owe everything, people who sacrificed and sometimes went without so that we could have happier and more complete lives. Today we remember and give thanks to our mothers. . . . I'd like to ask every woman who has a child graduating today to stand, if they would . . ." And they seemed to spring up, blossoming like morning glories in the early sun in every quarter of the great room as the applause exploded, growing into the happiest kind of roar. "Ladies, we honor your children today for their outstanding accomplishment, but we know that you deserve our accolades, as well. God bless you, and thank you all for all you've done to bring this happy day about."[90]

The president wasn't through. He brought Mrs. Pauline Punch to the rostrum, presenting her flowers in honor of her retirement from university service as secretary and executive assistant to three Tuskegee University presidents.

After drawing a comparison between the United States and Soviet Union relative to the ability of an individual to choose the direction of their lives, he spoke of the wonderfulness of freedom. Because of that hope, the graduating class to whom he spoke would have a role in ushering the world "into a new era of freedom and progress . . . when technology and . . . creativity will carry us beyond anything . . . we can now imagine." It is American ability to explore technology; conquering disease, engineering new aerospace craft and new discoveries in superconductivity. These graduates would have a hand in those developments because: "The legal sanctions of bigotry and discrimination were torn away, laws protecting the civil rights of all Americans were put in place, and racism was, in effect, outlawed."

And these things did not come easy, he reminded the audience, but "were the result of . . . struggle and commitment of generations and the outstanding leadership of individuals like Dr. Martin Luther King." In spite of continuing incidents of racial violence and interracial crime, these cannot be shrugged off, he continued. Perhaps the most important message of the president's entire address was couched this way: "Yet today, if black Americans are to progress socially and economically, if they are to be independent and upwardly mobile, it is imperative that they be part of the great technological and scientific changes now sweeping our country and the world. And it's just as vital for America that all her citizens march into the future together."

It was a variation on an old General Daniel "Chappie" James, Jr., theme. Chappie had lectured his American audiences on the need for unity because in unity there is strength and untrammeled progress. In point of fact, President Reagan continued, quoting Dr. George Washington Carver, pioneer in the field of agriculture: "Race and creed find no recognition in the eyes of the Deity when He bestows His general gifts . . ." "Tuskegee," he said, "made history with its agricultural research, which continues even now to be a source of pride. Yet let me suggest that this fame may someday be surpassed by contributions your institution will make in the field of aerospace engineering."

"*Yeah!*" exploded a member of the graduating class. Secret Service men flinched at the sudden outburst of the student. The audience guffawed.

"*He's* ready!" the president laughed.

The students' potential, he pointed out, was the reason the Department of Education was authorized to provide nine million dollars in support for the construction of their Aerospace Science and Health Education Center, now dedicated to General Chappie James. And there were other black American heros. The Tuskegee Airmen, destroying 261 enemy aircraft during World War II and earning a "basketful of Distinguished Flying Crosses." Dorie Miller, one of the first Americans to shoot down an enemy airplane at Pearl Harbor. Twenty-nine active duty army generals. Two black four-star generals and a third one pending, Bernard Randolph of the United States Air Force. Astronaut Guy Bluford. Ensign Jesse Brown, the navy's first black naval aviator, who lost his life over Korea. Proof positive that Chappie James's mother was right when she said: "Someday there will be so many black people doing so many things that are noteworthy that it will no longer be noteworthy."

The hope for the graduating class of 1987 as expressed by the president was that they "become part of the continuing saga, the history shaped by individuals like Dr. Carver, Chappie James, and Ensign Jesse Brown. What you do with your lives will keep America shining like a beacon of opportunity and freedom for all to see . . ."

Dr. Payton conferred the honorary degree of doctor of laws upon President Reagan and the Tuskegee University Alumni Merit Award to Dorothy Watkins James in honor of her loyalty and support she provided her husband, Daniel "Chappie" James, Jr., over thirty-six years of marriage. When it was over, five thousand people gave the president a standing ovation as he waved good-bye to the choir, the band, and the audience at large. A few minutes later, the whine of the Marine One helicopters could be heard as they began to ride upon the air. Students came out, holding a banner high. It read: "Good-bye, President Reagan . . . we're glad you could come and thanks for coming here today!"

Overhead, a flight of military jets flashed past in afterburner. The president and his entourage were airborne. The stifling dust barrage kicked up by the departing helicopters began to settle.

II

But perhaps there is still one more thing to do. Down in Pensacola, Florida, at 1606 Alcaniz Street where the Daniel "Chappie" James, Jr., saga began, the building housing the school in which his mother, Lillie Anna James, taught scores of black youngsters and him how to be better and accomplished Americans, is gone. All that is left are the concrete steps that led to its entrance. Someone built a flimsy, wooden watershed of a cover for them as protection against the elements and painted them white. On them is printed:

CHAPPIE'S FIRST STEPS
1920

Somehow, it isn't enough. It is an attempt at the instilling of a memory; a stab at a fleeting kind of permanency, and it is moving, but somehow incomplete. For this ground is almost hallowed, marking the place where a great, human oak was planted; a place where a kind of greatness amidst poverty and an immense and grand dream began its fulfillment. It is ground to be properly marked for coming generations of Americans to see; a place where elementary school teachers bring their classes to be reminded that here a concept about the importance of excellence and unflagging patriotism was taught and what that means to newer lives just beginning. Perhaps it could read:

This monument marks the spot where the life of Air Force General Daniel "Chappie" James, Jr., began on February 11, 1920. It is also the spot upon which his Mother, Mrs. Lillie Anna James, began her private school for black Pensacola children, bequeathing to America a gift of the talents of scores of responsible American citizens. . . . General James died on February 25, 1978.

It would be a fitting thing to do, because as Chappie's cousin, Mabel Bates has said: "What he did was not prejudiced to just black people. . . . He was a credit to the nation, and the total population of Pensacola should be proud of him. . . . And you'd be surprised at the number of black and white children and a lot of people who *don't know who you're talking about.*"

And if anyone is looking for a reason to properly close the circle on the life that was Daniel "Chappie" James, Jr., his widow, Dorothy Watkins James, said it best: "He loved people and he loved life and he liked to make people happy. He laughed. Yes, he was a happy person. And he wanted everyone to be happy. He could adjust to situations, and if he met someone who was unhappy, his goal was to make them smile—*'it's a wonderful world; let's enjoy it and live here together in Love and Peace!'* "

Appendix A

This is the text of *I Am an American,* the famous narration done by General James with the New Orleans Philharmonic Symphony Orchestra and with the United States Air Force Band on two different occasions.

"I am an American
Listen to my words!
Listen well, for my country
Is a strong country
And my message is a strong message—
I am an American!
And I speak for Democracy
And the dignity of the individual

"I am an American
And my ancestors have given their blood
for freedom—
On the green at Lexington
And the snow at Valley Forge
On the walls at Fort Sumter
And the fields at Gettysburg!
On the waters of the Marne
And in the shadows of the *Argonne!*

"On the beaches of Salerno
And Normandy, and the sands of Okinawa
On the bare, bleak hills called
Pork Chop and Old Baldy
And Heartbreak Ridge.
A million and more of my
Countrymen have died for Freedom!
I am an American!
And my country is their eternal monument!

"I am an American!
And my ancestors have bequeathed to me
The laughter of a small boy
As he watches the circus clown's antics,
The sweet, delicious cold bite
Of peppermint ice cream
On the Fourth of July . . .

The intenseness of a baseball crowd
As the umpire calls, 'Batter Up!'
The high school band's rendition
Of the Stars and Stripes Forever
In the Memorial Day Parade!
The clear, *sharp* ring of a school bell
On a crisp morning.
These, and many more things
They fought for and left for me.
I am an American!
And the fruits of my heart and labor
Are mine to enjoy

"I am an American
And my country is a land of many realms
And mansions—
It is the land of Ohio corn
And potatoes and pasture;
It is the realm of thousands of acres
Of golden wheat
Stretching across the flat miles of Kansas.
It is the land of precision,
Assembly lines in Detroit.
It is the realm of milling cattle
In the stockyards of Chicago.
It is the land of glowing skylines
Of Pittsburgh and Birmingham
Of San Francisco and New York
And in my churches and homes
Are mansions of heaven.

"I am an American
And in my churches and homes
Everyone worships God in his own *way!*
The young Jewish boy saying:
'Hear, Oh Israel, the Lord is One!'
The Catholic girl praying;
'Hail Mary, full of Grace,
The Lord is with thee!'
The Protestant boy singing:
'A mighty fortress is my God!'
Each one believing and praying as he must
And all joining in the universal prayer

'Our Father, who art in Heaven'
With the voice and the soul
Of every human being
That cries out to be free!

"I am an American
And I believe that America
Has answered that voice . . .
I am an American
and my country offers Freedom
And opportunity
Such as no land before her
has ever done!

Freedom to work
As mechanic or farmer,
Merchant or truck driver—
Freedom to think
As chemist or lawyer
As doctor or priest.
Freedom to love,
As a parent, as child,
Sweetheart, husband, wife!
Freedom to speak,
To pray, to read, to argue
To praise, to *criticize!*
Freedom to eat and sleep!
To work and play without fear!
Freedom to live one or two million
Different lives.

"I am an American!
And my heritage is
Of the land and of the spirit—
Of the heart and of the *soul*
Show me now
A country greater than my country
For I am an American!
I speak for Democracy
And the dignity of the individual!"

Appendix B

Awards and Medals

General James, a command pilot, was the recipient of numerous awards, both civilian and military. He was known internationally as an eloquent advocate of the American way of life. Excerpts from some of his speeches have been read into the *Congressional Record*.

The general was twice awarded the George Washington Freedom Foundation Medal, 1967 and 1968; the Arnold Air Society Eugene M. Zuckert Award for outstanding contributions to Air Force professionalism; Builder of a Greater Arizona Award; Phoenix Urban League Man of the Year Award; Distinguished Service Achievement Award from Kappa Alpha Psi Fraternity; American Legion National Commander's Public Relations Award; Veterans of Foreign Wars Commander in Chief's Gold Medal Award and Citation; Capital Press Club, Doolittle Chapter Man of the Year Award; Florida Association of Broadcasters' Gold Medal Award; American Veterans of Foreign World War II Silver Helmet Award; United Service Excellence Award; American Academy of Achievement Golden Plate Award; United Negro College Fund's Distinguished Service Award; Horatio Alger Award; VFW Americanism Medal; Bishop Wright Air Industry Award; and the Kitty Hawk Award. General James was awarded an honorary Doctor of Laws degree from the University of West Florida in 1971; the University of Akron in 1973; Virginia State College in 1974; Delaware State College in 1975; and St. Louis University in 1976. He was also named Honorary National Commander, Arnold Air Society in 1971.

As a command pilot, General James was a decorated war hero. His decorations include:

Distinguished Service Medal with Oak Leaf Cluster
Legion of Merit with Oak Leaf Cluster
Distinguished Flying Cross with two Oak Leaf Clusters
Meritorious Service Medal
Air Medal with thirteen Oak Leaf Clusters
Army Commendation Medal
Distinguished Unit Citations Emblem with one Oak Leaf Cluster (service before 1965 and later)
Air Force Outstanding Unit Award Ribbon with three Oak Leaf Clusters
Combat Readiness Medal
Good Conduct Medal
American Defense Service Medal
American Campaign Medal

World War II Victory Medal
National Defense Service Medal with one service star
Korean Service Medal with four service stars
Air Force Longevity Service Award ribbon with seven Oak Leaf Clusters
Vietnam Service Medal with four service stars
Armed Forces Reserve Medal
Small Arms Expert Marksmanship ribbon
Republic of Korea Presidential Unit Citation ribbon
United Nations Service Medal
Republic of Vietnam Campaign Medal

Endnotes

1. Jesse J. Johnson, *Black Armed Forces Officers, 1786–1971* (Hampton, VA: Carver Publishing Inc.), p. 1–2.
2. Ibid.
3. Jack D. Foner, *Blacks and the Military in America's History: A New Perspective* (New York: Praeger, 1974), p. 51.
4. Oral material in this chapter is based on interviews with Mrs. Dorothy Watkins James.
5. William Greider, "An American Success Story," *Washington Post,* 21 July 1975, p. A-16.
6. Martin Robinson Delaney, *The Conditions, Elevation, Emigration and Destiny of the Colored Peoples of the United States,* reprint of 1982 ed. (New York: Arno Press and *New York Times,* 1968), pp. 48–49.
7. Oral material in this chapter is based on interviews with Lilli Rollins, a student in Mrs. James's Pensacola school, 16 October 1986; Gloria Hunter, a niece, of Pensacola, Fla., 13 May 1988. An incomplete copy of Mabel Bates's unpublished typescript remains in the possession of Danice Berry, General James's daughter.
8. Duward S. Riggs, ed., "The Power of Individual Excellence," *The Commonwealth* (Commonwealth Club of San Francisco) n.d., p. 215–19.
9. Samuel R. Spencer, Jr., *Booker T. Washington and the Negro's Place in American Life* (Boston: Little, Brown and Co., 1955), p. 101.
10. Alan M. Osur, *Blacks in the Army Air Forces During World War II* (Washington, D.C., Office of AF History, 1977), pp. 2–5. Hereafter referred to as Osur, *Blacks in the AAF.*
11. Alan L. Gropman, *The Air Force Integrates: 1945–1964* (Washington, D.C., Office of AF History, 1978), p. 5. Hereafter referred to as Gropman, *The AF Integrates.*
12. Osur, *Blacks in the AAF,* pp. 21–22.
13. Material in this chapter has also been based on interviews with the following: Col. William Campbell, USAF (Retired), interview of 26 October 1986; Elaine Thomas, interview of 14 May 1987; Dorothy Watkins James, interview of 28 August 1986 and subsequent telephone conversations.
14. According to Robert A. Rose, *Lonely Eagles: The Story of America's Black AF in WWII* (1976), pp. 12–13; Moton Field was the third of several sites used for initial CPTP training. The first was a commercial airport, forty miles distant, in Montgomery, Alabama. Dr. Fred L. Patterson, Tuskegee president, with the help of Mrs. George L. Washington, director of Mechanical Industries, secured a lease of land about five miles away which

was called Kennedy Field. Moton Field, about four miles from Kennedy Field, was upgraded, construction monies contributed through the influence of Eleanor Roosevelt from the Julius Rosenwald Fund.

15. Osur, *Blacks in the AAF*, p. 22–25.
16. Some disagreement exists as to when the first blacks were inducted into the army air corps flying program. Rose, in *Lonely Eagles* (p. 14), cites the date as 19 July 1941. Gropman, in *The AF Integrates, 1945–1964*, cites the date used. The event did occur, however, in 1941. Also, Osur (p. 9) cites six men in the first class (i.e., one officer; five flying cadets); Rose (p. 15), maintains that the number was twelve cadets and one student officer. B. O. Davis, Jr., according to Rose, was the first black to solo as an officer of the army air corps on 2 September 1941, a full month before Osur indicates training began.
17. Other oral reference material in this chapter is based on interviews with the following: Archie Williams, interview of 3 February 1987; Danice Berry, interview of January 1987; "Chief" Alfred Anderson, interview of 14 May 1987.
18. Rose, *Lonely Eagles*, p. 19, and Osur, *Blacks in the AAF*, p. 44.
19. Gen. Daniel James, Jr., Pat Sampson Interview Tape J-105, Tuskegee University Archives, Tuskegee, Ala.
20. In addition to the notes listed, material for this chapter has been taken from interviews with the following: William B. Ellis, personal interview of 12 October 1986 and telephone interviews of 26 February 1987, et seq., hereafter referred to as WBE Interviews; Maj. Ted W. Johnson, USAF (Retired), interview of 28 June 1980; Roger C. Terry, interview of 26 July 1986 and telephone interviews of 1987/1988, hereafter referred to as RCT Interviews; Capt. Edward W. Woodward, USAF (Retired) interviews of January 1980 and subsequent telephone interviews; and "Chief Nurse" interviews via telephone 11 March 1987, anonomity requested and honored by author.
21. Slang: A Tuskegeeian provincialism meaning gossip, rumor. As in another provincialism: "What's happening?" and "What's going on?" Its most popular usage in this period is reported to have been: "Hey, what's the sprat?"
22. Mary Penick Motley, *The Invisible Soldier* (Detroit: Wayne State University Press, 1975), p. 201.
23. Ted Morgan, *FDR: A Biography* (New York: Simon and Schuster, 1985), pp. 536–37.
24. In addition to the above citations, material in this chapter is based on interviews with the following: John "Mr. Death" Whitehead, interview 22 March 1987; John Wilson, interview 22 March 1987; George W. Fordham

interview 22 March 1987; W. Leon, interview 22 March 1987; and R. Wilson, interview 22 March 1987.

25. History of FAF Army AB, Selfridge Field, Mich.: Chap. XIII, *War Takes a Holiday*, 1 Jan. 1943–31, Dec. 1943, p. 129, AFHRC Maxwell AFB, Ala.; J. Woodford, "McRae Tells His Story of Shooting by Colman," *Detroit Free Press*, 8 Sept. 1943; Osur, *Blacks in the AAF*, p. 54; *Detroit Free Press*, 8 Sept. 1943, p. 2, col. 4.; *Commanding Officer's Daily Ledger*, Appendix VIII, item 1., and Brig. Gen. Noel F. Parrish, *USAF Oral History Interview*. AFHRC, Maxwell AFB, Ala., p. 13.

26. Rose, *Lonely Eagles*, pp. 66–67.

27. History of Selfridge AB, 1943, Appendix XIII, item 9.

28. Willard A. Heaps, *Riots, USA, 1765–1965* (New York: Seabury, 1966), pp. 116–17.

29. In addition to the references cited, oral data is included from interviews with Edith Roberts of Sacramento, California.

30. History of FAF army AB, Selfridge Field, Mich., *The Colman Trial*, AFHRC, Maxwell AFB, Ala.

31. *Detroit Free Press*, "Who Is Being Protected? A Farce Trial," 16 Sept. 1943, p. 6.

32. Motley, *Invisible Soldier*, pp. 195–232.

33. WBE Interview. (Ellis, as of the interview date, was the sole survivor of this plot borne of frustration and anger. James died after an illustrious Air Force career in 1978; Daniels was killed in an aircraft accident. Taped account of this episode in possession of author. Ellis, in 1988, executed a sworn statement under penalty of perjury attesting to the truth of this episode after objections by the James family. Original statement in author's possession.)

34. Lt. Col. Spann Watson, *USAF Oral History Interview*, Albert F. Simpson Historical Research Center, AU, Maxwell AFB AC, p. 8.

35. Gropman, *The AF Integrates*, p. 17.

36. An allusion to an old military mess hall standby: "chipped beef on toast."

37. Osur, *Blacks in the AAF*, p. 113.

38. Osur, *Blacks in the AAF*, p. 113.

39. Osur, p. 111.

40. Record of Telephone Conversation, General Hunter to General Giles, 12 June 1944, AF Files 311.3, Office of AF History, Bolling AFB, Washington, D.C.

41. MacGregor and Nulty, *Blacks in U.S. Armed Forces: Basic Documents*, Vol. VIII, "A Broader Viewpoint," Office of AF History, Bolling AFB, Washington, D.C., pp. 176–80.

42. MacGregor and Nulty, p. 180.

43. MacGregor and Nulty, pp. 182–85.

44. WBE interviews.

45. Rose, *Lonely Eagles,* p. 127.

46. MacGregor and Nulty, p. 186.

47. Bryan LaPlante, 2d Lt., AC, Hq FAF Memo, "Report of Racial Situation, Freeman Field, Seymour, Ind., (19 Mar–21 Mar 45)" Office of AF History, Bolling AFB, Washington, D.C., pp. 4–5.

48. Freeman Field Letter Order, 1 Apr. 1945, "Assignment of Buildings and Areas at Freeman Field, Seymour, Indiana, Effective 1 April 1945," Office of AF History, Washington, D.C., p. 1.

49. Statement, 1st Lt. Joseph D. Rogers, assistant provost marshal, 24 Apr. 1945, *Record of General Court-Martial, 2/Lt Thompson, Marsden A., 0–0579458 and 2/Lt Clinton, Shirley R., 0–577152,* U.S. Army JAGO, CM #284024, 23 July 1945.

50. Statement, Capt. Franklin A. McLendon, air corps, 8 Apr 1945, *Record of General Court-Martial, (Thompson/Clinton),* JAGO, CM #284024, p. 1.

51. Testimony, 2d Lt. Coleman A. Young, Trial Transcript, *Record of General Court-Martial (Thompson/Clinton),* U.S. Army JAGO, CM #284024, p. 65.

52. Statement, Capt. Anthony N. Chiappe, air corps, 7 Apr 1945, *Record of General Court-Martial (Thompson/Clinton),* U.S. Army JAGO, CM #284024, p. 1.

53. Memorandum, director of intelligence, Freeman Field, "Racial Incidents: Summary of Information," 7 April 1945, Office of AF History, Bolling AFB, Washington, D.C., p. 2.

54. MacGregor and Nulty, pp. 198–99.

55. R. Buckminster Fuller, "Technology and the Human Environment" in *The Futurists,* ed. Alvin Toffler (New York: Random House, 1972), p. 299.

56. Indorsement courtesy 2d Lt. James V. Kennedy and Capt. Edward W. Woodward. Copies in Author's possession.

57. Greider, *Washington Post.*

58. Background Documents, *Record of Trial by General Court-Martial: Clinton, Shirley R.;* Thompson, Marsden A., JAGO, CM #284074, 23 July 1945 (in possession of Author).

59. Certified True Copy: *Administrative Reprimand to 2/Lt. Edward W. Woodward, "E" Squadron (Trainee),* 118 AAFBU CCTS, Freeman Field, Seymour, Indiana, 24 April 1945 (copy in Author's possession).

60. Floyd B. Barbour, ed., *The Black Power Revolt,* Frederick Douglass, in "No Progress Without Struggle: 1849," (Boston: Extending Horizons Books, 1968), p. 42.

61. To General Davis's credit, Spann Watson, in an oral interview, indicated that Davis "apparently on his own," began to check out in the B-25 before his return to the U.S., while still in Italy. Thus, these claims may not be all-inclusive.
62. In addition to the references cited, other material in this chapter is based on telephone interviews with the following: Fitzroy Newsom, telephone interview, 13 January 1988; James T. Wiley, telephone interview, 24 January 1988; Lt. Gen. Benjamin O. Davis, USAF (Retired), telephone interview, 26 August 1986; and James Shepherd, telephone interview, circa 1987.
63. Jane Roberts, *The Unknown Reality,* vol. 2. (Englewood Cliffs, N.J.: Prentice-Hall, Inc., 1979), p. 329.
64. Gropman, *The AF Integrates,* p. 30.
65. *Godman Field History,* 40–41 and Appendix, "Reconversion and the Negro: A 'GI-Town Hall' Topic," AFSHRC, p. 2.
66. Col. Benjamin O. Davis, Jr., in *Interview with Base Historian,* 30 September 1945, Appendix, *Godman Field History,* AFSHRC, p. 6.
67. In Toffler, *The Futurists.*
68. "Concerns over USAF Integration by Blacks at Lockbourne," and "Does Integration and Negro Screening Board Mean Progressive Elimination of Negro Personnel?" n.d., in A. L. Gropman Papers AFSHRC, Maxwell AFB, Ala.
69. The "Warrior" reference was common in most speeches made by General James during this era of his career.
70. Jack Broughton, *Going Downtown: The War Against Hanoi and Washington* (New York: Orion, 1988).
71. Greider, "An American Success Story," *Washington Post,* 21 July 1975.
72. Some oral material in this chapter is based on interviews with the following: Maj. Thomas J. Money, USAF (Retired), telephone interview, 14 Sept. 1988; Lt. Col. Jean K. Jones, USAF (Retired), interview, 1 Oct. 1988; Maj. Charles Hauver, USAF (Retired), telephone interview, 26 June 1988; and CM. Sgt. James H. Edmonson, USAF (Retired), telephone interview, June 1988.
73. Some oral material in this chapter is based on telephone and personal interviews with Deonice Lucky and Vernel Steen of Pensacola, Fla.
74. Thomas I. Pettigrew, *A Profile of the Negro American* (New Jersey: D. Van Norstrand Co., Inc., 1964), p. 46.
75. Pettigrew, p. 20.
76. "BNIC": A probable dilution of syntax. Many blacks of this air force period often referred to themselves using the acronym "HNIC" for "Head Nigger in Charge," after southern usage meant to describe a black placed in charge of other blacks and often referred to as the "Head Nigger."
77. Dr. Alfred J. Morrow, American Jewish Congress, testifying before the

Fahy Committee in Apr. 1945; in A. L. Gropman Papers, "Three Comments on Colored Troops;" "An Officer's Problems with Colored Troops," 26 Apr. 1941; 10 June 1942; 13 July 1945. AFSHRC, Maxwell AFB, Ala.

78. Walter J. Boyne, *Phantom in Combat* (Washington, D.C.: Smithsonian Institute Press, 1985), pp. 11, 14–15, 72, and 116.

79. Robert W. Ginsburgh, *U.S. Military Strategy in the Sixties* (New York: W. W. Norton & Company, Inc., 1968), p. 133.

80. Gen. William W. Momyer, USAF (Retired), *Air Power in Three Wars: WWII, Korea, Vietnam* (Washington, D.C.: U.S. Government Printing Office, 1978), p. 91.

81. Broughton, pp. 128, 129, and 171.

82. Michael Skinner, *USAFE: A Primer of Modern Air Combat in Europe* (Novato, Calif.: Presidio Press, 1988), p. 14.

83. Carlton Proctor, "James Never Forgot the People Back Home,: *Pensacola News-Journal,* pp. 1–7, quoting Dr. Donald Dale Spence, Pensacola, Fla.

84. James R. McGovern, *Black Eagle: General Daniel "Chappie" James, Jr.* (University: University of Alabama Press, 1985), pp. 115–16. According to McGovern, this story was verified by Melvin Laird, ex-secretary of defense in interview.

85. McGovern, *Black Eagle,* p. 113.

86. AF News Service feature, 7 February 1979, AFSHRC, Maxwell AFB, Ala.

87. Senator Barry Goldwater, letter to Author, 4 August 1986.

88. President Gerald R. Ford, in letter to Author, 11 August 1986.

89. *Pensacola News-Journal,* 28 February 1978, and *Congressional Record* (House) H1535, February 1978.

90. President Ronald W. Reagan: *Remarks at the Tuskegee University Commencement Ceremony,* 10 May 1987. In "The Administration of Ronald Reagan: 1987," pp. 509–14. Courtesy, chief of staff, Office of President Ronald Reagan.

Sources

Books

Barbour, Floyd B., ed. *The Black Power Revolt.* Boston: Extending Horizon Books, 1968.

Bishop, Jim. *FDR's Last Year: April 1944–April 1945.* New York: William H. Morrow and Company, Inc., 1974.

Blakesmore, Evon, et al. *The Tragedy of MacBeth: The Riverside Shakespeare.* Boston: Houghton-Mifflin Co., 1974.

Boyne, Walter J. *Phantom In Combat.* Washington, D.C.: Smithsonian Institute Press, 1985.

Broughton, Jack. *Going Downtown: The War Against Hanoi and Washington.* New York: Orion Books, 1988.

Carmen, Carl. *Stars Fell on Alabama.* New York: Rhinehart, Inc., 1934.

Churchill, Winston, *The Second World War.* New York: Houghton-Mifflin Co., 1959.

Coblenz, Stanton A. *From Arrow to Bomb.* New York: The Beechnut Press, 1953.

Cooley, John K. *Libyan Sandstorm.* New York: Holt, Rinehart and Winston, 1982.

Coonts, Stephen. *Flight of the Intruder.* Annapolis: Naval Institute Press, 1986.

Dalfiume, Richard M. *Desegregation of the U. S. Armed Forces: Fighting on Two Fronts.* Columbia, Missouri: University of Missouri Press, 1969.

Delaney, Martin Robinson. *The Conditions, Elevation, Emigration and Destiny of the Colored Peoples of the United States.* New York: Arno Press and The New York Times, 1982. Reprint.

Delury, George, and McGuire, Thomas J., et al. *The World Almanac and Book of Facts: 1976.* New York: Newspaper Enterprise Assn., Inc., 1985.

Fleming, Thomas J. *West Point: The Men and Times of the United States Military Academy.* New York: William Morrow and Company, Inc., 1969.

Foner, Jack D. *Blacks and the Military in America's History: A New Perspective.* New York: Praeger Publishers, 1974.

Friel, John P., ed. *Dorlund's Illustrated Medical Dictionary.* 25th ed. Philadelphia: W. D. Saunders Company, 1965.

Ginsburgh, Robert W. *U. S. Military Strategy in the Sixties.* New York: W. W. Norton and Company, 1968.

Glines, V. C. *The Compact History of the USAF.* New York: Hawthorne Books.

Gropman, Alan L. *The Air Force Integrates: 1945–1964.* Washington, D. C.: Office of Air Force History, 1977.

Hanak, Walter, ed. *Aces and Aerial Victories: The USAF in SEA 1965–1975.*

Montgomery, Alabama, and Washington, D. C.: Alfred F. Simpson Research Center and Office of Air Force History, 1976.

Havighurst, Walter. *The Heartland: Ohio, Indiana, Illinois.* New York: Harper and Row, 1974.

Heaps, Willard A. *Riots, U.S.A., 1765–1965.* New York: The Seabury Press, 1966.

Hynes, Samuel. *Flights of Passage: Reflections of a World War II Aviator.* Annapolis: Naval Institute Press, 1968.

Isaac, Arnold L. *Without Hanoi: Defeat in Vietnam and Cambodia.* Baltimore and London: The Johns Hopkins University Press, 1983.

Johnson, Jesse J. *Black Armed Forces Officers, 1796–1971.* Hampton, VA: Carver Publishing, Inc., n.d.

Jonas, Richard E. *The Dick Jonas Songbook,* Vol. I. Phoenix: Erosonic Enterprises, 1976.

Kane, Harnett. *The Golden Coast.* Garden City: Doubleday, 1959.

Karnow, Stanley. *Vietnam: A History.* New York: The Viking Press, 1983.

Kissinger, Henry A. *The Price of Power: Kissinger in the Nixon White House.* New York: Summit Books, 1983.

Kissinger, Henry A. *American Foreign Policy.* New York: W. W. Norton and Company, Inc., 1974.

Larson, Arthur. *When Nations Disagree: A Handbook on Peace Through Law.* Baton Rouge: Louisiana State University Press, 1961.

Lavien, Jack, and Lord, John. *Winston Churchill: The Valiant Years.* New York: Scholastic Book Services, Inc., 1963.

Lincoln, Eric C. *The Negro Pilgrimage in America.* New York: Bantam Books, 1967.

McGovern, James R. *Black Eagle: General Daniel "Chappie" James, Jr.* University: University of Alabama Press, 1985.

Manning, Robert, and Dreyfuss, Paul, et al. *Above and Beyond: A History of the Medal of Honor from the Civil War to Vietnam.* Boston: Boston Publishing Company, 1985.

Michener, James A. *Kent State: What Happened and Why.* New York: Random House, 1971.

Momyer, William W. *Air Power in Three Wars: WWII, Korea, Vietnam.* Washington, D.C.: U.S. Government Printing Office, 1978.

Morgan, Ted. *FDR: A Biography.* New York: Simon and Schuster, 1985.

Morocco, John. *The Vietnam Experience: Thunder from Above: 1941–1968.* Boston: Boston Publishing Company, 1984.

Motley, Mary Penick. *The Invisible Soldier: The Experiences of the Black Soldier in WWII.* Detroit: Wayne State University Press, 1975.

Osur, Alan M. *Blacks in the Army Air Forces During World War II.* Washington, D.C.: Office of Air Force History, 1977.

Pettigrew, Thomas I. *A Profile of the Negro American.* New Jersey: D. Van Nostrand Company, Inc., 1964.

Pierce, Neal R. *The Deep South of America.* New York: W. W. Norton and Company, Inc., 1944.

Roberts, Jane. *The Unknown Reality.* Vol. II. Englewood Cliffs, New Jersey: Prentice-Hall, Inc., 1979.

Rose, Robert A. *Lonely Eagles: The Story of America's Black Air Force in WWII.* Los Angeles: Tuskegee Airmen, Western Region, 1976.

Skinner, Michael. *USAFE: A Primer of Modern Air Combat in Europe.* Novato, California: Presidio Press, 1988.

Spencer, Samuel R., Jr. *Booker T. Washington and the Negro's Place in American Life.* Boston: Little, Brown and Company, 1955.

Stokesburg, James L. *A Short History of Air Power.* New York: William Morrow and Company, 1986.

Taylor, John W., ed. *Combat Aircraft of the World.* New York: G. P. Putnam's Sons, 1969.

Thornborough, Anthony M. *USAF Phantoms.* London and New York: Arms and Amour Press, 1988.

Thornbrough, E. L., ed. *Booker T. Washington: Great Lives Observed.* Englewood Cliffs, New Jersey: Prentice-Hall, 1969.

Toffler, Alvin, ed. *The Futurists.* New York: Random House, 1972.

Toliver, Raymond F., and Constable, Trevor. *Fighter Aces.* New York: MacMillan Company, 1965.

Villard, Henry Serrano. *Libya: The New Arab Kingdom of North Africa.* Ithaca, New York: Cornell University Press, 1956.

Wiesberger, Bernard A. *Booker T. Washington.* New York: The New American.

Letters to Author

1. Dorothy W. James, 21 September 1986.
2. Roger A. Jernigan, 10 February 1986 and 26 August 1986.
3. "Brenda," librarian, *Pensacola News-Journal,* 15 August 1986.
4. Senator Barry Goldwater, 4 August 1986.
5. George Spota, for Jonathan Winters, 22 August 1986.
6. President Gerald R. Ford, 11 August 1986.
7. Maj. William H. Austin, USAF, 26 February 1986.
8. Kevin Grace, University of Cincinnati, 11 July 1986.
9. Theodore M. Berry, 7 January 1980.
10. Howard P. Carter, 7 December 1979.
11. Col. H. E. Carter, USAF (Retired), 3 January 1980.
12. Congressman Ronald V. Dellums, 28 September 1979 and 27 September 1979.
13. Sherman L. Robinson, 19 September 1979.

14. Danice James Berry, 21 August 1987.
15. Brig. Gen. Robin Olds, 31 March 1987.
16. CM Sgt. James O. Helms, USAF, 6 July 1988.
17. Gloria Hunter, 21 September 1988.
18. Melvin R. Laird, 1 May 1987 and 17 November 1986.
19. Lilli Rollins, 13 November 1986.
20. Dick Johnson, *Kansas City Star,* 15 October 1986.
21. Nancy Leftenant-Colon, 17 March 1987.
22. Nancy L. Cunningham, secretary to Daniel Z. Henkin, 24 April 1987, and Daniel Z. Henkin, 2 February 1987.
23. T. Sgt. John J. Trammel USAF (Retired), 5 July 1988.
24. Lt. Col. A. J. Belisle, USAF (Retired), 7 February 1989.
25. Lt. Col. Theodore W. Jones, USAF (Retired), 23 May 1988 and 31 March 1988.
26. Lt. Col. Howard K. White, USAF (Retired), 7 November 1988.
27. Col. Dennis P. Sharon, USAF (Retired), 4 January 1989.
28. Al Downing, 5 July 1988.
29. Mark Boes, George Schlatter Productions, January 1988.
30. William D. Madsen, AF Academy, 17 December 1986.
31. Hank Basham, 4 April 1989 and 28 April 1989.
32. Melinda Manos, secretary to Bob Hope, 10 April 1989.
33. Pearlie M. Draughn, 23 March 1988.
34. Maj. William M. Austin, USAF, 2 June 1986.
35. Walter J. Boyne, author of *Phantom in Combat,* 10 April 1989.
36. Col. Dick Jonas, USAF (Retired), 15 April 1989.
37. Mark D. Weinberg, director of public affairs, Office of President Ronald Reagan, 20 April 1989.
38. Evelyn P. Fancher, Ph.D., director of libraries, Tennessee State University, 1 December 1986.
39. Pierre Hall, Hilversum, Holland, 21 April 1989.
40. Emmit H. Brooks, Enchantment Music, 1 May 1989.
41. Robert M. Kipp, 23 October 1986.
42. M. Sgt. Roger A. Jernigan, Office of AF History, 10 February 1987.
43. Sherman L. Robinson, principal, Washington High School, 19 September 1979.
44. Jack Rosner, Warner/Chappell Music, 2 April 1990 and 10 April 1990.
45. Bob McGruder, Managing Editor/News, *Detroit Free Press,* 11 April 1990.
46. William B. Ellis, *Affidavit,* 19 November 1988.

Interviews
1. Dorothy W. James, 28 August 1986.
2. Mabel Bates, 2 April 1989 and 6 April 1989.

3. Gloria Hunter and Cecil Hunter, 14 May 1988.
4. Col. Ralph Hodge, USAF, 3 October 1987.
5. Col. William McAdoo, 20 December 1988.
6. Maj. Roy J. C. Johnson, Canadian AF, 19 May 1988.
7. M. Sgt. Herbert C. Harper, USAF (Retired), 13 May 1988 and 26 June 1988.
8. Roger Terry, 26 July 1986 and 24 January 1988.
9. "Chief" Alfred Anderson, 14 May 1987.
10. Capt. Edward Woodward, USAF (Retired), 1985, 1986, and 22 March 1987.
11. Elaine Thomas, 14 May 1987.
12. Imelda Lovelace, May 1987.
13. Col. James Randell, USAF (Retired), 18 May 1988.
14. Col. Lloyd Thomas, USAF (Retired), 18 May 1988.
15. George Fordham, 22 March 1987.
16. W. Leon, 22 March 1987.
17. Robert Wilson, 22 March 1987.
18. John "Mr. Death" Whitehead, 22 March 1987.
19. Harold Beaulieu, 22 March 1987.
20. Danice James Berry, February 1987.
21. Lt. Gen. Benjamin O. Davis, Jr., 26 August 1986.
22. Vernel Steen, 15 May 1988.
23. James R. McGovern, Ph.D., 15 May 1988.
24. Maj. Charles White, USAF (Retired), 7 November 1988.
25. Dr. Maurice Brooks, Ph.D., 18 May 1988.
26. Hannibal Guidice, 19 October 1988 and 20 October 1988.
27. William B. Ellis, 12 October 1987, 1988, and March 1989.
28. CM Sgt. James O. Helms, USAF (Retired), 17 July 1988.
29. T. Sgt. John T. Trammel, USAF (Retired), 17 July 1988.
30. Lilli Rollins, 16 October 1986.
31. Edith Roberts, 11 March 1987 and 22 March 1987.
32. Maj. Charles Hauver, USAF (Retired), 26 June 1988.
33. M. Sgt. Herbert C. Harper, 26 June 1988.
34. Maj. Thomas J. Money, Jr., USAF (Retired), 14 September 1988.
35. William Phears, 10 May 1987.
36. Jerry Friedheim, 18 May 1987.
37. Fitzroy Newsum, 18 January 1988.
38. Col. James T. Wiley, 24 January 1988.
39. Col. William Campbell, 28 January 1988 and 26 October 1986.
40. Afc Tony Young, 13 December 1987.
41. Capt. Archie Williams, 3 February 1986.
42. Al Downing, June 1988.

43. Maj. Ted W. Johnson, USAF (Retired), 28 June 1980.
44. Sfc John Bayne, USAF, 18 February 1988.
45. Maj. Thomas J. Money, 14 September 1988.
46. Deonice Lucky, 18 May 1988.
47. CM Sgt. James Edmundson, USAF (Retired).
48. Milton Franklin, 7 April 1988 and 19 May 1988.
49. Johnny Ford, mayor, Tuskegee, Alabama, 10 April 1989.
50. Lt. Col. Ted Jones, USAF (Retired), May 1988.
51. Col. Dennis P. Sharon, USAF (Retired), December 1988.
52. Dr. Daniel Williams, Ph.D., archivist, Tuskegee University, 1986, 1987, 1988.
53. Lt. Col. Jean K. Jones, USAF (Retired), 1985, 1986, 1987.
54. Col. Dick Jonas, USAF (Retired), 13 April 1989.
55. James Shepherd, 25 June 1988.
56. Gordon C. Southall, 20 May 1989.

Index